SOCIETY FOR NEW TESTAMENT STUDIES

MONOGRAPH SERIES

General editor: John M. Court

148

THE POLITICS OF INHERITANCE IN ROMANS

SOCIETY FOR NEW TESTAMENT STUDIES

MONOGRAPH SERIES

Recent titles in the series

The Politics of Inheritance in Romans

DR MARK FORMAN

CAMBRIDGE
UNIVERSITY PRESS

CAMBRIDGE UNIVERSITY PRESS
Cambridge, New York, Melbourne, Madrid, Cape Town,
Singapore, São Paulo, Delhi, Tokyo, Mexico City

Cambridge University Press
The Edinburgh Building, Cambridge CB2 8RU, UK

Published in the United States of America by Cambridge University Press, New York

www.cambridge.org
Information on this title: www.cambridge.org/9780521769099

First published 2011

Printed in the United Kingdom at the University Press, Cambridge

A catalogue record for this publication is available from the British Library

Library of Congress Cataloguing in Publication data
Forman, Mark, 1972–
The politics of inheritance in Romans / Mark Forman.
    p.   cm. – (Society for New Testament Studies monograph series ; 148)
Includes bibliographical references and index.
ISBN 978-0-521-76909-9
1. Bible. N. T. Romans – Criticism, interpretation, etc.   2. Bible. N. T. Epistles of Paul –
Criticism, interpretation, etc.   3. Inheritance and succession – Biblical teaching.   I. Title.
BS2655.I63F67   2011
227'.1067 – dc22   2011006854

ISBN 978-0-521-76909-9 Hardback

For Luka and Oscar

CONTENTS

PREFACE

Completing a project of this length is both demanding and rewarding. There have been many stimulating moments as I have attempted to come to terms with Paul's thought world. But the process has also been taxing and I would like to acknowledge the support I have received along the way.

I am grateful to the John Baldwin Memorial Scholarship Fund, which contributed to financial needs during the first two years of this project.

This book began life as a thesis, which was supervised by Associate Professor Chris Marshall and Professor Paul Trebilco. They always found the right balance between offering much needed guidance and fostering independent thought. Despite the geographical distance, they provided me with encouragement and support as well as with creative and disciplined models of scholarship. I will never forget Chris' friendship during my fragile health in the early stages of the thesis.

Dr. Andrew Shepherd and Dr. Ingrid Shepherd contributed in practical ways to this book – Andrew offered stimulating conversation and musings, and Ingrid was a dedicated proofreader. Janelle sacrificed much during a seemingly endless, study-oriented phase of our relationship. I would like to acknowledge her support during the writing of this book.

Throughout the many phases of this project, Mum and Dad reminded me in myriad ways of what it means to show faith, hope and love. Duncan Philps helped with proofreading and I have appreciated his ongoing, gentle presence in my life. Reverend Jeremy Younger is a close and wise friend whose companionship continues to give me both lightheartedness and courage.

Finally, *The Politics of Inheritance* is dedicated to Oscar and Luka, whom I love with all I have.

ABBREVIATIONS

AB	Anchor Bible
ABD	*Anchor Bible Dictionary*. Ed. D. N. Freedman. 6 vols.
ACNT	Augsburg Commentaries on the New Testament
ANTC	Abingdon New Testament Commentaries
BAGD	W. Bauer, W. F. Arndt, F. W. Gingrich and F. W. Danker. *Greek–English Lexicon of the New Testament and Other Early Christian Literature*. 2nd edn.
BECNT	Baker Exegetical Commentary on the New Testament
BevTh	Beiträge zur evangelischen Theologie
BJRL	*Bulletin of the John Rylands University Library of Manchester*
BNTC	Black's New Testament Commentaries
CBQ	*Catholic Biblical Quarterly*
DPL	*Dictionary of Paul and His Letters*. Ed. G. F. Hawthorne, R. P. Martin and D. G. Reid
DSD	*Dead Sea Discoveries*
EBC	*Expositor's Bible Commentary*.
EDNT	*Exegetical Dictionary of the New Testament*. Ed. H. Balz and G. Schneider. 3 vols.
EGGNT	Exegetical Guide to the Greek New Testament
EKK	Evangelisch-Katholischer Kommentar zum Neuen Testament
EQ	*Evangelical Quarterly*
HR	*History of Religions*
HTKNT	Herders Theologischer Kommentar zum Neuen Testament
HTR	*Harvard Theological Review*
ICC	International Critical Commentary
IDBSup	*Interpreter's Dictionary of the Bible: Supplementary Volume*. Ed. K. Crim
Int	*Interpretation*

IVPNT	InterVarsity Press New Testament Series
JAAR	*Journal of the American Academy of Religion*
JBL	*Journal of Biblical Literature*
JCBRF	*Journal of the Christian Brethren Research Fellowship*
JETS	*Journal of the Evangelical Theological Society*
JJS	*Journal of Jewish Studies*
JQR	*Jewish Quarterly Review*
JRS	*Journal of Roman Studies*
JSJSup	Journal for the Study of Judaism Supplements
JSNT	*Journal for the Study of the New Testament*
JSOT	*Journal for the Study of the Old Testament*
JSNTSup	Journal for the Study of the New Testament: Supplement Series
JTS	*Journal of Theological Studies*
KJV	King James Version
KNT	Kommentar zum Neuen Testament
Louw–Nida	*Greek–English Lexicon of the New Testament Based on Semantic Domains.* Ed. J. P Louw and E. U. Nida. New York: UBS, 1989
NASB	New American Standard Bible
NCB	New Century Bible
NIB	New Interpreter's Bible
NIBC	New International Biblical Commentary
NICNT	New International Commentary on the New Testament
NICOT	New International Commentary on the Old Testament
NIDNTT	*New International Dictionary of New Testament Theology.* Ed. C. Brown. 4 vols.
NIDOTTE	*New International Dictionary of Old Testament Theology and Exegesis.* Ed. W. A. Van Gemeren. 5 vols.
NIGTC	New International Greek Testament Commentary
NIV	New International Version
NovT	*Novum Testamentum*
NovTSup	Novum Testamentum Supplements
NRSV	New Revised Standard Version
NTS	*New Testament Studies*
REB	Revised English Bible
RIC	*Roman Imperial Coinage*, vol. I: *Augustus to Vitellius 31 BC–AD 69.* Rev. edn. Ed. C. H. V. Sutherland. London: Spink, 1999
RSV	Revised Standard Version
SBLDS	Society of Biblical Literature Dissertation Series

SBLSP	*Society of Biblical Literature Seminar Papers*
SNTSMS	Society for New Testament Studies Monograph Series
STDJ	Studies on Texts of the Desert of Judah
TDNIV	Today's New International Version
TDNT	*Theological Dictionary of the New Testament.* Ed. G. Kittel and G. Friedrich. 10 vols.
THKNT	Theologischer Handkommentar zum Neuen Testament
TLOT	*Theological Lexicon of the Old Testament.* Ed. E. Jenni and C. Westermann. 3 vols.
TNIV	Today's New International Version
TNTC	Tyndale New Testament Commentaries
TSAJ	Texte und Studien um antiken Judentum
TynBul	*Tyndale Bulletin*
WBC	Word Biblical Commentary
WUNT	Wissenschaftliche Untersuchungen zum Neuen Testament

Dead Sea Scrolls

1QH	*Thanksgiving Hymns* from Qumran Cave 1
1QS	Qumran Community Rule
4QFlor	*Florilegium*
4Q501	*Words of the Luminaries* from Qumran Cave 4
11QMelch	*Melchizedek* text from Qumran Cave 11
CD	Cairo (Genizah text of) Damascus (Document)

1

INTRODUCTION: THE POLITICS OF INHERITANCE?

In the immediate aftermath of World War II, Colin McCahon, one of Aotearoa New Zealand's foremost artists, produced a painting called *I Paul, to you at Ngatimote*. In this painting McCahon, who is increasingly ranked as one of the masters of mid-twentieth-century modern art, did what Pauline interpreters have often attempted but have consistently struggled to do – to situate the apostle Paul within a particular landscape in order to tease out the significance of his message for a specific locale. McCahon does not offer many clues to the content of the scroll which Paul holds in his hand for the people of Ngatimote, New Zealand, but several aspects of the painting are revealing and unintentionally crystallize issues which have frequently been a concern of Pauline scholars, especially over the last century. The painting explores war and its devastating consequences. Flying above the figure of Paul is what appears to be a military aeroplane and behind Paul (as well as a self-portrait of McCahon) is barbed wire. In other words, for McCahon both the context of Paul's message and the content of his letters are of *this world*. In the midst of a landscape of war and violence Paul is to be found on the earth, with the people, presumably because he has a message which, despite the reality of the struggles of this world, may offer hope and solidarity to the community of which he is a part. In contrast to this, Paul's scholarly interpreters have often portrayed the apostle as hovering above the earth, detached from the social and political realities of the first century.

To juxtapose McCahon with Paul's interpreters is *not* to suggest that students of the apostle have failed to identify any aspects of hope in his writings. Often Paul's eschatological language is acknowledged as a source of expectation for his audience. One of the enduring insights of twentieth-century biblical scholarship is a recognition of the extent to which an eschatological milieu shapes and governs the NT writings in general and the Pauline corpus in particular. A seminal figure in this regard is Albert Schweitzer. His emphasis on the primacy of Paul's Jewish heritage and on the significance of the apostle's eschatological perspective are often described as Schweitzer's greatest contribution to Pauline studies.[1] It would not be an overstatement to refer to the twentieth-century as "the age of Schweitzer, that is, the age of eschatology."[2] Ernst Käsemann, a biblical scholar of equally far-reaching influence, walked a similar interpretive path to that of Schweitzer.[3] Although these two leading figures did not approach Pauline theology in identical fashion, there is much likeness in the terrain they traversed. Believing that "apocalyptic was the mother of all theology," Käsemann saw as one of his main purposes to renew the challenge emerging from the "rediscovery of primitive Christian apocalyptic," which Schweitzer and others had begun and which Käsemann argued had been "more or less industriously eliminated or pushed away to the outer fringes of our awareness."[4] Subsequent scholarship has given much reflection to Käsemann's challenge, but the interpreter who has given this the most sustained attention is J. Christiaan Beker.[5] Even if not all interpreters accept Beker's proposal that eschatology constitutes the "coherent center" of Paul's thought, many do now acknowledge that the apostle's eschatology could be identified as the starting point and one of the governing features of his writings.[6]

It is in light of the landscape sketched and shaded by Schweitzer, Käsemann and Beker in particular that an awareness has developed of the ways in which eschatology provides the background and foundation for many other strands of Paul's thinking, such as, for example, christology, pneumatology, ecclesiology and soteriology. In other words, it is possible to see eschatological concerns threaded through almost every letter within the Pauline corpus.

---

[1] See particularly A. Schweitzer, *The Mysticism of Paul the Apostle* (London: Black, 1931).

[2] B. Matlock, *Unveiling the Apocalyptic Paul: Paul's Interpreters and the Rhetoric of Criticism* (Sheffield Academic Press, 1996), 24.

[3] It is also the case that Käsemann's teacher, Rudolph Bultmann, has had a considerable influence on how Paul's eschatological language has been understood. See particularly R. Bultmann, "History and Eschatology in the New Testament," *NTS* 1 (1954): 5–16; R. Bultmann, *Theology of the New Testament* (London: SCM Press, 1956); R. Bultmann, *Jesus Christ and Mythology* (New York: Scribner's, 1958), *passim*.

[4] E. Käsemann, *New Testament Questions of Today* (London: SCM Press, 1965), 109 n. 2.

[5] J. C. Beker, *Paul the Apostle: The Triumph of God in Life and Thought* (Philadelphia: Fortress Press, 1980). There has been much debate over what exactly Käsemann meant by the term "apocalyptic." As Barry Matlock suggests, there is a sense in which the term functions as theological shorthand for whatever Käsemann wants it to mean. See Matlock, *Unveiling the Apocalyptic Paul*, 235. Similarly N. T. Wright, "A New Tübingen School? Ernst Käsemann and His Commentary on Romans," *Themelios* 7 (1982).

[6] For Beker's proposal see particularly Beker, *Paul the Apostle*, *passim*.

This is *not* to say that there has always been agreement amongst Paul's interpreters on how to understand and define this increasingly slippery term, with one interpreter asking whether it has now been devalued beyond recovery.[7] The word was formed from the Greek adjective *eschatos* and has traditionally been used to refer to that section of systematic theology which is concerned with "last things": Christian beliefs concerning the individual's death, judgment, the afterlife and resurrection. The term is now used more broadly than this. It often refers to the language, beliefs and concepts which relate to the end of history and which point to a new quality of existence, a world which is qualitatively different from the present.[8] In what follows, the focus will be on *describing* Paul's eschatology as it emerges in his writings rather than attempting to further *define* it. However, two observations are worth making at this stage: first, that a distinction will be assumed between the various expressions of Jewish apocalyptic phenomena and Paul's eschatology;[9] second, that Paul's eschatology encompasses how he understands the goal and destiny of history – both the *future* event of God's final intervention and the *quality* of that event.

Amidst the abundance of eschatological language and concepts which the apostle Paul employs, one word which has received relatively little attention within Pauline studies is that of "inheritance." What does Paul mean, for example, when he writes to the Christians in the capital of the Roman Empire insisting that they will one day "inherit the world" (Rom. 4:13)? How would such a grand claim to worldly dominion have sounded within the context of first-century imperial Rome? To ask this question is to enquire how one aspect of his eschatological thought (inheritance) might have been viewed against the backdrop of a particular landscape (first-century imperial Rome) and what it might have meant for a specific group of people (the Christians at Rome).

In Paul Hammer's 1960 article "A Comparison of *Klēronomia* in Paul and Ephesians," he identifies several characteristics of Paul's inheritance

---

[7] George B. Caird, *The Language and Imagery of the Bible* (London: Duckworth, 1980), 256.

[8] D. E Aune, "Eschatology (Early Jewish)," in *ABD* II (New York: Doubleday, 1992), 594.

[9] Following P. D. Hanson ("Apocalypse, Genre," in *IDBSup* 29 [Nashville: Abingdon, 1976], 27–34), there is a general consensus to divide the field of Jewish apocalyptic into three categories: apocalyptic (a literary genre), apocalyptic eschatology (a religious perspective not confined to apocalypses) and apocalypticism (a socio-religious movement or community that has recourse to apocalyptic eschatology as a way of dealing with social or political alienation). M. C. de Boer, "Paul and Apocalyptic Eschatology," in *The Encyclopedia of Apocalypticism*, ed. J. J. Collins (New York: Continuum, 1998), vol. I, 348.

language which set it apart from how *klēronomia* is used in Ephesians.[10] One of Hammer's conclusions is that inheritance in the undisputed Pauline letters (as opposed to its meaning in Ephesians, a disputed letter) refers both to Jesus Christ and to believers, and that both believers and Christ become "the means to and *the content* of the inheritance."[11] Hammer argues that "[a]lthough Paul does not say so directly, his argument leads us to assert that for him there is what approaches an identification between the heir and the inheritance. Christ is the *heir* of Abraham and the *content* of the promise to Abraham. He is both the historical *means* and the historical *end*."[12] In other words (although this is never stated explicitly by Hammer) what was typically understood in biblical and post-biblical Jewish tradition to refer to the land of Israel and to the inheritors of this land is now transmuted by Paul into a reference to individual Christians and their relationship to Christ.[13] Accordingly, the socio-political significance which the concept of inheritance carried in Jewish tradition, which will be discussed in due course, is no longer apparent when Paul uses the word.

In 1968, in his work *Paul's Concept of Inheritance*, James Hester engaged in an extensive study of inheritance and its cognates in Paul's letters.[14] In the decades since Hester's discussion there have been various forays into the territory of Pauline inheritance but there has been no other study which has examined the concept in such length.[15] Hester identifies a number of important themes conveyed by Paul's language of inheritance. At points he also identifies several problems with Hammer's treatment. Perhaps one of Hester's most significant findings is the conclusion (against Hammer) that when Paul uses inheritance language he maintains the focus on "land" which is so central to the Old Testament's use of the word. What Hester shows, however, is that for Paul "inheritance" includes the whole world, rather than referring to the specific land of Canaan. As Hester puts it, "The geographical reality of the Land

---

[10] P. L. Hammer, "A Comparison of *Klēronomia* in Paul and Ephesians," *JBL* 79.3 (1960).

[11] Ibid., 272; emphasis added.   [12] Ibid., 271; emphasis original.   [13] Ibid., 272.

[14] J. D. Hester, *Paul's Concept of Inheritance* (Edinburgh: Oliver & Boyd, 1968). See also J. D. Hester, "The 'Heir' and Heilsgeschichte: A Study of Gal 4:1ff," in *Oikonomia, Festschrift für Oscar Cullmann* (Hamburg-Bergstedt: Reich, 1967), 118–25.

[15] As Denton observes, Hester's monograph is "the most detailed study of inheritance in Paul"; D. R. Denton, "Inheritance in Paul and Ephesians," *EQ* 53.3 (1982): 158. For other discussions of the word, see, for example, F. Lyall, "Legal Metaphors in the Epistles," *TynBul* 32 (1981); J. Eichler, "Inheritance, Lot, Portion," in *NIDNTT* II (Grand Rapids: Zondervan, 1975–85), 295–304; J. H. Friedrich, "κληρονομία," in *EDNT* II (Grand Rapids: Eerdmans, 1993), 298–99.

never ceases to play an important part in Paul's concept of inheritance. He simply makes the Land the eschatological world."[16] Given Hester's emphasis on the earthly and physical nature of inheritance, it is surprising that the socio-political direction of his study has not been taken further in subsequent scholarship. As Walter Brueggemann points out, the promise of land within the biblical narrative is a pledge to secure socio-economic well-being for the people of God and such a guarantee carries with it inevitable socio-political implications: "The linkage of God and land makes the biblical tradition endlessly revolutionary in its social function. Every attempt to reduce the Bible to an otherworldly subject fails precisely on this accent on land."[17] If it is the case, therefore, that Paul is still referring to physical land, albeit extended to include the whole world, when he uses the word inheritance (as Hester argues), the question arises as to what degree such language is "endlessly revolutionary" for himself and his hearers in the context of first-century imperial Rome. At first glance Hester's reading of inheritance would seem to fit well within McCahon's painting since the word has the appearance of conveying a decidedly socio-political claim – like McCahon, Hester has painted Paul in earthy tones.

Not all interpreters, however, have understood Paul's language in this way. Many have concurred with Hammer's judgment that, although inheritance in the Hebrew scriptures refers primarily to physical land and the possession of this land, Paul's use of the word is entirely devoid of any such concrete reference. Particularly influential has been W. D. Davies' examination of "land" in the New Testament.[18] In Davies' study there is no mention of the phrase "inherit the world" as it occurs in Rom. 4:13 (τὸ κληρονόμον αὐτὸν εἶναι κόσμου) – a statement which has so much potential for an understanding of "land" in the New Testament – and neither is there any thought given to the use of "heir" in the context of Romans 8, a text which yields considerable insights into the future redemption of this world.[19] Davies acknowledges that "the notion of 'inheritance' is important and inseparable from our theme [of 'land']" [20] and yet he fails to give any attention to the *content* of the inheritance. What makes

---

[16] Hester, *Paul's Concept of Inheritance*, 82.

[17] W. Brueggemann, "Land," in *Reverberations of Faith. A Theological Handbook of Old Testament Themes* (Louisville and London: Westminster John Knox Press, 2002), 123.

[18] W. D. Davies, *The Gospel and the Land* (London: University of California Press, 1974).

[19] So E. Adams, *Constructing the World: A Study in Paul's Cosmological Language* (Edinburgh: T. & T. Clark, 2000), 170.

[20] Davies, *The Gospel and the Land*, 20 n. 12.

this omission particularly significant is that his work is arguably the most detailed treatment of the concept of "land" in the New Testament and it is certainly one of the most influential proponents of an apolitical and "spiritualized" reading of "land" in Paul.[21]

There are two interrelated aspects of Davies' study which have had a particularly significant influence on an understanding of inheritance in Paul. First there is Davies' observation that whereas in the Old Testament, inheritance and land are primarily focused on the territory of Canaan, for Paul, because of Christ, there is no longer any importance given to a particular territory. "To the contrary, fulfillment of the promise 'in Christ' demanded the deterritorializing of the promise."[22] Davies rightly points out that one of Paul's main purposes (especially in Galatians and Romans) is to argue *against* those who would continue to define the community of God in terms of ethnic traditions and observances. As Davies puts it, although Paul never makes explicit his perspective on the land, "In the Christological logic of Paul, the land, like the law, particular and provisional, had become irrelevant."[23]

There is one sense in which Davies' observation is accurate – there is little question that Paul, in the light of Christ, is insistent on the relativizing of the law. The implication of this would be that the land of Canaan no longer has any primary importance in the apostle's thinking. But the problematic nature of Davies' argument (and that of subsequent scholarship) is the deduction that since Paul's inheritance is non-territorial, inasmuch as it is not tied to one specific tract of terrain, it is therefore also necessarily non-material or spiritual in reference. For example, it is common for interpreters to suggest that because inheritance no longer refers to a particular territory then it is best understood as being, for Paul, a *symbol* of God's blessing – it is a word which connotes God's relationship with humanity rather than a concept which involves actual physical turf.[24] In other words, inheritance has little to do with the created order or tangible real estate and it is better conceived as transcending the present state of things on earth. One of the consequences of a non-material inheritance is the belief that, for Paul, the present created order (including the socio-political realm) is nothing but a transient stage on which believers play out the drama of life in preparation for the world which will follow. According to some of Paul's interpreters this is why he often appears to

---

[21] See Davies, *The Gospel and the Land*.   [22] Ibid., 179.   [23] Ibid.

[24] See, for example, L. Morris, *The Epistle to the Romans* (Grand Rapids: Eerdmans; Leicester: InterVarsity Press, 1988), 206; F. F. Bruce, *The Epistle of Paul to the Romans*, TNTC (Grand Rapids: Eerdmans, 1980), 116.

encourage the social and political status quo, for to engage at any level in the socio-political realm of the first century would be like "tinkering with the engines of a sinking ship."[25]

A second, closely allied deduction made by Davies and subsequent interpreters is the assumption that any elements of nationalistic hope and political expectation which were at the heart of inheritance and land in the Old Testament are entirely absent from Paul's thinking. The logic is that it was primarily the territory of Canaan that gave rise to the associated ideas of Israel's triumph over the surrounding nations. For Paul, Canaan is no longer important, therefore any ideas of worldly sovereignty, possession and ownership must also be missing when Paul uses the word "inheritance." In short, inheritance is non-territorial and therefore depoliticized.[26]

Although Davies' study of "land" has been influential, it is also important to outline the ways in which various other interpretive traditions have contributed to such an understanding. One particularly influential approach has been what is often now referred to as the Reformation or Lutheran reading of Paul. This understanding argues that the heart of his theology and the essence of his gospel revolve around concepts such as individual guilt, condemnation, righteousness and justification. It has been assumed that in using this language (especially in Galatians and Romans) the main theological problem Paul is dealing with is the question of how a sinful person can find acceptance before a righteous God. Paul's answer to this problem, it is argued, is faith: God reckons as righteous (i.e. he justifies) those who by faith accept the offer of forgiveness made possible through the atoning work of Christ. With this doctrine of justification by faith as his foundation, Paul opposes those who would seek to be justified by works, which is the attempt to claim acceptance of one's own meritorious achievement, whether moral or religious.[27] This governing Reformation approach to Paul in turn determines how

---

[25] J. Ziesler, *Pauline Christianity* (Oxford University Press, 1983), 120. For similar readings of Pauline eschatology in general, and the way in which this influences Paul's "social conservatism," see E. E. Ellis, *Pauline Theology: Ministry and Society* (Grand Rapids: Eerdmans, 1989), 18–23; J. P. Sampley, *Walking between the Times: Paul's Moral Reasoning* (Minneapolis: Fortress Press, 1991), 78, 113; H. Räisänen, "Did Paul Expect an Earthly Kingdom?," in *Paul, Luke and the Greco-Roman World*, ed. O. Christofferson, C. Clausen, J. Frey and B. W. Longenecker, JSNTSup 217 (Sheffield Academic Press, 2002), 19.

[26] See, for example, Davies, *The Gospel and the Land*, 164–220.

[27] For this reading of Romans see, for example, J. A. Fitzmyer, *Romans*, AB 33 (London: Doubleday, 1993), 369; D. J. Moo, *The Epistle to the Romans*, NICNT (Grand Rapids: Eerdmans, 1996), 94–96; B. Witherington, *Paul's Letter to the Romans. A Socio-Rhetorical Commentary* (Grand Rapids, and Cambridge: Eerdmans, 2004), 124.

the language of inheritance is understood: the focus is predominantly on *how* (for example) Abraham received the inheritance and therefore *how* believers receive the inheritance. Or, if any thought *is* given to the content of the inheritance, it is often understood in individualized and spiritualized terms, and there is believed to be no spatial, earthly or this-worldly dimension to the concept.[28]

This reading of Paul has undergone rigorous critique in the last twenty-five years with the result that there has emerged within NT scholarship a so-called "new perspective on Paul." This label was coined by James Dunn in his 1983 Manson Memorial Lecture, "The New Perspective on Paul and the Law,"[29] and it is now used to designate a diversity of revisionist readings of Paul which seek to do more justice to the first-century Jewish context Paul engages with.[30] One of the areas which has received extensive discussion in this new reading has been the law, not only Paul's view of the law and the "works of the law," but also first-century Jewish attitudes to the law. Whereas the traditional perspective understands Paul to be opposing Jews who believed they could be saved by legalistic observance of the law, the newer perspectives suggest that the principal problem with the law, for Paul, is that it is ethnically exclusive. If law remains central in Christian identity, then Gentiles, who do not possess the law, are either excluded from the Jewish community or they are considered to be inferior members of the community. Paul is therefore not opposed to works in general, but more specifically to "works of the law," understood as Jewish identity markers which produce rigid social boundaries between Jew and Gentile. This change in perspective can

---

[28] Identified by W. Brueggemann, *The Land: Place as Gift, Promise, and Challenge in Biblical Faith*, Overtures to Biblical Theology (Philadelphia: Fortress Press, 1977), 177. For a similar observation in relation to Romans 8 see B. J. Byrne, "Creation Groaning: An Earth Bible Reading of Romans 8:18–22," in *Readings from the Perspective of Earth*, ed. N. C. Habel (Sheffield Academic Press, 2000), 194.

[29] J. D. G. Dunn, "The New Perspective on Paul," in *Jesus, Paul and the Law*, ed. J. D. G. Dunn (London: SCM Press, 1990). Originally published as J. D. G. Dunn, "The New Perspective on Paul," *BJRL* 65 (1983). Dunn was also the first to demonstrate, in a NT commentary, the implications of the New Perspective. J. D. G. Dunn, *Romans 1–8*, WBC 38A (Dallas: Word Books, 1988); J. D. G. Dunn, *Romans 9–16*, WBC 38B (Dallas: Word Books, 1988).

[30] It was the work of E. P. Sanders which led to a re-evaluation of how first-century Judaism is understood. See particularly E. P. Sanders, *Paul and Palestinian Judaism: A Comparison of Patterns of Religion* (Philadelphia: Fortress Press, 1997), 33–428. However, John Barclay rightly notes that there are many before Sanders on whom he has drawn. See J. M. G. Barclay, "Paul and the Law: Observations on Some Recent Debates," *Themelios* 12 (1986): 6. Besides Dunn, the other primary contributor to the New Perspective approach has been N. T. Wright. See, for example, N. T. Wright, *The Climax of the Covenant: Christ and the Law in Pauline Theology* (Edinburgh: T. & T. Clark, 1991).

therefore be characterized (although this is only one aspect of a wider critique) as a shift from a predominantly soteriological reading of Paul to more of an ecclesiological understanding of his message. In other words, rather than being focused on how an individual is saved, Paul is more concerned with how the new community of God is to be defined. This change in perspective has had some effect on how inheritance is read in Paul's letters. Since Paul's focus is believed to be on the question of *who* are the heirs, there has been a welcome shift from understanding inheritance solely in individualized terms to recognizing that Paul uses the word in the course of discussing the make-up of the community. As James Dunn argues, "The question Paul has in view is 'Who are the heirs of the promise to Abraham?' "[31]

Despite this interpretive shift, however, there has still been comparatively little attention given to the importance of the category of inheritance in Paul's letters in general, and in particular to its possible socio-political significance for himself and his readers located in the context of the Roman Empire. In other words, the potentially suggestive nature of Hester's findings has not been capitalized on. In part this is understandable because it was not Hester's purpose to establish the degree to which Paul's inheritance language would have subverted the dominant imperial discourse of the day. Instead, Hester's primary intent was to describe the elements of salvation history found in certain passages in Paul's letters (primarily Romans 4 and 8; Galatians 3 and 4), using inheritance as a way of providing the focus and limits to this study. Even so, Hester's study includes some valuable insights which might have something to contribute to the growing interest regarding Paul and his socio-political context.

Over the last few decades there have been a number of isolated attempts to demonstrate the socio-ethical significance of Paul's letters. For example, there have been re-examinations of his apparently negative portrayal of women as well as readings of his work from a non-Western perspective. There have also been investigations into the significance of Paul's *principalities* and *powers* language. But what about Paul in relation to his socio-political context more broadly – to what degree does he confront or subvert the socio-political status quo? Pauline studies has, in recent times, begun to identify appropriate questions with regard to the Roman imperial context. Important work in this regard was started by the "Paul and

---

[31] Dunn, *Romans 1–8*, 213–14. See similarly R. B. Hays, "'Have We Found Abraham to Be Our Forefather According to the Flesh?' A Reconsideration of Rom 4:1," *NovT* 27 (1985): 83–84, 90–91, 93.

Politics" group in the Society of Biblical Literature and it is now increasingly adopted by other interpreters.[32] It is this sort of analysis which N. T. Wright considers to be the most exciting in Pauline studies today. He welcomes "the quite fresh attempts that are being made to study the interface, the opposition, the conflict between Paul's gospel . . . and the world in which his entire ministry was conducted, the world in which Caesar not only held sway but exercised power through his divine claim."[33]

In tandem with this increasing awareness of the tension between "Caesar" and Paul there has been a growing recognition of the ways in which material poverty affected Paul's assemblies and the extent to which such economic destitution might therefore have influenced how Paul's letters were understood in their first-century context.[34] Whereas over the last thirty years or so Pauline studies has tended towards a "cultivated detachment" regarding the social location of Paul's Christian audiences, there is now a slow (but growing) alertness to the possibility that "Paul's assemblies mostly comprised urban poor folks who lived near the line between subsistence and crisis" and that this should in turn shape how we interpret Paul's message.[35]

The politics of inheritance?

It is within this stream of Pauline socio-political scholarship that the present study finds its home. My intention in the ensuing discussion is to extend James Hester's research by giving sustained attention to the

[32] For the key contributors to the Paul and Politics group, see the essays in R. A. Horsley, ed., *Paul and Politics: Ekklesia, Israel, Imperium, Interpretation* (Harrisburg, PA: Trinity Press, 2000). See also N. Elliott, "Strategies of Resistance in the Pauline Communities," in *Hidden Transcripts and the Arts of Resistance. Applying the Work of James C. Scott to Jesus and Paul*, ed. R. A. Horsley (Atlanta: Society of Biblical Literature, 2004), 97–122; D. Harink, *Paul among the Postliberals. Pauline Theology beyond Christendom and Modernity* (Grand Rapids: Brazos Press, 2003).

[33] N. T. Wright, "Paul's Gospel and Caesar's Empire," in *Paul and Politics: Ekklesia, Israel, Imperium, Interpretation*, ed. R. A. Horsley (Harrisburg, PA: Trinity Press, 2000), 160.

[34] The first to put this question back on the agenda was J. J. Meggitt, *Paul, Poverty and Survival*, Studies of the New Testament and Its World (Edinburgh: T. & T. Clark, 1998). Meggitt's argument has sparked robust debate. For the responses, see further below, Chapter 2.

[35] Quotation from S. J. Friesen, "Poverty in Pauline Studies: Beyond the So-Called New Consensus," *JSNT* 26.3 (2004): 359. The approach to this issue over at least the last thirty years has been shaped by what has been called a "New Consensus." The primary advocates of this have been W. A. Meeks, *The First Urban Christians* (New Haven: Yale University Press, 1983); G. Theissen, *The Social Setting of Pauline Christianity* (Philadelphia: Fortress Press, 1982). For a more detailed discussion of these issues see Chapter 2 below.

potentially socio-political significance of Paul's inheritance language. What follows is therefore an exploration of the extent to which Paul's terminology of inheritance and its associated imagery, logic and arguments functioned to evoke socio-political expectations that were alternative to those which prevailed in contemporary Roman imperial discourse. In short, to what extent does inheritance contribute to a counter-imperial narrative? In order to address this question there are two areas which need to be teased out: the first-century Roman imperial *context* within which Paul uses the term, and the *content* which the word evokes.

Clearly, to examine the expectations conveyed by the language of inheritance as it occurs in each of Paul's letters in the same detail would be too big a task for a study such as this. Instead, the discussion will be directed in the first instance at Paul's letter to the Christians in Rome. There are five undisputed uses of κληρονόμος and its cognates in Romans – Rom. 4:13, 14; Rom. 8:17 (three times) – and there is one textual variant in Rom. 11:1, where the word κληρονομίαν is used in place of τὸν λαόν. With each of these uses, what is being conveyed by Paul and what would it have meant to utter such language within the context of imperial Rome in the first century? There are six occurrences of the κληρονόμος word group in Galatians, which will be examined in Chapter 6 below. Chapter 7 will consider the five occurrences of the word in 1 Corinthians and explore the two uses of the word in Colossians.

The Roman imperial context of inheritance

The first step, therefore, is to take seriously the context of Empire and the claims being made by the Roman Empire in the first century. In particular, what were some of the messages conveyed by the Roman Empire with regard to the structure and purpose, the hopes and expectations, of first-century society? After all, there is little doubt that Paul (although he had not yet visited Rome) would have been met at every turn by signs of Roman imperial power, each of which communicated something about how the world was to be structured. The roads he traveled on, the harbors he sailed from, and the soldiers whom he encountered were constant reminders of Rome's influence and control. Rome itself was an impressive city, ever more opulent in certain areas, with wealth intentionally visible so as to remind visitors of Rome's power and prosperity.[36] Anyone who could read would have been exposed to inscriptions, votive offerings,

---

[36] J. S. Jeffers, *Conflict at Rome. Social Order and Hierarchy in Early Christianity* (Minneapolis: Fortress Press, 1991), 3.

decrees and epitaphs, many of which (as will be shown in more detail in the next chapter) extolled the virtues of Rome and its rulers.[37] Furthermore, the regular festivals meant that all public spaces in cities such as Rome were involved in imperial-cult activities and that these spaces presented various images of Empire.[38] As Deissmann observes, to fail to pay attention to Paul's socio-political context would to be imply that "St. Paul and his fellow believers went through the world blindfolded."[39]

The Christians in Rome were daily exposed to and surrounded by the images and message of Caesar and his successors. There is therefore a need to consider how Paul's language of inheritance would have sounded to readers of Romans within this environment. Not only the rulers but also the general population of imperial Rome had hopes and expectations about the way their communities should be structured. It will be important to describe these in order to begin to uncover their political vision. It is vital that some consideration is given to these issues because (paraphrasing Richard Horsley's observation with regard to Jesus) trying to understand Paul's eschatology without an awareness of how Roman imperialism determined the conditions of life for Paul's communities "would be like trying to understand Martin Luther King without knowing how slavery, reconstruction, and segregation determined the lives of African Americans in the United States."[40]

The content of inheritance

As well as reading "inheritance" in its first-century Roman imperial context, there is a need to give more attention to the *content* of Paul's use of the word as it occurs in Romans.[41] To what extent does Paul retain

---

[37] P. Veyne, *Bread and Circuses. Historical Sociology and Political Pluralism*, trans. B. Pearce, Penguin History (London: Allen Lane, 1990), 128; R. J. Cassidy, *Paul in Chains. Roman Imprisonment and the Letters of St. Paul* (New York: The Crossroad Publishing Company, 2001), 2–13.

[38] S. J. Friesen, *Imperial Cults and the Apocalypse of John. Reading Revelation in the Ruins* (Oxford University Press, 2001), 75.

[39] G. A. Deissmann, *Light from the Ancient East*, trans. L. R. M Strachan (London: Hodder and Stoughton, 1910), 344. Similarly R. A. Horsley, "Paul and Slavery," in *Slavery in Text and Interpretation*, Semeia 83/4, ed. A. D. Callahan, R. A. Horsley and A. Smith (Atlanta: Scholars Press, 1998), 160.

[40] R. A. Horsley, *Jesus and Empire: The Kingdom of God and the New World Disorder* (Minneapolis: Fortress Press, 2003), 13.

[41] Hester says that rather than dealing with the "concept" of inheritance he is focusing only on the "language" of inheritance. In the discussion which follows, in order to limit the boundaries of the task, I am instead focusing solely on the specific references to inheritance and its cognates.

the OT and Intertestamental meaning or associations of the word, and to what degree is it altered or adapted by him? There are three interrelated aspects of his use of the word which warrant closer attention.

The this-worldly nature of inheritance

The first is the this-worldly and geographical nature of inheritance (as opposed to an entirely spiritualized or transcendent reading of the word). In short, this is a question about the degree to which Paul's use of inheritance has anything to do with land. In other words, this is to ask *what* the inheritance consists of. There is a need here to begin with Hester's findings but to ground these more rigorously within the particular Pauline passages where inheritance occurs – to what extent should Hester's this-worldly reading be adopted and what additional insights can be gained, for example, from the literary and logical contexts of inheritance in Paul?

The political nature of inheritance

Second, there is the closely related question of the political nature of inheritance.[42] This question stems from the first in that it asks: if it is the case that the language of inheritance is concerned with the renewal of the land, or of a restored world, then *who* inherits this land? One central aspect of inheritance in its OT usage is the guarantee it gives (or was supposed to give) that all in the community will be provided for. The concept of inheritance contributes to a social policy (if not realized, then at least envisaged) whereby wealth and power will not gather in the hands of a few families.[43] Israel's social well-being is thereby judged according to whether the needs and rights of the disadvantaged (particularly with regard to land) are taken care of and respected.[44] To be counted as one of the community is to be apportioned land, regardless of social status. The concept of inheritance and land in the Old Testament is therefore "political" in the sense that it includes who is entitled to the land and how is it distributed. As will be shown in Chapter 3, this question is then

---

[42] What follows assumes the conception of "politics" adopted below.

[43] This will be explored in more detail below. But see, for example, W. Brueggemann, "Land: Fertility and Justice," in *Theology of the Land* (Collegeville, MN: The Liturgical Press, 1987), 41–68; N. K. Gottwald, *The Hebrew Bible. A Socio-Literary Introduction* (Philadelphia: Fortress Press, 1985).

[44] W. Brueggemann, "Reflections on Biblical Understandings of Property," in *A Social Reading of the Old Testament: Prophetic Approaches to Israel's Communal Life*, ed. P. D. Miller (Minneapolis: Fortress Press, 1994), 277.

extended to the *whole world* in Jewish Intertestamental literature so that the question often becomes one of *who will reign* – that is, which group of people will *inherit* the world? The second question for this study is therefore the degree to which Paul, in Romans, continues the political tone of the inheritance word and concept.

The path to inheritance

But this in turn raises a third issue. To explore the *what* (what is the nature of the inheritance) and the *who* (who are the people that inherit) of inheritance unearths the question of *how* such an inheritance will come about. If it is the case that the combination of the *what* and the *who* of inheritance results in a politically oriented narrative then the question of *how* this transpires is just as important for exploring the counter-imperial nature of the concept. This is because there is a sense in which, if Paul's language mirrors the ideas and nature of imperial discourse, then rather than subverting the language of Empire, Paul would merely be replacing one kind of domination (Roman imperial) with another (that of God's people). If Paul's inheritance language contributes to notions of lordship, authority and universal sovereignty for the people of God, then what is the *path* to this dominion – does it carry the hegemonic intentions of imperial Rome, which envisages the triumph of one group of people (the strong) over another (the weak), or does it somehow undermine all claims to power and control?

Methodological considerations

The three categories of *what*, *who* and *how* will be used to assess the socio-political significance of inheritance in Romans. This task necessitates a comparison of two contrasting narratives – the narrative of first-century imperial Rome and the narrative of the inheritance of God's people. Put another way, this discussion sets Paul's theo-political stories alongside Roman imperial thought: what the leaders and general population of Rome expected for the future of the world.

What follows is therefore a literary or thematic study, rather than a lexical or technical analysis, of inheritance. This study is not an attempt to uncover a single, precise definition of inheritance from the six occurrences in Romans. Although the six uses of the κληρονόμος word group will be given intense scrutiny, these occurences do not constitute the entirety of what Paul wants to say about the notion of inheritance. Instead, there is considerable overlap between the κληρονόμος word group and other words such as, for example, the use of "glory" in Romans 8:17–39, or the person of Abraham in 4:13–25. Similarly, because Paul's argument in Romans is full of allusions to, and echoes of, various narratives from scripture, it is not possible to isolate a given word from its immediate and wider literary contexts. This is especially the case for a study of inheritance because a passage such as Rom. 4:13–25 (for example) evokes many concepts from the Old Testament. As will be shown, Genesis 15 and 17 are important sources for Paul's argument in Romans 4, and it is from these texts that the story of Abraham and Israel-in-relation-to-the-nations emerge. It is therefore inescapable that in the course of reading Romans 4, 8 and 11 consideration will need to be given to the narrative source(s) of Paul's argument.

Just as this is not a lexical analysis of inheritance in Romans, neither is it a study of the specific use of inheritance language in Roman society. Rather than searching for evidence of the actual vocabulary and categories of inheritance that were used in imperial ideology, this study is interested more in what might be termed the conceptual significance of Paul's language in its initial context, or what Bruno Blumenfeld refers to as an "affinity of concept." In his book *The Political Paul: Justice, Democracy and Kingship in a Hellenistic Framework*, Blumenfeld proposes to show that "Paul's views in general, and particularly in the letters to the Romans and the Philippians, are structurally, argumentatively and conceptually coherent with Classical and Hellenistic political thought."[45] In order to do this, Blumenfeld first examines the external sources which may have contributed to Paul's letters; he then considers the internal textual evidence of Paul's letters. While the content of Blumenfeld's study is not directly relevant to the present work, his methodology offers some important insights. He argues that it is not necessary to prove a direct linguistic connection between Classical political thought and Paul's letters in order to posit that Paul is influenced by Hellenistic philosophy: "In the absence of direct evidence, the burden of proof rests on *affinity of concept and analogy of lexis*. The assumption is that little is accidental and even less coincidental. Almost everything is the product of a context, of what critical theories call an intertext or a sociolect. Nothing is created ex vacuo."[46] Blumenfeld suggests that his thesis "subscribes to the critical view that regards Paul as a member of his political, social and cultural environment, that sees him as the result of a milieu."[47]

[45] Bruno Blumenfeld, *The Political Paul: Justice, Democracy and Kingship in a Hellenistic Framework*, JSNTSup 210 (London: Sheffield Academic Press, 2001), 12.
[46] Ibid., 448; emphasis added.   [47] Ibid.

Unlike Blumenfeld, I am not trying to show that Paul is necessarily *influenced* by Greco-Roman thought when he uses the word "inheritance." Instead I am proposing that the language of inheritance be read with closer attention to the political, social and cultural milieu of the first century and that, in the process, particular attention be given to the conceptual likeness between Paul and (for example) Nero with regard to how they conceive of the world and of the future of people, land and earth.

Given that elsewhere, through words such as εὐαγγέλιον, Ἰησοῦ Χριστοῦ τοῦ κυρίου ἡμῶν, πίστις and δικαιοσύνη, Paul *does* plainly evoke and revise key imperial concepts, it makes good sense to explore what affinity there is, at the conceptual level, between Paul's inheritance language and the terms and phrases used by the Roman Empire.[48] Bearing in mind the explicit lexical signals Paul sends throughout Romans that he is constructing a counter-imperial narrative, it is not necessary that every item in that subversive narrative, such as inheritance, needs to have direct parallels in imperial discourse in order for it to be viewed as counter-imperial.[49] Instead the proposal is that the *narrative echoes* which inevitably reverberate throughout Paul's argument whenever he uses the word "inheritance" contribute to an overall counter-imperial perspective in Romans.[50]

In the process of comparing these two contrasting narratives, insights begin to emerge into the socio-political significance of Paul's inheritance. If *politics* is understood in terms of the science and art of government then Paul's message seems to have little relevance to the political realm so defined. But if we adopt the definition of politics as *concern about the shape of a historical community – its structure and purpose, its formation and maintenance* – then this allows insights into the socio-political significance of inheritance in Romans.[51] As Neil Elliott observes, "We

[48] G. Stanton, *Jesus and Gospel* (Cambridge University Press, 2004), 25; G. Alföldy, "Subject and Ruler, Subjects and Methods: An Attempt at a Conclusion," in *Subject and Ruler: The Cult of the Ruling Power in Classical Antiquity*, ed. A. Small, Journal of Roman Archeology Supp. Series 17 (Alberta: Journal of Roman Archeology, 1996), 254–61.

[49] For the suggestion that "Christian use of the gospel word group may have formed part of a counter-story to the story associated with the imperial cult" see Stanton, *Jesus and Gospel*, 1–62. Quotation from p 25.

[50] Using the term "echoes" is not to suggest that it is necessary to apply R. B. Hays' methodological guidelines (*Echoes of Scripture in the Letters of Paul* [New Haven and London: Yale University Press, 1989]) in order to arrive at a solid understanding of inheritance in Romans.

[51] This definition of "politics" is adapted from D. G. Horrell, *Solidarity and Difference: A Contemporary Reading of Paul's Ethics* (London: T. & T. Clark, 2005), 1–2. Douglas Harink's work, which is influenced by (among others) Karl Barth, John Howard Yoder and Stanley Hauerwas, approaches Paul's theology from this perspective. See Harink, *Paul*

properly ask, not what Paul expected Christians to achieve in the political forum (which after all was the nearly exclusive domain of the powerful) but what contours he expected their life together to assume as they lived in anticipation of God's coming triumph."[52] To frame the question in these terms is to appreciate that in order for language to be subversive it does not always need to be explicitly confrontational. One of the observations which anthropologists and sociologists have made over the last few decades is that a narrative can be "hidden" or "covert" and yet still be sharply critical of the social and political status quo. The seminal study here is that of James C. Scott.[53] In the argument which follows I will not employ Scott's concept of "hidden transcripts" in any formal sense, but one of the related ideas which will often be returned to in the pages which follow is the extent to which eschatological language can sometimes be considered implicitly critical of the current status quo. To suggest that one day things will be different is to imply that the way things are at present is not sufficient and it is not final. What *ought* to be is always therefore a conceptual subversion of what currently *is*. This is not to say that explicit challenges to first-century imperial Rome are absent from Paul's letter to the Romans – these are present both in the overall narrative of Romans and sometimes specifically in the language of inheritance – but it is to acknowledge that there is often an implicit yet equally persuasive expectation which lies beneath the surface of these more direct socio-political references.

Summary of approach

In light of this definition, what can be learnt about the politics of inheritance in Romans? The discussion begins in Chapter 2 by considering the

---

among the Postliberals. Given this definition of "politics," I am using the term interchangeably with "socio-political."

[52] N. Elliott, *Liberating Paul: The Justice of God and the Politics of the Apostle* (Maryknoll, NY: Orbis, 1994), 174. One of the defining characteristics of Paul's inheritance language (particularly in Romans) is that it is oriented primarily towards the future. In other words, as will become clear, the references in Romans 4, 8 and 11 are predominantly to do with what believers will inherit in the age which is yet to come. This means that if there is any sense of an alternative vision for power and control then these are primarily postponed to the future – although, as will also become evident, this has ramifications for the present. This is contrary to Hammer, who argues that the word as it is used in Paul (in contrast to its use in Ephesians) refers exclusively to the present. Hammer, "*Klēronomia*," 267–72. This is inaccurate, as will be shown in the discussion of the Romans' texts below. Similarly see Denton, "Inheritance," 158–60.

[53] J. C. Scott, *Domination and the Arts of Resistance: Hidden Transcripts* (Yale University Press, 1990). See also J. C. Scott, *Weapons of the Weak: Everyday Forms of Peasant Resistance* (Yale University Press, 1987).

backdrop to Paul's world – in particular the Roman imperial cult which includes the beliefs, rituals, festivals, symbols and literature which were associated with, and disseminated by, the emperor Caesar Augustus and his successors. Chapter 3 is an examination of the use of inheritance in Rom. 4:13–25. Special attention will be given to Rom. 4:13 ("inherit the world") and the ways in which this coheres with the other key elements of the passage. This chapter will argue that inheritance in this context conveys decidedly political ideas such as the future universal sovereignty of the people of God on a renewed earth, and that the word evokes a this-worldly space and time where land is distributed equally. I will explore the possibility that such a vision entails a socio-political subversion of the imperial status quo not only in the *what* and *who* but also in the *how* of inheritance.

Interpreters often suggest that Rom. 4:13 can be read as anticipating the argument which Paul develops more fully in Rom. 8:17–39. Chapter 4 will examine the three uses of inheritance in Romans 8, with particular alertness to the degree of continuity between Romans 4 and Romans 8 and also to the relationship between the people of God and a renewed creation "inheritance" which is so central to the text. One of the significant themes of Romans 8 is that the path to future universal sovereignty will not come about through domination and subjection but through suffering love.

Chapter 5 begins by proposing that the textual variant of "inheritance" in Rom. 11:1 (instead of "people") should be adopted for both internal and external reasons. Given the discussion of Romans 4 and 8, this chapter is able to demonstrate the ways in which the context and themes of inheritance in these earlier Romans texts are present in Paul's use of inheritance in Rom. 11:1. The use of the word "inheritance" here, with its similar ideas of future restoration of people and earth, enables Paul to highlight the distance between the original intent of the promise and the current experience of it, a tension which is at the heart of Romans 9–11.

Following the examination of inheritance in these three texts in Romans, the next two chapters will make comparisons with the other uses of the concept in the indisputably Pauline letters and in Colossians. Chapter 6 will consider inheritance in its Galatian context and Chapter 7 will explore the word as it is used in 1 Corinthians. In this chapter thought will also be given to the use of inheritance in Colossians, a letter which is not indisputably Pauline but which seems to have some association with various "Pauline" themes and which therefore will help to round out an understanding of the word.

What follows is therefore an attempt to explore the politics of inheritance in Romans and to consider the extent to which it contributes to a counter-imperial vision. This attempt to locate Paul in his socio-political environment, therefore, is as much about recognizing broad brushstrokes as it is about specific detail – it is similar to paying attention to the background colors of a piece of art rather than its foreground detail. The artists, poets and sculptors of first-century Rome were covering their "canvas" with colors which they perceived would or should be (or already were) the colors of the future. What does it mean to situate inheritance language within, against or alongside this social landscape? In order to make such an assessment, it is necessary first to understand the light and shade of Paul's world. It is to this task that I now turn.

2

SOME FEATURES OF GRECO-ROMAN SOCIETY IN THE SYMBOLS, RITUAL AND LITERATURE OF PAUL'S TIME

If it is the case that interpretations of inheritance in Paul have made little or no attempt to situate this language within the social and political context of the Greco-Roman first century, then it is not surprising that readings of inheritance typically give little thought to the extent to which it was subversive of its wider socio-political environment. In order to redress this tendency, I will describe some aspects of the social, political and religious environment of the city of Rome and the Roman Empire during the time when Paul wrote Romans. As noted in the Introduction, one of the arguments of the present study is that the language of inheritance evokes ideas about God's future renewal of this world and (in broad terms) what such a world might look like. It will also be suggested that the language of inheritance conveys expectations as to who inherits the land and how land (and by extension, power, control and sovereignty) should be distributed and managed in society. If this is an accurate understanding of inheritance in Romans (a question which remains to be explored in this study) then there are aspects of Greco-Roman imperial society with which the inheritance language will have jarred and clashed. What were the expectations of the Roman leaders and the general population with regard to an ideal society and empire? What did they want for society and how did they think this would come about (or had already been achieved)? The element of first-century Greco-Roman society which provides the clearest path to addressing these questions is the Roman imperial cult, which includes the beliefs, rituals, festivals, symbols and literature which were associated with, and disseminated by the emperor Caesar Augustus and his successors.

While a survey of aspects of the imperial cult has potential, however, it is also not without its problems. Richard Horsley points out that until recently studies have discounted the imperial cult as religiously superficial and politically insignificant.[1] There are several interrelated reasons

---

[1] R. A. Horsley, "The Gospel of Imperial Salvation: Introduction," in *Paul and Empire: Religion and Power in Roman Imperial Society*, ed. R. A. Horsley (Harrisburg, PA: Trinity Press International, 1997), 20.

for this. Interpreters often assume that in order to obtain the most accurate and genuine insights into the imperial cult it is necessary to understand the attitudes of individuals and the kinds of views they expressed in private. This more "personal" material, interpreters suggest, is likely to reveal more than sources which are public and formal in nature especially with regard to the "religious" dimension of the imperial cult. In other words it is common for studies to assume a clear separation between the "religious" (which is understood to be personal, private and more spontaneous) and the "political" (which is believed to be corporate, public and formal). In terms of the symbols of the Greco-Roman imperial cult, therefore, the conclusion is often that its symbols (such as coins or public monuments or city festivals) provide little insight into the "real" attitudes of first-century Roman society.[2] The assumption is often that because these sources are public and formal, rather than private and spontaneous, they are therefore devoid of any "true" substance or meaning. Furthermore these symbols are understood primarily to be evidence of what society as a whole thought and they do not address the more important question of what individuals in society thought.

This observation, however, is itself open to critique. S. R. F. Price challenges the way in which private responses are often prioritized over public responses. He points out that even if we did have information about how individuals in the first century responded to the imperial cult, this would not necessarily provide a more accurate record of the society's worldview; the information we require is more delicate and complex than a simple answer would give: "There is in fact no reason to think that the public and formal documents are necessarily misleading. There might be private exegetical responses to these official conceptions, but one should not privilege such private responses. Nor should their absence lead us to believe that the cult has no meaning for individuals."[3]

Price also challenges the "realist epistemology" which leads to an emphasis on the individual and personal at the expense of the corporate and societal. This methodology assumes that society is essentially "an aggregate of individuals" and that explanations of society have to

---

[2] This approach is evident, for example, in A. D. Nock, "Deification and Julian," *JRS* 47 (1972): 121. Nock grudgingly concedes that there is some sentiment present in the sources.

[3] S. R. F. Price, *Rituals and Power: The Roman Imperial Cult in Asia Minor* (Cambridge University Press, 1984), 5. As Price acknowledges, "this does not mean that there are no problems with the sources we have access to – there are. For example, they are largely sources which originate from the elite. Thus we cannot be sure of the tension between ideology and practice" (p. 6). Justin Meggitt adopts a "bottom up" approach which includes studies of epitaphs, defixiones and graffiti; Meggitt, *Paul, Poverty and Survival*, 30.

be viewed from the perspective of the individual. Price argues that such "methodological individualists" "draw a sharp distinction between symbolism and the 'real' world of individuals and they cannot treat ritual as an articulation of collective representations."[4] He suggests that a preferable approach, and one adopted from Durkheim onwards, is an insistence on the *social* as the primary area of analysis. Such an emphasis invests cultural symbols with new significance.

A third assumption which needs to be re-examined is the belief that in the first century religion could be thought of as entirely separated from politics. Many modern interpreters have questioned whether the imperial cults constituted a religious or a political phenomenon. Stephen Friesen points out, however, that "the very notion that politics can be severed from the sacred is a misconstrual."[5] The challenge, suggests Friesen, is to examine the evidence from the first century without using inappropriate notions of "religious" and "political" in the process of considering the sources. This is not to say that such separate categories should be entirely abandoned – it is sometimes helpful, as evidenced in the study which follows, to separate the "social," "religious" and "political" in order to aid clarity – but there needs always to be the recognition of the inextricable relationship between such terms.[6] Most importantly in terms of the imperial cult, there needs to be an acknowledgment of the ways in which the "political" and "social" can only be fully understood as tightly interwoven with the "religious."

Considering the cultural symbols of a society is therefore no less important than exploring the views and expectations of individuals in society. But to what extent were the symbols to which we have access only an indication of the ideals which the rulers themselves wanted to convey? Were symbols and ritual merely the voice of the powerful? There is often an assumption that the imperial cult was "propaganda" disseminated from the elite in Roman society and that the general populace were passive recipients of this message. According to this understanding, these sources are only an indication of how the emperors wished to be perceived and do not offer any insights into the attitudes of society as a whole. Such a criticism has some validity. It is true that there was often a strongly controlling approach to the Empire's use of symbol and ritual in first-century Greco-Roman society. Through visual imagery a new mythology

---

[4] Price, *Rituals and Power*, 11.   [5] Friesen, *Imperial Cults*, 4–15.
[6] See also J. Rives, "Religion in the Roman World," in *Experiencing Rome. Culture, Identity and Power in the Roman Empire*, ed. J. Huskinson (London: Routledge, 2000), 266; Horsley, "Paul and Slavery," 162.

of Rome and a new ritual of power was created. "Built on relatively simple foundations, the myth perpetuated itself and transcended the realities of everyday life to project onto future generations the impression that they lived in the best of all possible worlds in the best of all possible times."[7]

But while it is important to note the degree of "propaganda" from above, it is equally vital to acknowledge the complex role which symbols play in a society. The work of Paul Zanker,[8] S. F. R. Price[9] and Karl Galinsky,[10] for example, shows that, in first-century Greco-Roman society, symbols and ritual were integral to the beliefs and praxis of *all* groups in society. Price argues that when there were festivals in a city which celebrated imperial rule, the whole of the city participated. He shows that the imperial cult did not mean something entirely different for the elite and the common people but that it involved the whole city.[11] Why was this? What function did cultural symbols fulfil in ancient Greco-Roman society?

One of the primary purposes was to help people make sense of the significant changes which had occurred in society and to find what Zanker terms "a new visual language" for the "new order" which was being established.[12] This was especially so for those in the Empire who did not have access to power. For these people the influence of the Roman Empire was overwhelming and the imperial cult pervaded all aspects of people's lives. In the surrounding Greek cities in particular, subjects had to make sense of a foreign rule in their land. How were they to conceptualize the new relationship between themselves as subjects and the new powerful ruler? As Price notes, these Greek citizens used their traditional symbolic system to represent

> the Emperor to themselves in the familiar terms of divine power. The imperial cult, like the cults of the traditional gods, created a relationship of power between subject and ruler... That is, the cult was a major part of the web of power that formed the fabric of society. The imperial cult stabilised the religious order of the world. The system of ritual was carefully structured; the symbolism evoked a picture of the relationship between

[7] P. Zanker, *The Power of Images in the Age of Augustus*, trans. Alan Shapiro, Jerome Lecture Series 16 (University of Michigan Press, 1988), 3–4.

[8] Ibid. [9] Price, *Rituals and Power*.

[10] Karl Galinsky, *Augustan Culture: An Interpretive Introduction* (Princeton University Press, 1996).

[11] Price, *Rituals and Power*, 248.

[12] Zanker, *The Power of Images*, 1–10. See similarly Veyne, *Bread and Circuses*, 378, 463 n. 287.

the Emperor and the gods. The ritual was also structuring; it imposed a definition of the world. The imperial cult, along with politics and diplomacy, constructed the reality of the Roman Empire.[13]

One function of symbols, therefore, was to make sense of a new situation, particularly the relationship between ruler and subject. Rather than being primarily about "meaningless" honors given towards the ruler, symbols were as much about the subjects of the emperor trying to describe a new system and administration. In part the population's participation in imperial festivals and ritual may have been a recognition that the dominant order could not change and a consequent need to acknowledge that order as well as articulating their own place within it.

It was also evident that the use of symbols and ritual involved a spontaneous response of gratitude. Once certain directions had been put in place by the rulers, there was often no need for further instructions or coercion. As Zanker puts it, "What appears in retrospect as a subtle program resulted in fact from the interplay that the Emperor himself projected and the honors bestowed on him more or less spontaneously, a process that evolved naturally over long periods of time."[14] Rather than seeing the symbols and rituals of the imperial cult as a hierarchical "organization of opinion" it is better to see them as a "complex system of multiple autonomous interactions, more spontaneous than organised."[15] This was even the case during Augustus' reign when the imperial cult was founded. Throughout his reign Augustus enjoyed a close relationship with many poets, especially Virgil. Yet as Galinsky shows, this did not mean that the poets were merely reacting to the tone which Augustus set. Instead, much of their poetry was a free response to their times and the poets often helped to shape culture as much as Augustus did.[16] Similarly, in subsequent periods of Roman rule, the imperial family played a significant role in proliferating shrines, temples and festivals in honor of the emperor, and this was met with a spirit of gratitude from the Greek cities which in turn led to initiatives by the cities to build temples and establish games in the emperor's honor.

The symbols of a society therefore reveal important insights about the attitudes and views of many groups in that society and there is clearly

---

[13] Price, *Rituals and Power*, 248.   [14] Zanker, *The Power of Images*, 4.
[15] Horsley, *Jesus and Empire*, 13. Similarly Veyne, *Bread and Circuses*, 378, 463 n. 287.
[16] Galinsky, *Augustan Culture*, 239.

much to be gained from such an investigation. But it is not the purpose of this chapter to attempt to describe all aspects of a first-century Greco-Roman worldview – the task is more focused than this. Although Rome's influence was vast, only some aspects of imperial presence are of relevance to a study of inheritance in Romans. Three questions will be the focus of this chapter. First, *what* were the features which the Roman leaders and the general population believed would characterize the ideal society they desired? What would be the characteristics of this time? Second, *how* would this (or for some first-century observers, how had this already) come about? Who were the people who would create these ideals for society, who would make it happen? Third, *had this time occurred*, or was it yet to happen? Although separating the first two questions of *what* and *how* is almost impossible, it is helpful to recognize them here as distinct questions, at least conceptually, before examining specific examples and sources.

The expectations of Empire

So *what* kinds of ideals and expectations were evident in the cultural symbols of Paul's time, the period when Claudius and then Nero were the emperors? While it is true that the themes evident during this period are complex and nuanced, it is still possible to express these themes in simple terms. The belief of the Roman emperors and the expectation of many of the people living in Rome was that they would experience a time of material blessings on earth, in this life. These blessings were thought of in very concrete terms and included the hope of fertility and abundance for people and crops, the hope of the welfare of the people of the Empire, which included the blessings of peace, stability, order, abundance and tranquility. The means (*how?*) by which these blessings would eventuate was equally clear. The peace, stability and consequent abundance which (most of) those under Roman rule expected would come about through the Roman emperor "savior" as he was guided and blessed by the gods.[17] The gods would enable the emperor to achieve military victory and thus to subdue and dominate other people groups. In other words, the emperor was the one who created the "peaceful" conditions for his subjects to work towards the society they desired.[18] This conviction

---

[17] J. R. Harrison, *Paul's Language of Grace in Its Graeco-Roman Context*. Wissenschaftliche Untersuchungen zum Neuen Testament (Tübingen: Mohr-Siebeck, 2003), 214, 228.
[18] Ibid., 232.

of the importance of the emperor did not therefore lead to passivity from the general populace. Instead the poets of the day such as Virgil reminded people that the blessings of this world would also be achieved through the hard toil and moral improvement of the general population. These themes emerge in at least three types of cultural symbols – how *time and space* are ordered in the cities and towns; the *coins* of the time; and the *literature* of the day, particularly but not limited to poetry.

The ordering of time and geographical space

The way in which *time* was ordered, structured and given meaning in imperial Rome prior to and during the first century offers important insights into who and what were highly valued in Roman society. This is particularly the case with regard to the type of calendar model adopted. The Roman calendar, which had been somewhat idiosyncratic, was renovated by Julius Caesar in 46 BCE so that it was based on a solar model. Augustus then ordered a number of adjustments to this model in 9 BCE so that from 8 CE onwards the Roman calendar functioned with regularity and predictably. At the same time as Augustus was fine-tuning the solar calendar, his proconsul of Asia, Paulus Fabius Maximus, proposed that the province also adjust its own calendars so that they were aligned with the calendar of Rome. This recommendation was not made for pragmatic reasons but was primarily to do with the meaning of time.[19] Augustus' proconsul pressed for the change in calendar because he believed that time had been so profoundly shaped by the birth and accomplishments of Augustus. The koinon agreed. As Friesen observes, "Augustus was a cosmogonic and cosmological deity. He had saved the world from itself, ending warfare and returning order to the world. The beginning of the year and the beginning of each month were to become a commemoration of his birth. Augustus would make sense of time."[20]

The influence which Augustus had on the management of time is an important reminder of the significance of his reign, both for the provinces of the Empire and for subsequent Roman emperors. Augustus' rulership was a turning point for the Roman Empire and many of the ideals and hopes for Roman society which it created were then adopted and adapted by the rulers who followed. While the primary focus of the present study

---

[19] Friesen, *Imperial Cults*, 125. See further G. Woolf, "Inventing Empire in Ancient Rome," in *Empires: Perspectives from Archeology and History*, ed. S. E. Alcock *et al.* (Cambridge University Press, 2001), 321. For more on the so-called Priene inscriptions, which record these changes in calendar models, see below, pp. 34–35.

[20] Friesen, *Imperial Cults*, 125.

is the time during Claudius' and Nero's rule, understanding the ideals of these emperors necessarily involves looking at themes which emerged from Augustus' rule. Just as it is important to consider examples specific to Claudius and Nero, it will also become apparent that these rulers must be understood within the wider historical context of Augustus' reign for it was this period which gave birth to and nourished many of the expectations expressed in the Rome of Paul's day. Not surprisingly, Augustus' successors often deliberately emphasized the continuity between their own reign and that of Augustus before them.[21]

Closely related to this realignment of calendars of time in first century Rome is the organization of space. How space is used and ordered in a society provides important insights into what the society considers significant and gives clues to its dominant ideas. Price draws on the work of anthropologists who have shown that "the ordering of space can be seen both as a representation of social ideas and as a part of the fabric of reality. Political and social changes are likely to consist in part in the reordering of space."[22] What can be learned from the ordering of space in the cities and towns of first-century Greco-Roman society?

First, the city of Rome was believed to be at the centre of the world. Whereas (as will be described below) the internal structure of cities could literally be transformed so as to reflect the values of the imperial cult, this was clearly impossible with regard to the location of Rome. Instead, the city of Rome *conceptually* became the centre of all things. It became the "shop window" of the Empire, at least ideologically.[23] A good example of this is the procedures which were put in place for the creation of imperial temples in the provinces of the Empire. If one of the provincial cities wanted to establish an imperial cult, it was not allowed to do so on its own initiative. Instead, officials from the city in question would make the journey to Rome to present the city's case at the imperial centre. The emperor and senate would then make a verdict and representatives would travel to Asia (or elsewhere) to deliver the decision. If there was disagreement over the decision then advocates would return to the capital for a reconsideration of the matter. Such a procedure was one way in which Rome was established as the centre of the world.[24] This policy contributed to the belief that reality revolved around the imperial city. While there was still room for diversity within the surrounding cities,

[21] V. Rudich, *Political Dissidence under Nero. The Price of Dissimulation* (London: Routledge, 1993), 6. Galinsky argues persuasively for Augustus' reign as a turning point in the history of the Roman Empire; Galinsky, *Augustan Culture*.

[22] Price, *Rituals and Power*, 136. Similarly Meggitt, *Paul, Poverty and Survival*, 31.

[23] Veyne, *Bread and Circuses*, 385.   [24] Friesen, *Imperial Cults*, 124.

even these variations reinforced the main theme that there was a "sacred geography" to the Empire: Rome was at the heart of the world.[25]

As well as the pre-eminence of the city of Rome, the cities themselves were structured in such a way as to reinforce particular ideals. The clearest feature is the ways in which images of the emperors as well as buildings and monuments which supported the imperial cult were given priority and prominence. This not only included gates, fountains, porticoes and other monuments of honor, but also the imperial temples and sanctuaries. All of these were often located in positions of prestige and pre-eminence within the larger cities, while in smaller cities the temples were positioned in the civic centre.[26] In Greek cities in particular, where the traditional arrangements were modified to honor the emperor, this frequently had the effect of transforming the physical framework of the city.

A good example of this during Claudius' reign is the entrance to the Antioch Temple built in 50 CE and dedicated to Claudius. Stephen Mitchell notes that the massive design on the entranceway to the temple "provides one of the most notable examples of the transformation of civic space, whereby imperial buildings literally took over and dominated the urban landscape, thus symbolizing unequivocally the central position that Emperor worship occupied in city life, and the overwhelming manner in which the Emperor dominated the world view of his subjects."[27] The message this conveyed daily to the people of Antioch was clear: the one who will bring (or perhaps has already brought) the desired society is the emperor Claudius. He has transformed the city and it is this which needs to be acknowledged and honored.

Coins

Coins are a second important indicator of the stories and themes which undergirded the Greco-Roman worldview during Paul's time.[28] Again several interrelated images emerge from this coinage, ideas which symbolically express the Roman hopes for their society.[29] Once more the

---

[25] Ibid., 125. The phrase is Friesen's.   [26] Price, *Rituals and Power*, 136–37.

[27] Stephen Mitchell, *Anatolia: Land, Men, and Gods in Asia Minor*, 2 vols., vol. I (New York: Oxford University Press, 1993), 107. Mitchell insists that despite Price's argument, there is no doubt that this dedication dates to the Julio-Claudian period.

[28] R. Miles, "Communicating Culture, Identity and Power," in *Experiencing Rome. Culture, Identity and Power in the Roman Empire*, ed. J. Huskinson (London: Routledge, 2000), 42.

[29] Meggitt, *Paul, Poverty and Survival*, 30; C. Howgego, *Ancient History from Coins* (London: Routledge, 1995), 70–73.

strongest message conveyed is that there would be a time of lasting peace and happiness and that the emperor was the person who would bring this.

Lugdunum 64–67 CE

This is evident, for example, in a coin issued by the imperial mint in Lugdunum between 64 and 67 CE.[30] The bronze sestertia show the Altar of Peace which Augustus had ordered to be erected and which was one of the most significant artistic monuments surviving from the Julio-Claudian period. The words ARA PACIS stand at the base of the scene.[31] This altar, the *Ara Pacis Augustae*, was situated on the Field of Mars and dedicated on January 30, 9 BCE in celebration of Augustus' return from Spain and Gaul in 13 BCE.[32] The Tallus Relief on the Ara Pacis is particularly revealing, conveying images of peace, tranquility and lasting happiness.[33] At the center of the composition is a goddess sitting at ease with fruit and two small children in her lap. There are reeds, poppies and ears of grain sprouting up next to her, and a cow (or an ox) and a sheep lie peacefully at her feet. On both sides she is flanked by two female companions, one on a swan, the other on a sea animal.[34]

Heightened significance is given to this suggestive idyll by the complementary panels on the monument. In the case of the goddess, the complementary panel is the goddess Roma, sitting on a pile of arms (probably with a spear and shield).[35] Similarly the relief of Aeneas' sacrifice on one side is complemented by the presence of Mars, the god of war, on the other side.[36] The way these scenes are combined suggests a clear message that tranquility is made possible only through war, victory and military dominance. Indeed Augustus' own comment on the Ara Pacis was that "Peace was achieved through victories (*parta victoriis pax*)."[37] This theme is reinforced by the larger architectural ensemble alongside which the Ara Pacis is positioned in Rome.[38] There is the Augustan Mausoleum which is positioned in order to establish a "direct

---

[30] *RIC*, Nero, 418. See also *RIC*, Nero, 456–61, 526–31.
[31] L. J. Kreitzer, *Striking New Images: Roman Imperial Coinage and the New Testament World*, JSNTSup 134 (Sheffield Academic Press, 1996), 120–21.
[32] Ibid.
[33] E. Gren, "Augustus and the Ideology of War and Peace," in *The Age of Augustus*, ed. R. Winkes (Louvain: Brown University Press, 1985), 61–63.
[34] See Galinsky, *Augustan Culture*, 108 fig. 41.   [35] Ibid., 108 fig. 42.
[36] Ibid., 109 fig. 43.
[37] P. Brunt and J. M. Moore, eds., *Res Gestae Divi Augusti* (Oxford University Press, 1967), 13; Galinsky, *Augustan Culture*, 106–107.
[38] See Galinsky, *Augustan Culture*, 147 fig. 64.

link between the princeps' birth and world peace"[39] and there is the monumental sundial, the tip of which contained a small globe symbolizing world domination. In other words the entire piazza, which was certainly one of the most impressive public spaces in Rome, is a glorification of conquest, of peace through war, in this case the conquest of Egypt.[40]

It is this image which Nero chose for the coin issued in Lugdunum in 64–67 CE. In doing so, he was presenting himself as a ruler, like Augustus, who would bring peace through war. As Kreitzer concludes, "The role of the Julio-Claudian house as a peacemaking force in the Roman world is thereby asserted."[41]

Caesarea 54–55 CE

Such an explicit attempt to build on the life and "peaceful" ideals of previous emperors was common. In a series of didrachma minted in Caesarea in Cappadocia 54–55 CE, Nero commemorated the life of Claudius (his father through adoption). The obverse of the coin has a portrait of Claudius with the inscription DIVOS [the deified one] CLAVD AVGVST [Claudius Augustus] GERMANIC[42] PATER [father of] AVG [an imperial title adopted by all ruling emperors from 27 BCE onwards]. Nero's portrait is on the reverse of the coin with the inscription NERO CLAVD [Nero Claudius] DIVI CLAVD F [having a family relationship – "Filius" to the divine Claudius] CAESAR AVG [Caesar Augustus – common titles for reigning emperors or their designated heirs] GERMANI. Nero was consciously marking the family connection which he had both to the deified Julius Caesar and to the deified Augustus, and part of his purpose in doing so was to establish himself as one who also would bring peace through military victory.[43]

Rome and Lugdunum 64–65 CE

This theme of "peace" through domination is similarly evident in an imperial coin dated between December of 64 CE and December of 65 CE and issued in the mints in Rome and Lugdunum. The obverse portrait is that of Nero with an inscription reading NERO CAESAR AVG(ugustus)

---

[39] Claude Nicolet, *Space, Geography, and Politics in the Early Roman Empire*, trans. Helene Leclerc, Jerome Lecture Series 19 (University of Michigan Press, 1991), 16.

[40] Galinsky, *Augustan Culture*, 107, 147.

[41] Kreitzer, *Striking New Images*, 120–21.

[42] "This title declares that its bearer was recognized to have achieved some military victory over the peoples of Germanica. To a certain degree it was also a hereditary title and was passed on from one succesful military commander to his heir"; ibid., 16.

[43] Ibid., 82.

IMP(erator) TR(ibunicia) P(otestas) [a title referring to the tribunical power given to the emperor: describes his position as civil head of state] P(ater) P(atriae) [father of the Empire]. The reverse of the coin symbolically depicts the closing of the doors of the temple of Janus, an event which could only occur when war had ceased.[44] The particular event which Nero's coin refers to is Tiridates' visit to Rome. The king of Armenia's visit was seen as an act of submission to Rome after a period of warring and it is this victory which Nero is celebrating.[45]

Sesterius 64–65 CE

Closely linked to this commemoration of victory is a sesterius dating to 64–65 CE.[46] The obverse of the coin bears Nero's portrait with the inscription NERO CLAVD(ius) CAESAR AVG(ustus) GERM(anicus) P(ontifex) M(aximus) [a title declaring the emperor as the supreme head of the Roman religion] TR(ibunicia) P(otestas) IMP(erator) P(ater) P(atriae) [father of the Empire]. On the reverse is an ornamental triumphal arch and a figure of the emperor riding in a quadriga. The figures of Victory and Pax are alongside the quadriga. On the right is Victory, a wreath and palm in hand. On the left is Pax holding a caduceus and a cornucopia. The arch itself is decorated with the figure of Mars holding a spear. As Kreitzer concludes, "it seems certain that the Triumphal Arch has an integral link to the Tiridates incident."[47] Once more the connection between peace and victory is strong.

Portrait of Claudius 46–47 CE

Honors such as the coins and triumphal arch were rarely granted by the Roman senate, although Nero's predecessor had received a similar triumph.[48] In 44 CE Claudius' campaigns in Britain were honored with gold coins which represented the triumphal arch to be erected in Rome in 51–52 CE. These were first issued by the imperial mint in Rome in 46–47 CE. "These aurei have an obverse portrait of Claudius surrounded by the inscription TI CLAVD [Tiberius Claudius] CAESAR AVG [titles used for ruling emperors from 27 BCE onwards] P(ontifex) M(aximus) TR(ibunicia) P(otestas) VI IMP(erator) P(ater) P(atriae) [father of the Empire]. The reverse has a single-span arch topped by a figure riding a horse with trophies on either side; the words DE(victis) BRITANN(is) are

---

[44] For this decree see Suetonius, *Augustus* 22; Cassius Dio, *Histories* 51.20.4 and 53.27.1.
[45] L. Hardwick, "Concepts of Peace," in *Experiencing Rome. Culture, Identity and Power in the Roman Empire*, ed. J. Huskinson (London: Routledge, 2000), 335–68.
[46] *RIC*, Nero, 143. [47] Kreitzer, *Striking New Images*, 120. [48] Ibid., 129.

on the architrave."[49] With these and other coins the symbolism is again clear: the Pax which people long for has been and will continue to be achieved through Claudius' and Nero's military dominance.[50] And such imagery was not at all unusual within the time in which Paul wrote. The idea of peace through Roman military triumph was well known within the ancient world and was celebrated not only in coins but in "various literary works, as well as a host of artistic media, including sculpture, painting, engraving and metal-working."[51]

These themes were not new to Paul's time but had existed as early as Pompey's time. Often the idea was that of universal domination and was signified through the symbol of a globe. Nicolet points out that the globe, and the symbols of Roman domination which were placed alongside it, were not so much a sign of the concrete domination of the earth but rather were to do with "cosmic" sovereignty. After all, no empire during this time period could reasonably intend to rule the entire terrestrial sphere.

> Three-quarters of it remained literally unattainable in ancient cosmogony, out of reach of all human enterprise. A universal domination could not claim more than the one known *oikoumene*. Nevertheless, they could claim to fit in the order of the cosmic destiny – either they were under the protection of or they held a covenant with the gods, they were in some way divine. They became therefore an element, or the guarantee, of world order.[52]

In other words the citizens of Rome carried with them daily the coins which asserted that Caesar is the ruler of all and that the well-being of the inhabitants of the Empire depends on Caesar's genius.[53] While many of the finer points of the imperial images expressed in coins could have gone unnoticed, it remains true that "these images had a powerful symbolic value as a representation of the legitimacy and success of a particular emperor's reign. Thus coins, like inscriptions, were common currency in the legitimization of imperial power."[54]

Literature

A third source which provides evidence of the worldview of Paul's Greco-Roman society is literature, especially, but not limited to, poetry. Claude

---

[49] Ibid., 130–31.   [50] Ibid., 136–38.   [51] Ibid., 142–43.

[52] Nicolet, *Space, Geography, and Politics*, 35.

[53] A. Kee, "The Imperial Cult: The Unmasking of an Ideology," *Scottish Journal of Religious Studies* 6 (1985): 122.

[54] Miles, "Communicating Culture, Identity and Power," 44.

Nicolet suggests that from the 30s BCE onwards, poetry (both official and semi-official) claims universal domination as Rome's destiny. The expectation that Rome is the one divinely ordained to ensure the prosperity of the human race, and that the emperor is the primary means through which this will happen, is expressed in the formative period of the Roman Empire – Augustus' reign – and it is also evident in the years following the time of Paul. Most importantly for the present study, it is also deeply embedded in the literature and inscriptions associated with Claudius' and then Nero's rule. But before looking at the sources which relate most directly to the time when Romans was written, it is important first to note examples from the time of Augustus' rule, a period with which both Claudius and Nero were anxious to be connected.

Augustus and the Julian family were believed to be the ones who would achieve the sovereignty over the earth which the Roman people and its rulers desired. Virgil's *Aeneid* was an important contributor to this belief, creating a myth of how this family was divinely ordained to bring peace and order to the Roman state. Dihle observes that Virgil presents the whole sweep of Aeneas' story as "foreshadowing the global rule of the Imperial state and the destiny of the Roman people as foreseen in the divine universal order."[55] According to Virgil's story, the Julii had always been Rome's most significant family and it would be this family who would produce Rome's savior.[56] As Virgil puts it: "This, this is he whom so often you hear promised to you, Augustus Caesar, son of a god, who shall again set up the golden age in Latium amid the fields where Saturn once reigned and shall spread his empire past Garamat and India, to a land that lies beyond the stars."[57] Virgil's *Aeneid* has the Roman supreme god Jupiter appoint Romulus the founder of Rome and its Empire. Young Romulus,

> Will take the leadership, build walls of Mars,
> And call by his own name his people Romans.
> *For these I set no limits, world or time,*
> *But make the gift of empire without end.*[58]

---

[55] A. Dihle, *Greek and Latin Literature of the Roman Empire: From Augustus to Justinian*, trans. M. Malzahn (London: Routledge, 1994), 115. Similarly Woolf, "Inventing Empire," 319.
[56] Zanker, *The Power of Images*, 211.
[57] *Aeneid* 6.791–5, trans. R. Fitzgerald (London: David Campbell Publisher, 2000). Similarly Seneca, *De Clementia* 1.4.1f.
[58] *Aeneid* 1. 373–76, trans. Fitzgerald. Greg Woolf observes that the phrase *imperium sine fine*, translated above as "empire without end," could also be rendered "limitless power" or "an empire with no frontier"; Woolf, "Inventing Empire," 317.

In a phrase which forms an intriguing backdrop to Romans 4 and 8 (see, for example, the discussion in Chapter 3 below of Rom. 4:13 – "heirs of the world") Jupiter then refers to the "toga-bearing Romans" as "heirs of heaven" and "Lords of the world."[59] The nature of this "lordship" or sovereignty is then described further in Book 6 of the *Aeneid* when Virgil has Anchises tell his son, Aeneas,

> Roman, remember by your strength to rule
> Earth's peoples – for your arts are to be these:
> To pacify, to impose the rule of law,
> To spare the conquered, battle down the proud.[60]

Horace (born 65 BCE; died 8 BCE) conveys in his poetry a similarly idyllic description of the Augustan age, replete with the motifs of redemption, restoration and fertility.

> [the] country yearns for Caesar. For when he is here, the ox in safety roams the pastures; Ceres and benign Prosperity make rich the crops; safe are the seas over which our sailors course; Faith shrinks from blame; polluted by no stain, the home is pure; custom and law have stamped out the taint of sin; mothers win praise because of children like unto their sires; while Vengeance follows closely on guilt.[61]

These poetic descriptions are matched by various other inscriptions around or in close proximity to, the time of Augustus. The most well known is the so-called Priene inscription, which, in terms of its impact in the first century CE is only superseded by the emperor's own catalogue of achievements, *Res Gestae Divi Augusti*.[62] This inscription encouraged the replacement of the local lunar calendar with the Julian solar calendar as described above. The calendar replacement was initiated in a letter written by the Proconsul of Asia, Paulus Fabius Maximus, to the Provincial Assembly in about 9 BCE. Maximus' letter opens as follows:

> (It is hard to tell) whether the birthday of our most divine Caesar Augustus spells more of joy or benefit, this being a date that we could probably without fear of contradiction equate with the beginning of all things . . . he restored stability, when everything was collapsing and falling into disarray, and gave a new look

---

[59] *Aeneid* 1. 359.   [60] *Aeneid* 6.1151–54, trans. Fitzgerald. *Aeneid* 6.851–3.
[61] *Carmen saeculare* 4.5.16–24, trans. Sherk. More generally see A. Wallace-Hadrill, "The Golden Age of Sin in Augustan Ideology," *Past & Present* 95 (1982).
[62] Stanton, *Jesus and Gospel*, 30.

to the entire world that would have been most happy to accept its own ruin had not the good and common fortune of all been born, Caesar Augustus. (Lines 4–9)[63]

In response to this letter the Provincial Assembly issued two decrees which were inscribed numerous times on huge blocks of stone and were then set up in cities throughout Asia Minor.[64]

> In her display of concern and generosity on our behalf, Providence, who orders all our lives, has adorned our lives with the highest good, namely Augustus. Providence has filled Augustus with divine power for the benefit of humanity, and in her beneficence has granted us and those who will come after us [a Saviour] who has made war to cease and who shall put everything [in peaceful order] . . . And Caesar, [when he was manifest], transcended the expectations of [all who had anticipated the good news], not only by surpassing the benefits conferred by his predecessors but by leaving no expectation of surpassing him to those who would come after him, with the result that the birthday of our god signaled the beginning of good news for the world because of him. (Lines 34–41)[65]

These interrelated notions of universal sovereignty and the blessing which Rome brings to the world are also evident in the attitudes of certain Jewish leaders towards the Roman Empire. One example of this is in a tapestry given by Queen Cyprus, wife of King Agrippa I (10 BC–44 CE).[66] This tapestry, which is a physical "map" of the world presented to the reigning Roman emperor, is described in a first-century epigram of Philip of Thessalonica. He says that the "map" contains "a perfect copy of the harvest-bearing earth, all that the land-encircling Ocean girdles, obedient to great Caesar, and the gray sea too."[67] It seems likely that the

---

[63] Quoting here from F. W. Danker, *Benefactor* (St. Louis, MS: Clayton, 1982), 216–17.

[64] Many fragments of the inscription have now been discovered. There are thirteen in all, from five cities in Asia Minor: Priene, Apamea, Maeonia, Eumenia and Dorylaeum. See R. K. Sherk, ed. and trans., *The Roman Empire: Augustus to Hadrian*, Translated Documents of Greece and Rome (Cambridge University Press, 1988), 328–37.

[65] Quoting here from Danker, *Benefactor*, 216–17.

[66] See J. M. Scott, "Luke's Geographical Horizon," in *The Book of Acts in Its First-Century Setting*, ed. D. W. T. Gill and C. Gempf (Grand Rapids: Eerdmans, 1994), vol. II, 492–93. Scott shows that the queen who gave the tapestry would be Cyprus, a granddaughter of Herod.

[67] *Anthologia Graeca* 9.778: A. S. F Gow and D. L. Page, *The Greek Anthology: The Garland of Philip and Some Contemporary Epigrams*, vol. I: *Introduction, Text and Translation* (Cambridge University Press, 1968), 300–301.

epigram is describing the appreciation of a Roman emperor (probably Gaius Caligula, 12–44 CE) for a Jewish representation of the Roman world – a map which is regarded as a perfect copy of the earth.[68]

Another example of this conception of the Roman world is that put in the mouth of King Agrippa II by Josephus at the beginning of the Jewish war. Agrippa says that the Romans rule "the universe" (*ta panta*) and that the imperialistic ambition of the Empire drives them to the ends of the inhabited world. In order to emphasize this universal sovereignty Agrippa observes that whereas the Jewish forces have constantly been defeated by the surrounding nations, the Roman forces have never suffered defeat throughout the whole inhabited world.[69] Agrippa then describes an impressive list of nations which are under Roman control.[70] James M. Scott points out that the claims of universal sovereignty made by Rome and by Rome's subjects are often exaggerated and are commonly divorced from reality.[71] Although the extent of Rome's control and power was vast, Scott concludes that Rome's frequent boasts of having achieved dominion over the whole inhabited world (for example Augustus' claims) are overstated and ostentatious.[72] But this does not take away from the fact that Rome's reach *was* still extensive and that the rulers and (many of) the subjects of the Empire were eager to speak of this far-reaching rule. For the purposes of a study of inheritance in Romans (and this is what Scott implies also) the important feature to note is that although these claims were not necessarily the reality, they do hold considerable significance for an understanding of the attitudes and expectations held in imperial Rome.

There are further examples from the post-Nero period which convey the notion of Rome's destiny to bring peace and prosperity to the world through the rulership of the divinely appointed emperors. For example in Tacitus' *Annals* he has a Roman governor announce to the leader of a German tribe that, "all men had to bow to the commands of their betters; it had been decreed by those gods whom they implored that with the Roman people should rest the decisions what to give and what to take away."[73] Similarly, writing in the mid second century, Aelius Aristides says: "Since the very beginning you (viz. the Romans) were born free and in a sense directly to rule, you admirably provided for all that serves this end, founded a form of state such as no one yet had, and established

---

[68] J. M. Scott, "Luke's Geographical Horizon," 493.

[69] *Bellum Judaicum* 2.362. See further J. M. Scott, "Luke's Geographical Horizon," 494.

[70] *BJ* 2.358–87.   [71] See J. M. Scott, "Luke's Geographical Horizon," 490–91.

[72] Ibid., 491.   [73] Tacitus, *Annals* 13.51, trans. Sherk.

firm laws and rules for all."[74] This destiny of ruling the earth is believed to be the will of the gods. Aristides declares that "the gods beholding, seem to lend a friendly hand to your empire in its achievement and to confirm you in its possession." He therefore invokes the gods' blessing that "this empire and this city flourish forever and never cease."[75] Pliny (63–113 CE) conveys similar sentiments. Praising the emperor Trajan, Pliny calls the gods "the guardians and defenders of our empire" and prays to Jupiter for "the safety of our prince" since human "security and happiness depends on your safety."[76] Similarly Pliny asserts that: "By protecting and sustaining the Roman empire the gods secure the safety of the world. That stands in peace, concord, security, riches and honour, all aspects of the Pax Romana which this empire provides. The gods protect and sustain it in the person of the emperor, who stands surety for all these benefits."[77]

These ideas of universal sovereignty and the blessings which this had brought to the world are not only evident in the literature before and after Paul's letter to the Romans. Similar hopes for society are expressed in the poetry and inscriptions of Paul's time. A good example of the poetic expression of these expectations is found in the Einsiedeln manuscripts (or eclogues or pastorals) which almost certainly date from the early years of Nero's reign (54–68 CE).[78] In the first of these two incomplete poems (so called after the tenth-century manuscript at Einsiedeln from which H. Hagen first published them in 1869) Nero is compared to the supreme god Jupiter and to Jupiter's son Apollo. In this poem there are two contending shepherds, Thamyras and Ladas, who are testing their skills of "minstrelsy" before the "umpire," who is Midas. Thamryas says of Nero:

> Here flourishes the wealth of Helicon; here is your own Apollo!
> You too, O Troy, raise your hallowed ashes to the stars and
> display this work to Agamemnon's Mycenae! Now has it proved
> of such value to have fallen! . . . Lo! Homer too had come . . . So
> when he filled the poet's ears with accents divine, he undid the

---

[74] Aristides, *Eulogy of Rome,* 91, trans. Sherk. Also Virgil, *Aeneid* 7.258: according to an oracle the coming race of Romans will "occupy the whole earth with troops."

[75] Quotation from *Roman Oration* 89, 104–105, 109. See further W. Carter, "Vulnerable Power: The Roman Empire Challenged by the Early Christians," in *Handbook of Early Christianity: Social Science Approaches,* ed. J. Anthony, Duhaime Blasi and P.-A. Turcotte (Walnut Creek, CA: AltaMira Press, 2002), 463.

[76] Pliny *Panegyricus,* 72.   [77] Pliny, *Panegyricus,* 72, trans. Sherk.

[78] J. W. Duff and A. M. Duff, "Introduction to Einsiedeln Eclogues," in *Minor Latin Poets,* ed. J. W. Duff and A. M. Duff (London: William Heinemann Ltd, 1954), 319.

golden circlet from his fair brow and veiled the emperor's head
with its deserved attire . . . [79]

In the second poem (which is a dialogue between two shepherds, Glyc-
eranus and Mystes) one of the shepherds, Mystes, is convinced that with
the emperor's accession the golden age has returned.

> The days of Saturn have returned with Justice the Maid: the age
> has returned in safety to the olden ways. With hope unruffled
> does the harvester garner all his corn-ears; the Wine-god betrays
> the languor of old age; the herd wanders on the lea; we reap with
> no sword, nor do towns in fast-closed walls prepare unutterable
> war: there is not any woman who, dangerous in her motherhood,
> gives birth to an enemy. Unarmed our youth can dig the fields,
> and the boy, trained to the slow-moving plough, marvels at
> the sword hanging in the abode of his fathers. From us is the
> luckless glory of Sulla and the threefold crisis when dying Rome
> despaired of her final resources and sold her martial arms. Now
> doth earth untilled yield fresh produce from the rich soil, now
> are the wild waves no longer angry with the unmenaced ship:
> tigers gnaw their cubs, lions endure the cruel yoke: be gracious,
> chaste Lucina: thine own Apollo now is King.[80]

In these two poems therefore (for which there is no named author) Nero is
compared to the gods Apollo and Jupiter and he is described as restoring
the golden age. Nero is said to be the one who will bring peace between
people and within nature, and the emperor who will return justice to the
earth. There will be the end of all violation of nature so that people can
be fed bountifully without having to till the soil. As Dihle observes of
these poems: "[t]o be monarch of a global empire is to play a role of
cosmic dimension, or at least it justifies the claim to such a role: thus
the emperor may without any hesitation be placed alongside the highest
gods, or even be identified with them."[81]

Similar ideas are conveyed in the poetry of Calpurnius Siculus in
an eclogue apparently written soon after Claudius' death. This poem
welcomes the coming golden age of the reign of Nero, "the youthful
prince," "a very God."

> Nay, laws shall be restored;
> right will come in fullest force; a kinder god

---

[79] *Einsiedeln Eclogues* 1, 36–49, trans. Duff and Duff.
[80] *Einsiedeln Eclogues* 2, 15–38, trans. Duff and Duff.
[81] Dihle, *Greek and Latin Literature*, 107.

will renew the former tradition and look of the Forum
and displace the age of oppression.[82]

As well as these expectations expressed in the poetry of Paul's day, there
is also evidence from various inscriptions of this time which suggests
that Nero claimed the status of, and was in turn proclaimed as, the "lord"
of the Roman people, "savior" of the entire "world." For example there is
a papyrus from Oxyrhynchus in Egypt which is a draft of a proclamation
of Nero as emperor (54 CE):

> Fulfilling the debt | to his ancestors, the ma | nifest god Caesar
> | has departed to them, || and the expected and hoped | for
> imperator | of the world has been pro | claimed: the good | spirit
> of the | world, the *origin* | of [[the greatest of]] all | good things,
> Nero | has been proclaimed Caesar.[83]

A similar sentiment is found on a marble slate, damaged at the top and
on the right side, containing a speech of Nero and a decree of Acraephiae
in Boeotia, where it was found (67 CE). The first inscription is "to noble-
minded Greece" to whom Nero grants that "all Greeks" inhabiting Achaea
[and what is now known as the Peloponnesus] will receive freedom with
no taxation. The response from Acraephiae is one of overwhelming praise
for Nero:

> The high-priest of the Augusti for life and of Nero | Claudius
> Caesar Augustus, Epameinondas | (son) of Epameinondas, made
> the motion: he moved that a preliminary decree || be forwarded
> to the Boule and the People: | Since the lord of the whole
> world, Nero, Imper | ator supreme, holding the tribunician
> power for the thir | teenth time (AD 67) designate (?), father
> of his country, | New Sun shining upon the Greeks, has || cho-
> sen to be a benefactor of Greece, requiting | and receiving our
> gods who stood by him . . . Greece-loving [[Nero]]Zeus the Deli-
> verer . . . [84]

Nero also appears in the Greek athletic games, Athens (61 CE), and is
hailed as "the new Apollo."[85] Similarly, in what appears to be a rough
draft for an official proclamation for Nero's accession, thanks are given
to the gods for their beneficence:

---

[82] *Ecl.* 1.59–64; 1.69–73, trans. Sherk. See further Rudich, *Political Dissidence under Nero*, 4.
[83] Sherk, ed., *The Roman Empire*, 102–3. [84] Ibid., 111–12. [85] Ibid., 115.

> The Caesar who had to pay his debt to his ancestors, god mani-
> fest, has joined them, and the expectation and hope of the world
> has been declared Emperor, the good genius of the world and
> the source of all things, Nero, has been declared Caesar. There-
> fore ought we all wearing garlands and with sacrifices of oxen
> to give thanks to all the gods.[86]

Such praise was heaped on Nero not only in the provinces but also in
the capital city. On his return to Rome in 68 Cassius Dio recounts the
acclamation which Nero receives:

> The city was decked with garlands, was ablaze with lights and
> reeking with incense, and the whole population, the senators
> themselves most of all, kept shouting in chorus, "Hail, Olympian
> Victor! Hail, Pythian Victor! Augustus! Augustus! Hail to Nero,
> our Hercules! Hail to Nero our Apollo! The only Victor of the
> Grand Tour, the only one from the beginning of time! Augustus!
> Augustus! O, Divine Voice, Blessed are they that hear thee."[87]

While Cassius Dio does tend towards exaggeration, it is also the case
that other ancient historians describe Nero in similar terms. Furthermore
there are numerous occasions described by Cassius Dio in which Nero
is obsessed about such matters.[88] Suetonius paints a similar picture of
Nero:

> He had a longing for immortality and undying fame, though it
> was ill-regulated. With this in view he took their former appel-
> lations from many things and numerous places and gave them
> new ones from his own name. He also called the month of April
> Neroneus and was minded to name Rome Neropolis.[89]

Perhaps one of the most staggering accolades given to Nero is the reference to him as the "good god" (ὁ ἀγαθὸς θεὸς) included in an inscription
recovered from the Mediterranean island of Cos.[90] Along similar lines
is a votive inscription for Emperor Nero on a marble slab at Magnesia
on the Meander between his adoption by Claudius and his accession to
the throne. Nero is here referred to as "Son of the greatest of the gods,
Tiberius Claudius."[91] In addition there are numerous references to Nero

---

[86] J. R. Harrison, *Paul's Language of Grace*, 87.   [87] Hist. 62.20.5, trans. Sherk.
[88] Cassidy, *Paul in Chains*, 157.   [89] *Lives of the Caesars: Nero* 55, trans. Sherk.
[90] Deissmann, *Light from the Ancient East*, 349. See further Cassidy, *Paul in Chains*,
160.
[91] Deissmann, *Light from the Ancient East*, 351.

as "the Lord" during Paul's time. One example is from an ostracon which is dated to around 63 CE. The small document concludes with the phrase: "In the year nine of Nero the Lord, Mesore 11th."[92] Another example from Cassius Dio describes the language which the Parthian leader Tiridates used of Nero. He traveled to Rome to be officially venerated as ruler of Armenia by Nero. Upon meeting Nero, Tiridates "obsequiously knelt on the ground, crossed his arms, and petitioned Nero as *despoten* ('lord')." But this display at Naples was only a prelude to a more elaborate ceremony at Rome. His speech included the following exalted language: "Lord, I am the descendant of Araces, brother of the kings Gologaesus and Pacorus, and thy slave. And I have come to thee, my god, to worship thee as I do Mithras. The destiny thou spinnest for me shall be mine; for thou are my Fortune and my Fate."[93]

These declarations about Nero feed into a pool of beliefs concerning the ways in which the emperor will bring well-being to the world. But there are statements which are even more grandiose than this and are particularly suggestive when read alongside similar phrases in Romans. Nero is sometimes referred to as "savior of the world" and as "savior and benefactor of the world."[94] Above, in relation to Virgil's *Aeneid*, it was noted that the phrase "lords of the world" is used, a phrase which bears an intriguing likeness to Rom. 4:13. But this phrase is not isolated to Augustus' reign. The marble tablet of Acraephiae in Boeotia includes a proclamation of honor by the Boeotian town in which Nero is called "lord of the whole world" and then "lord Augustus."[95]

For the purposes of the present study it is not necessary to assess the degree to which Nero thought himself comparable to the gods and it is obviously not possible to know this. What *can* be established from the inscriptions, papyri and ostraca is that Nero at least highly prized such divinity-resonating titles and enjoyed having himself portrayed in such terms.[96] Such phrases are important for a reading of inheritance in Romans because they are not isolated instances but take their place within the wider social and political landscape of first-century Rome.

When would this time arrive?

This description of three cultural symbols in Greco-Roman society during Paul's day shows that one of the messages which emerged clearly was that

---

[92] Ibid., 105. Cassidy, *Paul in Chains*, 160. [93] Hist. 62:5.2, trans. Sherk.
[94] Cassidy, *Paul in Chains*, 160; Deissmann, *Light from the Ancient East*, 369.
[95] Deissmann, *Light from the Ancient East*, 358. [96] Cassidy, *Paul in Chains*, 160.

the emperor (in this case Claudius and Nero) had been ordained by the gods to bring material blessings to the earth and that through the emperor the Romans would be "lords of the earth." To what degree was this period of happiness and fulfillment believed to have already been achieved? Did the people of first-century Greco-Roman society believe that they were already living in a "golden age"? Exploring these questions is important because I will argue that just as Paul's eschatology is describing a time partially inaugurated but mostly yet to be, so also Greco-Roman society, although aware of present "blessings," was rife with expectations of what was yet to come.

But this is not how the sources have always been understood. Traditional interpretations of the symbols examined above have been understood as proclaiming a time which has already arrived. According to this reading, the emperor and the images surrounding him are examples of an ideology which claims present fulfillment. This, for example, is how Dieter Georgi reads these sources. He suggests that this is the pervasive mood from the work of Virgil's *Fourth Eclogue* and Cicero's *Somnium Scipionis* to the poems of Statius.[97] But the source on which Georgi particularly focuses is Horace (who Georgi suggests is the major theologian prophet of the imperial cult or what Georgi refers to as the "Caesar religion") and his *Carmen Saeculare*. Horace's poem, which is relatively contemporary with the New Testament, was commissioned for the official celebration of the Secular Games, the official jubilee for the founding of the republic. In Horace's ode, Georgi identifies a close relationship between "personal quietude, idyll, and world peace . . . Peace is not merely seen as political status but is put into the light of cosmic processes. Election, inspiration, experience and linguistic magic are all personal realizations of this cosmic process."[98] Georgi argues that in this poem the golden age is described as already present, already fulfilled.

> The *Carmen Saeculare* celebrates the miracle which occurred: the salvation of the republic. The hope expressed in the *Carmen* is miraculous, no doubt, but present, indeed fulfilled. The confidence about the realization of what has been desperately expected before is concrete, and the materialism of the expectation indicates the degree of reality. There are many eschatological themes: the eschatological language of *Urzeit–Endzeit*, the

[97] Dieter Georgi, "Who Is the True Prophet," in *Paul and Empire: Religion and Power in Roman Imperial Society*, ed. R. A. Horsley (Harrisburg, PA: Trinity Press International, 1997), 37.
[98] Ibid., 40.

ideal of the miraculous return of the golden age and paradise, and even the ideal of the eschatological savior – in line with the heroes of old.[99]

Similarly, when Horace engages with Augustus' marital legislation the poet prays for stability, prosperity and peace, and he makes it clear that "these things are not bloodless dreams but present reality." The *Carmen* prays for the increase of these experiences.[100]

Recent interpretation of this material, however, questions the degree to which it should be read as an age which had already arrived. Karl Galinsky argues persuasively that the themes of happiness and bliss which are expressed in many of these symbols and in poetry, were not believed to have already been experienced. After investigating the iconography of this period Galinsky suggests that no icons exist which would point to a "golden age" of easy bliss. The reason is simple enough: there was no intention to convey such an impression. Although this was to be the time of happiness (*felicia saecula*) "there was no attempt to obscure, through a plethora of blissful images, the realities of the age . . . "[101] Instead it is preferable to interpret these writings and symbols as a longing for a better time, a desire for an age when things would improve from the way they had been. Virgil's outlook was profoundly shaped by the turmoil of the late republic and the civil wars. The generation in which Virgil grew up "yearned for peace, stability, and a restoration of basic Roman values . . . there is no question that he and his contemporaries had seen the fullness of human suffering, helplessness, and displacement."[102] It is this context, Galinsky argues, which contributed to the longing for a better society. He describes the ideas in Virgil's *Eclogues* and proposes that "after many grim decades, the world of Italy and Rome was *rife with soteriological expectations* and that even the faintest hope could be greeted with enthusiastic success."[103] This is particularly so in Virgil's *Fourth Eclogue*, which was not meant to be a depiction of the way things already were but an "evocative expression of the yearning for peace and tranquillity after decades of civil wars (with no complete assurance as yet that they will come to an end)."[104] Galinsky points out that the utopian images presented in the poem were "far removed from the realities and the ethos of the Augustan age and calls for considerable suspension of

---

[99] Ibid., 41.
[100] Ibid., 41–42. See also Zanker, *The Power of Images*, 215; Woolf, "Inventing Empire," 319.
[101] Galinsky, *Augustan Culture*, 118.   [102] Ibid., 226.
[103] Ibid., 313; emphasis added.   [104] Ibid., 91.

disbelief."[105] Similarly the *Aeneid* does not celebrate the fulfillment of the golden age but instead stresses the ongoing process that will ultimately lead to the society for which Romans have longed.

A good example of this perspective is the language surrounding the Secular Games of 17 BCE. Contrary to Georgi's argument noted above, these games did not celebrate a millennial bliss which had already arrived nor did they assume that there was no role for the people to play. Instead the games took place after Augustus' legislation on marriage and morals had been passed in 18 BCE. This implied that "the health of the new *saeculum* was not merely an automatic, god-given blessing but was to depend on the moral effort of the Romans, the ruling classes in particular."[106] The phrase *melius aevum* is particularly suggestive. It does not have overtones of a millennium or golden age but could be an age or lifetime or generation and may include the idea that it could be co-extensive with Augustus' reign. However, "It more generally expressed a hope for better time ahead especially as the preceding decades had been singularly ruinous. And the new era was not one of automatic blessings but was grounded in moral and even military effort."[107]

If, therefore, the poets, artists and inscribers of Augustus' time were *not* claiming that the time of bliss had arrived in full, how *should* these sources be understood in Paul's time? For example, were the coins of Nero's time suggesting that the emperor had finally brought peace and prosperity to the earth, or are these inscriptions and images better understood as another way of expressing the perpetual longing of the Roman people? More particularly, what about the people of Rome to whom *Paul* is writing? If (as will be explored in the chapters below) the language of inheritance includes a promise of a better life and world, then how did such promises sound alongside the ideas expressed in relation to the imperial cult? In part, the answer to these questions is determined by the situation of those to whom Paul writes. It may be, for example, that one's place in the social strata of society affects one's assessment of the claims being put forward by Nero – the view from "below" is quite likely to look different than the perspective from "above."

The social structure of the Christians in Rome?

What, therefore, was the social make-up of the first Christians at Rome? In recent years there has been considerable debate within Pauline studies with regard to the social structure of each of the communities to whom

---

[105] Ibid.   [106] Ibid., 99–100.   [107] Ibid., 105.

Paul writes.[108] In an attempt to summarize this discussion, Justin Meggitt suggests that over about the last thirty years there has emerged a so-called "New Consensus" within NT studies.[109] This view (advanced in relation to the Pauline epistles by G. Theissen and W. A. Meeks) argues that the early churches consisted of individuals from a cross section of first-century society.[110] According to this "consensus," the early Christian communities included individuals from the higher stratas of society who were often financially well off. While there is some variety within the "New Consensus," the view continues to dominate NT sociological studies and, until recently, has gone largely unchallenged.[111] Meggitt both challenges the "New Consensus" and also contrasts this "consensus" with what he terms the early twentieth-century view, advanced initially by Deissmann, that Christianity was "a religion of the slaves and the oppressed, made up of poor peasants and workers."[112]

While Meggitt's assessment is useful in broad terms, Steven Friesen points out that the term "New Consensus," which Meggitt and others use, is factually wrong.[113] The primary problem is that it is a misrepresentation of Deissmann's position. Whereas Deissmann is often believed to have argued that Paul's communities were made up of Christians mostly from the lowest classes of society, Friesen shows that in fact Deissmann

---

[108] The book which has done most to catalyze this debate has been Justin Meggitt, *Paul, Poverty and Survival*. See in response to this D. B. Martin, "Review Essay: Justin J. Meggitt, *Paul, Poverty and Survival*," *JSNT* 84 (2001): 51–64; G. Theissen, "The Social Structure of Pauline Communities: Some Critical Remarks on J. J. Meggitt, *Paul, Poverty and Survival*," *JSNT* 84 (2001): 65–84; G. Theissen, "Social Conflicts in the Corinthian Community: Further Remarks on J. J. Meggitt, *Paul, Poverty and Survival*," *JSNT* 25.3 (2003): 371–91. See also B. Holmberg, "The Methods of Historical Reconstruction in the Scholarly 'Recovery' of Corinthian Christianity," in *Christianity at Corinth: The Quest for the Pauline Church*, ed. E. Adams and D. G. Horrell (Louisville: Westminster John Knox Press, 2004); J. J. Meggitt, "Response to Martin and Theissen," *JSNT* 84 (2001): 85–94; Friesen, "Poverty in Pauline Studies."

[109] The phrase was first used by A. J. Malherbe, *Social Aspects of Early Christianity* (Baton Rouge: Louisiana State University Press, 1977), 31. See similarly Meeks, *The First Urban Christians*, 51–52. For further discussion of these developments see B. Holmberg, *Sociology and the New Testament: An Appraisal* (Philadelphia: Fortress Press, 1990), 21–76.

[110] Theissen, *The Social Setting of Pauline Christianity*. Meeks, *The First Urban Christians*.

[111] See Meggitt, *Paul, Poverty and Survival*, 100–101.

[112] See ibid., 101. This is how the earlier position is described in Holmberg, *Sociology and the New Testament*. Meggitt notes that this position was persuasively argued by Adolf Deissmann.

[113] Theissen also argues that in fact the "new consensus" is not new since it is evident from the end of the nineteenth century; Theissen, "The Social Structure of Pauline Communities," 66.

held that Paul's assemblies included a cross-section of society.[114] Friesen argues that instead of a new consensus within Pauline studies, there was simply a twentieth-century consensus that the members of Paul's assemblies "represented a cross-section of society, coming mostly from the middle and lower sectors of society, with some members from the higher sectors."[115] In other words, the "New Consensus" is a more nuanced understanding of how Paul has been interpreted but it does not change the conclusions which were reached regarding the social structure of Paul's communities.

It is these "New Consensus" conclusions which are beginning to be challenged. Three recent critiques of this view have been particularly influential – those of Justin Meggitt (directly) in his *Paul, Poverty and Survival* and Peter Lampe (more indirectly) in *From Paul to Valentinus: Christians at Rome in the First Two Centuries* and Steven Friesen's article "Poverty in Pauline Studies: Beyond the So-Called New Consensus."[116] Meggitt argues strongly that the evidence presented in support of the "New Consensus" (or what Friesen refers to as "the twentieth-century cross-section consensus") does not stand up to close scrutiny and that its interpretations are often anachronistic and inappropriate.[117] Even when the critiques of Meggitt's study have been taken into account there remains good evidence to suggest that the Pauline communities (in Rome and abroad) "shared fully in the bleak material existence that was the lot of the non-elite inhabitants of the Empire."[118] There are several aspects which merit discussion here and it is worth summarizing their findings (alongside the similar conclusions reached by, for example, Steven

[114]   See, with good evidence, Friesen, "Poverty in Pauline Studies," 325–26.

[115]   Ibid., 325. Friesen advances a strong case for reading Deissmann and subsequent Pauline interpreters as evidencing a shift "from one capitalist orientation to another: from Deissmann's perspective of bourgeois industrial capitalism of the early twentieth century, to the new consensus perspective of bourgeouis consumer capitalism in the late twentieth century"; ibid., 326–37. Quotation from page 336.

[116]   P. Lampe, *From Paul to Valentinus. Christians at Rome in the First Two Centuries*, trans. Michael Steinhauser (Minneapolis: Fortress Press, 2003); Meggitt, *Paul, Poverty and Survival*; Friesen, "Poverty in Pauline Studies," 323–61.

[117]   Meggitt, *Paul, Poverty and Survival*, 100. For a critique of the methodology of the "New Consensus" and a detailed examination of the evidence commonly put forward see Meggitt, *Paul, Poverty and Survival*, 100–53.

[118]   Meggitt, *Paul, Poverty and Survival*, 153. For this understanding of the first-century Roman Empire in general see, for example, P. Garnsey, *Food and Society in Classical Antiquity* (Cambridge University Press, 1999), 32–33; C. R. Whittaker, "The Poor in the City of Rome," in *Land, City, and Trade in the Roman Empire* (Aldershot: Ashgate, 1993), 301–33; For what this means regarding Paul's assemblies see, for example, T. L. Carter, "The Irony of Romans 13," *NovT* 46.3 (2004): 209–28; Jeffers, *Conflict at Rome*, 3; N. Elliott, "Strategies of Resistance."

Friesen, T. Carter, Neil Elliott and J. S. Jeffers) because of the potential significance which their conclusions have for a study of inheritance in Romans.

To begin with, Meggitt questions the assumption by NT scholars that there was, in the words of J. Becker, "a self confident, urban bourgeoisie with entrepreneurial spirit and sizeable wealth."[119] Meggitt argues instead that the economy of the Roman Empire was "essentially pre-industrial in character and incapable of sustaining a mid-range economic group."[120] Meggitt demonstrates that there were enormous disparities of wealth in the first-century Greco-Roman world and that it is likely that 99 percent of the population lived in brutal poverty.[121] Such poverty meant that people lived at or near subsistence level and that there was a continual struggle to obtain the minimum food, clothing and shelter necessary to sustain life.[122] The group of particular interest to a study of Romans is the urban poor. What was life like for this group? In terms of employment, the skilled artisans were the most wealthy group among the urban poor but even they lived at, or slightly above, subsistence level.[123] The existence of the semi-skilled or unskilled was even more destitute, living in constant fear of unemployment and its consequences. There is of course a close relationship between employment and food. Hunger was a continuous complaint for the *plebs urbana* and many people sold themselves and their families into slavery in order to avoid starvation.[124] The clothing of the poor in Rome was similarly a constant source of anguish. The urban poor of Rome lived in a broad spectrum of housing. The poorest had no housing and therefore slept in the open air or in tombs, cellars and vaults, lean-tos or in spaces under the stairs of apartment houses. Those who were slightly more economically successful would be able to afford an *insula* or a shared house. Often the apartment blocks were squalid and overcrowded. Meggitt therefore concludes, along with Brunt, that the entire *plebs urbana* lived in "appalling slums."[125] For women and children and the aged, the experience of poverty was intensified even further.

---

[119] J. Becker, "Paul and His Churches," in *Christian Beginnings: Word and Community from Jesus to Post-Apostolic Times*, ed. J. Becker (Louisville: John Knox Press, 1993), 168.
[120] Meggitt, *Paul, Poverty and Survival*, 153.   [121] Ibid., 41–73.
[122] Ibid.; Meggitt acknowledges that there are of course differences within this group of people and that some lead more precarious lives than others. But he does use the term without too many qualifications.
[123] Ibid., 54.   [124] Ibid., 59–60.
[125] Ibid., 66. Similarly T. L. Carter, "The Irony of Romans 13," 211; Jeffers, *Conflict at Rome*, 4.

One of the criticisms leveled at Meggitt's argument is the way he describes Roman society in exclusively binary terms – wide-scale destitution (99 percent of the population) and a small super-wealthy elite (1 percent of the population of the Empire).[126] What is needed, as Friesen observes, is a poverty scale with more than two categories. While Meggitt's categories are useful in that they allow him to crystallize the issues involved, there is certainly a need to consider a more differentiated model of social structure in first-century Roman society.[127] Towards this purpose Friesen proposes seven categories for thinking about poverty in the Roman Empire. His summary of these categories, with the estimated percentages of the urban population in larger cities, is as follows:[128]

Poverty Scale 1 (PS1)	Imperial elites	0.04%
Poverty Scale 2 (PS2)	Regional elites	1.00%
Poverty Scale 3 (PS3)	Municipal elites	1.76%
Poverty Scale 4 (PS4)	Moderate surplus	7%?
Poverty Scale 5 (PS5)	Stable near subsistence	22%?
Poverty Scale 6 (PS6)	At subsistence	40%
Poverty Scale 7 (PS7)	Below subsistence	28%

In broad terms these categories can then be gathered into two main groups – the super-wealthy (PS 1–3, totaling around 3 percent of the population) and the poor (PS 5–7, totaling 90 percent of the population) – and one small remaining category (PS 4). This means that the vast majority of people in the city of Rome lived near the subsistence level (PS 5–7), with "subsistence level" defined as "the resources needed to procure enough calories in food to maintain the human body."[129] Within Rome, 22 percent (PS 5) were able to rise marginally above the subsistence level for a time and 40 percent (PS 6) remained at a level of resources which meant they were able to obtain enough calories to survive. Those who lived below this level – the people "incapable of earning a living" and

---

[126] See, for example, Holmberg, "The Methods of Historical Reconstruction," 264.

[127] Friesen, "Poverty in Pauline Studies," 339. Meggitt himself acknowledges that his study is "undifferentiated" but suggests that this is helpful as long as we understand its limitations. He argues that his differentiation was deliberate so as not to obscure the nature of the widespread poverty of first-century Rome; Meggitt, *Paul, Poverty and Survival*, 41–73.

[128] Friesen, "Poverty in Pauline Studies," 347 fig. 3. Friesen points out that although this poverty scale is "rough in the details" it is a better guide to poverty questions "than are the assumptions of the twentieth-century cross-section consensus." For a description of the calculations which Friesen uses to arrive at these figures see ibid., 340–47 and Appendix.

[129] Ibid., 343.

those "permanently in crisis" – would fit into category PS7, which made up just over a quarter of the city of Rome (28 percent).[130]

At the other end of the scale a little less than 3 percent (PS 1–3) of the population were considered super-wealthy families. While estimating the incomes of these families is difficult, it is possible to gain some idea of the disparity between their existence and the lives of those at the other end of the poverty scale. For example, it is estimated that a family of four in the city of Rome would require an annual income of around 4,000 sesterces (= 1,000 denarii) in order to sustain themselves at the subsistence level.[131] In contrast we know that to be enrolled in the equestrian order (PS 2) one had to own property worth at least 400,000 sesterces and to be enrolled as a senator one needed property worth at least 1,000,000 sesterces. Friesen points out that, of course, the actual fortunes of such individuals would normally have been much larger.[132] Friesen then draws on the work of Duncan-Jones, who has provided a list of documented private fortunes of twenty-nine individuals, most of whom are from the early imperial period.[133] The documented fortunes of these individuals range from 1.8 million to 400 million sesterces.[134] Most of the wealth of these people would have been based on land, with income generated by farming and rent.[135]

There were very few people who had incomes between these two main groups of super-wealthy and poor. Those who did fit into this category (PS 4) did not comprise a "middle class" as it is defined in modern industrial or post-industrial economies.[136] The income of this small group of people (estimated at 7 percent of the population) is the most difficult to estimate since little is known about those who were near, but safely above, the subsistence level (which is why PS 4 and PS 5 have question marks by them in the summary above). Friesen reasons, however, that PS 4 was probably much smaller than PS 5 "because of the endemic nature of poverty in the Roman Empire, because of structural impediments in the

[130] Ibid., 344. Here Friesen notes particularly the study of Whittaker, "The Poor in the City of Rome."
[131] E. W. Stegemann and W. Stegemann, *The Jesus Movement: A Social History of Its First Century* (Minneapolis: Fortress Press, 1999), 81–85.
[132] Friesen, "Poverty in Pauline Studies," 345. See also G. Alföldy, *The Social History of Rome*, 2nd edn. (Baltimore: The Johns Hopkins University Press, 1998), 115–16.
[133] R. Duncan-Jones, *The Economy of the Roman Empire: Quantitative Studies*, rev. edn. (Cambridge University Press, 1982); R. Duncan-Jones, *Structure and Scale in the Roman Economy* (Cambridge University Press, 1990).
[134] Duncan-Jones, *Economy of the Roman Empire*, 343–44.
[135] Friesen, "Poverty in Pauline Studies," 345.   [136] Ibid., 346.

economy, and because of the large amounts of wealth required to move up the poverty scale."[137]

If a good case can therefore be made for the majority of the population of the Roman Empire living at or around a subsistence level, what of the Christians to whom Paul was writing in Rome? Which areas of Rome did these Christians live in and what does this reveal about the social status of these first Christian communities? Here the magisterial work of Peter Lampe has much to offer. Lampe first sets out to investigate where the urban Roman Christians in the first two centuries lived. In order to do this he examines five sources: local traditions (the primary evidence used here are the Tituli of late antiquity); the earliest archaeologically available graves (cemeteries on the radial roads outside the city offer clues to where their users lived in the city); Jewish quarters (because urban Roman Christianity developed out of Judaism we can expect that Christians of this period would be found in those areas of the city in which Jews also lived); concentrations of the Tituli (at which places in the city?); contemporary literary information concerning businesses of Christians that can be localized (where, for example, would one have opened a bank if hoping for Christian customers? – where Christians were clustered).[138] Lampe appreciates that each of these sources has only limited validity and therefore what he is looking for are the points at which there is overlap – which of these areas, for example, arise from more than one of these sources? His conclusions are that "we are able with great certainty to identify Trastevere, the XIVth Augustan region, as an early Christian quarter."[139] The same is true for the area within the city to the left and right of the Via Appia: "the Appian lowland from the Porta Capena to the Almone River."[140] The other two areas of the city which are evident from the sources (but with less overlap and therefore less certainty) are the Aventine and the Lesser Aventine (to the left of the Via Appia) and Mars Field (on both sides of the Via Lata/Flaminia).

In light of these findings Lampe then considers the question of which particular strata of the population predominated in these quarters (particularly Trastevere and the Via Appia). What is known about these areas that might offer insights into the social make-up of the Christian community in Rome? Lampe shows that both Trastevere and Appia/Porta Capena are lowlands between the hills of the city and that whereas the rich dwelt in the hills, the poor lived in these unhealthy, moist lowlands of

---

[137] Ibid.   [138] Lampe, *From Paul to Valentinus*, 19–47.
[139] Ibid., 42.   [140] Ibid.

the city.[141] "Trastevere was a harbor quarter, a workers' quarter. It accommodated harbor workers . . . porters . . . sailors . . . and also workers from the brickyards on the Vatican slopes . . . potters . . . millers," along with tanners and leatherworkers whose workshops "spread a penetrating odor" of urine and refuse.[142] Lampe demonstrates that Trastevere was the most densely populated area of the capital and had the highest percentage of apartment buildings. The "traders, craftsmen and transport workers" of the densely populated Appian Way outside of Porta Capena were of a similarly low social standing.[143] Both of these sections of the city attracted most of the city's immigrants because the areas were on the major traffic arteries and on the fringes of the city, outside the Pomerium.[144] In terms of the other two areas – the Aventine and Mars Field – the results are not totally clear cut. There seems to have been, for example, more variation in the social strata of these areas, although Christians living in Mars Field, for example, most probably lived in insulae.[145]

Further support for these conclusions is provided by Lampe's analysis of the twenty-eight individual persons introduced by Paul in Rom. 16:3–16 (twenty-six are named, two are unnamed). One of the questions which Lampe directs at these names is that of the social strata of the people listed: do these names belong to specific classes?[146] His conclusions serve to reinforce his earlier findings regarding the location of the Roman Christians. Lampe observes that of the thirteen persons about whom it was possible to make conclusions, "over two-thirds with a degree of probability show indications of slave origins."[147] Of these thirteen, most probably four persons are freeborn and at least nine are of slave origin.

The work of Lampe and Meggitt and others, therefore, strongly challenges the conclusion that the first Christian communities at Rome were made up primarily of a cross-section of society. Instead it seems that the majority of Christians to whom Paul was writing are likely to have lived in the poorest areas of the city and would have been in a continual struggle for survival. One of the problems with these conclusions, however, is the specific texts from (especially) Romans which seem to suggest that there were in fact wealthy individuals in the churches to whom Paul wrote. For example the specific NT texts which are often drawn on in support of the "twentieth-century cross-section consensus" are: 1 Cor. 1:26; 4:10; 5:1–13; 1 Corinthians 8–10; Rom. 16:3 (Prisca and Aquila); Rom. 16:23

---

[141] Ibid., 46.   [142] Ibid., 50.   [143] Ibid., 56–58.
[144] Ibid., 43–44. Similarly T. L. Carter, "The Irony of Romans 13," 211; Jeffers, *Conflict at Rome*, 8.
[145] Lampe, *From Paul to Valentinus*, 65.   [146] Ibid., 170–83.   [147] Ibid., 183.

(Erastus); and Rom. 16:1–2 (Phoebe).[148] Of these, the two which have the most significance for a study of Romans are the references to Phoebe and to Prisca and Aquila in Romans 16.[149]

There is not a lot to go on from the Romans 16 text itself with regard to Prisca and Aquila but the argument often presented is that elsewhere there are indications that this couple hosted an assembly in their home (1 Cor. 16:19). Also Acts 18:3 (which in this case seems to be an accurate tradition) indicates that they gave Paul accommodation and that they worked in the same trade as him.[150] It is therefore *possible* that Prisca and Aquila had (once more using Friesen's categories) moderate surplus resources (PS 4). But Friesen shows that it is just as likely that this couple were further down the poverty scale. In a major urban city such as Rome, housing was usually crowded and noisy.[151] It is possible that Prisca and Aquila lived in a tenement or in rented quarters near their workshop and it is also possible that both were manual laborers (Acts 18:3).[152] In other words, it is by no means certain that because Prisca and Aquila hosted a meeting at their house they had reasonable wealth. It is just as possible that the meetings were hosted in a shared housing area such as the shared space between tenements or in shanties or tents.[153] Friesen therefore concludes that Prisca and Aquila were not "relatively wealthy"[154] but were more likely to be in either category 4 (possibly) or category 5 (more likely) of the poverty scale.[155]

Paul's reference to Phoebe in Rom. 16:1–2 is also thought to be evidence for the existence of wealthy people in the Roman Christian community. The deductions which are commonly made are that she was an independent woman and a "patron" and someone who traveled. All of this is believed to indicate that she was therefore a wealthy woman. Meggitt questions the connection which is often made between a first-century person's independence and their wealth. It is "simply erroneous," he insists, to assume that autonomy was restricted to the most affluent people in

---

[148] Meggitt, *Paul, Poverty and Survival*, 102–53.

[149] Also mentioned in Romans 16 are "Erastus" and "Gaius," both of whom are often believed to be from the super-wealthy of Roman society. Neither of these is amongst the Christians at Rome, however, as indicated in Rom. 16:23.

[150] For the reliability of Acts here see Friesen, "Poverty in Pauline Studies," 353 n. 92.

[151] Whittaker, "The Poor in the City of Rome," 8–12; Jeffers, *Conflict at Rome*, 4.

[152] R. Jewett, *Paul, the Apostle to America: Cultural Trends and Pauline Scholarship* (Louisville: Westminster John Knox Press, 1994), 73–86.

[153] Meggitt, "Response to Martin and Theissen," 93. As Meggitt observes, "We may need to engage our imaginations a little more when we try to envisage the meetings of the early Christians."

[154] As argued by Meeks, *The First Urban Christians*, 59.

[155] Friesen, "Poverty in Pauline Studies," 353. Meggitt, *Paul, Poverty and Survival*, 145.

first-century society.[156] Neither does the term often translated "benefactor" (προστάτις) unequivocally indicate that Phoebe was wealthy. To begin with, as Friesen notes, προστάτις is not the normal term for a benefactor.[157] It is unusual too that Paul asks the Romans to assist her when she arrives, which would be inappropriate behavior for a client (in this case Paul) on behalf of a benefactor. Further, Paul's request for help also indicates that Phoebe's financial standing was not high.[158] As Meggitt observes, "It is one thing to say that Paul referred to Phoebe as a patron, it is another thing entirely to argue that she must have been in some sense an *elite* patron who enjoyed a position similar, for example, to that of the celebrated Theodora in first-century Corinth."[159] In light of this, Meggitt concludes that Paul's words suggest little about her social status in first-century Rome:

> It is much more likely that in Rom. 16:1–2 the apostle is engaged, as he so often is elsewhere in his letters, in manipulating socially emotive language (rather than using it in a straightforward, descriptive sense). It is quite probable that by his choice of words he intended to play Phoebe a powerful, public, compliment, and to indicate to the Roman Christians something of her importance to the church at Cenchreae.[160]

What significance does the work of Lampe, Meggitt and Friesen therefore have for an exploration of inheritance in Romans? These and other studies marshal considerable evidence to suggest that most people who lived under Roman imperialism were poor and that the Christian communities in the city of Rome were largely composed of the urban poor, people who lived close to the line between subsistence and crisis. What difference does it make, therefore, that the majority of the people to whom Paul is writing were amongst the poorest in Rome and that this poverty was often brutal and gruelling? How would a situation of poverty affect the response of these Roman Christians to the ideals and expectations being presented by the imperial cult? It seems likely that these people will have been aware of the disparity between what the Empire was proclaiming and what they experienced on a day-to-day basis. Whereas the imperial cult claimed that the emperor had brought peace, prosperity, order and fruitfulness to society, the urban poor to whom Paul wrote had

---

[156] Meggitt, *Paul, Poverty and Survival*, 145.
[157] Friesen, "Poverty in Pauline Studies," 355.   [158] Ibid.
[159] Meggitt, *Paul, Poverty and Survival*, 147.
[160] Ibid., 148. Friesen, "Poverty in Pauline Studies," 355.

experienced very little of this. Although saturated by images of well-being, Paul's Roman Christians were in reality destitute. The question for the present study therefore becomes how they would have responded to Paul's message of inheritance. In the midst of a daily struggle for survival, how would a promise of future inheritance have sounded?

With these questions in mind two qualifications need to be made. First, this is not to suggest that the study which follows would collapse if the argument regarding social strata at Rome (above) is not accepted – the arguments regarding inheritance remain. But what it does do is intensify the message which Paul evokes because of the alternative message of hope and well-being which it contains.

Second (to reiterate the methodology of this study, described above), to ask these questions is not to suggest that this thesis is interested in whether there is a direct linguistic connection between the language of inheritance in Roman society and Paul's use of inheritance. To attempt to uncover the perceptions of inheritance by Rome's urban poor would be highly problematic. This is because such inheritance laws are exclusively to do with the elite in Roman society.[161] Justin Meggitt is one of the first to address this problem by using epitaphs, defixiones and graffiti as a way of exploring the perspective of Rome's urban poor.[162] This is no easy task, given that most of the sources available reveal more about the elite than the poor. Even more difficult would be to attempt to uncover how Rome's poor perceived the inheritance laws – as Meggitt's study shows, no such evidence exists. Although the task is difficult, however, it is not impossible. It is not possible to dig up evidence specifically concerned with how Rome's poor perceived inheritance but there *is* evidence which provides insights into the perspective of the poor in more general terms. This will be explored in Chapter 3.

Of course it is not a new observation to propose that there were some people in first-century Rome who were resistant to the claims of the Empire and who longed for something different. At the time of the first century there are many examples of figures and texts which resisted Rome's Empire: the German prophetess Veleda;[163] a large number of Jewish prophetic figures attested to by Josephus;[164] and magi and astrologers who foretold various disasters and were consequently expelled by the emperors Vespasian and Domitian.[165] In addition to this, There was also

---

[161] Price, *Rituals and Power*, 5.   [162] Meggitt, *Paul, Poverty and Survival*, 30.
[163] Tacitus, *Histories* 5.13.
[164] W. Carter, *Matthew and the Margins. A Socio-Political and Religious Reading*, JSNTSup 204 (Sheffield Academic Press, 2000), 557 n. 2.
[165] Ibid.

the text of Revelation and other apocalyptic texts which predicted the victory of God over all oppression, including Rome's (*1 Enoch* 37–71; *4 Ezra*; *2 Baruch*).[166] But perhaps the most well known of resistance texts were the Sibylline Oracles. These oracles usually focused on prophecies of future, frequently political events, and were often virulent attacks on Roman power. One example is from Sibylline Oracles Book 4:

> Great wealth will come to Asia which Rome itself once plundered and deposited in her house of many possessions. She will then pay back twice as much and more to Asia, and then there will be a surfeit of war.[167]

So there is some evidence to suggest that various people and groups in Rome did not believe that things in society were exactly as they should be or that the golden age had arrived in full. Yet it is also the case, as seen in the sources examined above, that there were some claims being made that the Roman people were already living in the best of times. Perhaps it is important, therefore, to hold in tension these two realities. This is what Mark Clark seems to do in his study of *Spes Augusta*, "the hope of Augusta." This legend first appeared on a coin in 41 CE, issued by Claudius.[168] The concept of Spes was not unique to the imperial cult – it was also used in relation to deities such as Fortuna and other goddesses. (The concept was also used in Latin literature, although there was not always a consistent and dependable quality to it.) When the concept was used in relation to the Roman Empire, it had both political and religious importance, with the two categories converging in the person of the emperor – the cult of Hope was focused on the emperor.[169] The focus on the emperor meant that it was both a private and public hope. "We should imagine here the virtue as proceeding from the hope of a

[166] See further N. Elliott, "The 'Patience of the Jews': Strategies of Resistance and Accommodation to Imperial Cultures," in *Pauline Conversations in Context. Essays in Honor of Calvin J. Roetzel*, ed. J. C. Anderson *et al.* (London: Sheffield Academic Press, 2002), 32–41; A. Y. Collins, *Crisis and Catharsis. The Power of the Apocalypse* (Philadelphia: Westminster Press, 1984), 90–93.

[167] *Sib. Or.* 4.145–48. This oracle was either composed or taken over by a Jew in about 80 CE; A. Y. Collins, *Crisis and Catharsis*, 91. Realizing the threat of such oracles to the status quo, Augustus had two thousand books of this kind confiscated and burned in 12 BCE. R. MacMullen, *Enemies of the Roman Order* (Harvard University Press, 1966), 148–49. See further J. J. Collins, "Sibylline Oracles," in *Dictionary of New Testament Background*, ed. C. A. Evans and Stanley E. Porter (Leicester InterVarsity Press: 2000).

[168] Mark Edward Clark, "Images and Concepts of Hope in the Early Imperial Cult," in *Society of Biblical Literature: Seminar Papers*, ed. K. H. Richards (California: Scholars Press, 1982), 41.

[169] Ibid.

great name to the hope of the Empire and down to the expectations of all Romans. The emanation of *spes* was a single process, for the hope of the imperial family was also the personal hope of private citizens."[170] Clark shows that this concept was then used by subsequent emperors. These later emperors evoked the Augustan concept in order to convey the idea of dynasty, and perpetuity. What emerges from this concept is *both* a present realization *and* a future hope. For example, Clark notes Horace's *Carmen Saeculare* (which was discussed earlier), written for the secular games of 17 BCE. There are twenty-seven young boys and girls in this poem who represent hope for their parents' future. The poem

> is a look to the future from a panoramic view of Roman history
> and it ends up with an affirmation of good hope for the present:
> *spem bonam certamque domum reporto* (line 74). Though not
> one of Horace's best, the ode does suggest that the Romans were
> concerned with their future, represented by children, and that
> this concern took on new confidence under Augustus.[171]

A later example noted by Clark is the adoption of Tiberius by Augustus. This is described by Velleius Peterculus (2.103), written before 30 CE. In this passage Fortuna returns her protection to the state of Rome through Tiberius' arrival at just the right time:

> On the day of the adoption the city was filled with joy and the
> *realized hope* of the perpetual security and eternity of the empire;
> parents had hope of children, men of matrimony, masters of
> patrimony, and all men had the hope of salvation, quiet, peace
> and tranquility, so much so that one could not hope for more,
> nor could it be accorded hope more fortunately.[172]

For many in the Empire there was little evidence of such peace. Despite this, it was still the case that the emperor and his family often engendered hope for society, both realized and delayed.

Conclusions

Through the coins and literature of first-century imperial Rome, and through the way cities were organized and structured, the message was clear – the blessing of peace and stability would come about through the actions of the Roman emperor. Often referred to as the "savior," the emperor was looked to as the one who would subdue and dominate

---

[170] Ibid., 42–43.   [171] Ibid., 42.   [172] Ibid.; emphasis added.

other people groups through military victory. There would be "peace" on the earth, a tranquility and stability understood in very concrete terms. It would include the fertility and abundance of crops and the hope of the welfare of the people of the Empire. What these sources show is that in the Greco-Roman society and ritual of Paul's day there was an acknowledgment that in part the material blessings had been fulfilled. And yet at the same time it continued to be a society rife with soteriological expectations, especially for those (such as the majority of the Roman Christians) who were from the lowest strata of society.

It is within this context that Paul writes his letter to the Christians in Rome. In light of this, how should his language of inheritance be read? As noted in the Introduction, against the backdrop of first-century Rome described above, this study is an exploration of the content of the inheritance in Romans. Three sub-questions serve to sharpen further this enquiry: to what extent does Paul have in mind a this-worldly inheritance (*what* is the inheritance?); to what degree is this political in nature (*who* will inherit?) and what is the path to this inheritance (*how* does this transpire?)? The next chapter considers Romans 4 with these questions in mind and examines the extent to which this subverts the features of first-century imperial Rome described above.

3

PROMISING THE WORLD: INHERITANCE IN ROMANS 4:13–25

Introduction

This description of some of the features of Greco-Roman society provides a backdrop for a reading of inheritance (κληρονόμος) language in Romans. In what follows I will explore the nature and characteristics of the inheritance and the degree to which this contributes to an overall counter-imperial narrative in Romans. The present chapter takes the first steps towards this goal, examining κληρονόμος in Rom. 4:13–25 in order to consider the contribution this term makes to Paul's argument and to begin to understand his message within its first-century social, religious and political context.[1]

> (13) For the promise that he would inherit the world(τὸ κληρονό-μον αὐτὸν εἶναι κόσμου) did not come to Abraham or to his descendants (σπέρματι) through the law but through the righteousness of faith. (14) If it is the adherents of the law who are to be the heirs (κληρονόμοι), faith is null and the promise is void. (15) For the law brings wrath; but where there is no law, neither is there violation. (16) For this reason it depends on faith, in order that the promise may rest on grace and be guaranteed to all his descendants (σπέρματι), not only to the adherents of the law but also those who share the faith of Abraham (for he is the father of all of us [ὅς ἐστιν πατὴρ πάντων ἡμῶν], (17) as it is written, "I have made you the father of many nations [Πατέρα πολλῶν ἐθνῶν])" – in the presence of the God in whom he believed, who gives life to the dead and calls into existence the

---

[1] In Romans 4 and 8 κληρονόμος ("heir") is used but in Romans 11 the variant κληρονομία ("inheritance"). There is an inseparable connection between the two forms of the word – it is not possible to explore the meaning of "heir" without also understanding the meaning of "inheritance." In what follows, the focus will therefore be on both the content of the inheritance and also the recipients of the inheritance. Biblical quotations are from the NRSV unless otherwise indicated.

things that do not exist. (18) Hoping against hope, he believed
that he would become "the father of many nations (πατέρα
πολλῶν ἐθνῶν)," according to what was said, "So numerous
shall your descendants (σπέρμα) be." (19) He did not weaken
in faith when he considered his own body, which was already as
good as dead (for he was about a hundred years old), or when
he considered the barrenness of Sarah's womb. (20) No distrust
made him waver concerning the promise of God, but he grew
strong in his faith as he gave glory to God, (21) being fully
convinced that God was able to do what he had promised. (22)
Therefore his faith "was reckoned to him as righteousness." (23)
Now the words, "it was reckoned to him," were written not for
his sake alone, (24) but for ours also. It will be reckoned to us
who believe in him who raised Jesus our Lord from the dead,
(25) who was handed over to death for our trespasses and was
raised for our justification.

Rom. 4:13–25, which offers the highest concentration of κληρονόμος
language in Romans (4:13, 14),[2] provides a rare insight into what Paul
understands to be the *content* of the inheritance.[3] While usually Paul
seems to assume that his audience will know what he intends to convey
by these terms, in 4:13 he employs a highly compressed but suggestive
phrase which explicitly defines the promised inheritance as "the world"
(κόσμος). This is important because, as James Hester observes in his
study of inheritance in Paul's letters, usually Paul never bothers to define
the concept of inheritance since there is no dispute over its contents.[4]

---

[2] The word "promise" (ἐπαγγελία) is a prominent term in this section of Romans and
is virtually synonymous with κληρονομία (Rom. 4:13, 14, 16, 20, 21). There is a general
consensus that in the context of Romans 4 "promise" refers to "the promise to Abraham,"
i.e. the promised "inheritance." See, for example, B. J. Byrne, *Romans*, Sacra Pagina 6
(Collegeville, MN: The Liturgical Press, 1996), 158; Dunn, *Romans 1–8*, 215.

[3] In Rom. 4:13 the subject ἐπαγγελία has no verb expressed. Frequently a verb is
supplied by translators, such as "the promise that was granted." Sam Williams shows,
however, that while this makes some sense, it is better to understand the word ἐπαγγελία
as either (1) designating the pledge itself or (2) refering to the content of the pledge. Rom.
4:21, where Paul writes "God was able to do what he had promised (ὃ ἐπήγγελται),"
offers some clues to the interpretation of Rom. 4:13. It suggests that in at least some parts
of Romans 4, ἐπαγγελία means "what was promised." As Williams concludes, it seems
likely that in Rom. 4:13 ἐπαγγελία refers to the content of the promise; S. K. Williams,
"The 'Righteousness of God' in Romans," *JBL* 99 (1980): 279.

[4] Hester, *Paul's Concept of Inheritance*, 69. While the phrase "kingdom of God" is often
directly linked to "inheritance" in Paul's writings, the apostle does not have much to say
about the kingdom and the phrase is therefore difficult to define. See the discussion of these
texts in Chapters 6 and 7.

Given the significance which this text has for understanding Paul's concept of inheritance, it is surprising that little attention has been given to the phrase. This interpretive neglect has been shaped in part by Davies' influential discussion of "land" in the New Testament and in part as a consequence of the Reformation approach to Paul which has, until recently, been the prevailing reading of the apostle. For example, C. K. Barrett gives little thought to the significance of the content of the inheritance in verse 13, and chooses instead to interpret verses 13–18 through his reading of verses 1–12: "[the section vv. 13–18] provides a further argument for the view (already set forth in vv. 1–12) that God's relation with Abraham was not on the basis of law."[5]

Although the so-called "new perspective(s)" on Paul have shifted the focus from *how* one becomes an heir to an emphasis on *who* are the heirs, this interpretive modification has had little effect on how the *content* of inheritance is understood. One of the weaknesses of these approaches is an inability to identify a demonstrable connection between the highly suggestive phrase in verse 13 "inherit the world" and Paul's argument in the verses which follow – interpreters have not made a lot of headway in explaining how "inherit the world" might relate to the rest of Paul's argument in the chapter. While commentators observe the boldness of Paul's use of this phrase there is often no attempt to inquire into the reason for his audacious statement – typically it is regarded as an intriguing anomaly that has little direct connection to the substance of Paul's argument. There is seldom any attention given to how this phrase might shed light on Paul's other uses of "promise" and "inheritance" in Romans 4 (and other contexts in Romans) or on the insights it might offer in understanding the immediate context (4:13–25).

The perceived disconnection between verse 13 and what follows is most noticeable when interpreters want to argue that Paul's message was subversive of the Roman Empire. This is the case, for example, with the work of N. T. Wright. In his article "Paul and Caesar: A New Reading of Romans," Wright begins by noting that in recent years Pauline scholarship has started to appreciate the decidedly political nature of Paul's letters with the result that interpreters, rather than seeking only to tease out certain political "implications," have become increasingly aware of the possibility of socio-political critique at the very heart of Paul's message.[6] Wright believes this approach is worth exploring further and

[5] Davies, *The Gospel and the Land*; C. K. Barrett, *The Epistle to the Romans*, BNTC (London: A. & C. Black, 1957), 93.
[6] N. T. Wright, "Paul and Caesar: A New Reading of Romans," in *A Royal Priesthood? The Use of the Bible Ethically and Politically. A Dialogue with Oliver O'Donovan*, ed.

in his initial pursuit of this perspective proposes that in both the thematic introduction to Romans (1:1–17) and in its thematic conclusion (15:7–13) Paul is directly challenging the ruler of the Empire, Caesar himself.[7] Wright therefore poses the question: "[I]f Paul has framed this great letter with an introduction and a theological conclusion which seem so clearly to echo, and thus to challenge, the rule of Caesar with the rule of Jesus Christ, is the rest of the letter in some sense about this as well, and if so, how?"[8] Most importantly for our purposes, to what degree does Wright see this political subversion as evident in the detail of Romans 4?[9] In his commentary's concluding reflections on Romans 4 Wright suggests that

> when examining Paul's gospel and the way it reveals God's justice, this message offers an implicit challenge to the world Paul and his readers inhabited – the world in which Caesar ruled supreme, in which his justice had rescued the world from chaos and had established a single Empire embracing all nations. Paul is not ashamed of the gospel of Jesus, because in it God's saving justice, his covenant faithfulness, is revealed. The living God thereby upstages Caesar.[10]

In what sense, then, does Paul in Romans 4 understand God to have upstaged Caesar? Wright comes closest to showing how this is so when he begins to unpack verse 13. Commenting on the phrase "inherit the world," Wright suggests that

> In Paul's thought ethnic, national Israel will not rule the world. God will rule the world, and will do so through Jesus the Jewish Messiah, in such a way as to bring all nations equally into God's family (see 9.5; 10.13). Paul's development of the inheritance theme, so important in Genesis 15 and elsewhere in the Pentateuch, here takes a decisive turn that looks ahead to 8.12–30.[11]

As will be argued below, the phrase "inherit the world" (v. 13) is indeed a provocative one for Paul to utter in this context. Wright's reading of inheritance as a this-worldly renewal is here helpful. However, his

C. Bartholomew (Grand Rapids: Zondervan, 2002). See also the introductory comments in Wright's commentary on Romans: N. T. Wright, "Romans," in NIB 10 (Nashville: Abingdon Press, 2002), 404–405.

[7] N. T. Wright, "Paul and Caesar," 177. See further N. T. Wright, "Coming Home to St Paul? Reading Romans a Hundred Years after Charles Gore," *Scottish Journal of Theology* 55.4 (2002): 402.

[8] N. T. Wright, "Paul and Caesar," 177.

[9] The best example of Wright's reading of the detail of Romans 4 is from his commentary on Romans; N. T. Wright, "Romans."

[10] Ibid., 505.   [11] Ibid., 496.

argument needs to be taken further in order to comprehend the full scope and force of inheritance and promise in Rom. 4:13–25. It is particularly noticeable in Wright's exegesis of this text (and this is also the case with other "new perspective" readings of the passage) that there is little demonstrable connection between verse 13 and the verses which follow, particularly verses 16–17, which Wright insists is the climax of Romans 4. According to Wright's reading, Rom. 4:13 is a suggestive phrase but one ultimately disconnected from the primary focus of Paul's argument. For Wright, in verse 13 "Paul speaks *almost casually* about Abraham's family 'inheriting the world,' "[12] and Paul's phrase is "included here almost as a throwaway line."[13] But is this the case? Is Paul's provocative use of κληρονόμος a passing comment which bears little substantial connection with the subsequent argument?

One way of addressing this question might simply be to insist that for Paul there is no disjunction between the *who* and the *what* of inheritance in Romans 4. Ernst Käsemann, for example, asserts that it is inconceivable that there would be a division in Paul's mind between the two ideas – the content of the promise and the inheritors of the promise – as is often assumed. The view, "which sees the text as a general discussion (Kuhl) in which the specific content of the promise is not at issue (Nygren), appears ridiculous (Juchler; Kuss)."[14] And yet while Käsemann rightly exposes the artificial dichotomy (between the specific content of the promise and the beneficiaries of the Abrahamic promise) which is often assumed in readings of this text, and although he hints at the this-worldly nature of the inheritance, it is not his purpose to show the ways in which the *who* and the *what* of inheritance are combined in this text.[15]

The brief survey above suggests that neither the content of κληρονόμος and "promise" in Rom. 4:13 (and following) nor how this coheres with the immediate context (vv. 14–25) has been given sufficient attention. In light of this, I will advance three proposals in this chapter. First, that the "promise" of "inheritance" in verse 13 refers to a this-worldly geographical reality, not to a spiritualized blessing and that it simultaneously conveys ideas of universal sovereignty and political themes because of the way it deals with the question of *who* will inherit the world. Second,

---

[12] N. T. Wright, "Paul and Caesar," 189; emphasis added.

[13] N. T. Wright, "New Exodus, New Inheritance: The Narrative Substructure of Romans 3–8," in *Romans and the People of God: Essays in Honour of Gordon D. Fee on the Occasion of His 65th Birthday*, ed. N. T. Wright and S. K. Soderland (Grand Rapids: Eerdmans, 1999), 31.

[14] E. Käsemann, *Commentary on Romans* (Grand Rapids: Eerdmans, 1980), 120.

[15] See ibid., esp. 120–21, 123.

that verse 13 is not a curious anomaly but is closely connected with the verses which follow (13–25) – that "inherit the world" is the first clue that this section concerns a whole complex of ideas associated with the Abrahamic tradition, and subsequent Jewish interpretation of this tradition, ideas such as the people of God inheriting and receiving sovereignty over actual physical territory in order that the nations might be blessed. These ideas are equally present in verses 14–25. Third, I will explore what it might have meant for Paul to make such claims in the first-century Roman imperial context.

Romans 4:13

In Rom. 4:13 Paul writes: "For the promise that he would inherit the world" or, more literally, "the promise that he should be the heir of the world (τὸ κληρονόμον αὐτὸν εἶναι κόσμου) did not come to Abraham or to his descendants through the law but through the righteousness of faith." What does Paul mean here when he writes of Abraham's descendants and "the world" (κόσμος) of which he will be κληρονόμος?[16] In the few other instances where the content of inheritance is mentioned in Paul or in the Pauline tradition, it is often referred to as "the kingdom of God"[17] or "the kingdom of [God's] beloved Son,"[18] phrases which offer helpful clues to what Paul means. Although there is no mention of "kingdom" language in Romans 4, there are other conceptual clues to the meaning of inheritance. For example, commenting on the wider context of this verse (Romans 4), Walter Brueggemann observes that "While the [Abrahamic] image undoubtedly is transformed [in Paul's thinking], it is inconceivable that it should have been emptied of its reference to land. The Abraham imagery apart from the land promise is an empty form. No matter how

---

[16] In posing this question I make two syntactical judgments. First, to whom does "his seed" here refer – to "Christ" or to "all who have the faith of Abraham"? On the basis of Gal. 3:16 it would be possible to read Paul as here referring to Christ, but Rom. 4:14 and 16 make clear that in this context Paul uses the noun as a collective so that "his seed" refers to "all who are from the faith of Abraham"; S. K. Williams, "'Righteousness of God,'" 279. Second, to whom does the pronoun αὐτόν refer and thus who inherits the world – Abraham (so Barrett, Harrison, Watson) or Abraham's posterity? As Williams rightly concludes, although the more likely is Abraham's posterity, the distinction amounts to little: "since from a Jewish perspective Abraham 'includes' his posterity and his posterity represents him. In fact, the word ἤ which cannot here be disjunctive (either Abraham *or* his descendants), may indicate that in Paul's mind 'Abraham' and Abraham's 'seed' are virtually interchangeable"; ibid. Similarly James M. Scott, *Adoption as Sons of God. An Exegetical Investigation into the Background of YIOTHEZIA in the Pauline Corpus*, WUNT 48 (Tubingen: J. C. B. Mohr [Paul Siebeck], 1992), 135.
[17] 1 Cor. 15:50. Also Gal. 5:2.   [18] Col. 1:12–13.

spiritualized, transcendentalized, or existentialized, it has its primary focus undeniably on land."[19] To what degree is this the case? Would Paul's reference to Abraham have brought to mind for his readers ideas such as physical land and of the sovereignty of Abraham's heirs? Everett Harrison argues that there is no such reference to universal sovereignty in this verse – "nothing in the section we are considering suggests the thought of dominion. To be sure, Abraham received a promise that his descendants would possess the gate of their enemies (Gen. 22.17) but that concept is not introduced here."[20] It is easy to understand why interpreters have not given much attention to the content of inheritance in this context and why Harrison insists that the idea of sovereignty is absent from Paul's mind. After all, up to this point in Romans 4, Paul's language has primarily revolved around terms such as "circumcision," "uncircumcision," "faith," "works" and "righteousness," none of which appear to lay the foundation for anything to do with the universal sovereignty of the heirs of Abraham. However, Paul's use of the term "world" (κόσμος), with its connotations of physicality and universality, is an indication that κληρονόμος may in fact bear close relation to the traditions and perspectives identified above. Since ideas associated with the Abrahamic tradition are so central to this context, then what can be learnt from this tradition, in particular the OT and LXX background to the κληρονόμος word group?

In the LXX the word group which includes κληρονόμος, συγκληρονό-μος, συγκληρονομέω, κατακληρονομέω and κληρονομία is mostly used for נָחַל ("to have or get as a possession") and בַהֲלָה ("inheritance," "property," "permanent possession"). Theologically, the investigation of the whole κληρονόμος word group finds its focus in נָחַל and בַהֲלָה.[21]

The verb נָחַל occurs 59 times in its various forms in the Old Testament and its meanings are influenced by the noun בַהֲלָה, which occurs 220 times.[22] Several ideas are commonly denoted by the term בַהֲלָה. It encompasses property, especially land, which is inalienable and enduring, something which individuals or groups usually receive as a grant

[19] Brueggemann, *The Land*, 170. Similarly, Christopher Wright, *God's People in God's Land. Family, Land and Property in the Old Testament*, rev. edn. (Carlisle: Paternoster Press, 1997), 111.

[20] E. Harrison, "Romans," in *EBC*, ed. Frank Gaebelein (Grand Rapids: Zondervan, 1976), 51. Note Barrett, however, who suggests that although Paul never quotes directly from Gen. 22:17f., he doubtless has it in mind; Barrett, *The Epistle to the Romans*, 94.

[21] L. J. Coppes, "Nahal, Naḥ^aLâ," in *Theological Wordbook of the Old Testament*, ed. R. L. Harris (Chicago: Moody Press, 1980), 569–70.

[22] G. Wanke, "Nahal, Naḥ^aLâ," in *TLOT* II, ed. E. Jenni and C. Westermann (Peabody, MA: Hendrickson Publishers, 1997), 731.

or an inheritance and thereafter possess indefinitely.[23] The most common literal application of both נְחַל and בַהֲלָה is to the property divided permanently according to the social structure of Israel in fulfillment of Yahweh's promise to Abraham – the allotment given to the extended family or to the tribes and clans[24] or to the nation as a whole.[25] The land that belonged to an individual Israelite and his family, within the tribal division of territory, was therefore his בַהֲלָה.[26] Christopher Wright points out that the prophets often strongly attacked those whose actions threatened the family בַהֲלָה, because everyone should have a share in the land, and they even wanted to ensure that the aliens had a share in the blessing of Israel by being allotted their own בַהֲלָה.[27]

Less common is the portrayal of the land as being the בַהֲלָה of Israel as a whole. Sometimes the term refers to the possession of a geographical area by the nation of Israel and sometimes "the use of inheritance language of the land as a whole is verging on the metaphorical [in comparison with the concrete meaning discussed above] since it draws attention to that unique relationship between Yahweh and Israel of which the possession of this particular land was proof."[28] To enter this land promised to Abraham and his descendants was to enjoy the inheritance.[29]

This concept of בַהֲלָה as national territory receives an eschatological focus in the prophetic writing, especially in Ezekiel 40–48, and parts of Isaiah. In Ezekiel 40–48 the prophet predicts that there will again be a time when the tribes of Israel will divide the land (בַהֲלָה) so that each will receive its בַהֲלָה by lot.[30] Similarly in Deutero-Isaiah Yahweh (48:19) will restore the land in the day of salvation, apportioning the devastated land as בַהֲלָה.[31]

---

[23] Ibid.

[24] Gen. 48:6 and especially Num. 26:52–56; 32:18f.; 34:14–18; 36:2–12; 34:29; 18:20ff.; 26:62; 27:1ff.; Deut. 19:14; Josh. 13:1, 7.

[25] Christopher Wright, "Nahal, NaḥᵃLâ," in *NIDOTTE* III, ed. W. A. Van Gemeren (Grand Rapids: Zondervan, 1997), 78.

[26] The בַהֲלָה, which was the special privilege of the firstborn son, could include not just a piece of real property (Ruth 4:3), but also possibly a vineyard (1 Kgs. 21:1–19), a "field and a vineyard" (Num. 16:14) or more generally "landed property" (Mic. 2:2) or "slaves" (Lev. 25:44–46) "money" (Eccl. 7:11–12a) or "chattels" (Prov. 19:14).

[27] C. Wright, *God's People in God's Land*, 104–109.

[28] C. Wright, "Nahal, NaḥᵃLâ," 78. Hester, *Paul's Concept of Inheritance*, 4.

[29] For example Deut. 1:7, 8, 21, 35, 38; 2:12, 29; 3:18, 20, 28; 4:1, 5, 14, 21, 26, 38, 40; 6:1, 10, 23; 7:1, 13. In some of these texts there is an overlap with individuals, tribes and clans.

[30] Ezek. 47:13, 14; 48:29; 45:1.

[31] See further Isa. 19:25; 63:17; Zech. 2:16; 8:12; Joel 1:2; 2:17, 18, 26, 27; 3:3, 16.

Similar emphases are conveyed when κληρονόμος is used in the LXX. Basic to the concept of inheritance in the Greek is "'heir' in the sense of the natural heir and the one named by a will or by legal provisions."[32] But the meaning of κληρονόμος in the LXX goes beyond this. Norman Habel, in *The Land Is Mine: Six Biblical Ideologies*, argues that the term בְּהֲלָה is best rendered with expressions such as "portion," "share," "entitlement," "allotment," and "rightful property." His reasoning is that בְּהֲלָה "in its primary meaning, is not something simply handed down from generation to generation, but the entitlement or rightful property of a party that is legitimated by a recognized social custom."[33] In other words, one of the problems with using the word "inheritance" to render the word בְּהֲלָה is that it conveys the idea of the transfer of land or property from parent to child or ancestor to progeny. But, as Habel shows, this is misleading. The word בְּהֲלָה certainly includes such generational transfers of land and property but it extends further than this.[34] The idea which characterizes both the verb κληρονομέω and the noun κληρονομία in the LXX is the element of rightful grant or share or allotment which thereafter becomes a lasting possession. For example, this is conveyed through the verb when Joshua asks, "How long will you be slack about going in and taking possession of the land that the LORD, the God of your ancestors, has given you?"[35] Here and throughout the LXX "κληρονομεῖν denotes the actual taking of the land in possession."[36] With regard to the noun, there are instances where it can mean *inheritance* or *the inheritance*.[37] But this is not the primary meaning. Instead, like the verb κληρονομεῖν, the decisive point is once more that of a legal grant or share which results in enduring possession.[38] Strong evidence for this is the fact that even when the whole of the land of Canaan could no longer be considered to be the patrimony of Israel, it was still referred to as the κληρονομία of Israel.

Why, then, is this word group used for נָחַל and בְּהֲלָה if the essential Greek element of inheritance is relegated to the background? The reason seems to be that other related words, such as κτήτωρ (owner) or κτᾶσθαι (owner, gainer) all convey the idea of one possession changing owner

---

[32] W. Foerster, " κληρονόμος," in *TDNT* III (Grand Rapids: Eerdmans, 1964–76), 768.

[33] N. C. Habel, *The Land Is Mine: Six Biblical Ideologies*, Overtures to Biblical Theology (Minneapolis: Fortress Press, 1995), 35.

[34] Ibid, 33–35. See further R. O. Forshey, "The Hebrew Root Nhl and Its Semitic Cognates" (Harvard University Press, 1972).

[35] Josh. 18:3. Cf. also Exod. 23:30; Num. 14:24.

[36] Foerster, " κληρονόμος," 779.

[37] See, for example, the story of the daughters of Zelophehad in Num. 27:8.

[38] Foerster, "κληρονόμος," 779. Habel, *The Land Is Mine*, 35.

in exchange for another possession. In other words, the process can be reversed if desired. But in the cases where the LXX uses κληρονομεῖν, there is not the possibility of reversible processes. Only with force can a people be removed from the territory which it ἐκληρονόμησεν. The type of acquisition inherent in בְּהֵלָה confers a lasting right of ownership, a process which cannot be reversed at will – for families and individuals, and as expressed in the legislation of the year of jubilee (see p. 68).[39] From this investigation of the sources for Paul's use of κληρονόμος several themes emerge. First, the sources refer almost exclusively to the possession of land.[40] Most significantly, "land" in the Old Testament denotes the "actual physical turf where people can be safe and secure, where meaning and well-being are enjoyed without pressure or coercion."[41] According to the Old Testament, it is this "concrete particularity of land" which Yahweh commits to providing for Israel.

Second, בְּהֵלָה is "the keyword of a rich cluster of ideas concerning Yahweh, Israel, and the land."[42] At the heart of these three interrelated realities in the Old Testament is Yahweh who owns the land. The inheritance of Israel is therefore a grant or a gift from Yahweh, who is committed to the welfare of his people. And such a commitment is not just "a good idea" but an assurance that Israel will possess actual real estate and therefore will be able to live and be provided for in the material socio-political-economic world.[43] By pledging to provide and secure a particular piece of land for Israel, Yahweh is guaranteeing that Israel will be permanently loved and cared for and that the people of Israel will have what they need to make their way materially and economically in the world. Closely linked with this concept is the understanding that this promise cannot be reversed – Yahweh's provision of land will endure forever.[44] This theological conviction of Israel's lasting possession of land is what fuelled the religio-political aim of the Maccabees. Their desire was to recapture the land, in its entirety, because it had been given to Israel as a lasting possession.[45]

An inseparable third theme which emerges is the belief that because Yahweh is the owner and provider of the land, this must determine how the land is to be used – in particular, whether all in the community

---

[39] The words κληρονομεῖν and κληρονομός are therefore integrated into the more developed theological usage of נָחַל and בְּהֵלָה in the Old Testament. Foerster, "κληρονόμος," 778–79.
[40] Ibid., 774. Hester, *Paul's Concept of Inheritance*, 5.
[41] Brueggemann, *The Land*, 3.   [42] C. Wright, *God's People*, 19 n. 29.
[43] Brueggemann, "Land," 120.   [44] Hester, *Paul's Concept of Inheritance*, 5.
[45] 1 Macc. 15:33f.

are provided for. In other words, the property law and ethics which are attached to the concept of inheritance in the Old Testament are always based on the belief in God's ownership of the land.[46] The clearest example of this is in the theological rationale for the "jubilee" system of land tenure which is expressed in Lev. 25:23: "The land must not be sold permanently, because the land is mine and you are but aliens and my tenants." It is similarly on this basis that the OT prophets rebuke the people of Israel – because if some groups in the community do not have access to land then this is an indictment of Israel's relationship with God:

> The theological status of Israel was earthed and rooted in the socio-economic fabric of their kinship structure and their land tenure, and it was this fabric which was being dissolved by the acids of debt, dispossession, and latifundism. The prophetic protest against these evils, therefore, must be illumined by the fact that there was an essential link between the social and economic facts of life and the theological self-understanding of Israel.[47]

To what degree, then, does Paul stand in continuity with this under-standing of κληρονόμος? More particularly, what about the reference to κόσμος and κληρονόμος in Rom. 4:13? As mentioned above, one way of understanding the phrase "inherit the world" is that Paul has here spiritualized the original Abrahamic promise and subsequent interpretation of this promise. The promise has been spiritualized, in the sense that it is understood now to apply to Abraham's *spiritual* descendants, the worldwide "family of faith."[48] Certainly, there is a degree of truth in this reading. The Abrahamic promise *is* spiritualized by Paul to the extent that it no longer applies only to the physical descendants of Abraham. One of Paul's primary purposes in this chapter is to argue that the promise comes by "faith" and that Abraham's descendants are therefore those who follow him in this faith (4:1–12). Similarly, this understanding of the phrase is correct in suggesting that the promise is in some sense "de-territorialised." But what of the geographical reality inherent in the original promise and the inseparable concepts of permanent possession and universal sovereignty? Are these completely abandoned? To insist that Paul de-territorializes the promise does not necessarily lead to the conclusion that he thereby removes any reference to geographical reality and its related concepts.

---

[46] C. Wright, *God's People*, 115–82.   [47] Ibid., 109.
[48] So, for example, Morris, *The Epistle to the Romans*, 206.

A second main understanding of "inherit the world" is that κόσμος here refers to the future restoration of creation and the natural order which is the rightful inheritance of the people of God. For example, Bailey concludes that here "Paul means a restoration of humankind's responsibility for all of nature. All Christians are thus called on to look at the natural world as their 'inheritance' and care for it, guard it, and protect it. In this manner they will fulfill God's command to Adam to till and keep/guard/protect the earth (Gen 2:15)."[49]

While this line of interpretation has much to commend it because of its emphasis on the renewal of creation, it is not without its weaknesses. In particular, it is difficult to see how such an understanding of "inherit the world" has any substantial connection with its immediate context. Although it might be that the phrase anticipates the conclusions of Romans 8 it bears little relation to Rom. 4:14–25. One of the consequences of this lack of contextual fit is that the specific content of the promise is usually forgotten or lost amidst what are perceived to be the weightier concerns of the chapter.

A closely related interpretation is suggested by James Hester and also by Edward Adams. These proposals go beyond the ones mentioned above in their insistence on the geographical reality of the phrase Paul uses. As Hester puts it, "The geographical reality of the Land never ceases to play an important part in Paul's concept of inheritance. He simply makes the Land the eschatological world."[50] Far from understanding Paul to have "de-territorialised" the promise, Hester insists that the inheritance "will be located in a definite territory – the New Creation."[51] Similarly, in his comprehensive study of Paul's use of cosmological language (κόσμος and κτίσις), Adams concludes that in Rom. 4:13b Paul is referring "not just to the environment of human beings, but to the *eschatological* environment of the people of God, the 'world' which is to be the eschatological inheritance of God's elect, that is to say, the new or restored creation."[52]

While such approaches to "inherit the world" are helpful, there is an important aspect of the phrase which has remained largely unaddressed. One of the dimensions of land and inheritance which is present in later Jewish traditions and is arguably embedded in the original Abrahamic promise (see below) is an emphasis on the expectation of an eschatological *universal sovereignty* for one particular group of people. In other

---

[49] Kenneth E. Bailey, "St Paul's Understanding of the Territorial Promise of God to Abraham. Romans 4:13 in Its Historical and Theological Context," *Theological Review* 15.1 (1994): 68. Similarly Dunn, *Romans 1–8*, 213.

[50] Hester, *Paul's Concept of Inheritance*, 82.   [51] Ibid., 115.

[52] Adams, *Constructing the World*, 169; emphasis original.

words, the language of inheritance has at its heart the political question of *who* will inherit the land. If this is the case, and if Paul in Rom. 4:13 is referring to actual physical land then in what sense is the universal sovereignty aspect retained in Paul's usage? As Walter Brueggemann points out, the promise of land is a pledge to secure socio-economic well-being and such a guarantee carries with it inevitable socio-political significance.[53] To be sure, for Paul it is no longer the case that only the physical descendants of Abraham are eligible for such inheritance (4:1–25). Similarly, even a casual glance at Rom. 4:13 indicates that the inheritance has been extended by Paul far beyond the physical bounds of Palestine. But none of this necessarily means that the claim to sovereignty embedded in the original promise is absent in Paul and neither does it suggest that the question of *who* inherits has lost its political edge.[54]

A second way I propose to extend the argument of Adams and Hester, therefore, is by suggesting that verse 13 is a catalyst for unearthing a possible wider narrative context for Paul's argument in 4:13–25. This is to suggest that although the references to κληρονόμος in this text are highly compressed and initially appear puzzling, they are best understood as the primary indicator that there is a perspective embedded within these verses which is often neglected and which needs to be teased out. This entails, therefore, asking how such a reading of verse 13 coheres with the verses which follow. Some commentators acknowledge the ways in which Rom. 4:13 anticipates the argument of Romans 8. This is important, but does Paul do more than this? Is there any sense in which inheritance in this context conveys ideas of the universal sovereignty of the people of God?

One of the chief barriers to integrating this reading of inheritance into the section which follows is how interpreters often understand Paul's use of the example of Abraham, particularly the relationship between Abraham and his descendants. Often, interpreters observe that one of Paul's primary purposes in 4:13–25 is to demonstrate the universal nature of the original promise to Abraham.[55] If Paul can do this, then he can establish his point that now both Jews and Gentiles can be considered part of the people of God. But what is the *nature* of Paul's universalism? Here,

---

[53] W. Brueggemann, "Land," in *Reverberations of Faith. A Theological Handbook of Old Testament Themes* (Louisville and London: Westminster John Knox Press, 2002), 123.

[54] See James M. Scott, *Paul and the Nations: The Old Testament and Jewish Background of Paul's Mission to the Nations with Special Reference to the Destination of Galatians*, WUNT 84 (Tubingen: J. C. B. Mohr (Paul Siebeck), 1995), 63 n. 33, 128, 132 n. 499.

[55] Byrne, *Romans*, 159–60; R. Pesch, *Römerbrief*, Die Neue Echter-Bibel 6 (Wurzburg: Echter-Verl, 1994), 47.

amidst the variety of approaches to understanding Romans 4, there is common ground. There is widespread agreement that when Paul refers to the descendants of Abraham he is meaning the *spiritual* descendants. So, for example, when Paul writes of Abraham as the "father of all of us" (v. 16) or "the father of many nations" (vv. 17, 18) he means that Abraham has numerous "spiritual children" or a worldwide spiritual family of faith.[56] This reading has considerable significance for the present study. If it is true that phrases such as "father of many nations" (which are often accepted as being at the heart of what Paul is wanting to argue in this chapter) are entirely spiritual in their meaning, then this is determinative for how the language of inheritance is understood. Most importantly, if concepts such as "descendants" and Abraham's fatherhood are read in spiritualized terms only, then the content of inheritance in verse 13 remains an intriguing but ultimately disconnected anomaly. This is because if there is no demonstrable direct inner connection between "inherit the world" and "father of many nations," then it can be assumed that "inherit the world" has less importance in Paul's thinking.

To question the nature of Paul's argument regarding the universal application of the Abrahamic promise is not to suggest that the spiritual dimension is not present. Certainly, for Paul, the family of Abraham is no longer limited to Abraham's physical descendants. But what is the connection between this reading as it is traditionally expressed, and "inherit the world" in verse 13? Most interpretations of this section proceed as if, until Romans 8, the heirs of Abraham are floating in a disembodied state outside space and time. In what follows I will argue that Paul's universal application of the promise is not only spiritual but physical as well and that it therefore has a deep connection with verse 13. While there is little doubt that Abraham's "faith" in God and the subsequent "faith" of believers is central to this section, I suggest that Paul is also evoking here the universalistic promise–fulfillment trajectory which was set in motion by the Abrahamic promise tradition and which included decidedly physical and social dimensions. I will explore the original context and subsequent interpretive traditions of three concepts which are determinative for how this section is understood – the two closely related phrases, "father of many nations" and "so numerous shall your descendants be," and the extended nature of the original Abrahamic promise ("inherit *the world*"). I will argue that each of these concepts encompasses God's universal socio-physical-spiritual blessing of the world and the associated ideas of

---

[56] See, for example, J. Cottrell, *Romans*, The College Press NIV Commentary (Missouri: College Press, 1996), 298.

Israel's permanent possession of land and Israel's constant interplay and engagement with "the nations."

Romans 4:14–18: descendants, nations and possessing the land

In verses 16–18 Paul draws together a number of the threads of his argument so far. This is signaled by the phrases "For this reason" (διὰ τοῦτο, 16a) and "in order that" (ἵνα, 16a),[57] alerting his audience to the fact that he is about to give the reason for his argument in verses 1–12. He says that the reason "it [the promise]"[58] depends on faith (v. 16a) is "in order that the promise (ἐπαγγελία) may rest on grace and be guaranteed to all his descendants, not only to the adherents of the law but also those who share the faith of Abraham (for he is the father of all of us)." This continues into verse 17 and then resounds with great volume in verse 18 where, echoing both Genesis 15 and Genesis 17, Paul concludes that Abraham "believed that he would become 'the father of many nations,' according to what was said, 'So numerous shall your descendants be.'"[59] The first quotation is from Gen. 17:4 – that Abraham would become "the father of many nations." The second is from Gen. 15:5 – "so numerous shall your descendants be" (which also closely resembles Gen. 17:2).

The concept of "descendants" (σπέρμα) is therefore a central one, both linguistically and thematically, for this section (vv. 13–25). Paul explicitly uses the word σπέρμα three times in the passage (vv. 13, 16, 18) and there is little doubt that as well as these references, the word and the questions associated with it pervade his argument at every turn. Interpretation of this concept is generally determined by whether Paul's central question is understood to be *how* entry into the community happens or *who* are the heirs of Abraham. According to either reading, the content of inheritance is marginalized and any thought of physical earth and universal sovereignty is not appreciated.[60] But this approach

---

[57] Cf. 5:12; 2 Cor. 4:1. N. T. Wright, "Romans," 497.

[58] The word "it" in verse 16 could refer either to "promise" or "promised inheritance." Esler suggests "promise" is more likely because of the parallel with verses 13–15; P. Esler, *Conflict and Identity in Romans. The Social Setting of Paul's Letter* (Minneapolis: Fortress Press, 2003), 192. Similarly Dunn, *Romans 1–8*, 215.

[59] The first explicit reference to Genesis 17 comes in Rom. 4:11, where Paul recounts Abraham's receiving of circumcision (Gen. 17:10). This example holds considerable importance for the argument which has progressed up to that point (vv. 1–10). There are four other instances where Paul either directly quotes or alludes to Genesis 17 (4:13, 17, 18, 19).

[60] So, for example, Moo concludes that Paul's use of "seed" here has a spiritual meaning; Moo, *The Epistle to the Romans*, 284.

is challenged when the language of "descendants" is placed within its wider narrative setting. It is the context of Genesis, in this case Genesis 15, which is particularly instructive for readings of Rom. 4:13–25.[61]

In Gen. 15:5 (which Paul cites in 4:18) there is an important clue to one aspect of the concept that was conveyed by the word "descendants." There, God says to Abraham to "Look toward heaven and count the stars, if you are able to count them . . . So shall your descendants be." The idea is similar in Gen. 17:8, where God's promise to Abraham is that "I will give to you, and to your offspring after you, the land where you are now an alien, all the land of Canaan, for a perpetual holding; and I will be their God." Particularly revealing is the close connection between "land" (obviously understood in terms of physical turf) and "descendants." Both in Genesis 15 and 17 (which are pivotal to Paul's argument in Romans 4)[62] and in the texts immediately preceding and following these passages, there is often a very close association between "land" and the "offspring" of Abraham, so that the two words are commonly used in the same sentence. An almost identical expression is found earlier in Gen. 12:7, "To your offspring I will give this land." Similarly Gen. 13:15: "for all the land that you see I will give to you and to your offspring forever." This close connection between land and descendants is expressed also in Gen. 22:17–18, "I will indeed bless you, and I will make your offspring as numerous as the stars of heaven and as the sand that is on the seashore. And your offspring shall possess the gate of their enemies." The concept similarly pervades the promise when it is reiterated to Jacob in Gen. 28:14, "and your offspring shall be like the dust of the earth, and you shall spread abroad to the west and to the east and to the north and to the south; and all the families of the earth shall be blessed in you and in your offspring."

Why, then, is there such a close connection between the two concepts? Crucial here is understanding that the concepts take their place within the interrelated complex of ideas including, for example, Israel being a "great nation"; bringing blessing to "the nations"; possession of "land"; and numerous offspring. There seems to have been an understanding

---

[61] M. A. Seifrid, "Unrighteousness by Faith: Apostolic Proclamation in Romans 1:18–3:20," in *Justification and Variegated Nomism. The Paradoxes of Paul*, ed. D. Carson *et al.* (Grand Rapids: Baker Academic, 2004), 62; N. T. Wright, "New Exodus, New Inheritance," 30.

[62] Paul's argument in Romans 4 relies heavily on OT texts. For example, in the twenty-five verses which make up this chapter Paul quotes directly from the Old Testament five times: 4:3 (Gen. 15:6); 4:7ff. (Ps. 32:1f.); 4:17 (Gen. 17:5); 4:18 (Gen. 15:5); 4:23 (Gen. 15:6). He echoes or alludes to at least five other OT sources: 4:11 (Gen. 17:10); 4:13 (Gen. 17:4–6; 22: 17–18); 4:19 (Gen. 17:17); 4:25 (Isa. 53:11–12).

that the promise of a great nation (12:2), or many descendants, was dependent on Abraham having a land of his own (13:14).[63] As Hester observes, "Always the fulfillment of the promise to make of Abraham and his descendants a great nation is predicated on the possession of the Land which God had sworn to give them." [64] Similarly one of the ideas signified by the word ἔθνος is "the whole population of a particular land," [65] which is why the promise to Abraham of nationhood includes a promise of land – "The land cannot be possessed and held without a large group of people to do so, and the descendants of Abram cannot be a great nation without a land in which a national existence can be established."[66] This is why when Abraham questions YHWH about Eliezer, who is to be his successor, God's promise of a son for Abraham and subsequent numerous offspring is followed by a covenant detailing the borders of the land which YHWH will provide. In a similar way, one of the reasons why the exile was considered so horrific was that without land Israel could not be God's effective instrument.

It is within this mix of ideas that the concepts of "land" and "descendants" take their place. Understood within this perspective it is clear that the two ideas cannot be separated – the "descendants" of Abraham must have "land" in order to be the "great nation" they are expected to be: "Never again in the testimony of Israel will the sovereignty of Yahweh be separated from the legitimacy of land. The two are joined by the concreteness and specificity of utterance that has the force of oath."[67]

Given the inseparability of the two words, how should Paul's pervasive use of the term "descendants" in Romans 4 be read? Understandably, interpreters do not usually suggest that the idea of "land" is intended when "descendants" is used. The word "land" is not explicitly used in Romans 4, nor is the closely related concept of Israel and the nations (as traditionally understood). By this stage, however, it should be clear that while such terms do not always explicitly surface in Paul's argument, this does not mean that they are not present in his thinking.[68] Given that in verse 13 Paul refers to inheriting the physical earth and in verse 18

---

[63] W. Brueggemann, *Theology of the Old Testament. Testimony, Dispute, Advocacy* (Minneapolis: Fortress Press, 1997), 168–69.

[64] Hester, *Paul's Concept of Inheritance*, 23. L. A. Snijders, "Genesis XV. The Covenant with Abram," *Oudestamentische Studien* 12 (1958).

[65] J. M. Scott, *Paul and the Nations*, 61–62.

[66] Hester, *Paul's Concept of Inheritance*, 23.

[67] Brueggemann, *Theology of the Old Testament*, 169.

[68] Pesch, *Römerbrief*, 48.

(immediately preceding "descendants") he evokes the whole Israel-in-relation-to-the-nations perspective (as will be argued below), it is highly likely that his use of σπέρμα here is intended to evoke further ideas of the heirs of Abraham reigning in the land God has gifted to them.[69]

A second important concept in this text is expressed by the phrase "many nations" (πολλῶν ἐθνῶν), and in particular the word ἔθνος. James Scott has provided a comprehensive investigation of Paul's use of ἔθνος,[70] showing that throughout his letters the usage follows that of the LXX and other Hellenistic-Jewish literature of the Greco-Roman period.[71] Reflecting the original use of the word, Paul uses the plural in three related senses. First, ἔθνος is used in the sense of all the "nations" of the world, including the nation Israel.[72] Second, the plural is used to refer to the non-Jewish *nations* – "all the nations" of the world apart from the "nation" of Israel. The citations of Deut. 32:43 and Ps. 117:1 in Rom. 15:10–11 are good examples of this second usage.[73] Third, Paul uses the plural of the "Gentiles," that is, *individuals within a nation*, other than the nation of the Jews.[74] In Rom. 4:17 and 18 it seems most likely that πολλῶν ἐθνῶν is used in the first sense and that it therefore refers to Paul and other Jews as well as Gentiles and is best translated as "many nations."[75]

Given that this is how the word ἔθνος would normally be understood in the context of the citation, what can be learnt from the Genesis tradition and subsequent interpretation of this tradition? In what sense was ἔθνος part of a wider OT tradition and to what extent is this perspective evident in Rom. 4:18 and in the wider context of Rom. 4:13–25? Scott persuasively demonstrates that the word provides insights with regard to one of the most fundamental dimensions of the Old Testament: the interaction and interplay between the nation of Israel and the other nations of the

---

[69] Pesch points out that in Rom. 4:13–16 the promise of land is treated more explicitly, while in verses 17–22 the promise of seed is in view; Pesch, *Römerbrief*, 48.

[70] J. M. Scott, *Paul and the Nations*. Scott's overall purpose is to assess the geographical horizon of Paul's missionary enterprise – in particular the possible destination of Galatians. Scott persuasively shows the ways in which Paul was influenced by the Table of Nations tradition (see below, pp. 76–80) in the Old Testament and in Jewish tradition. It is in the course of doing so that he examines ἔθνος in Paul's letters.

[71] Ibid., 121.

[72] Paul does not call Israel a nation, per se, but he often refers to it as a λαός. Scott shows that this term is often synonymous with ἔθνος in the Old Testament. (cf. Exod. 19:5–6; 23:22; Deut. 4:6–8; Ezek. 37:21–23; Esth. 3:8; 1 Macc. 13:6; also Zech. 12:3); J. M. Scott, *Paul and the Nations*, 122.

[73] J. M. Scott, *Paul and the Nations*, 122.   [74] Ibid., 123.

[75] As further examples see Ps. 134:10; Ezek. 38:12; Zech. 8:22; *Jos. Asen.* 15:6; *Sib. Or.* 3.598.

world.[76] In the Old Testament ἔθνος is often used in connection with, or in order to express, a perspective which was at the heart of the Table of Nations tradition, a tradition first described in the genealogy of Genesis 10 and in 1 Chron. 1:1 – 2:2. This tradition was pervasive in the Old Testament and the Jewish literature of the Second Temple Period continues and modifies it.[77] Of particular importance is Scott's conclusion that the word ἔθνος and the Table of Nations tradition "provided the fundamental point of orientation for describing Israel's place among the nations of the world and the basis for envisioning world geography and ethnography for both the present and the eschatological future."[78]

What is this "fundamental point of orientation"? There are many expressions of it – some negative and some positive. The negative stream of the tradition suggests that Israel's restoration will result in the destruction of the nations of the world. Ezekiel 38–39, for example, describes the nations waging war against the returned exiles and experiencing defeat in a final eschatological battle. As Ezek. 30:3 states: "the day of the LORD is near; it will be a day of clouds, a time of doom for the nations."[79]

Co-existing with this tradition is the positive stream which expects that all nations of the world will experience and participate in the eschatological pilgrimage to Jerusalem. It is this perspective which seems to undergird Paul's thinking in Romans 4. This is the belief that, through Israel, God would bring blessing to the rest of the world. Implicit in this tradition was the belief that the descendants of Abraham had been chosen by God to bring blessing to the world, to bring well-being to the earth.[80] It seems clear from the Genesis account that Israel was supposed to be, or to become, God's intended true humanity for the sake of the nations.[81] This divine intention is first signaled in the command given to Adam (Gen. 1:28), which then reappears in a new guise later in the Genesis account.

At critical points in the Genesis story Abraham appears to inherit the role of Adam and Eve, which is to be God's true humanity for the world.[82]

---

[76] J. M. Scott, *Paul and the Nations*, 58. See further Brueggemann, *Theology of the Old Testament*, 430–34, 495–98; Donald Gowan, *Eschatology in the Old Testament* (Philadelphia: Fortress Press, 1986), 48–57; D. W. van Winkle, "The Relationship of the Nations to Yahweh and to Israel in Isaiah XL-LV," *VT* 35 (1985): 446–58.

[77] See J. M. Scott, *Paul and the Nations*, 5–56.   [78] Ibid., 135.

[79] See further Brueggemann, *Theology of the Old Testament*, 495–97.   [80] Ibid., 430.

[81] See Hans Walter Wolff for the ways in which "blessing to the nations" runs as a leitmotif throughout the ancestral narrative; H. W. Wolff, "The Kerygma of the Yahwist," *Int* 20 (1966): 131–58.

[82] See, for example, Gen. 12:2; 17:2, 6, 8; 22:16ff.; 26:24; 28:3; 5:11; 47:27; 48:3ff. N. T. Wright, *The Climax of the Covenant*, 21–26.

In Gen. 12:2ff. and Gen. 22:16ff., Abraham and his family are understood to be God's way of dealing with the sin of Adam and with the evil of the world. In this way they would be a blessing to the nations. "The holiness and salvation that was centred in Palestine stretched out over the whole world. The whole world was inherited because of the effective holiness of Israel. This holiness made the rest of the earth holy, and, therefore, inheritable."[83] This theme, which is begun in Genesis, is also evident in other parts of the Pentateuch, the Prophets and the Wisdom Literature, where "the underlying point, time after time, is that Israel, the family of Abraham, is God's true humanity."[84] As Isa. 60:3 puts it, "Nations shall come to your light, and kings to the brightness of your dawn."[85] Similarly Isa. 2:2–4: "In the days to come the mountain of the LORD's house shall be established as the highest of the mountains, and shall be raised above the hills; all the nations shall stream to it."[86] This expectation pervades the final text of Isaiah.[87] In Zion "the Lord of Hosts will be for all nations on this Mount; they will drink gladness" (Isa. 25:6). The expectation is that as Israel spreads out from Zion and the land of Canaan it will become a great nation and will gradually take over possession of all the nations of the earth (Isa. 54:3). In other words, Israel's numerous descendants will gradually bring blessing to the nations.[88]

The concept is particularly clear in Isa. 54:1–3 (a text which will be examined in more detail below). In this text Zion is addressed as a barren mother and the expectation is that this situation will be reversed: "The children of the desolate woman will be more than the children of her that is married, says the LORD" (v. 1). What this text suggests, therefore, is that the Abrahamic promise of descendants and of becoming a populous nation is the way by which Israel will gradually "inherit" all the nations of the world, beginning by first spreading out from Zion.[89] Similarly, Isa. 66:18–20 envisages, following the Table of Nations tradition, that God will gather "all nations and tongues" to Jerusalem. Likewise in Jeremiah, the "prophet to the nations": "all nations" will come to Jerusalem "and they shall no longer stubbornly follow their own evil will"

---

[83] Hester, *Paul's Concept of Inheritance*, 32.

[84] N. T. Wright, *The New Testament and the People of God*, Christian Origins and the Question of God 1 (London: SPCK, 1992), 262–66.

[85] Cf. Isa. 51:4. The expression is applied to the Servant of the Lord in Isa. 42:6; 49:6.

[86] Cf. Mic. 4:1–3.

[87] See, for example, 60:1–6; 49:22; 66:18–20. Cf. also Zech. 8:22–23.

[88] James Scott points out that this expectation is expressed in Isa. 54:1–3. Scott notes the ways in which Philo understood the tradition this way; see J. M. Scott, *Paul and the Nations*, 94.

[89] Ibid., 63–64.

(Jer. 3:17).[90] The ultimate goal of this eschatological restoration, then, is that Israel and the nations, together would worship the Lord in Zion: "Save us, O God of our salvation, and gather and rescue us from among the nations, that we may give thanks to your holy name and glory in your praise" (1 Chron. 16:35).[91]

That Paul is familiar with this orientation and that it undergirds his thinking is evident at various points throughout his letters. James M. Scott argues that in Paul's letters and also in Acts, the apostle's missionary strategy was based on the Table of Nations.[92] The earliest evidence of this tradition is in Gal. 3:8, where Paul recounts the promise in Gen. 12:3 that "all the nations of the earth" (which most likely refers to all the nations in the Table of Nations of Genesis 10) will be blessed through Abraham and his seed.[93] "The missionary strategy that results from this understanding of the gospel can be seen in the outcome of the so-called Apostolic Council in Gal. 2:7–9, where the apostles agree to observe territorial jurisdictions in their respective missions, probably drawn along the lines of the sons of Noah in the Table of Nations."[94] Following the Apostolic Council, territoriality is an increasingly significant factor for Paul's missionary strategy. The clearest example of this is in Romans 15, where Paul explains that his mission is to the "nations" and that it proceeds from Jerusalem and "in a circle" (κύκλῳ μέχρι, 15:19b).[95] Also, Paul's announcement of his plans to continue his mission as far as Spain (Rom. 15:24, 28; cf. 2 Cor. 10:16) suggests that he has "evidently focused his mission on his territory of the Japhethites, that is, of the descendants of the third son of Noah, who settled in the region of Asia Minor and Europe from Cilicia to Spain."[96]

If it is the case, therefore, that for Paul (as in OT and subsequent Jewish tradition) the word ἔθνος and the interrelated Table of Nations tradition

---

[90] The nations, which will come from "the end of the earth" will acknowledge that their idols have no value. Jer 16:19; cf. Zech 2:15.

[91] See also Ps. 105:47; Jer. 4:2; Deut. 32:43; Ezek. 36:22–24; 39:23, 28.

[92] J. M. Scott, *Paul and the Nations*, 135–215. See further C. H. H. Scobie, "Israel and the Nations: An Essay in Biblical Theology," *TynBul* 43.2 (1992): 283–305. Scott points out that there are only a few monographs available on the theme of Israel and the nations.

[93] Note that while some of the promises in Genesis read "by you shall all the nations of the earth *bless themselves*" (Gen. 22:16; 26:3), Paul draws from Gen. 12:3 "In you shall all the nations of the earth *be blessed*."

[94] J. M. Scott, *Paul and the Nations*, 179. Scott suggests that the book of Acts seems also to be structured along these lines.

[95] "The expression 'in a circle' can be explained in terms of Ezek. 5:5, which states that God has set Jerusalem 'in the middle of the nations' and the countries in a circle around her"; Scott, *Paul and the Nations*, 179; see further, 136–49.

[96] Scott, *Paul and the Nations*, 179.

provide the fundamental orientation regarding the interplay between the people of God and the nations of the world, then what does all this mean for a reading of the key phrase, "father of many nations," which is used in verses 17 and 18 and which is also indirectly signaled in verse 16 ("the father of all of us" – πάντων ἡμῶν – πάντων emphatic here)? Taken by itself, Paul's use of the concept of ἔθνος refers back to the perspective of Israel at the center of the nations. But used within the phrase "father of many nations" it refers to the *culmination* of Israel's engagement with the nations. The spiritual meaning of the phrase (i.e. the spiritual father of many nations) is of course present, but the phrase also goes beyond this and refers to the expected fulfillment of the Abrahamic promise which would bring socio-political-spiritual blessings not just for Israel but for all the nations of the world. In this way Abraham would be "father of many nations," because the blessings he experienced (in the fullest sense of the concept)[97] would now be experienced by "many nations."[98]

In other words, the interrelated OT concepts of "descendants" and "father of many nations" reverberate throughout the verses, each informing and being informed by the other. Significantly, there is a third clue which reinforces this reading of Rom. 4:13–25. In verse 17, wedged between two references to the "father of many nations," Paul writes of the God "who gives life to the dead and calls into existence the things that do not exist" (v. 17b). Romans as a whole "is suffused with resurrection" and it seems that in using this phrase in verse 17 Paul is similarly alluding to resurrection.[99] In his monumental work *The Resurrection and the Son of God*, Wright shows that within the early Christian movement there is virtual unanimity about future hope. Strongly influenced by Judaism, "resurrection" for the early Christians meant literal bodily resurrection and it is this concept which is similarly evoked by Paul in Romans 4. As Wright concludes, "There can be no doubt, from this passage, that Paul envisages the resurrection of Jesus as bodily. Anything less than

---

[97] As Byrne says, "in a more eschatological and transcendant sense, the promise can refer to 'the age to come', including *all the blessings of salvation within its scope*"; Byrne, *Romans*, 143; emphasis added.

[98] One of the OT traditions which may have contributed to this broad understanding of the promised inheritance is the concept of the messianic King who was expected to rule the world. Since the King was often understood as the seed of Abraham this meant that the Abrahamic promise of land was expanded to include the whole world. Examples of such a link between the King, the Abrahamic promise and the universal sovereignty of Israel abound in OT tradition. For example Ps. 2:8; Isa. 55:5; Ps. 72; Gen. 27:29; Deut. 15:6; Ps. 46:2–3, 9–10; Isa. 54:3; 60:11, 16; Jer. 38:7.

[99] N. T. Wright, *The Resurrection and the Son of God*, Christian Origins and the Question of God 3 (Minneapolis: Fortress Press, 2003), 246–47. Quotation from 241.

that would simply not fit the parallel with Abraham and his 'resurrection faith.' It would not take a special, unique act of divine power to trans- late Jesus' soul into a glorious heavenly existence."[100] This suggests that when in verse 17b Paul alludes to resurrection he is evoking the expec- tation of a renewed body and that such reference stands in continuity with the surrounding references to "descendants" and "father of many nations."

But how does all of this relate to the phrase Paul uses in Rom. 4:13, "inherit the world"? Within the tradition surveyed above, there does seem to be the implication that the Abrahamic promise was always intended for the entire world, not exclusively for Israel. As Scott observes, "The Abrahamic Promise sets in motion a trajectory whose ultimate fulfillment takes place in the time of Israel's Restoration, when Israel will again become a great nation, and all nations (i.e. all those listed in the Table of Nations) will be blessed in Abraham and his seed."[101] But at no stage in the Old Testament is the phrase "inherit the world" explicitly used; it is never put in such bold, expansive terms. There is therefore a consensus amongst Paul's interpreters that in using this expanded version of the promise Paul is instead drawing from an Intertestamental interpretive tradition.[102]

References to Israel's future "inheritance" of *the world* are scattered throughout the Intertestamental literature, as is the more general concept of Israel in relation to the nations.[103] For example *4 Ezra* 6:59 uses the phrase this way:

> If the world has indeed been created for us, why do we not possess our world as an inheritance? How long will this be so?

---

[100] Ibid., 247.

[101] J. M. Scott, *Paul and the Nations*, 121. Byrne suggests that "Here we see an inter- section of what might be called the 'Adamic' and the 'Abrahamic' trajectories with respect to 'promise,' 'inheritance' and the lordship of the world"; Byrne, *Romans*, 157.

[102] U. Wilckens, *Der Brief an die Römer: Röm 1–5*, EKK, 3 vols., vol. I (Zurich: Benziger, 1974), 269; O. Michel, *Der Brief an die Römer* (Göttingen: Vandenhoeck & Ruprecht, 1978), 168; Dunn, *Romans 1–8*, 213; Pesch, *Römerbrief*, 47; Fitzmyer, *Romans*, 384; Adams, *Constructing the World*, 168; Hester, *Paul's Concept of Inheritance*, 69; S. K. Williams, "The *Promise* in Galatians: A Reading of Paul's Reading of Scripture," *JBL* 107.4 (1988): 718–19.

[103] For similar concepts with different language used see, for example, *Bar.* 14:13; *Bar.* 51:3. The concept of the promised land also undergoes a transformation in the writings of Josephus, where it no longer refers only to the land of Canaan but to the whole world. See, for example, B. Halpern-Amaru, "Land Theology in Josephus' *Jewish Antiquities*," *JQR* 71 (1981): 202–29; M. Weinfeld, *The Promise of the Land. The Inheritance of the Land of Canaan by the Israelites* (Berkeley: University of California Press, 1993), 214–15.

Similarly *1 Enoch* 5:7

> But to the elect there shall be light, joy, and peace, and they
> shall inherit the earth.

In Sir. 44:21 inheritance is used alongside words such as "nations" and
numerous "descendants":

> Therefore the Lord assured him with an oath
> that the nations would be blessed through his offspring;
> that he would make him as numerous as the dust of the earth,
> and exalt his offspring like the stars,
> and give them an inheritance from sea to sea
> and from the Euphrates to the ends of the earth.

Amidst these references, however, there is one book in particular, the
Book of Jubilees, which has much to offer to an understanding of "inherit
the world" in Rom. 4:13 and the tradition from which this stems. There
are several reasons why *Jubilees* is especially instructive.[104] To begin
with, there are three direct references to the inheritance of Israel: inherit
"the land" (17:3); "inherit the entire earth" (22:14); and "gain the entire
earth and inherit it forever" (32:19). In itself, this makes these references
particularly illuminating for a reading of Rom. 4:13. But what adds to
the import of these phrases is the broader framework within which the
word inheritance is used: the land of Israel, together with the role it
fulfills within the purposes of God, is one of the primary concerns of
Jubilees.[105] In other words the concept of inheritance takes its place
within the broader expectation of Israel's future.[106] This is not to say that
Rom. 4:13 should be understood exclusively in relation to *Jubilees* but
that the use of inheritance here does bear close resemblance to Romans
and is therefore instructive.

---

[104] Work on the book of *Jubilees* is burgeoning. For the purpose and themes of *Jubilees*
see especially the prodigious work of James C. VanderKam, for example "The Origins
and Purposes of the *Book of Jubilees*," in *Studies in the Book of Jubilees*, ed. M. Albani
et al. (Tübingen: Mohr-Siebeck, 1997). See also J. M. Scott, *On Earth as in Heaven. The
Restoration of Sacred Time and Sacred Space in the Book of Jubilees*, JSJ Sup 91 (Leiden:
Brill, 2005), 1–15.

[105] The centrality of land in *Jubilees* is not accepted by all scholars, but persuasive arguments for it come from D. Mendels, *The Land of Israel as Political Concept in Hasmonean
Literature: Recourse to History in Second Century BC. Claims to the Holy Land*, TSAJ 15
(Tübingen: Mohr-Siebeck, 1987); see esp. 57–88. Also J. M. Scott, *On Earth as in Heaven*,
162–66.

[106] VanderKam, "The Origins and Purposes of the *Book of Jubilees*," 22. J. M. Scott,
On Earth as in Heaven, 165.

Through the revelation received by Moses on Mount Sinai, *Jubilees* shows the ways in which the inheritance of land occurs at momentous chronological points in Israel's history.[107] Crucial here is the law of jubilee in Leviticus 25, which is foundational to the whole chronological scheme in the *Book of Jubilees*.[108] *Jubilees* seeks to demonstrate that at the jubilee of jubilees (i.e. at the fiftieth jubilee from the creation of the world) YHWH redeemed Israel from slavery and returned to Israel the land which was theirs by inheritance.[109] This moment is the climax of the narrative of *Jubilees*.[110] But the book also implicitly expects a time in the future when there will be another jubilee of jubilees, a period when Israel will again be redeemed from slavery (in this case the experience of exile) and will once more be restored to the land of the inheritance.[111] In other words, *Jubilees* brings together sacred time with sacred space in order to reveal that things will eventually be done on earth as they are in heaven.

In the course of conveying these themes *Jubilees*, in a similar way to the OT tradition noted above, often uses the term "descendants." This is the case, for example, in *Jub.* 19:21–24, where the concept of numerous descendants is clear:

> Let your hands be strong and let your heart rejoice in your son, Jacob. Because I love him more than all of my sons. He will be blessed forever and his seed will be one which fills *all of the earth*. If a man is able to count the sand of the earth, then his seed will be counted. And all of the blessings with which the Lord blessed me and my seed will be for Jacob and his seed always.

The concept is similar in *Jub.* 22:17–23:

> (17) My daughter, take care of my son, Jacob, because he will occupy my place on the earth and (will prove) a blessing among mankind and the glory of all the descendants of Shem. (18) For I know that the Lord will choose him as his own people (who

---

[107] *Jub.* 1:4; 1:26–27.

[108] As VanderKam puts it, "By calling a major unit of his chronology a *jubilee,* the writer naturally invokes the biblical associations of that term"; J. C. VanderKam, *Calendars in the Dead Sea Scrolls: Measuring Time* (London: Routledge, 1998), 102.

[109] J. C. VanderKam, "Studies in the Chronology of the Book of Jubilees," in *From Revelation to Canon: Studies in the Hebrew Bible and Second Temple Literature*, ed. J. C. VanderKam, JSJSup 62 (Leiden: Brill, 2000), 522–44.

[110] For this, see especially J. M. Scott, *On Earth as in Heaven,* 73–158.

[111] VanderKam, "The Origins and Purposes of the *Book of Jubilees*," 22. See, for example, *Jub.* 1:15–18, 27–29.

will be) special from all who are on the surface of the earth.
(19) My son Isaac now loves Esau more than Jacob, but I see
that you rightly love Jacob. (20) Increase your favor to him still
more; may your eyes look at him lovingly because he will prove
to be a blessing for us on the earth from now and throughout
all the history of the earth. (21) May your hands be strong and
your mind be happy with your son Jacob because I love him
much more than all my sons; for he will be blessed forever and
*his descendants will fill the entire earth. (22) If a man is able to
count the sands on the earth, in the same way his descendants,
too, will be counted.* (23) May all the blessings with which the
Lord blessed me and my descendants belong to Jacob and his
descendants *for all time.*

One of the points at which *Jubilees* differs from the OT tradition, however,
is in the connection which is made between this overflow of "descendants" and the universal sovereignty which Israel will eventually have
over the '"nations." In *Jubilees* there seems to be a merging of the Adamic
and Abrahamic promises. According to *Jub.* 2:14 (cf. Gen. 1:26, 28), after
God had made the animals on the sixth day, he accomplished one final act
of creation: "he made mankind – as one man and a woman he made them.
He made him rule everything on earth and in the seas and over flying
creatures, animals, cattle, everything that moves about on the earth, and
the entire earth. *Over all these he made him rule.*" Thus Adam was created to rule as universal sovereign over the whole world.[112] This theme
of Israel's numerous descendants gradually gaining sovereignty over the
world is similarly apparent in *Jub.* 22:11b–12a, 13–14 and in this context
is also closely allied to the concept of inheritance.

> May my son Jacob and all his sons be blessed to the most
> high Lord throughout all ages. May the Lord give you righteous
> descendants, and may he sanctify some of your sons within the
> *entire earth. May the nations serve you, and may all the nations
> bow before your descendants.* (12) *Be strong before people and
> continue to exercise power over all Seth's descendants . . .* (13)
> May the most high God give you all the blessings with which
> he blessed me and with which he blessed Noah and Adam.
> May they come to rest on the sacred head of your descendants
> throughout each and every generation and forever. (14) May he
> purify you from all filthy pollution so that you may be pardoned

---

[112] H. T. Fletcher-Louis, *All of the Glory of Adam: Liturgical Anthropology in the Dead
Sea Scrolls*, STDJ 42 (Leiden: Brill, 2002); esp. 93–94, 97, 435–37.

> for all the guilt of your sins in ignorance. May he strengthen
> and bless you; may you *possess the entire earth [inherit all of
> the earth]*.

But perhaps the clearest example of the relationship between Abraham's
"descendants" and Israel's future sovereignty is in *Jub.* 32:18–19 where
the Lord blesses Jacob and gives this promise, the culmination of which
is referred to as an inheritance:

> (18) I am the Lord who created heaven and earth. I will increase
> your numbers and multiply you very much. Kings will come
> from you, and they will rule wherever mankind has set foot. (19)
> I will give your descendants all of the land that is beneath the
> sky. They will rule over all the nations as they wish. Afterwards,
> they will gain the entire earth, and they will possess it [inherit
> it] forever.[113]

What does such sovereignty or possession or inheritance therefore
involve? How does it come about? Here, similar to the OT tradition,
Jubilees conveys the idea that first Zion will be renewed and then the
rest of the earth will similarly be restored. *Jub.* 1:28 says, "Then [at the
time of Israel's restoration] Zion and Jerusalem will become holy." *Jub.*
4:26 describes what will happen subsequent to Zion's renewal: "Mount
Zion . . . will be sanctified in the new creation for the sanctification of the
earth. For this reason the earth will be sanctified from all its sins and from
its uncleanness into the history of eternity." At that time, when Israel will
be purified from sin, "Then they will live confidently in the entire land.
They will no longer have any satan or any evil person. The land will be
pure from that time until eternity" (50:5).

All of this suggests, therefore, that in using the phrase "inherit the
world" Paul stands in continuity with this Intertestamental literature. In
these texts the language of inheritance takes its place within a wider
perspective of the descendants of Israel and the relationship which they
will one day have with the whole earth. Just as in Rom. 4:13, so scattered
throughout *Jubilees* we find the expansion of the original Abrahamic
promise beyond the land of Canaan to include the whole world. And it is
easy to see why Paul does this. One of Paul's intentions in this chapter is
to demonstrate that the community of God should not be narrowly defined
in terms of certain ethnic observances. By choosing the expanded version
of the promise Paul is able to sever the tie between the land of Palestine

---

[113] See also *1 Enoch* 5:7; *Jub.* 17:3; 22:14; 32:19; *4 Ezra* 6:59. S. C. Keesmaat, *Paul and
His Story: (Re)Interpreting the Exodus Tradition* (Sheffield Academic Press, 1999), 83.

and the definition of who are the people of God. Or as Kenneth Bailey puts it: "The promise *had to expand*, because the very 'people of God' had expanded! Gentiles across the known world *had become a part of 'the people of God.'*"[114]

What makes this reading particularly attractive is the way it coheres with verse 13a as outlined above. There it was shown that Paul is referring to a time when the heirs of Abraham will inherit the world, the eschatological world of a restored creation, an earth where the heirs of Abraham will reign. If the phrases "father of many nations" and "descendants" are allowed to carry with them their original contextual referents, then the concept of the heirs of Abraham (many nations) reigning over a healed and restored world is begun in verse 13 and climaxes in verse 18, with each verse informing the other. This way of reading verse 18 is not therefore suggesting a completely new way of understanding Paul's purpose in Romans 4 but rather arguing that the promise depends on faith so that the original intent of the Abrahamic promise (understood in its full social-physical-spiritual scope) will be realized. Wright hints at the full significance of what Paul is arguing when he suggests that this section is "about the *extent* of Abraham's family", which includes more than just spiritual blessings.[115] But still this does not go far enough. Brendan Byrne's reading is more helpful: "What is at stake, then, in this discussion concerning Abraham is nothing less than the definition of God's eschatological people. To determine who is and who is not 'progeny of Abraham' and thus heir to the promise is to determine who gets a share in the world to come and upon what terms."[116] Of course, implicit throughout all of the chapter, and made explicit again in verses 24–25, is Paul's belief that the promise is now open to all because of the death and resurrection of Jesus Christ. For Paul, the promise–fulfillment trajectory of the Abrahamic promise culminates in Christ.

Romans 4:19–21: Isaiah 54 and the subversion of the Empire

If this approach to Rom. 4:13–18 is valid, then why does Paul follow these verses with a description of Abraham's faith in God despite the barrenness of Sarah (vv. 19–21)? In these verses Paul recounts the story

---

[114] Bailey, "St Paul's Understanding of the Territorial Promise," 68; emphasis original. Related to this, it may be that Paul uses κόσμος rather than γῆ here because it eliminates any possibility of a connection to Palestine.

[115] N. T. Wright, "Romans," 495.

[116] Byrne, *Romans*, 143. Similarly, though less clear, is Käsemann, *Commentary on Romans*, 120.

from Gen. 17:15–17, where God tells Abraham that his wife will bear a child. According to the Genesis text, Abraham falls on his face and laughs: "Can a child be born to a man who is a hundred years old? Can Sarah, who is ninety years old, bear a child?" (Gen. 17:17). Paul's version sees Abraham as rather more confident, recounting that Abraham "did not weaken in faith when he considered his own body, which was already as good as dead . . . or when he considered the barrenness of Sarah's womb. No distrust made him waver concerning the promise of God, but he grew strong in his faith as he gave glory to God" (Rom. 4:19–20). Paul says that it was because Abraham was "fully convinced that God was able to do what he had promised" (v. 21) that Abraham's faith "was reckoned to him as righteous" (v. 22).

At first glance, then, there appears to be little relationship between the "inheriting the world" perspective of verses 13–18 and the trusting-in-God-for-descendants perspective of verses 19–21. If it is the case that verses 19–21 are primarily concerned with the personal faith of Abraham, this would seem to undermine any argument that verses 13–18 are concerned with the inheritance of a restored creation.

On closer examination, however, the connection between these two ideas is not without precedent in Jewish interpretive tradition. In Isa. 54:1–3 a connection is made between these two concepts which may help to illuminate Paul's purpose in 4:19–21.

Isaiah 54:1–3

(1) Rejoice, O barren one who does not bear;
break forth, and shout,
you who are not in labor!
Because more are the children
of the desolate woman
than of her that has a husband,
for the Lord has spoken.

(1) εὐφράνθητι στεῖρα ἡ οὐ τίκτουσα,
ῥῆξον καὶ βόησον,
ἡ οὐκ ὠδίνουσα·
ὅτι πολλὰ τὰ τέκνα
τῆς ἐρήμου
μᾶλλον ἢ τῆς ἐχούσης τὸν ἄνδρα.
εἶπεν γὰρ κύριος.

(2) Enlarge the site of your tent,
and the coverings of your curtains;

make it firm; do not hold back;
lengthen your cords
and strengthen your stakes.

(2) πλάτυνον τὸν τόπον τῆς σκηνῆς σου
καὶ τας δέρρεις τῶν αὐλαιῶν σου·
πῆξον μὴ φείσῃ·
μάκρυνον τὰ σχοινίσματά σου,
καὶ τοὺς πασσάλους σου κατίσχυσον,

(3) because you must spread out to the right
and to the left,
and your offspring will inherit the nations
and will inhabit the cities that have become desolate.

(3) ἔτι εἰς τὰ δεξιὰ
καὶ τὰ ἀριστερὰ ἐκπέτασον,
καὶ τὸ σπέρμα σου ἔθνη κληρονομήσει
καὶ πόλεις ἠρημωμένας κατοικιεῖς.

The first phrase here ("Rejoice, O barren one who does not bear") seems to be a reminder of Sarah and her barrenness, with imagery appealing directly to the stories of Genesis.[117] It then progresses from Sarah's barrenness (στεῖρα, v. 1), to numerous children and to their "descendants" (σπέρμα), who will "possess" or "inherit" (κληρονομήσει) "the nations" (ἔθνη) and settle "the desolate towns" (πόλεις ἠρημωμένας κατοικιεῖς – v. 3). In other words, the passage draws on the Abrahamic promise and subsequent interpretation of this tradition which envisaged that, as Israel became a more populous nation, it would gradually inherit the nations.

The existence of this reinterpretation of Genesis 17 might therefore suggest that the connection between Rom. 4:13–18 (where the phrase "inherit the world" is closely linked to the "descendants" of Abraham) and 4:19–21 would not have been entirely unexpected for his audience and that Paul might have intentionally evoked this earlier tradition. But in order to explore further whether this is the case there is a need to consider Richard Hays' work on the use of OT texts in Paul's letters. In his seminal work *Echoes of Scripture in the Letters of Paul*, Hays explores

---

[117] Trans. M. Silva from A. Pietersma and B. G. Wright, *A New English Translation of the Septuagint* (Oxford University Press, 2007). See, for example, K. Baltzer, *Deutero-Isaiah: A Commentary on Isaiah 40–55*, trans. M. Kohl, Hermeneia (Minneapolis: Fortress Press, 2001), 434; W. Brueggemann, *Hopeful Imagination: Prophetic Voices in Exile* (Philadelphia: Fortress Press, 1986), 115. Baltzer points out that in Isa. 51:1–3 the link between Sarah and Jerusalem has already been made; Baltzer, *Deutero-Isaiah*, 434.

the much-debated issue of how Paul uses the scriptures of Israel.[118] Hays persuasively argues that rather than understanding Paul to be appealing to the "authority" of the Old Testament in order to "prove" his point, it is more helpful to see the apostle as working within the "symbolic world" of Israel's scriptures, grappling his way "through to a vigorous and theologically generative reappropriation of Israel's scriptures."[119]

Using Hays' method as a guide, what evidence is there to suggest that throughout Rom. 4.13–21 Paul echoes Isa. 54:1–3? There are several aspects of Paul's argument which meet Hays' criteria, to varying degrees. To begin with, there is the criterion of *recurrence*. This relates to whether the alleged echo has been used in other contexts by the author. In our case, has Paul explicitly quoted Isa. 54:1–3 in other letters? If it can be established that the author has a pattern of using the alleged source text then this obviously strengthens the case for a proposed echo.[120] In Gal. 4:27 Paul quotes from the first verse of the Isaiah text (54:1), and the wording is identical to that of the LXX: "For it is written, 'Rejoice you childless one, you who bear no children, burst into song and shout, you who endure no birth pangs; for the children of the desolate woman are more numerous than the children of the one who is married.'"

Galatians 4:27
　　Εὐφράνθητι, στεῖρα ἡ οὐ τίκτουσα·
　　ῥῆξον καὶ βόησον, ἡ οὐκ ὠδίνουσα·
　　ὅτι πολλὰ τὰ τέκνα τῆς ἐρήμου
　　μᾶλλον ἢ τῆς ἐχούσης τὸν ἄνδρα.

Isaiah 54:1 (LXX)
　　εὐφράνθητι στεῖρα ἡ οὐ τίκτουσα
　　ῥῆξον καὶ βόησον ἡ οὐκ ὠδίνουσα
　　ὅτι πολλὰ τὰ τέκνα τῆς ἐρήμου
　　μᾶλλον ἢ τῆς ἐχούσης τὸν ἄνδρα

Although there is no *pattern* of direct quotation of the Isaiah text throughout Paul's letters, Paul is certainly aware of the text; it is important to him, and connections between the Isaiah text and the

---

[118] Hays, *Echoes of Scripture in the Letters of Paul*. For an appreciative critique of Hays' work see C. A. Evans and J. A. Sanders, eds., *Paul and the Scriptures of Israel*, JSNTSup 83 (Sheffield Academic Press, 1993).

[119] Hays, *Echoes of Scripture in the Letters of Paul*, 2.

[120] See Ibid., 212. Also J. Ross Wagner, *Heralds of the Good News: Isaiah and Paul "in Concert" in the Letter to the Romans*, NovTSup 51 (Leiden, Boston and Cologne: Brill, 2002), 12.

present Christian communities are not far from his mind.[121] The criterion of *recurrence* also asks whether the wider context of the alleged echo is familiar to the author. It is certainly so for Paul. As will be argued in more detail below, at the heart of the Isaiah text and context is the perspective of Israel-in-relation-to-the-nations. That such a perspective is familiar to Paul and is used by him is evident not only from his other letters and from other places in Romans[122] but, as shown above, from its being at the very heart of his argument in Romans 4, particularly verses 13–18.

Pertinent to the criterion of *recurrence* is also the passage which Paul quotes in Rom. 4:25 (the verse almost immediately after 4:19–21): "[Jesus] who was handed over to death for our trespasses and was raised for our justification." Here Paul's source is undoubtedly Isa. 53:1–12, the passage which immediately precedes Isa. 54:1–3.[123] Isa. 53:1–12 expresses hope in "the righteous one" who "was wounded for our transgressions, crushed for our iniquities; upon him was the punishment that made us whole, and by his bruises we are healed." It is the "righteous one" who "bore the sin of many and made intercession for the transgressors" (Isa. 53:12). The close literary connection between the text to which Paul directly alludes (Isa. 53:1–12) and the proposed echo (Isa. 54:1–3) – one immediately preceding the other – strengthens the case that Paul intends his readers to make the connection.[124]

A second criterion to consider at this stage is *volume*. This refers to the degree of *verbal and conceptual correspondence* between a passage and its alleged source. What can be said about the volume of the alleged echo in Romans 4? To begin with, it is worth noting that Second Isaiah is very important to Paul. As Richard Hays puts it, Isaiah is "statistically and substantively the most important scriptural source for Paul."[125] There are particularly strong verbal links between the LXX text of Isa. 54:3 (ἐκπέτασον καὶ τὸ σπέρμα σου ἔθνη κληρονομήσει) and the language Paul uses in verse 13 and in verses 16–18. Paul uses the word "descendants" (σπέρμα) three times in the passage (vv. 13, 16, 18)[126]

---

[121] This also addresses the criterion of *availability* – which is whether the text was available to Paul. Clearly it was.

[122] See J. M. Scott, *Paul and the Nations*, 135–80.

[123] Dunn, *Romans 1–8*, 224–25.

[124] On this basis Wright suggests that Isaiah 40–55 has been implicit throughout the chapter; N. T. Wright, "Romans," 503.

[125] Hays, *Echoes of Scripture in the Letters of Paul*, 162. See also Wagner, *Heralds*, 14–15.

[126] σπέρμα, the word used for "descendants" in Isa. 54:3, is a word which occurs in Gen. 12:7 ("to your offspring I will give this land"); J. N. Oswalt, *The Book of Isaiah: Chapters 40–66*, NICOT (Grand Rapids and Cambridge: Eerdmans, 1998), 417.

and he also uses the word "nations" (ἐθνῶν) twice in this context (vv. 17–18). But perhaps the most significant link for our purposes is the "inherit" word group which is used in Isa. 54:3 (κληρονομέω) and which similarly occurs twice in Romans 4 (vv. 13–14).[127] The fact that this word group is *not* used in the Genesis 17 context suggests that when Paul appropriates the story of Sarah and Abraham he has in mind both the Genesis 17 context and its interpretation in Isaiah 54. For both Paul and the author of Second Isaiah this language is not selected arbitrarily but seems to be drawn from and to echo the Abrahamic promise tradition.[128] In keeping with the original promise to Abraham, both texts apply to their own contexts the theme of Abraham as a father of many nations.[129] The fact that the Abrahamic promise tradition and language are so central to Paul's argument in Romans 4 and are clearly important in the Isaiah 54 passage further suggests that Paul may intend his audience to make the connection between the two texts.

As well as these echoes in verses 13–18, the narrative of Sarah's barrenness and subsequent childbirth is similarly evoked by Paul. While the word which Paul uses for barrenness (νέκρωσιν) is different from that used in the LXX of Isa. 54:1 (στεῖρα), there is an obvious conceptual connection between the two and both appeal directly to the stories of Genesis.[130] Just as Isaiah 54 refers to a time when "the barren one" will rejoice because she has so many children, so Paul briefly narrates the story of Abraham, Sarah and their faith in God's ability to bring new life out of barrenness.

A third criterion that Hays suggests is *historical plausibility*. This entails taking seriously the author's inherited traditions of interpretation and the cultural environment of the author. In the case of Paul, for example, is an alleged echo plausible for the first century, considering its historical and cultural context? A strong indication that this is the case is the ways in which Philo appropriates the Isaiah passage. James M. Scott shows that in line with early Judaism, which frequently interpreted the promise in terms of sovereignty over the whole world, Philo reads Isa. 54:1–3 as an expectation that Israel will steadily become a populous

---

[127] In Isa. 54:3 this is translated as "possess the nations" (NASB, NRSV) or "inherit the nations" (KJV) or as "dispossess the nations" (NIV).

[128] J. Blenkinsopp, *Isaiah 40–55: A New Translation with Introduction and Commentary*, AB 19A (New York, London, Toronto, Sydney and Auckland: Doubleday, 2000), 362.

[129] Brueggemann, *Hopeful Imagination*, 116.

[130] See, for example, ibid., 115; Seters, "The Problem of Childlessness in Near Eastern Law and the Patriarchs of Israel," *JBL* 87 (1968): 401–408.

nation and subsequently rule over many nations.[131] Philo's appropriation of the Isaiah text stands in continuity with the way he reads Gen.
28:14, where the Abrahamic promise is reiterated to Jacob. Philo explains
the Genesis text in this way: "And this, in accordance with the Divine
promises, is broadening out to the very bounds of the universe, and renders its possessor inheritor of the four quarters of the world, reaching to
them all, to East, and West, and South, and North; for it is said, 'It shall
spread abroad to the West and to the South and to the North and to the
East.'"[132]

Clearly, therefore, there is good evidence that Paul is intentionally
echoing this passage from Isa. 54: the passage explicitly occurs in Galatians; there is a degree of verbal and conceptual correspondence between
the two passages; and use of the passage in this way is plausible within the
context of the first-century Greco-Roman world. But perhaps the crucial
question is whether Paul's allusion to Isaiah 54 makes sense within the
immediate context of 4:13–25. If Paul intentionally echoes this passage,
then to what degree does it fit with the argument of verses 13–18, or as
Hays puts it, to what extent is there *thematic coherence* and *satisfaction*
if the proposed echo is adopted?

The traditional understanding of these verses is that they are about the
personal faith of Abraham and that they further develop Paul's argument
regarding the superiority of faith over works. But while this interpretation
accounts for the surface detail of the text, it fails to grasp the full scope and
significance of the context from which this narrative is drawn (Genesis
12–17). Paul's primary emphasis in verses 19–21 is the *promise of God*
to Abraham: "no distrust made [Abraham] waver concerning the *promise*
(ἐπαγγελίαν) of God." Instead, Abraham was "fully convinced that God
was able to do what he had *promised* (ὃ ἐπήγγελται)." The discussion of
verses 13–18 above showed that the language of promise and κληρονόμος
in this context includes the interrelated concepts of "descendants," "land"
and being a "great nation." In verses 13–18 Paul's argument is that
the original intent of the promise to Abraham is now being fulfilled:
the Roman Christians he is writing to are all now considered to be
"descendants" of Abraham and they will therefore "inherit the world,"
an expression which encapsulates a perspective including physical land
and sovereignty. There is no indication that the "promise of God" is used

---

[131] Philo, *De Praemiis et Poenis* 158: "for she that was desolate, as the prophet says
(Isa. 54:1), is now become happy in her children and the mother of a large family"; *The
Works of Philo*, trans. C. D. Yonge (Peabody, MA: Hendrickson Publishers, 1993), 679.
[132] J. M. Scott, *Paul and the Nations*, 94.

in the later section of this text (vv. 20–21) in a different way from in the first part (vv. 13–14). Instead, the story of Abraham's faith in God is partly a continuation of the belief that one day the people of God would become a populous nation and gradually inherit the world.[133]

Isaiah 54:1–3 and the experience of Christians in Rome

Importantly, however, it is also more than this. I suggest that by echoing Isa. 54:1–3 Paul also invites his readers to reflect on the promised inheritance in light of their current socio-political context. My proposal is that Paul is aware that what he has just written is likely to create considerable cognitive dissonance for his audience in the face of their current experience of life under Rome. It seems *unlikely* that Paul would have been able to make such a bold claim regarding the inheritance of the world (in v. 13) without simultaneously reflecting on what such a statement meant for the Roman Christians to whom he was writing. For the Christians at Rome there would have been a significant difference between Paul's vision for the future and Rome's supposed "blessing" of the world and what they were experiencing in the present. It will be helpful to tease out this dissonance before returning to the way Isa. 54:1–3 can be read as a response to it.

The catalyst for this conceptual clash is the claims which Paul has made in verses 13–17 when they are heard within the context of first-century urban imperial Rome. These Christians were confronted daily with images which stated very boldly and clearly (as the previous chapter established) the vision of the world which the Empire wanted to perpetuate and which many of its citizens wanted to believe. The imperial images proclaimed that there had been peace and justice in Augustus' time and that there would be similar times of security and order through the military victories of Claudius and Nero. Or perhaps in even more jarring terms for Paul's readers, the Roman poets wrote that it was the Romans, above all other people, who were now and would be forever, the true "lords of creation."[134] And as was established in Chapter 2, there was a small group in the city and in the Empire who *had* experienced

---

[133] It is in this sense that the world can be promised to Abraham and his seed. As Williams points out, the key "lies in the Hebraic concept of the inclusion of the descendants in the progenitor. In a sense foreign to us, a people's ancestor and the ancestor's offspring are identical. The offspring are incorporated in the ancestor and the ancestor is later present as his offspring. Thus Abraham can possess the world though his offspring – or better, *as* his offspring"; S. K. Williams, "The *Promise* in Galatians," 717.

[134] Virgil, *Aeneid* 1. 281–82.

the so-called "blessings" of Rome. As Steven Friesen has shown, there were a small number of "super-wealthy elites" in the city of Rome who possessed vast amounts of land and wealth.

Within this context of wealth, prosperity and "blessing" for a few, Paul makes a bold counter-claim. At the heart of the language of inheritance is the question of *who* determines who has a share in the world. Who is the one who decides who has a portion in the land and earth? This is a decidedly political question. Paul's answer, as has been shown, is unmistakable in Romans 4: it has always been and still is God who grants the inheritance of the world. Equally clear from the discussion above is the belief that it is the people of God who will one day receive this inheritance from God. In other words, Paul follows the OT linking of land and God and in doing so emphasizes that it is God, not Caesar, who determines who has a share in the world and that it is the people of God, not necessarily the wealthy and powerful of Rome, who will receive this renewed earth. This is not to suggest that the concept of inheritance in the Old Testament contributed to specific social policy and neither am I suggesting that this is how Paul's concept should be understood. The way in which Paul uses the language of inheritance is not a direct prophet-like naming of the social and political realities of first-century Rome. The specific detail of the OT inheritance laws is not intended when Paul refers to inheritance in this context. Clearly, for Paul, the particular land of Canaan and the allotment of boundaries within that land are no longer important. But Paul does evoke the issue of *which* groups of people have a share in the world to come and in doing so he is inviting his audience to critique the current social, economic and political situation and, by implication, to reflect on the causes of the disparities which exist. For Paul to use the language of inheritance is to refuse to allow the imperial narrative to be the only story by which the Roman Christians are shaped.

For the Christians at Rome, therefore, there are likely to have been at least two reasons why a message of life in the midst of apparent "death" was needed. First, whereas the imperial cult claimed that the emperor had brought peace, prosperity, order and fruitfulness to society, the urban poor to whom Paul wrote knew very little of this. Although saturated by images of well-being, Paul's Roman Christians were, in reality, destitute. And they were powerless to do anything about it. As argued above, there is good evidence to suggest that the majority of Christians in Rome were struggling to live at, or just above, the subsistence level. Many would have experienced brutal poverty and ongoing destitution. To imagine that things could ever be different may well have been unthinkable. It is within this situation of apparent despair that Paul declares to the urban poor that they will one day "inherit the world." And yet it is just as likely that Paul's words would have been met with disbelief, because the idea that these people would one day inherit anything may well have been unimaginable and there was little realistic hope of the situation changing in the near future. The people to whom Paul writes are those who lie outside the realms of power and they are therefore non-participants in the history of the Roman Empire. In other words there is a vast gap between what Paul's inheritance language invokes and what was realistically possible in the first century.

It is also possible that the means by which Paul expects the inheritance to come about will have compounded the incomprehensibility of the situation. In other words, just as jarring for Paul's audience will have been the question of *how* this future inheritance would happen. As will be demonstrated in Chapter 4, this question is made still more explicit in Romans 8. But even in Romans 4 there are indications that the inheritance involves a political vision which is very different from that of Rome.

This is suggested firstly through the language of gift and grace in Romans 4: the concept of inheritance as a gift from God reverberates throughout. Just as in the Old Testament the notion of inheritance was inextricably linked to the concept of inheritance as *gift* from YHWH rather than as a possession which is earned, so in Rom. 4:13–25 the theme of grace weaves its way in and out of the language of inheritance. Paul is insistent that "the promise" of inheritance rests entirely on the "grace" of God (4:16). The promise that Abraham would become the "father of many nations" (4:16) was made "in the presence of the God in whom he believed, who gives life to the dead and calls into existence the things that do not exist" (4:17). Abraham did not waver with distrust concerning the promise because it was the "promise *of God*" and Abraham was "fully convinced that God was able to do what he promised" (4:20–21). Traditionally, of course, these verses have been read almost exclusively as relating to the issue of entry into the community of God. However, the discussion of inheritance (above) should alert us to the fact that while "grace" and "faith" are key themes in this passage they should not be understood exclusively in terms of individual salvation. Instead, it is likely that when Paul refers to the promise which "depends on faith" and rests "on grace," one of his intentions is to remind his audience that the future inheritance is not something which is earned or deserved but (as is conveyed by the OT meaning of the word) is always a grant or gift from God. This certainly fits well with the survey above of the language of inheritance (nahala) in the Old Testament, where it was noted that the concept of land in general and inheritance in particular is the fulcrum for the relationship between Yahweh and Israel.[135] The inheritance is expressed as a grant from Yahweh to Israel, which is the primary way in which Yahweh provides and cares materially and economically for Israel. The inheritance concept includes the conviction that land can be given to Israel because the land already belongs to YHWH (it is YHWH's inheritance). As noted above, the land is therefore a special, permanent and precious possession because it is a legal grant from God.[136]

Of course, even the language of "grace" and "faith" could conceivably be appropriated in ways which result in hegemony and inappropriate power. Such a claim *could be* heard as theological legitimation for one group of people's taking over the land of another group. But at the heart of Romans 4 is also the concept that God's intention was always that Abraham and his descendants would bring blessing to the nations. As has been established above, woven throughout Paul's argument here is the idea that the descendants of Abraham had been elected by God to bring well-being to the earth and all people. Abraham is considered the "father of many nations" in the sense that the blessing which he experienced would now be experienced by "many nations."

This suggests that when Paul uses the language of inheritance in Romans 4 he is drawing from one particular stream of land ideology in the Old Testament. Norman Habel, in his discussion of Old Testament land ideologies, points out that there is not a monolithic concept of land but contrasting voices.[137] For example, one stream of land ideology sought to provide theological legitimation, through the language of inheritance, for land policies which showed little concern for a fair distribution of land and wealth. Habel calls this a "Royal Ideology."[138] K. Whitelam describes the concept:

> Royal ideology provided a justification for the control of power and strategic resources; it proclaimed that the king's right to rule was guaranteed by the deities of the state. A heavy emphasis was placed on the benefits of peace, security and wealth for the population of the state which flowed from the king's position in the cosmic scheme of things.[139]

---

[135] C. Wright, *God's People*, 19 n. 29.   [136] C. Wright, "Nahal, NahᵃLâ," 79.

[137] See similarly W. Lempke, "Review of *The Land Is Mine*," *JBL* 116 (1997): 334; W. Scott, "Review of *The Land Is Mine*," *CBQ* 58 (1996): 708–709; H. Spykerboer, "Review of: *The Land Is Mine*," *Colloquium* 28.2 (1996): 122–23.

[138] See further Habel, *The Land Is Mine*, 17–32.

[139] K. Whitelam, "Israelite Kingship: The Royal Ideology and Its Opponents," in *The World of Ancient Israel*, ed. R. Clements (Cambridge University Press, 1989), 121.

The account of Naboth's vineyard in 1 Kgs. 21:1–16 is one instance where this kind of royal ideology stands in tension with an ideology which seeks to protect the rights of small family landholders. Here "Ahab is apparently caught between the ideal of the strong monarch, who takes whatever lands are needed to promote the wealth of the palace, and the ideal of the just monarch, who upholds the rights of the peasant."[140] Arguably the final form of this narrative can be read as a critique of the royal ideology which appropriates Naboth's family inheritance. Despite this, however, it is still the case that threaded throughout the Old Testament is an ideology which supports the interests of the monarchy and the royal court at the expense of the rights of other people.[141]

It is conceivable, therefore, that in drawing on the language of "descendants" and "nations" Paul reflects a "royal ideology" which envisages the eventual domination of the people of God over, for example, the Empire of Rome. But the Abraham narrative which Paul evokes in Romans 4 suggests that such a perspective is not the one which Paul has in mind here. Significantly, Habel identifies a tradition which he terms an "immigrant ideology." Whereas many of the land ideologies of the Old Testament seek to provide legitimation for Israel's conquering and dispossession of the land of Canaan, the Abraham narratives "reflect a distinctive immigrant ideology that views the land as a host country and its inhabitants as potentially friendly peoples."[142] Habel shows that embedded in the Abrahamic narrative is the promise of "a great nation" who will obtain "the land" and who will mediate "blessing" to the nations.

There is the expectation, therefore, that in the future the Abraham family will expand beyond a small social group and become a political power with control of the land. Significantly, however, the implication is that this future which is envisaged for Israel will not come about through the domination of other nations but through the blessing which Abraham will mediate both to the ancestral families of the host country, including the Canaanites, and potentially, to all nations of the earth.[143] There is no thought here of the expulsion or destruction of the inhabitants of Canaan. Instead, woven throughout the Abraham narratives is the idea that Abraham provides "a model of how to live at peace with the host peoples of the land and share ownership of the land. In this ideology, possessing the land does not demand annihilation or expulsion of these people."[144] This means that Abraham respects the rights and cultures of

---

[140] Habel, *The Land Is Mine*, 30.   [141] Ibid., 17–32.   [142] Ibid., 115.
[143] Ibid., 121.   [144] Ibid., 125.

the host country, including the right to share, sell and negotiate the use of land.[145] Such an ideology, of course, exists in tension with the militant Joshua story where the expectation is clear that to become a great nation Israel must first annihilate the existing inhabitants. But as Habel argues, there is not a monolithic ideology of land in the Old Testament; there are only ideologies which stand in tension with each other and which are appropriated at different times in Israel's history.[146]

It is clear from the discussion above that in Romans 4 Paul draws heavily on the Abraham narrative and that this is especially so with regard to the language of inheritance. This has obvious significance for the question of *how* the process of inheriting the land should be understood. Identifying the "immigrant ideology" which threads its way throughout the Abraham story is an important reminder that although (following the Intertestamental literature) there is the notion of universal sovereignty conveyed by the phrase "inherit the world," the original intent of the Abrahamic promise was not that this would come about through conquering annihilation but that this would happen in the course of the people of God bringing "blessing to the nations." In keeping with the original intent of the Abrahamic narratives, therefore, Paul rejects the kind of ideology which sought theological legitimation for the violent overthrow of people and their land. The echoes of Abraham are therefore a further indication that the inheritance is not meant to gather in the hands of a few select people but is to be mediated to "all" the peoples of the earth. This way of understanding the *how* of the future inheritance of the people of God fits well with how Paul concludes the text, in Rom. 4:24–25. There he refers to "Jesus our Lord" who was "handed over to death." In other words the concept of self-giving to the point of death seems to stand in continuity with the proposed reading of an "immigrant ideology" in Romans 4; it is not a world where one group oppresses another but where groups of people live at peace with one another.

I propose that Rom. 4:19–21 takes on a new significance when read as a response to the socio-political situation of first-century Roman society described above. If Paul is here echoing Isa. 54:1–3, it is likely that he is doing so because the passage and its context illuminate the historical and socio-political situation of the Christians to whom he writes in first-century Rome. More specifically, for the urban poor at Rome simultaneously to be bombarded with the message that they were already

---

[145] Ibid., 132.
[146] See similarly Davies, *The Gospel and the Land*, 157; C. Wright, *God's People*, 44.

"blessed" (by Rome) and to be told that they would one day "inherit the world" (by Paul) would have created considerable cognitive dissonance. As Robert Jewett puts it, "Given the marginal social circumstances of most of the Christians in Rome, and their ongoing troubles with persecution, poverty and conflict, how could anyone imagine they would inherit the earth?"[147] Paul's language of inheritance and its associated concepts are likely to have raised this inevitable question for his audience: how is it possible to believe such a vision (and to embody such a lifestyle) while living in the heart of the Roman Empire? The Roman Christians were therefore ripe for a message of hope and it is precisely this which is evoked by Paul's use of Isa. 54:1–3.

Walter Brueggemann points out that when the author of Isa. 54:1–3 refers to the "barren one" it is likely that, as well as evoking the Sarah tradition and the pervasive OT theme of barren women surprised by births,[148] he is primarily making connections with Israel's present situation of exile. As Brueggemann observes, in the context of Isaiah 54, "the imagery of Sarah refers to exilic Israel, whose barrenness signifies the hopelessness of exile ... Thus the imagery of barrenness – birth in context concerns the despair of exile and the happy prospect of restoration."[149] The author intends to evoke the possibility that, just as (in ancient society) the shame of a woman's barrenness can miraculously turn to joy, so Israel's experience of exile can result in a return to her home.[150] Brueggemann teases out how this text encouraged the Jewish exiles that things would not always be as they were. One of the ways in which Isaiah 54 does this is by being deeply subversive of the empire of the day. For example, the allusion to the Abrahamic promise and the suggestion that exilic Israel would be "the father of many nations," "is a remarkably bold offer in the face of a situation in which Israel seems to be the servant of many nations. The poetry articulates the deep inversion and reversal which are

---

[147] R. Jewett, "Impeaching God's Elect: Romans 8.33–37 in Its Rhetorical Situation," in *Paul, Luke and the Greco-Roman World*, ed. O. Christofferson *et al.*, JSNTSup 217 (Sheffield Academic Press, 2002), 43. Jewett's observation is made with regard to Romans 8 but (as his use of the phrase "inherit the earth" indicates) it could be made equally accurately with regard to Romans 4.

[148] For example Rebekah (Gen. 25:21), Rachel (Gen. 29:31) and Hannah (1 Sam. 1:2). Brueggemann suggests that "The whole history of Israel is a history of barren women surprised by births"; Brueggemann, *Hopeful Imagination*, 115–16.

[149] W. Brueggemann, *Isaiah 40–66*, Westminster Bible Companion (Louisville: Westminster John Knox Press, 1998), 1–15, 151; M. Thompson, *Isaiah 40–66*, Epworth Commentaries (London: Epworth Press, 2001), xvii–xviii.

[150] For the social and economic consequences of barrenness in ancient society see, for example, Baltzer, *Deutero-Isaiah*, 435; Blenkinsopp, *Isaiah 40–55*, 361.

necessary for life beyond empire."[151] Just as the promise to Abraham was for Sarah the end of a season of humiliation, so the suggestion that Israel would "possess the nations" was "surely heard by exiles as an end to the season of political-cultural displacement and humiliation . . . The promissory word of birth and hope breaks and nullifies all of the weighty, oppressive claims of the Babylonian Empire."[152]

The author of Isaiah 54 is evoking the memory of the Abrahamic promise, with its sweeping claims of land, progeny and blessing, and inviting exilic Israel to consider anew these promises. As John Oswalt observes, the Isaiah author is posing the following question to his audience: is God "really able to keep those promises given geopolitical realities and the more horrid reality of human sin? That is the question that the Egyptian bondage raised, and it is the same question that the exile raises."[153]

The message of Rom. 4:13–18 invites similar questions for the first-century Roman Christians and this is why Paul returns to the Sarah tradition in verses 19–21. While in Isaiah 54 there is a movement from Sarah's barrenness (v. 1) to numerous descendants (v. 1) to inheriting the nations (v. 3) the progression in Paul's argument is reversed but the point seems to be similar. Isa. 54:1–3 appropriates the story of Sarah and Abraham and connects it with the "land" and "inheritance" themes of the Abrahamic tradition in order to make available to Israel a way of thinking about God and empire.[154] Paul reminds his readers that Abraham was "fully convinced that God was able to do what he had promised" (v. 21) and in doing so Paul is inviting his readers to consider the ways in which God will also do what he has promised despite appearances to the contrary in first-century Rome. Both the author of Isaiah and Paul in Romans 4 therefore make available to the people of God a memory which can be worked towards in the present in order to subvert the empire of the day.

On the one hand, Paul implicitly acknowledges that there is little evidence of inheritance in the present for those Christians at Rome. But on the other, he reminds his audience of Sarah and Abraham and of the potential for life in the midst of death which always exists for God's people. This is not to suggest that Paul's language of inheritance is in any way intended to contribute to specific social policy, but rather that it

---

[151] Brueggemann, *Hopeful Imagination*, 117.
[152] Ibid. Similarly Blenkinsopp, *Isaiah 40–55*, 361.
[153] Oswalt, *Isaiah*, 416.
[154] Brueggemann, *Hopeful Imagination*, 115.

functions as a vision of the way things were meant to be and thus as a critique of the ways things currently are. In his study of eighth-century prophets, D. N. Premnath points out that the purpose of a vision is to reveal the contradictions between what is and what ought to be.[155] A vision "enables us to distance ourselves from reality so that we can begin to perceive alternative ways of living. The world of possibilities is opened up. Alternatives to the present system and orderings are unfolded."[156] It is of course easy to dismiss visions as utopian or as unreliable. But this is to miss the function of visions and it would be to misunderstand the way in which Paul's language of inheritance would have functioned in the city of Rome. In this context, inheritance helps the Christians at Rome to perceive society in alternative ways and thus it exposes the supposedly permanent and immutable character of the present order of the world. By evoking a world where land is granted by God and is managed in line with the character of God, the language of inheritance calls into question and subverts the present situation of land and landlessness in Rome.

Conclusions

All of this suggests, therefore, that far from being tangential to Paul's theology, or a sideline to his main argument, Paul's reference to the content of the inheritance in verse 13 is a product of how he, as a Jew, understands himself and Abraham's descendants in relation to God and the world. Verse 13's "inherit the world" is no casual reference, but instead an integral part of a typical Jewish perspective which undergirds Paul's thinking. As has been shown, when the citations in verse 18 are understood as referring to the original intent of the promise – that all the world would one day experience God's blessing through Israel and the land of Canaan – then verse 13 is not a curious anomaly but a compressed and inevitable reference to a broader perspective which is signposted in verse 13 and continues through the verses which follow. This reading of verses 13–18 also suggests that while the particular land of Canaan is not important in Paul's thinking (this is extended to include the whole "world"), his inheritance language quite clearly refers to a geographical reality and undoubtedly retains a claim to sovereignty: there is in this text a clear sense that the question of *who* will inherit the world is a central one. Importantly, however, Paul indicates that the *how* of the inheritance

---

[155] D. M. Premnath, *Eighth Century Prophets. A Social Analysis* (St. Louis, MO: Chalice Press, 2003), 184.
[156] Ibid., 184–85.

also subverts the hegemonic and militaristic approach of Rome. Finally, Paul (in vv. 19–21) deliberately alludes to Isa. 54:1–3, a text which was originally used in order to provide hope in the midst of exile. Paul appropriates this text and the interpretive tradition associated with it in order to remind his audience that although they are currently in the midst of a world fraught with inequality and injustice, and despite dwelling in the heart of an Empire which claims otherwise, it is the people of God, consisting now of believing Jews and Gentiles, who are the ones who will one day inherit the earth.

4

SUFFERING "CONQUERORS": INHERITANCE IN ROMANS 8:17–39

Introduction

The discussion of inheritance (κληρονόμος) in Rom. 4:13–25 concluded that it refers to a geographical reality which includes the concept of the people of God living on the restored earth, and that the term also carries with it political significance. The only other undisputed use of κληρονόμος and its cognates in Romans is in Rom. 8:17,[1] which takes its place within the following text:

> (14) For all who are led by the Spirit of God are children of God. (15) For you did not receive a spirit of slavery to fall back into fear, but you have received a spirit of adoption. When we cry, "Abba! Father!" (16) it is that very Spirit bearing witness with our spirit that we are children of God, (17) and if children, then heirs (κληρονόμοι), heirs of God (κληρονόμοι μὲν θεοῦ) and joint heirs with Christ (συγκληρονόμοι δὲ Χριστοῦ) if, in fact, we suffer with him so that we may also be glorified with him. (18) I consider that the sufferings of this present time are not worth comparing with the glory about to be revealed to us. (19) For the creation waits with eager longing for the revealing of the children of God; (20) for the creation was subjected to futility, not of its own will but by the will of the one who subjected it, in hope (21) that the creation itself will be set free from its bondage to decay and will obtain the freedom of the glory of the children of God. (22) We know that the whole creation has been groaning in labor pains until now; (23) and not only the creation, but we ourselves, who have the first fruits of the Spirit, groan inwardly while we wait for adoption, the redemption of our bodies. (24) For in hope we were saved. Now hope that is

---

[1] See Chapter 5 for a discussion of the use of κληρονομίαν in some manuscripts in Rom. 11:1.

seen is not hope. For who hopes for what is seen? (25) But if we have hope for what we do not see, we wait for it with patience.

(29) For those whom he foreknew he also predestined to be conformed to the image of his Son, in order that he might be the firstborn within a large family. (30) And those whom he predestined he also called; and those whom he called he also justified; and those whom he justified he also glorified.

(31) What then are we to say about these things? If God is for us, who is against us? (32) He who did not withhold his own Son, but gave him up for all of us, will he not with him also give us everything else?

(35) Who will separate us from the love of Christ? Will hardship, or distress, or persecution, or famine, or nakedness, or peril, or sword? (36) As it is written,

"For your sake we are being killed all day long;
we are accounted as sheep to be slaughtered."

(37) No, in all these things we are more than conquerors through him who loved us. (38) For I am convinced that neither death, nor life, nor angels, nor rulers, nor things present, nor things to come, nor powers, (39) nor height, nor depth, nor anything else in all creation, will be able to separate us from the love of God in Christ Jesus our Lord.

For some interpreters the common use of κληρονόμος in Romans 4 and Romans 8 is sufficient evidence to conclude that κληρονόμοι in Rom. 8.17 continues the themes of Rom. 4:13 with regard to the heirs to the Abrahamic promise. Adolf Schlatter, for example, suggests that the promise that "you will inherit the world" receives its "premise and interpretation" in Rom. 8:17.[2] However, not all interpreters agree. There is disagreement whether Paul intends any thematic connection with the use of κληρονόμος in Romans 4 and 8. One of the main reasons for this is that the phrases which Paul uses in Rom. 8:17 – "heirs of God" and "joint heirs with Christ" – appear to be referring to something separate from the inheritance concept in 4:13. One of the most notable differences between the two uses of κληρονόμος (Romans 8 and Romans 4) is the absence in Rom. 8:17 and in the wider context (8:18–39) of any reference to Abraham or of God's promise of land to Abraham. The contrast with

---

[2] A. Schlatter, *Gottes Gerechtigket. Ein Kommentar zum Römerbrief* (Stuttgart: Calwer, 1935), 267.

Romans 4 seems particularly clear (at least at first glance), where the example and story of Abraham is central to Paul's argument. Not only this, but in Romans 4 Abraham plays an important role in how κληρονό-μος is understood and explained. The promise of inheriting the earth was made "to Abraham and his descendants" (4:13) and in the verses which follow Paul insists that *inheriting* is connected with being Abraham's seed. As Cranfield points out, in Romans 4 heirship is connected with sonship "but the sonship referred to is sonship *of Abraham*: nothing is here said of being sons or heirs *of God* [as it is in Rom. 8:17]."[3] On this basis, Cranfield concludes that the uses of inheritance in the three main passages (Galatians 3–4; Romans 4; Romans 8) bear little relation to each other: "The differences between these three passages are such that it is better not to assume that Rom. 8:17 is to be explained simply on the basis of one or other or of both the other two passages, but to explain it independently of them."[4] He suggests that any attempt to compare, for example, Romans 4 and Romans 8, will result in both passages being scrambled: "The effect of scrambling (by explaining the use in Romans 8 on the basis of Romans 4 and/or Galatians 3–4) is seriously to obscure the transcendent significance of what is being said in Romans 8."[5]

This is not to say that all interpreters are so explicit about the difference between κληρονόμος in Romans 4 and in Romans 8 or so adamant about the need to deal with the two occurrences separately. But the assumption is often that there is little lexical or thematic continuity between the use of inheritance in Rom. 4:13 and Rom. 8:17. For example, James Dunn suggests that while in Romans 4 κληρονομία refers to the "whole earth,"[6] in Rom. 8:17 the term refers to "the idea of Israel itself as God's inheritance."[7] On the one hand such an understanding of the term has some merit because the phrase which Paul uses, "heirs of God" (κληρονόμοι μὲν θεοῦ), is "a recurring theme in Jewish literature and was a basic datum of Jewish self-understanding."[8] But there is also a need to explore whether Paul's different phrasing in Romans 4 and 8 is meant to convey a distinct idea or whether they are instead two ways of expressing a similar theme.

[3] C. E. B. Cranfield, *A Critical and Exegetical Commentary on the Epistle to the Romans,* ICC 1 (Edinburgh: T. & T. Clark, 1975), 405.

[4] Ibid., 406–407.   [5] Ibid., 405 n. 3.   [6] Dunn, *Romans 1–8,* 213.

[7] Ibid., 455. Similarly P. Stuhlmacher, *Paul's Letter to the Romans: A Commentary,* trans. S. J. Hafemann (Louisville: Westminster John Knox Press, 1994), 130.

[8] Dunn, *Romans 1–8,* 455. Dunn lists the following references: Deut. 32:9; 1 Kgs. 8:51, 53; 2 Kgs. 21:14; Pss. 33:12, 74:2; Isa. 63:17; Jer. 10:16; Mic. 7:18; Jdt. 13:5; Sir. 24:8, 12; *Jub.* 1.19–21; 22:9–10, 15; 33:20; *3 Macc.* 6.3; *2 Apoc. Bar.* 5.1; *Ps. Philo* 12.9; 21.10; 27:7; 28:2; 39.7; 49.6.

It is not only the phrase "heirs *of God*" which has led interpreters to suggest a thematic discontinuity between Rom. 4:13 and Rom. 8:17. Similarly distracting has been the accompanying phrase "joint heirs with Christ" (συγκληρονόμοι δὲ Χριστοῦ). One assumption made in explaining this phrase is that Paul is downplaying the physical nature of κληρονομία especially in comparison with 4:13. For example, P. Hammer argues that Paul conceives of Christ as both the "heir" and the inheritance in this passage – that Christ is not only the *means* but also the *end* of the inheritance, so that once more the content of inheritance in the two contexts should be understood as separate and distinct expressions.[9]

In light of all this, how should the three occurrences of κληρονόμος in Rom. 8:17 be understood? If κληρονομία is to be understood entirely separately in Romans 8 from in Romans 4, then what consequences does this have for an overall understanding of the concept and what does it mean for the argument presented for inheritance in the previous chapter? One response could be that there need not be a problem with reading the two texts as independent of each other since they could simply be expressing different aspects of the single theme of inheritance. While in theory this is possible, I propose that Paul intends no such separation between the two texts and that keeping the two distinct from each other has significant negative consequences for how one of the central themes of Paul's eschatological worldview in Romans is understood.

One of the effects of keeping the texts conceptually separate is that Rom. 4:13 continues to be interpreted as an intriguing statement but one ultimately disconnected from Paul's "main" argument. In the previous chapter I argued that although Paul's phrase in Rom. 4:13 "inherit the world" is brief and compressed, it is nevertheless indicative of a much broader eschatological worldview which has many connections with the rest of his argument in 4:13–25. However, although there is a degree to which that text is a significant statement on its own, I will argue that when it is read in tandem with Rom. 8:17–39 the full scope and force of κληρονόμος in Romans becomes apparent.

Another consequence of cutting loose Rom. 4:13 from Romans 8 is that κληρονόμος in Romans 8 tends to be read in spiritualized and individualized terms. This, for example, is how Luke Timothy Johnson understands κληρονόμος in 8:17. He suggests that Paul completely redefines the original Jewish understanding of κληρονόμος, "identifying it not with the possession of the *land* but specifically with *the gift of the Holy Spirit* (see, e.g., Acts 3:37–42). Once this slight (!) [*sic*] adjustment

---

[9]   Hammer, "*Klēronomia*," 272.

is made, then it follows that everyone who has the Holy Spirit is also an heir of the promise made to Abraham."[10] Not surprisingly, Johnson's discussion of Romans 4 gives no thought to what Paul might mean by the phrase "inherit the world." In similar fashion, John Ziesler fails to detect the possible connection between Romans 4 and Romans 8 and therefore concludes that in Rom. 8:17–39 "there is nothing about land, and even the reference to Abraham is no more than an allusion."[11] Even the highly suggestive phrase "joint heirs with Christ," which, I will argue, has a ring of universal sovereignty about it, is consequently spiritualized and individualized. For example Leon Morris suggests, "It is difficult to see what possessions we share as fellow heirs with Christ; the title is surely one of dignity, assuring us of our place in the *heavenly family* where he is the Son."[12]

These brief observations suggest that while it may be possible to understand κληρονόμος in Romans 4 and 8 as two different ways of expressing a this-worldly concept, the more common tendency is for an assumed disconnectedness to weaken the socio-political aspects of both. To what degree is this proposed disjunction warranted? One of the arguments commonly put forward for the alleged discontinuity is the apparent lack of any mention of Abraham or the Abrahamic tradition in Romans 8. But this observation needs to be questioned. Although Abraham is not explicitly mentioned in Romans 8, the tradition is not entirely absent. James M. Scott points out that the Abrahamic tradition in fact lies close to the surface of Romans 8.[13] Evidence for this lies in verse 32a, "He who did not spare his own Son but gave him up for us all," a phrase which many interpreters identify as an allusion to the story of Abraham's sacrifice of Isaac in Genesis 22.[14] The question *why* Paul alludes to this story is not essential to our purposes here. There has been some dispute whether Jewish teaching regarding the binding of Isaac included vicarious soteriological connotations. Some

---

[10] L. T. Johnson, *Reading Romans: A Literary and Theological Commentary* (New York: The Crossroad Publishing Company, 1997), 125. The exclamation mark enclosed within parentheses in this quotation is original.

[11] J. Ziesler, *Paul's Letter to the Romans* (Harrisburg, PA: Trinity Press, 1989), 216. Similarly C. H. Dodd, *The Epistle of Paul to the Romans*, Moffat New Testament Commentary (London: Hodder and Stoughton, 1932), 132.

[12] Morris, *The Epistle to the Romans*, 317; emphasis added.

[13] J. M. Scott, *Adoption*, 249.

[14] Examples of those who identify this as an intentional echo include U. Wilckens, *Der Brief an die Römer: Rom 6–11*, EKK, 3 vols. (Zurich: Benziger, 1980), vol. II, 172; D. Campbell, "The Story of Jesus in Romans and Galatians," in *Narrative Dynamics in Paul. A Critical Assessment*, ed. B. W. Longenecker (London: Westminster John Knox Press, 2002), 114. Hays, *Echoes of Scripture in the Letters of Paul*, 61–62.

interpreters have argued that there is little evidence for the existence of a pre-Christian Jewish understanding of Isaac's binding in vicarious terms and that it therefore seems unlikely that Paul is here drawing from this story in order to describe the atoning sacrifice of Christ.[15] More recently, however, evidence has become available which suggests that the tradition can in fact be dated as pre-Christian.[16] Whether or not Paul is intending to compare Christ with Isaac in terms of atoning sacrifice, it does seem likely that Paul is consciously alluding to the Abraham and Isaac story. Paul's phrase, "God did not spare (ἐφείσατο) his own Son" is very similar to Gen. 22:12[17] and 16[18] where God extols Abraham for not "sparing" (the same verb as is used in the LXX is used here) his much loved son.

Further evidence that the Abrahamic tradition is not far from Paul's thinking in this text comes from his argument in Romans 9, a passage which has traditionally been seen as a separate unit of thought but which may well be the inevitable response to Paul's argument in Rom. 8:17–39.[19] In Rom. 9:4, for example, Paul insists that to the people of Israel "belong the adoption, the glory, the covenants, the giving of the law, the worship, and *the promises.*" The Abrahamic tradition permeates Romans 9, with Paul in verse 7 echoing some of the language used in Romans 4: "not all of Abraham's children are his descendants; but 'It is through Isaac that descendants shall be named after you.'"

By itself, of course, this evidence for the Abrahamic tradition is not enough to demonstrate that the themes attached to κληρονομία in Romans 4 are similarly associated with the concept in Romans 8. But it should at least signal the prospect that the word may convey similar concepts in both contexts. To begin with, it raises the possibility that the idea of physical geography and this-worldly space, and the consequent political implications which are attached to this, might be included within Paul's use of inheritance in Romans 8.

In this chapter, therefore, I propose to explore this possibility. My intent is to show that the three occurrences of κληρονόμος in Rom. 8:17

---

[15] See Fitzmyer, *Romans*, 531–32; Moo, *The Epistle to the Romans*, 582.

[16] See for example G. Vermes, "New Light on the Sacrifice of Isaac from 4Q225," *JJS* 47 (1996): 140–46.

[17] καὶ εἶπεν μὴ ἐπιβάλῃς τὴν χεῖρά σου ἐπὶ τὸ παιδάριον μηδὲ ποιήσῃς αὐτῷ μηδέν νῦν γὰρ ἔγνων ὅτι φοβῇ τὸν θεὸν σὺ καὶ οὐκ ἐφείσω τοῦ υἱοῦ σου τοῦ ἀγαπητοῦ δι' ἐμέ.

[18] λέγων κατ' ἐμαυτοῦ ὤμοσα λέγει κύριος οὗ εἵνεκεν ἐποίησας τὸ ῥῆμα τοῦτο καὶ οὐκ ἐφείσω τοῦ υἱοῦ σου τοῦ ἀγαπητοῦ δι' ἐμέ.

[19] This will be argued in Chapter 5. See N. Elliott, *The Rhetoric of Romans. Argumentative Constraint and Strategy and Paul's Dialogue with Judaism*, JSNTSup 45 (Sheffield: JSOT Press, 1990), 261.

should be read as continuing the themes of the renewal of the physical earth and the reign of the people of God in this restored world.[20] The argument which will be advanced in this chapter is that instead of understanding Rom. 4:13–25 and 8:17–39 as separate and distinct expressions, they should be interpreted as two strands of the same fiber. Such a reading, I suggest, adds even greater force to the proposal that Paul's language of κληρονόμος and κληρονομία is contributing to a narrative which subverted the Roman imperial worldview disseminated by Nero.

Inheritance, creation and the children of God

At first glance, Paul's use of κληρονόμος in Rom. 8:17 could be considered to be as compressed as that in Rom. 4:13 and therefore as allegedly elusive. Just as Rom. 4:13–25 does not elaborate on the concept of κληρονομία, so the three occurrences of the word in Rom. 8:17 do not lend themselves to any sort of precise definition of the word, such as a detailed account of what it entails or how it might come about. But as was demonstrated with Rom. 4:13, brevity does not necessarily mean that the word is insignificant or inconsequential. Although in the verses following Rom. 8:17 Paul does not explicitly use the language of κληρονόμος or κληρονομία, it becomes apparent that the concept is at the forefront of his thinking and that the word dovetails with at least three other important ideas in this text: "glory," "creation" and "the children of God."

One of the most important observations to make when unpacking the meaning of inheritance in this context is its relationship to the concept of "glory." While the two words are not identical in Paul's thinking, it seems that he uses them almost synonymously in verse 17, where he begins with the concept of "heirs of God and joint heirs with Christ" and implies that

---

[20] Francis Lyall proposes that the concept of κληρονομία has its background in Roman law. F. Lyall, *Slaves, Citizens, Sons. Legal Metaphors in the Epistles* (Grand Rapids: Acadamie Books, Zondervan Publishing House, 1984), ch. 5. See, similarly, D. J. Williams, *Paul's Metaphors. Their Context and Character* (Peabody, MA: Hendrickson Publishers, 1999), 64–66. Such a suggestion does not challenge or weaken the conclusions of the present study – that the language is best explained with reference to an OT/Jewish background. While the term may have been understood as referring in some way to the system of Roman law, the question still remains as to what the content of this "inheritance" entails. For this it is necessary to turn to contextual clues. It seems clear, as the present chapter argues, that an OT background, in particular the story of Israel, informs Paul's argument at every turn. For a comprehensive case for an OT/Jewish background as more likely than a Greco-Roman background for a closely related Pauline word, "adoption," see J. M. Scott, *Adoption*.

this is only the case (one is only considered an heir) "if" (εἴπερ) one suffers "with him" (v. 17b).[21] The logic of the phrase means that Paul could conceivably have concluded the verse with: "if we suffer with him in order that we may also receive the inheritance." But instead of using the word "inheritance" at the end of the verse (after setting out the proviso of "suffering with Christ")[22] Paul instead writes of being "glorified with him." In other words, Paul seems to be using the terms "inheritance" and "glorified" interchangeably here. As Schreiner observes, "Suffering is the path to future glorification, and συνδοξασθῶμεν is *just another way* of describing the future inheritance of believers."[23] The synonymous nature of inheritance and glory has obvious importance for the present study. By tracing Paul's use of "glory" in the verses which follow, a word which is central to his purpose in 8:17–30, it is possible to understand more about inheritance.

Following the use of συνδοξασθῶμεν in verse 17 (a uniquely Pauline construction), the δόξα word group occurs three more times in Rom. 8:17–39. The two most important references for understanding inheritance are in verse 18, where Paul writes of the "glory (δόξαν) about to be revealed to us," and in verse 21, where Paul refers to creation which will obtain "the freedom of the glory of the children of God (τὴν ἐλευθερίαν τῆς δόξης τῶν τέκνων τοῦ θεοῦ)." It is not possible to arrive at a precise definition of "glory" in these references because such detail is not Paul's purpose here.[24]

Paul's use of the word in this context and elsewhere follows the general early Christian usage which is concerned with the basic nature of God and of heaven.[25] The "glory of God" refers to the splendor, beauty and power of God, with an abstract meaning of honor and worthiness and a concrete meaning of a fiery phenomenon which comes forth from radiance and brilliance.[26] Paul uses the word in Romans 8 in the context of describing the eschatological destiny of believers, and his point in broad terms is that this will be a time when humanity reflects the splendor and radiance

---

[21] εἴπερ here denotes a condition not yet fulfilled. In other words one is only considered an heir, *if one suffers*. R. W. Funk, *A Greek Grammar of the NT and Other Early Christian Literature*, rev. edn. (Cambridge University Press, 1961), 237.

[22] Witherington, *Romans*, 219.

[23] T. R. Schreiner, *Romans*, BECNT 6 (Grand Rapids: Baker Books, 1998); emphasis added, 428. Similarly N. T. Wright, "Romans," 594.

[24] Dunn, *Romans 1–8*, 468.

[25] Elsewhere, the goal of God's salvation is that humanity will experience and share in God's glory. For example, Rom. 2:7, 10; 5:2; 8:21; 9:23; 1 Cor. 2:7; 15:43; 2 Cor. 3:18; 4:17; Phil. 3:21; Col. 1:27; 3:4; 1 Thess. 2:12; 2 Thess. 2:14.

[26] Hegermann, "δόξα," in *EDNT* II (Grand Rapids: Eerdmans, 1993), 344–49.

of God and will therefore entail "a much different quality of existence"[27] than that which they currently experience. But as well as this more general sense, it is possible to identify two concepts (the "children of God" and "creation") which help to clarify the meaning of "glory" in this context and throw further light on the meaning of inheritance.

The underlying logic of Rom. 8:18–25 is that first "the children of God" will be liberated by God through Christ and that as a direct result of this freedom, "the creation" will in turn "be set free from its bondage to decay." In order to better understand this logic it will be helpful first to clarify one of the key terms here, namely κτίσις. The meaning of the word in this passage has been the focus of much debate.[28] Edward Adams' exploration of Paul's "cosmological language" helps to clarify the meaning of κτίσις in this text.[29] Adams points out that the three main options which have been proposed in the modern period of NT study are that κτίσις refers to (1) the unbelieving human world;[30] (2) unbelievers and the non-human creation;[31] or (3) the non-human creation.[32] Adams concludes that in this context the most likely meaning of κτίσις is "non-human creation."

To build his case for this reading, Adams first investigates the established usage of the term prior to Paul's appropriation of it. The common Jewish senses of the word are: "act of creation," "creature," "created universe," and "non-human creation." Since the meaning "act of creation" or "creature" are not possible within the context of 8:19–22, the only plausible, previously established, options are "non-human creation" and "created universe." Adams points out, however, that the broad sense of "created universe" (the whole creation embracing heaven, earth and every human being) is unlikely because in verses 22–23 believers are distinguished from the κτίσις. Paul states that "the whole creation (πᾶσα ἡ κτίσις) has been groaning" until now (v. 22), "and not only (οὐ μόνον δέ) the creation (κτίσις), but we ourselves (ἀλλὰ καὶ αὐτοὶ) (v. 23)." Of

---

[27] Dunn, *Romans 1–8*, 468.

[28] For the history of research see O. Christofferson, *The Earnest Expectation of the Creature: The Flood Tradition as Matrix of Romans 8:18–27*, Coniectanea Biblica 23 (Stockholm: Almqvist and Wiksell, 1990), 33–36.

[29] Adams, *Constructing the World*, 175–85.

[30] For example, J. G. Gager, "Functional Diversity in Paul's Use of End-Time Language," *JBL* 89 (1970): 325–37.

[31] For example, J. G. Gibbs, *Creation and Redemption: A Study in Pauline Theology*, NovTSup 26 (Leiden: Brill, 1971), 40; E. Käsemann, *Commentary on Romans*, 223; C. Hoegen-Rohls, "Ktisis and Kaine Ktisis in Paul's Letters," in *Paul, Luke and the Greco-Roman World*, ed. O. Christofferson *et al.*, JSNTSup 217 (Sheffield Academic Press, 2002), 114.

[32] For example, Byrne, *Romans*, 256; Adams, *Constructing the World*, 176.

the three main possibilities put forward for the meaning of κτίσις in this section, therefore, only "non-human creation" is an established sense prior to Paul's use of it.[33] This is not to say that the sense of "unbelieving humanity" or "believers together with the natural world" can be ruled out. But if Paul is using κτίσις in this way, it is a non-conventional use of the word. On this basis, Adams suggests that "lexical priority" should be given to "non-human creation" in this context.[34]

In addition to the established sense of the term, the logic of these verses renders unlikely the other two proposals put forward for κτίσις: "unbelievers" or "unbelievers and the non-human creation." In verse 19 Paul writes that κτίσις "waits with eager longing for the revealing of the children of God." As Adams points out, this seems an unlikely way for Paul to describe the present disposition of non-Christians. It is similarly improbable that Paul would go on to suggest (v. 20) that "unbelieving humanity" was "subjected to futility, not of its own will." Earlier in the epistle (Romans 3), for example, Paul insists on the culpability of all humans before God. Understanding κτίσις as referring to non-Christians or "unbelievers and the non-human creation" is therefore less likely and Adams' conclusion seems appropriate: "The linguistic evidence thus adds support to the consensus view that κτίσις in 8:19–22 denotes the 'non-human creation.' It is an established sense of the term (Wis. 2.6; 5.17; 16.24; 19.6); it fits the linguistic context; and it coheres with the traditions upon which it is generally accepted, Paul is drawing in these verses, especially the cursing of the earth in Gen. 3.17–19."[35]

It is therefore the fate of non-human creation which is so tightly inter-woven in Paul's thinking with "the children of God," so that the situation of one affects the experience of the other. This is clearest in verse 19, where he states that "creation waits with eager longing for the revealing of the children of God," and the thought is picked up again in verse 21 when he says that "creation itself will be set free from its bondage to decay and will obtain the glorious freedom of the glory of the children of God." In these two verses the future tense of the verb Paul uses in verse 21 "it will be freed" (ἐλευθερωθήσεται) connects closely with the phrase "revealing of the children of God" in verse 19, the implication being that creation's fate is closely tied to the fate of humanity.[36] It is likely that this concept is similarly being expressed through the use of a

---

[33] Adams, *Constructing the World*, 176.   [34] Ibid.

[35] Ibid., 177–78. Similarly Byrne, *Romans*, 256; Wilckens, *Rom 6–11*, 153.

[36] R. Jewett, "The Corruption and Redemption of Creation. Reading Rom 8:18–23 within the Imperial Context," in *Paul and the Roman Imperial Order*, ed. R. A. Horsley (Harrisburg, PA: Trinity Press International, 2004), 39.

collection of genitives following ἐλευθερωθήσεται in verse 21 (τῆς δόξης τῶν τέκνων τοῦ θεοῦ). While the first genitive in this group (τῆς δόξης) is often translated as a genitive of quality (i.e. "glorious freedom"),[37] it seems preferable to read it in a "loosely possessive sense,"[38] so that it is the freedom "which is associated with the glory of the children of God."[39] Likewise, the final two genitives in the phrase (τῶν τέκνων τοῦ θεοῦ) are genitives of possession, so that the idea being expressed is of the glory "that belongs to" the children, who in turn "belong to God."

This reading of the phrase rightly understands that for Paul the renewal of creation is tied up with the transformation of the children of God – that the healing of creation is contingent upon the restoration of believers. As Byrne puts it, for Paul, "because human beings were created along with the non-human created world and given responsibility for that world, they share a common fate with that world. When the situation of human beings deteriorates, so does that of the rest of creation, and, vice versa, when it goes well, the creation shares in the blessing."[40] The second of these scenarios (when humanity positively affect creation) appears in certain prophetic texts. For example Isa. 11:6–9:

> (6) The wolf shall live with the lamb,
> the leopard shall lie down with the kid,
> the calf and the lion and the fatling together,
> and a little child shall lead them.
> (7) The cow and the bear shall graze,
> their young shall lie down together;
> and the lion shall eat straw like the ox.
> (8) The nursing child shall play over
> the hole of the asp,
> and the weaned child shall put
> its hand on the adder's den.
> (9) They will not hurt or destroy
> on all my holy mountain;
> for the earth will be full of the
> knowledge of the LORD
> as the waters cover the sea.

[37] For example KJV, NIV, RSV.

[38] Moo, *The Epistle to the Romans*, 554; Similarly Byrne, *Romans*, 255–61.

[39] Byrne, *Romans*, 261. Cf. The TNIV translation: "the freedom and glory of the children of God."

[40] Byrne, "Creation Groaning," 197. N. T. Wright, "Romans," 597. Similarly Jewett, "The Corruption and Redemption of Creation," 35–36.

Similarly Isa. 43:19–21:

> (19) I am about to do a new thing;
> now it springs forth, do you not perceive it?
> I will make a way in the wilderness
> and rivers in the desert.
> (20) The wild animals will honor me;
> the jackals and the ostriches;
> for I give water in the wilderness,
> rivers in the desert,
> to give drink to my chosen people,
> (21) the people whom I formed for myself
> so that they might declare my praise.[41]

Understanding why Paul makes this connection between κτίσις and the children of God takes us to the heart of κληρονόμος in Romans 8. In expressing this union, Paul is presupposing a Jewish tradition which understands non-human creation to be closely bound up with the fate of humanity: what Brendan Byrne refers to as "the common fate principle."[42] The tradition can be traced back to the Genesis narrative, in particular the story of Adam, of his intended role of displaying the image of God through his care of creation and of his sin and the consequences which this disobedience had upon the garden.[43] The allusion is particularly evident in verse 20, where Paul says that "the creation was subjected to futility (ματαιότητι)." This is most probably a reference to Gen. 3:17–19, where Adam and the earth are cursed because of Adam's sin.[44] Paul says that creation was subjected "to futility (ματαιότητι)," a word which carries the sense of "emptiness, futility, purposelessness, transitoriness"[45] – "the futility of an object which does not function as it was designed to do . . . or, more precisely, which has been given a role for which it was not designed and which is unreal or illusory."[46] Paul's point is that because of Adam's sin, the original purpose of creation, which was to be a place for the human glorification of God, was frustrated. Whereas in Romans 1 Paul described humanity as making creatures the

---

[41] See also Isa. 55:12–13; cf. Ps. 114; Ezek. 34:25–31; Hos. 2:18; Zech. 8:12.

[42] Byrne, *Romans*, 256. See also Byrne, "Creation Groaning."

[43] Paul's allusion to the Adam narrative is commonly recognized. See, for example, Wilckens, *Rom 6–11*, 154; Keesmaat, *Paul and His Story*, 103.

[44] Fitzmyer, *Romans*, 508.   [45] ματαιότης, BAGD, 495.

[46] Dunn, *Romans 1–8*, 470. See also Jewett, "The Corruption and Redemption of Creation," 36.

objects of worship and reverence, "exchanging the glory of God" for the "images" of mortal things (1:23), in Romans 8 he conceives of humanity as experiencing God's redemption which leads to the restoration of creation. "So what the creation awaits with eager longing is the emergence of this triumph of divine righteousness (cf. Rom. 1:17) which will begin to restore a rightful balance to the creation, overcoming the Adamic legacy of corruption and disorder that fell as a calamitous curse upon the ground (Gen. 3:17–19)."[47] Paul believes that through Christ God has redeemed humanity and therefore creation also will experience liberation. In Rom. 8:17 Paul writes that those who are children of God are also "heirs of God" and "joint heirs with Christ." The relationship between Christ and believers is essential for Paul because those who "suffer with Christ" will also "be glorified with him."

In light of this survey of κτίσις, δόξα and τῶν τέκνων τοῦ θεοῦ, the specific meaning of "glory" becomes clearer. When Paul uses the word "glory" in this context (vv. 18, 21, 30), it carries the usual sense of God's radiance and brilliance but it is applied particularly to "the whole creation" (πᾶσα ἡ κτίσις, v. 22) which will be liberated by God. While Paul does not elaborate on exactly what this liberation means, it is clear that there is a continuity in his mind between the present creation and the creation which will be renewed. According to Paul it is "the creation itself" (καὶ αὐτοὶ ἐν ἑαυτοῖς) – the use of καί with αὐτοί emphasizing the point[48] – which will be set free from its slavery and bondage. In other words, *this* creation will not pass away or be followed by another creation but will be redeemed and renewed.[49] For Paul, nature is included in the redemptive process.[50] Creation is not to be "redeemed *from*" but is to be "redeemed" in *continuity with* its present form.[51] Paul's words "point unambiguously to the restoration of the present creation. This creation will be freed from its present, but temporary, subdued and enslaved condition so that it may at last fulfil the purpose for which it was made."[52] Before this can happen, however, humanity must first be liberated by God through Christ (v. 17). There is therefore an inseparable

---

[47] Jewett, "The Corruption and Redemption of Creation," 35–36. Similarly Byrne, *Romans*, 258.

[48] Dunn, *Romans 1–8*, 471.   [49] Gibbs, *Creation and Redemption*, 44.

[50] Jewett, "The Corruption and Redemption of Creation," 38. As Jewett notes, this renders implausible Barrett's comment that Paul "is not concerned with creation for its own sake"; Barrett, *The Epistle to the Romans*, 165.

[51] Dunn, *Romans 1–8*, 471.

[52] Adams, *Constructing the World*, 182. J. C. Beker, "Vision of Hope for a Suffering World: Romans 8:17–30," *The Princeton Seminary Bulletin* 3 (1994): 29.

connection in Paul's mind between redeemed humanity and liberated creation.

All of this offers insights into the meaning of "heirs of God (κληρονόμοι μὲν θεοῦ)" in Rom. 8:17. Given the nature of Paul's argument and language in Romans 8, it is not possible to arrive at a precise definition of κληρονόμος. But much can be deduced from the discussion above of κτίσις, δόξα and τῶν τέκνων τοῦ θεοῦ ("children of God"). Most important, as noted above, is the fact that Paul uses the word "glorified" almost synonymously with κληρονόμος in verse 17. As was observed, the content of "glory" is then explicated in the verses which follow.[53] "Glory," for Paul, includes the reflection of God's radiance, splendor and power through the redemption of κτίσις, the cosmic and this-worldly renewal of all things. For Paul, the whole earth will display God's glory when the children of God are set free and the whole of creation is healed. This is what Paul means by "glory" and, given the almost synonymous use of the two words in 8:17, it seems likely that this is similarly what Paul refers to when he uses the phrase κληρονόμοι μὲν θεοῦ.[54] While some interpreters suggest that θεοῦ here should be understood as the *object* of κληρονόμοι, so that God's very self is what is inherited[55] the phrase is better read as a *source* or *subjective* genitive.[56] In other words, the idea expressed is that of believers who inherit the promises of God: God is the *bestower* of the inheritance rather than the inheritance itself. When creation experiences liberation, when the people of God are redeemed and therefore ruling wisely, there will be a return to the originally intended glory of creation and humanity together, an environment which reflects God's own glory. It is this that the heirs of God will inherit; it is this that constitutes κληρονόμος in 8:17.[57]

---

[53] Robert C. Tannehill, *Dying and Rising with Christ. A Study in Pauline Theology* (Berlin: Alfred Töpelmann, 1967), 110.

[54] Keesmaat, *Paul and His Story*, 111.

[55] So, for example, J. Murray, *The Epistle to the Romans: The English Text with Introduction, Exposition and Notes*, NICNT (Grand Rapids: Eerdmans, 1968), 298–99; Cranfield, *A Critical and Exegetical Commentary on the Epistle to the Romans*, 407.

[56] Moo, *The Epistle to the Romans*, 541.

[57] Brueggemann, *The Land*, 178. Crucially, as Wright points out, part of the meaning of "glory" in this text – "the glory that has been promised to all God's children in Christ – is precisely that they are to receive this inheritance ..."; N. T. Wright, "Romans," 597. Keesmaat has argued for an exodus background for these verses. The exodus was, of course, one of the ways in which the promise to Abraham was fulfilled (the various texts that refer to Israelites entering the land often add "as promised to Abraham, Isaac and Jacob"), and the land itself, goal of the exodus event, was the inheritance promised. This adds support to what has been argued above.

Once more, by understanding κληρονόμος in this fashion, its subversive nature becomes apparent. This concept was unmistakably political in the sense that it subverted the claims of Nero and Claudius and of the emperors who proceeded them. These emperors, as has been shown previously, were claiming that the redemption of the world was a present political achievement. Paul, instead, talks of "inheritance" which will be "of God" and will come about "with Christ." Furthermore, it is a renewal which, while worked towards in the present, is mostly yet to happen. The eschatological nature of κληρονόμος and its associated concepts is unmistakable. Paul's emphasis is clearly on redemption as a future hope rather than present reality. Again it may be that Paul is echoing those earlier Jewish sources which envisaged a time when the glory which Israel had lost would be restored in the day of God's salvation.[58] This language of restoration is particularly striking in the Qumran Scrolls, where it is connected directly with the glory of Adam. "And all the glory of Adam shall be theirs" (1QS 4.22–23; CD 3.19–20); "Thou wilt keep thine oath and wilt pardon their transgressions; thou wilt cast away all their sins. Thou wilt cause them to inherit all the glory of Adam and abundance of days" (1QH 17.14–15; 4QpPS 37 3.1–2); Sir. 4.13 envisages that those who follow the path of wisdom will inherit glory. Similarly in 1 *Enoch* 90.37–38 there is a transformation of humanity so that it reflects the glory of Adam.[59]

Far from the emperors bringing about bliss to the natural world, Paul claims that creation has been "subjected to futility" (ματαιότητι), a word used in Rom. 1.20 and which is drawn from a biblical tradition that in part refers to the abuse of the natural world by Adam and his descendants. As Robert Jewett observes,

> Paul's audience would have thought about how imperial ambitions, military conflicts, and economic exploitation had led to the erosion of the natural environment throughout the Mediterranean world, leaving ruined cities, depleted fields, deforested mountains, and polluted streams as evidence of this universal vanity. That such vanity in the form of the pax Romana had promised the restoration of the age of Saturn appears utterly preposterous in the light of this critical biblical tradition.[60]

[58] See for example Isa. 61:3. Also 46:13; 60:29; 2 *Bar.* 15:8; 50:48, 49; 51:1–6; *4 Ezra* 7:60, 95.

[59] Keesmaat, *Paul and His Story*, 87.

[60] Jewett, "The Corruption and Redemption of Creation," 37. Similarly, Horsley, "Paul and Slavery," 175.

In other words, as in Rom. 4:13–25, in Rom. 8:17–30 Paul is again nurturing a worldview for his audience which would inevitably clash with the one being put forward by Nero.[61]

Inheritance and universal sovereignty

The reading of κληρονόμος advanced above is, however, not always how the word is understood. Partly because the imperial context has not been acknowledged and partly because the this-worldly nature of the language has been neglected or underplayed, the concept has tended to be understood in terms of the individual and in relation to the "spiritual" dimension. The discussion above has demonstrated, however, that the concept suggests a claim to the future universal sovereignty of the people of God.

This is reinforced when the phrase "joint heirs with Christ" (8:17) is situated within the wider context of 8:17–39. Elsewhere Paul can refer to the risen Christ as the "Last Adam" (1 Cor. 15:45) and the one who is "above every name" in heaven and on earth, the Christ who is "Lord" (Phil. 2:9–11).[62] In these instances it is Christ's lordship which enables believers to receive the benefits of salvation. In 1 Cor. 3:21b–23, for example, Paul expresses the idea that by virtue of believers belonging "to Christ," then "all things" belong to the Christians at Corinth, including "life or death or the present or the future." One of the implications of being united with Christ, the "Last Adam" and "the Lord," is that believers participate in the lordship of the universe, God's original design for humanity, which was set out in Gen. 1:26–28 and developed in subsequent Jewish tradition. The relationship is particularly clear in Gal. 3:29, where Paul expresses it in terms of the promised inheritance: "And if you belong to Christ, then you are Abraham's offspring, heirs according to the promise."

To what degree is this idea being expressed in verse 17 through the phrase "joint heirs with Christ" (συγκληρονόμοι δὲ Χριστοῦ)? While the universal sovereignty aspect of this verse is not immediately apparent, there is embedded within the phrase an idea which appears later in the passage in more explicit fashion. In verse 32 Paul writes: "He who did not withhold his own Son, but gave him up for all of us, will he not with

---

[61] Horsley, "Paul and Slavery," 164.
[62] Byrne, *Romans*, 253. For the ways in which this claim can be understood as a comparison with the emperor Nero, see particularly P. Oakes, *Philippians. From People to Letter*, SNTSMS 110 (Cambridge University Press, 2001) 147–74.

him also give us everything else (τὰ πάντα)?" To what degree could it be the case that τὰ πάντα here is meant to denote the idea of universal sovereignty – that giving us "all things" or "everything else" "with him" [Christ] includes the eventual reign of Christ over the earth?

Some interpreters do not understand such connotations to be present in the phrase τὰ πάντα. For example, Cranfield suggests that although a comparison with 1 Cor. 3:21–23 might indicate that verse 32 involves "giving a share in Christ's lordship over the universe" and although verse 17 could be used to support this view, "it seems more probable that 'all things' should be understood as denoting the fullness of salvation (cf. 5.10) or else 'all that is necessary for our salvation.'"[63] In a similar way Leon Morris recognizes the connection between τὰ πάντα and verse 17's "joint heirs with Christ" but concludes that the better understanding of this phrase is "all things connected with salvation."[64]

While these interpreters understand τὰ πάντα in terms of salvation, usually individual and spiritual, there are good reasons for interpreting it more concretely as referring to "the universe."[65] For example, in the list which follows (vv. 35–39) there is a similar universal scope to Paul's argument – the sovereign reign of Christ is described as including ruler-ship over "'death' . . . 'life' . . . 'angels' . . . 'rulers' . . . 'powers' . . . 'all creation.'"[66] This, together with the Adam christology which is threaded throughout verses 18–30, makes it likely that τὰ πάντα in verse 32 denotes the rule of Christ over the universe and that the phrase is there-fore best read in conjunction with Rom. 4:13 and 8:17.[67] Certainly the phrase often has this sense in Paul.[68] The clearest example of this is in 1 Cor. 3:21–23, where Paul assures the Corinthian Christians that "all things are yours" (21b).[69]

A closely related phrase and one which reinforces this reading of τὰ πάντα is found in Rom. 8:29c: "in order that he might be the *first-born* (πρωτότοκον) within a large family." What makes this particularly

---

[63] Cranfield, *A Critical and Exegetical Commentary on the Epistle to the Romans*, 437. Quotation from W. Sanday and A. C. Headlam, *A Critical and Exegetical Commentary on the Epistle to the Romans*, ICC, 5th edn. (Edinburgh: T. & T. Clark, 1902), 219.

[64] Morris, *The Epistle to the Romans*, 336. Similarly Witherington, *Romans*, 232.

[65] J. M. Scott, *Adoption*, 251–54. S. K. Williams, "The *Promise* in Galatians," 718; Wilckens, *Rom 6–11*, 173–74.

[66] Byrne, *Romans*, 275. Similarly Wilckens, *Rom 6–11*, 177 n. 800.

[67] S. K. Williams, "The *Promise* in Galatians," 718. Cf. also 1 Cor. 15:27; Phil. 3:21; Eph. 1:22.

[68] See, for example, Rom. 11:36; 1 Cor. 8:6; 11:12; 15:27–28; Phil. 3:21; Col. 1:16–17, 20; Eph. 1:10–11, 23; 3:9; 4:10.

[69] Byrne, *Romans*, 275.

relevant to an understanding of inheritance is the phrase which immediately precedes it, where Paul refers to those who are "to be conformed (συμμόρφους) to the image of his Son" (29b). It is likely that the term συμμόρφους which "harks back to the earlier flurry"[70] of συν compounds in 8:17, is meant to recall the phrase "joint heirs with Christ (συγκληρονόμοι δὲ Χριστοῦ)." Not only do both sections of the passage refer to "glorification," but the way in which it is referred to is similar, with both explaining it, using συν formulations, as a participation in Christ's glory.[71] Given the understanding of "glory" in 8:17 argued above, it is likely that the term "firstborn (πρωτότοκον)," which follows it, should be read against the background of Ps. 89:27, where the psalmist writes: "I will make him the firstborn, the highest of the kings of the earth."[72] In this psalm God promises the messiah that he will be made the firstborn son of God, which means that the messiah will be foremost among other rulers and kings of the earth. It is highly likely that Paul's words in 8:29c are an allusion to this messianic psalm. But as well as emphasizing Christ's universal sovereignty the verse is referring to the status which believers now have by virtue of their relationship with Christ. Christ is the first-born "within a large family (πολλοῖς ἀδελφοῖς)." This suggests that in the process of being conformed to Christ believers become "brothers and sisters" of God's Son, a relationship which means the people of God participate in Christ's reign over creation.[73] The thought here is of "the resurrected Christ as the pattern of the new humanity of the last age, the firstborn (of the dead) of a new race of eschatological people in whom God's design from the beginning of creation is at last fulfilled."[74]

Such an understanding would certainly fit well with Rom. 8:34, where Christ Jesus is the one "who was raised, who is at the right hand of God." This verse, perhaps echoing the vision of Ps. 110:1, looks forward to a time when the messiah will reign with God until God has put all enemies under his feet (cf. 1 Cor. 15:25).[75] Together, these two phrases – "firstborn within a large family" (8:29c) and "at the right hand of God" (8:34) – contribute to the concept of Christ's universal sovereignty. Paul's point is that Christ, as the Messiah, reigns over the cosmos. "The messianic Son of God is heir to the Abrahamic promise of universal sovereignty, because, just as in Gal. 3–4, the 'seed' of David (Rom. 1.3)

---

[70] Dunn, *Romans 1–8*, 485.   [71] Tannehill, *Dying and Rising*, 110.
[72] Moo, *The Epistle to the Romans*, 535 n. 158.
[73] J. M. Scott, *Adoption*, 255; Byrne, *Romans*, 273.   [74] Dunn, *Romans 1–8*, 483.
[75] J. M. Scott, *Adoption*, 253–54.

fulfills the Abrahamic promise (Gen. 15.18) and the Davidic promise (2 Sam. 7.12, 14)."[76]

There are therefore close lexical and thematic connections between "joint heirs with Christ" (v. 17) and certain phrases in the verses which follow (vv. 18–39): "everything" (τὰ πάντα, v. 32); "firstborn within a large family" (v. 29); and "at the right hand of God" (v. 34). Each of these phrases offers insights into how "joint heirs with Christ (συγκληρονόμοι δὲ Χριστοῦ)" should be interpreted, suggesting that it is intended to convey the idea of universal sovereignty which believers will share with the Son.[77] As Dunn concludes, what seems to be envisaged "is a sharing in Christ's lordship (Ps. 110:1 alluded to in v. 34) over 'the all' (Ps. 8:6 being regularly merged with Ps. 110:1 in earliest Christian thought); Christ again being understood as the one who fulfills God's mandate for man (Ps. 8:6) but precisely as the head of a new humanity who share his sonship and his devolved authority."[78] This is not to say that the contextual links between 8:17 and verses 29, 32 and 34 are always given the weight they deserve. As noted previously, for example, P. Hammer proposes that in 8:17 Christ is both the means and the end of "inheritance," both the "heir" and the "inheritance" itself. The result of this reading is that there is no thought of believers and their future reign with Christ. In proposing such a reading, Hammer is perhaps following the pattern of the genitive with συγκληρονόμοι elsewhere in the New Testament, which indicates *what* one inherits.[79] But this pattern is not evident in Rom. 8:17, because συγκληρονόμοι δὲ Χριστοῦ is expressed as a deliberate parallel to κληρονόμοι μὲν θεοῦ and also as a parallel to τέκνα θεοῦ. As discussed above, it is clear that τέκνα θεοῦ expresses the concept of the relationship of believers to God. This suggests that all three of these phrases are to be taken as genitives of relationship or possession and, most importantly for the present study, συγκληρονόμοι δὲ Χριστοῦ should be read as "joint heirs" or "fellow heirs" *with* Christ, rather than *of* Christ.[80]

One of the strengths of this reading is that it is entirely in keeping with the distinction Paul makes between the inheritance itself and Christ as the means by which people inherit.[81] Also, as Hester observes in his study of

---

[76] Ibid., 254. For a discussion of how Paul develops this theme in Rom. 11.29 see O. Betz, *Jesus und das Danielbuch, vol. I.i: Die Menschensohnworte Jesu und die Ziekunftserwartung des Paulus (Daniel 7, 13–14)* (Frankfurt: Peter Lang, 1985), 168–69.

[77] J. M. Scott, *Adoption*; Stuhlmacher, *Romans*, 139.   [78] Dunn, *Romans 1–8*, 502.

[79] Cf. Eph. 3:6; Heb. 11:9; 1 Pet. 3:7. Tannehill, *Dying and Rising*, 112. In this it follows the pattern of the genitive with κληρονός: Rom. 4:13; Heb. 1:2; 6:17; 11:7; James 2:5.

[80] Tannehill, *Dying and Rising*, 112.

[81] Hester, *Paul's Concept of Inheritance*, 65 n. 1.

inheritance in Paul, one of the most significant features of the concept in the New Testament is the connection between "sonship" and "heirship" and the claim that these are grounded in the person and work of Christ.[82] The phrase συγκληρονόμοι δὲ Χριστοῦ in Rom. 8:17 is continuing this line of thinking and in doing so seems to be similarly following the less compressed argument of Gal. 3:26 – 4:7. In both of these texts there is the language of "sonship" and "inheritance." In both passages the Spirit is the one who witnesses to believers being "sons" and "heirs." Most importantly, "in both cases being son and heir means sharing in the status of Christ, who is the *one* seed and heir."[83] It is this concept of "sharing in the status of Christ" which gets to the heart of Paul's use of the phrase in Rom. 8:17. The expression συγκληρονόμοι δὲ Χριστοῦ, like Galatians 3–4 and like the subsequent phrases in Rom. 8:18–30, is describing the close relationship which Paul understands there to be between Christ as reigning Lord and the believers at Rome as the heirs of Christ. Those who are "in Christ" (8:1) and are "conformed to the image of his Son" (29b) and are "heirs with Christ" are the ones who will one day "inherit the world" (4:13) and have dominion over it, as was originally intended (8:29, 32, 34, 37–39).[84] To be an heir with Christ is to participate in his divine sonship and his Abrahamic heirship. As Käsemann puts it: "The heir of God is he who participates in his rule, as in 5:17. One can do this only as a co-heir with Christ, the future cosmocrator, who as the exalted one already rules in a hidden way."[85]

Inheritance and suffering conquerors

There are therefore significant continuities between the concepts of κληρονόμος in Rom. 4:13 and the ways in which it is used in Romans 8. Both contexts suggest that Paul uses the language of κληρονόμος (and the implied κληρονομία) to refer to the time when those "in Christ" will take possession of a renewed earth and will reign with Christ over the world. It is important, however, to point out once more that there would probably have been a degree of cognitive dissonance for the communities in Rome who heard Paul's vision for the future.[86] Although they may well have understood what was *intended* for God's people in the future,

---

[82] Ibid., 38.   [83] Tannehill, *Dying and Rising*, 114.

[84] J. M. Scott, *Adoption*, 254.

[85] Käsemann, *Commentary on Romans*, 229. Also Schreiner, *Romans*, 454.

[86] Elliott notes a similar cognitive dissonance which Paul may have experienced: the belief that God was sovereign in heaven alongside the knowledge that Rome ruled the earth; N. Elliott, *Liberating Paul*, 125.

this would not have been what they were *currently experiencing.* Paul is encouraging these communities to think of themselves as "heirs of the world," but there was considerable evidence to the contrary for those who lived in the heart of the Roman Empire. The future expectation of a restored earth was far from the present experience of the Christians at Rome.

One of the first indications (in this text) that the Christians at Rome may have been experiencing persecution is Paul's use of the word "sufferings" (παθήματα) in verses 17–18, a concept which then undergirds much of his subsequent argument (vv. 19–39).[87] He writes that believers must "suffer" with Christ (συμπάσχομεν, v. 17) in order to be glorified with him and that he considers "the sufferings" of the present time to be nothing compared with the glory which will follow (v. 18). Using language which seems to continue this theme of suffering, Paul also refers to the "groaning" (συστενάζει) of creation (v. 22) and of believers (v. 23) and even to the groaning of God's Spirit (v. 26).

As well as the language which expresses more general experiences of suffering there is the use of language which seems specifically to refer to "persecution." In 8:26, for example, Paul writes, "Likewise the Spirit helps us in our weakness (ἀσθενείᾳ)." Michael Barre argues, based on his examination of the LXX and Intertestamental usage of ἀσθενεία, that Paul uses ἀσθενεία here to refer to "persecutions" which are experienced by the believer as part of the "eschatological ordeal."[88] In the LXX ἀσθενεία is used to translate the Hebrew word for "stumble." In Intertestamental literature, this stumbling happens against the backdrop of the eschatological ordeal which brings persecution.[89] In his discussion of 2 Cor. 11:29 Barre suggests that Paul understands his own suffering in the context of an eschatological trial. Barre concludes that when Paul uses ἀσθενεία, he is referring to "concrete events, specifically events in which one is the object of hostility, not merely the ways in which one lacks strength."[90] It is likely that in Rom. 8:26 Paul is using ἀσθενείᾳ in a similar way: not meaning "weakness" in a broad and undefined way,[91] but more specifically the stumblings which believers experience as a consequence of

---

[87]   Keesmaat contends that suffering could be considered the centre of the whole passage. Keesmaat, *Paul and His Story,* 89. See further Pesch, *Römerbrief,* 71.

[88]   M. Barre, "Paul as 'Eschatological Person': A New Look at 2 Cor 11:29," *CBQ* 37 (1975): 510–12.

[89]   See 1QS 3:21–24 and the Theodotionic recension of Dan. 11:33–35; 12:10. Keesmaat, *Paul and His Story,* 120–21.

[90]   Barre, "Paul as 'Eschatological Person,'" 512.

[91]   Dunn, *Romans 1–8,* 477; G. Fee, *God's Empowering Presence. The Holy Spirit in the Letters of Paul* (Peabody, MA: Hendrickson Publishers, 1994), 578.

persecution, all of which are a part of the ordeals of the eschatological age.[92]

This way of interpreting ἀσθενεία certainly fits well with the list of trials in verses 35–39. In particular Paul's references to "hardship" (θλῖψις), "distress" (στενοχωρία), "persecution" (διωγμός), "peril" (κίνδυνος) and "sword" (μάχαιρα) (v. 35), as well as "death," "rulers" and "powers" (v. 38) suggest a context of persecution. Käsemann points out that μάχαιρα may refer concretely to execution: the citation (v. 36) which follows μάχαιρα was often used by the rabbis to refer to the martyrdom of the pious.[93] John S. Pobee's study of *Persecution and Martyrdom in the Theology of Paul* similarly seems to back up this reading. Pobee points out that πάσχειν, as used in 8:17, often has martyrological overtones in Paul's writings and in the rest of the New Testament. Given Paul's subsequent trial list in verse 35, it therefore seems likely that these verses were written against the backdrop of persecution and suffering, whether this had actually occurred, or was expected to happen in the future.[94]

Paul's use of "groaning" (συστενάζει), mentioned above, has similar overtones of persecution, especially when its OT roots are acknowledged. Time and again in the Old Testament God is said to have intervened on behalf of Israel because he has heard their groaning. The most common reason for the language of groaning in these texts is a situation of oppression: the people groaning under the weight of oppressive circumstances. Commonly this oppression was a consequence of living under the rule of a foreign empire. As Keesmaat points out, "This language of groaning originated in Israel's first experience of empire, and was repeatedly used when Israel found herself suffering under imperial control during her history."[95] It is likely that in using the language of "groaning" Paul therefore is echoing this idea of calling out to God in the midst of the oppression of the Roman Empire.

Historical evidence may confirm this proposal. It is quite possible that the Christians to whom Paul is writing had already experienced persecution in the form of harassment and deportation through the Claudian Edict.[96] Claudius expelled the Jews from Rome because of disturbances

---

[92] Keesmaat, *Paul and His Story*, 122.

[93] Käsemann, *Commentary on Romans*, 249. Similarly John. S. Pobee, *Persecution and Martyrdom in the Theology of Paul*, JSNTSup 6 (Sheffield: JSOT Press, 1985), 5.

[94] Pobee, *Persecution*, 112.

[95] S. C. Keesmaat, "The Psalms in Romans and Galatians," in *The Psalms in the New Testament*, ed. S. Moyise and M. Menkes (Edinburgh: T. & T. Clark, 2004), 149.

[96] Jewett, "The Corruption and Redemption of Creation," 32.

"at the instigation of *Chrestus*,"[97] according to Suetonius (*Claud.* 25). However, Suetonius gives no date for this event, and it needs to be acknowledged that there is no consensus on the reason for this expulsion or the nature of it or of the year in which the expulsion occurred.[98] Cassius Dio (*Hist.* 60.6.6) states that Claudius did not expel the Jews but that he ordered them not to hold meetings. Claudius' order is dated in 41 CE. A third piece of evidence comes from Acts 18:2, where Aquila and Priscilla are recorded as recently coming to Corinth from Italy "because Claudius had ordered all Jews to leave Rome." Although there are problems with the historical reliability of this Acts description the date of the expulsion from Rome is estimated to be around 49 CE.[99]

The evidence therefore sometimes appears contradictory. But we can piece together a possible scenario of persecution which the early Roman Christians suffered at the hands of the Empire. The most probable scenario is that Claudius, in 41 CE, acted to repress the Jews in Rome (in the form of a ban on synagogue gatherings) and that at the later date of 49 CE he expelled some Christian Jews from the city.[100] Thus, although there is not a consensus as to how many Jews were expelled from Rome in 49 CE, it seems clear that the Jews were on the receiving end of an edict at that time and that they were therefore subjected to the power of the imperial authorities.[101] If nothing else, Claudius' actions emphasize the insecurity of the political status of Jewish Christians in Rome.[102] It is possible that the Jewish exiles returning to Rome (after the ban had lapsed) had previously suffered the confiscation of their property and now faced restrictions on gathering together, homelessness, and the difficulty of obtaining kosher food.[103]

---

[97] *Iudaeos impulsore Chresto assidue tumultuantis Roma expulit.* As Adams points out, "It is generally accepted that *Chrestus* is a misspelt reference to Christ"; Adams, *Constructing the World*, 196. See similarly Lampe, *From Paul to Valentinus*, 11–16. Note however S. Benko, "The Edict of Claudius of AD 49 and the Instigator Chrestus," *Theologische Zeitschrift* 25 (1969): 406–18.

[98] J. M. G. Barclay, *Jews in the Mediterranean Diaspora. From Alexander to Trajan (323 BCE–117 CE)* (Edinburgh: T. & T. Clark, 1996), 303–306.

[99] Ibid., 303.

[100] So, for example, F. F. Bruce, "Christianity under Claudius," *BJRL* 44 (1961); A. Momigliano, *The Emperor Claudius and His Achievement*, rev. edn. (Oxford University Press, 1961). Also, tentatively, Barclay, *Jews in the Mediterranean Diaspora*, 305.

[101] Keesmaat, "Psalms in Romans," 151; B. Abasciano, *Paul's Use of the Old Testament in Romans 9:1–9. An Intertextual and Theological Exegesis*, Library of New Testament Studies 301 (London: T. & T. Clark, 2005), 27–28. Adams suggests that it is more likely that only those most directly involved in the disturbances were ejected; Adams, *Constructing the World*, 196.

[102] Barclay, *Jews in the Mediterranean Diaspora*, 306.

[103] N. Elliott, *The Rhetoric of Romans*, 51–55.

Given the oppressive circumstances of the Christians at Rome, it is not surprising to find that there are elements of the lament tradition evident in Rom. 8:14–39. Sylvia Keesmaat advances this possibility, arguing that while Paul does not necessarily employ the *specifics* of lament technique, it is likely that Paul is describing the *process* of lament.[104] For example, one of the formal characteristics of lament in the Old Testament is that of invocation, a crying out to God. That Paul may be encouraging the believers at Rome similarly to cry out to God is suggested in Rom. 8:15 when he says that we cry "Abba! Father!" Likewise, in verse 26 the language of prayer seems to suggest that God is the one for whom our cries are intended. A second element common to the lament tradition is that of appeal. The concern of the lament is not only to describe suffering but also to pray for its removal or alleviation. This certainly seems to be the intent of Paul's words when he describes the groaning of believers and creation. His concern is not only to describe a situation of suffering but to encourage believers to eagerly expect its removal (vv. 19, 23, 25). This passage is permeated with the hope that the experience of the present will not be permanent because creation and the children of God will one day be redeemed. Finally, just as the lament tradition in Israel's scriptures often concludes with a song of thanksgiving, so it is possible to read Rom. 8:28–39 as Paul's celebration that all things will one day be transformed. For Paul there is an assurance that in the face of death and persecution, there can be life and love. Overall, therefore, Paul follows the process and dynamic of the lament tradition by moving from pain to praise, from despair to hope.[105]

One of the metaphors used by Paul which is indicative of the lament process is that of "labor pains" or "travail": he says that the whole creation "has been groaning in labor pains until now" (v. 22). In using this language, Paul seems to be drawing on two interrelated traditions from Israel's scriptures. First, there is a direct verbal connection between "labor pains" and the Genesis 3 passage which likely underlies this text. In Gen. 3:16 Eve is told by God that her pains and groaning in childbirth will increase. Paul echoes this tradition and in doing so adds depth to his description of the creation which suffers in bondage.[106] The second "travail" tradition which Paul seems to be echoing is those texts in the Old Testament and in later Jewish sources which use the word in an eschatological sense. In these the language of "travail" is connected with

---

[104] Keesmaat, *Paul and His Story*, 26–28.   [105] Ibid., 127.
[106] Ibid., 18. Similarly D. T. Tsumura "An OT Background to Rom 8:22," *NTS* 40 (1994): 620–21.

the day of the Lord's judgment or salvation. For example, in Isa. 13:8 those who experience Yahweh's judgment on Babylon are said to be "in anguish like a woman in labor." Similarly, the destruction of Moab in Jer. 48:41 is described using the language of "the heart of a woman in labor."[107] Often when this imagery is used to describe the punishment which will be experienced, it is followed by a promise of renewal and restoration: "they [the whole earth] break forth into singing. I The cypresses exult over you, I the cedars of Lebanon, saying I 'Since you were laid low, I no one comes to chop us down'" (Isa. 14:7, 8).[108] In Jewish apocalyptic literature, the imagery is often associated with the coming of God's kingdom and the new age; the language is a call for liberation, and therefore hope, in the midst of oppressive rulership.[109] Paul echoes both of these traditions when he describes creation as experiencing the pains of childbirth. He is not only echoing the language of the curse but also drawing from language which was associated with God's act of liberating Israel from bondage and oppression, ideas which often carried notes of hope and optimism, especially for those suffering persecution in the midst of empire.[110]

But how would the Christians at Rome have understood such language, especially when heard in conjunction with the bold language of inheritance? On the one hand, they seem to have been experiencing persecution at the hands of the Roman Empire, but at the same time Paul is reminding them that they are heirs of "the world" and "joint heirs" with the sovereign Christ. In the midst of such dissonance Paul echoes a lament tradition and the language of "travail," all of which would have brought to mind for his audience thoughts of overthrowing one's enemies or petitioning God to alter the present situation, often through violent and cataclysmic means. Similar to many elements of the lament tradition, some features of Paul's arguments could be understood to be encouraging protest against the injustice of the Empire and a call for redemption from the violence of the Empire.[111] Take, for example, the language of "conquering" that Paul uses later in the text. His proclamation in verse 37 that "in all these things we are more than *conquerors*" could easily be understood in terms of the

---

[107] See similarly Isa. 21:3; 26:17–18; 66:7–8; Jer. 4:31; 22:23; 30:5–6; Hos. 13:13; Mic. 4:9–10; 1Q 3:7–18.

[108] The parallel with Romans 8 is particularly strong in Jeremiah, where creation is said to be suffering the same punishment as the people.

[109] Eg. 1QH 3:6–19; *1 Enoch* 62:4; cf. *4 Ezra* 5:46–55. For a thorough analysis of this language in Intertestamental literature, see D. C. Allison, *The End of the Ages Has Come* (Philadelphia: Fortress Press, 1987), ch. 2; Dunn, *Romans 1–8*, 472–73.

[110] Adams, *Constructing the World*, 128.   [111] Keesmaat, "Psalms in Romans," 149.

triumph of God's people over their enemies. At the very least, it is likely that the language of "conquerors" would have reminded Paul's audience of images frequently used by the Roman Empire. As Keesmaat points out, "What else was Rome than the conqueror of the whole world, the victor over the pagan hordes, whose status as conqueror was celebrated on coin and portal where subjugated peoples were depicted in positions of subservience to victorious Roman conquerors. For a small beleaguered community in Rome, the power of such conquerors was all pervasive."[112]

In light of all of this, could it be argued that the language of inheritance, connected so closely to the process of lament in this text, encourages the Christians at Rome to raise similar questions to those being asked in the lament tradition? As Keesmaat asks, in the face of the violence of the Empire, do the people of God "take up the cry of the psalms of lament and demand that God come in salvation to grind the nations into dust, that God defeat the evildoer, that God once again enable his people to oppress their foes?"[113]

While the proposed reading of κληρονόμος in Romans 8 – the universal sovereignty of the people of God in particular – could certainly lead in this direction, it is clear that Paul has quite a different understanding of the role of the "heirs of God and joint heirs with Christ." Paul is not calling for his communities to imitate the conquering with which they will have been most familiar – the conquering of the Roman Empire. Instead, they will be conquerors, but through the suffering of self-giving love, not violence. To put it another way, not only the *what* and the *who* of inheritance but also the *how* undermines the narrative being perpetuated by Rome.

This subversive concept is embedded within the language of κληρονό-μος in verse 17, where Paul says that those who are "joint heirs with Christ" must *suffer with Christ* in order that they will be glorified with him. Central to this verse is the insistence that suffering is integral to the life of those "in Christ." While Paul uses the word εἰ at the start of the verse to denote "a necessary and sufficient condition fulfilled"[114] (in other words, "since it is the case that . . . "), his use of εἴπερ to introduce the clause about suffering is significant. Dunn points out that εἴπερ denotes a condition not yet fulfilled and therefore a consequence dependent on

[112]   Ibid., 151; See also Jewett, "The Corruption and Redemption of Creation."

[113]   S. C. Keesmaat, "Crucified Lord or Conquering Saviour: Whose Story of Salvation?" *Horizons in Biblical Theology* 26.2 (2004), 87. See for example, Pss. 10:15–16; 94:23; 140: 10–12; cf. Pss. 18:30; 34:17; 69:23–29.

[114]   Dunn, *Romans 1–8*, 456.

the fulfillment of the condition.[115] Paul then says "so that we may also be glorified with him," which, combined with the use of εἴπερ, suggests that "suffering with Christ is not an optional extra or a decline or lapse from the saving purpose of God. On the contrary, it is a necessary and indispensable part of that purpose."[116]

The idea of suffering which precedes glory is not unique to Paul. Common to the OT prophetic literature, for example, is the belief that the people of God will suffer before they experience redemption and glory.[117] This is particularly explicit in the servant song of Isa. 52:13–53:12. The servant is one who was "despised and rejected by others; a man of suffering and acquainted with infirmity" (53:3) yet "Out of his anguish he shall see light . . . The righteous one, my servant, shall make many righteous, and he shall bear their iniquities" (53:11). Similarly, the vision in Daniel 7 is that the saints will experience a period of suffering and trial before receiving the kingdom (Dan. 7:21–22). This theme is similarly evident in Intertestamental literature.[118] Although texts such as Wisdom of Solomon, *1 Enoch*, *Jubilees*, *4 Ezra* and *2 Baruch* were written after Paul wrote Romans, they do suggest that there was continuity with a theme which was already evident in Israel's scriptures.[119] These Intertestamental sources show that the concept of suffering prior to redemption was expressed within Judaism both before and after the time of Paul.[120]

In order to explore the depth of the suffering-as-a-prelude-to-glory concept in verse 17, it is necessary first to note the way verse 17 connects with verses 35–39. There is a particularly significant link between verse 17 ("suffer with" Christ) and verse 36, where Paul writes, "As it is written, 'For your sake we are being killed all day long; we are accounted as sheep to be slaughtered.'" The purpose of this quotation from Ps. 44:22 (LXX 44:23) and the important connection it has with κληρονόμος in verse 17 (where this section of Paul's argument was initiated) are often missed. For example, Moo suggests that the verse (v. 36) "is something of an interruption" in the flow of Paul's thought and that while it is common for the apostle to argue that Christians should not be surprised by suffering,

---

[115] Ibid.; Dunn points out that "seeing that" (Cranfield) and "since, as is the case" (Black, Lietsmann, Lagrange, Michel, Schmidt) are inadequate translations. Better translations should include the hortatory sense of verses 12–13. Also Funk, *A Greek Grammar*, 237; Käsemann, *Commentary on Romans*, 229.

[116] Dunn, *Romans 1–8*, 456. So also Schreiner, *Romans*, 428.

[117] See for example Isa. 40:1–5.   [118] Byrne, *Romans*, 256.

[119] See, for example: 3:4–8; *1 Enoch* 102–105 and *Jub.* 23:23–31; *4 Ezra* 6:25–28; *2 Bar.* 15:7,8; 25.

[120] Keesmaat, *Paul and His Story*, 100.

the citation seems to add little to his main point.[121] Even when interpreters do understand verse 36 to be an important part of Paul's argument, there is seldom any serious attempt to explore the degree to which it relates specifically to the situation faced by the Christians in Rome. Instead, the most common understanding is that Paul is here offering a general encouragement to his audience, a reminder that the suffering they are experiencing is nothing new – that, as Schreiner puts it, "such mockery and suffering are inevitably the lot of Christians."[122]

While Paul's words are undoubtedly intended on one level to offer encouragement in a general sense to Christians who are experiencing suffering, there is something more specific going on here. To begin with, as Richard Hays has shown, one of the reasons for Paul's quoting this particular psalm is because it raises doubts about whether God can be considered just and faithful to his covenant with Israel.[123]

> Because of you we are being killed
> all day long,
> and accounted as sheep for the slaughter.
> (Ps. 44:22)

The psalmist has doubts because the community he is a part of is currently experiencing suffering, most probably the suffering of exile. The central question of the psalm is whether, on the basis of this present oppression, the conclusion can be made that God has abandoned his people. So Paul most probably echoes this psalm because it relates closely to one of his central concerns in Romans, in particular the question of God's integrity and faithfulness in upholding his promises to Israel.[124] As Hays points out, Paul's quotation of this psalm "serves to intensify the depiction of suffering and to sharpen the question of God's faithfulness."[125] Having used this psalm to heighten the tension in his argument, Paul then responds with a resounding conclusion: "in all these things we are more than conquerors . . ." (v. 37).

But is it possible that Paul's argument is even more specifically related to the socio-political situation of the Christians at Rome? Some commentators move towards such an understanding when they point out that the psalm quoted in verse 36 was often used by rabbis in reference to the martyrs of the Maccabean and Hadrianic times.[126] This reading of the verse rightly acknowledges the psalm's application to a specific context

---

[121] Moo, *The Epistle to the Romans*, 586.   [122] Schreiner, *Romans*, 464.
[123] Hays, *Echoes of Scripture in the Letters of Paul*, 58.   [124] Ibid., 59.
[125] Ibid., 59.   [126] Dunn, *Romans 1–8*, 504; Byrne, *Romans*, 280.

of persecution. At the same time, however, especially given Paul's references to persecution and suffering surveyed above, it is surprising that interpreters have not given more attention to the possibility that verses 35–39 are directed specifically to the situation of Christians living in the capital of imperial Rome. If the description of the socio-political backdrop to Romans (Chapter 2 above) is correct, and the probable persecution outlined above, then it should be expected that any mention of persecution in the epistle might be a result of oppression which Paul's readers are experiencing (or might potentially experience) under the Roman Empire. As Neil Elliott observes, there is little doubt that the afflictions mentioned in 8:35 "would have evoked sharp echoes of very recent events in Rome itself."[127]

If it is indeed the case that verse 36 is intended directly to address the socio-political situation of Christians in Rome, what does this add to an understanding of κληρονόμος in verse 17, particularly Paul's insistence that the "joint heirs with Christ" will undergo suffering? I propose that verses 35–39 (especially v. 36) are meant to be read intratextually with verse 17: that verse 36 informs an understanding of verse 17, and that verse 17 in turn helps to illuminate the use of Ps. 44 in verse 36.

Like most readings of "suffering" in Romans, the reference in 8:17 to the heirs of God "suffering with" Christ is usually understood in a very general sense. However, it seems likely that something more specific is going on here. If, as argued above, the references to "suffering" and "persecution" (vv. 18–30) are concrete socio-political terms, and if verse 36 is similarly to do with the suffering of those in the midst of Empire, then it is likely that "suffer with him" in verse 17 expresses a parallel concept. Such an understanding of "suffer" should be entirely expected, given what has been observed with regard to κληρονομία above, both in relation to 4:13 and with regard to "heirs of God" in 8:17. To be an "heir of God" is, as Paul sees it, to be one of the people who will inherit a renewed earth and will be given sovereignty, with Christ, over this world. There are at least two reasons why such a claim in the capital of Rome would have been highly provocative.

First, to describe the present state of creation as "groaning" for a new world, would have been offensive to those in power who were proclaiming that the golden age had already arrived because of the work of Caesar and his successors. In direct contrast to Nero's carefully chosen images

---

[127] N. Elliott, "Romans 13 in the Context of Imperial Propaganda," in *Paul and Empire*, ed. R. A. Horsley (Harrisburg, PA: Trinity Press, 1997), 194. Also Käsemann, *Commentary on Romans*, 249–50.

of the abundance and prosperity of the earth, Paul refers to creation as being "subjected to futility" (v. 20) and as in "bondage to decay" (v. 21). Paul's portrayal of an earth which groans with the pains of labor (v. 22) as it waits for "freedom" (v. 21) is in bold contrast to Nero's version of the world. It is not difficult to imagine why Paul's perspective would have upset those in power.

Second, as noted in the discussion of inheritance in Romans 4, the vision of a renewed and restored earth raises the inevitable question of what *kind* of earth this will be. More particularly, if inheritance retains its original this-worldly dimension, then who will be classed among the "landed" and who will be amongst the "landless"? In other words, how (in broad terms) is the land to be distributed, or, *who* inherits the land? It was argued above that there are good grounds for reading the language of inheritance in Romans 4 as, in part, echoing the OT concept of land as a grant from God rather than "possession." Included within this concept is the principle that, as "gift," land is not a commodity to be traded but is to be received as God's guarantee of the socio-economic well-being of his people. It was suggested that the language of inheritance in Romans 4 is therefore visionary in the sense that it exposes the disparity between the current state of things with regard to land and the reminder of how things ought to be. Similarly, in Romans 8 there is a vision evoked of a time when the children of God and also the entire creation will be renewed and restored. Once more, therefore, such an alternative picture of land and people invites a critique of the status quo with regard to ownership and distribution of the land.

It therefore seems likely that suffering is so closely connected with inheritance in verse 17 because persecution at the hands of the Empire is an inevitable consequence of the beliefs and praxis of the heirs of God. As Nero's reign demonstrated, those who offered an alternative to the message of the Empire were likely to suffer the fate described in 8:36. "Suffer with him" (v. 17) should by no means be understood in generalized and spiritualized terms, therefore, but rather as expressing the expected result of being "heirs of God" and "joint heirs with Christ" in the midst of the oppressive Empire.

Verse 17 also informs a reading of verse 36. In addition to the direct citation of Psalm 44 noted above, a second echo present in Rom. 8:36 is that of Jeremiah's lament in Jer. 11:18–12:6.[128] In this lament the prophet is crying out to God for vengeance. Describing the suffering of the prophet, Jeremiah asks God to reverse the situation by killing the

---

[128] Keesmaat, *Paul and His Story*, 130–31.

guilty like "sheep for the slaughter." Paul answers the plea of Psalm 44 (which he directly quotes) and the call for retribution of Jeremiah 12 (to which he alludes) with the paradoxical claim that those who suffer, those who experience persecution, are not the defeated, but are "more than conquerors" (v. 37). In a startling reversal of Jeremiah's lament, Paul claims that all of the suffering and persecution he has alluded to actually "works for good for those who love God" (v. 28) and that it is through their being counted as "sheep to be slaughtered" that believers are more than conquerors (v. 37). In a profound turnaround, therefore, Paul insists that those who "are being killed all day long" are the ones who are "more than conquerors through him who loved us."[129]

It is not immediately apparent from the surrounding context of verse 36 how Paul can make such a claim. But the concepts in 8:17 elucidate Paul's possible reasoning. Central to this verse is the idea of the intimate relationship between believers and Christ. Being an heir of God means being a "joint heir with Christ" (συγκληρονόμοι δὲ Χριστοῦ), suffering "with him" (εἴπερ συμπάσχομεν) and being glorified "with him" (συνδοξασ-θῶμεν). The συν prefixes here express the closeness of the relationship between Christ and his followers. This is why Paul concludes in verse 37 that those who suffer are actually the ones who are conquerors. It is by virtue of union with Christ that one is considered a suffering conqueror and an afflicted victor. Paul is implicitly referring to Jesus' crucifixion at the hands of the Roman authorities, the only people who had the power to carry out this form of execution.[130] Whereas in other contexts Paul is more explicit about the relationship between the crucified messiah and the rulers and powers of the day (for example 1 Corinthians 1–2), here the thought is present in a more implicit form. Paul says that the messiah who suffered and died (verses 32, 34) at the hands of the Roman Empire, is now "at the right hand of God" (v. 34) and is our "Lord" (v. 39). The thought is once more of the power of Rome being turned on its head.[131] Consequently those who "suffer with him" (v. 17) are also "glorified with him" (v. 17) and therefore "conquerors" through Christ (v. 37). "These victors, as v. 32 declared, inherit 'the all,' but only in the midst of their ongoing vulnerability and suffering on behalf of Christ."[132]

Together, then, verses 17 and 36 convey the idea that by virtue of their union with Christ believers will experience persecution, and yet this suffering, far from representing defeat, is in fact evidence that they are

---

[129] Keesmaat, "Psalms in Romans," 152.   [130] Cassidy, *Paul in Chains*, 181.

[131] For the political significance of crucifixion and Paul's theological reflection see further ibid., 181–83.

[132] Jewett, "Impeaching God's Elect," 57.

reigning with Christ. Significantly, this means that the language of inheritance in 8:17 should be understood not only as a direct confrontation to other *claims* to rule, but also as a reversal of all other *paths* to lordship and rule.[133] The exploration of the word "inheritance" above acknowledged the tones of universal sovereignty present in Paul's use of this word. Just as in Romans 4 there are hints that the path to inheritance is peaceful and will not be one which imitates the violence of Rome, so here it is evident that Paul rejects the traditional ways of evaluating who is the victor and who is the conquered.[134] The "conquering" or "supervictory" of the Christians at Rome is

> vastly different from Roman imperialism, as embodied in the goddess "Victoria" and in the ceremonies of victory parades, triumphal arches, and gladiatorial games that feature the vanquishing of barbarians. Rather than a victorious general leading the vanquished in triumph and receiving the lion's share of the glory, here is a community of victors whose glory is shared equally.[135]

For Paul, "the logic of sacred violence" has been replaced by the life-giving power of Jesus, who has been raised from the dead.[136] As Keesmaat argues:

> Paul is rejecting the imperial categories here of victory, categories beloved by both Israel and Rome, and is replacing them with the category of suffering love. He is rejecting the narratives of salvation that link the saviour with conquest and is replacing them with the story of a saviour who died and was raised. In this story, the way to respond to the violence of the Empire is to bear it; and in that bearing to reveal that one is part of the family of Jesus (Rom. 8:17, 29), and therefore one of those who cannot be separated from God's love. It is such love, such "relentless solidarity" that enables the Roman Christians to bear the suffering that they experience at the hands of their persecutors (Rom. 12:12–21).[137]

The presence of these themes of suffering in Romans 8 leads Richard Hays to point out that it would have been logical for Paul to draw directly on Isa. 53:7 as a way of making even more explicit the concept of Jesus

---

[133] Keesmaat, "Crucified Lord?," 76. Stanton, *Jesus and Gospel*, 40.
[134] Keesmaat, "Crucified Lord?," 88.
[135] Jewett, "Impeaching God's Elect," 57. The phrase "supervictory" is Jewett's.
[136] N. Elliott, *Liberating Paul*, 174.   [137] Keesmaat, "Crucified Lord?," 88.

and the people of God as prefigured in the suffering-servant narrative.[138] While the apostle hints at this throughout the passage, he does not directly draw this conclusion.[139] The result, suggests Hays, is a profound example of metalepsis, the reader being compelled to "complete the trope."[140] Those with ears to hear will understand that to be an "heir of God" is a bold counter-imperial claim which will result in persecution from the Empire. To be "joint heirs with Christ" is therefore to be counted as sheep to be slaughtered, to suffer with Christ under a violent Empire. But this echo also invites the Christians at Rome to understand that in the midst of experiencing this suffering they will be living out the vocation prefigured for them in the scriptures. Perhaps reaching back to verses 18–21 and the concept of creation's renewal subsequent to the redemption of humanity, this metalepsis in verse 36 suggests that "[u]pon them is the chastisement that makes others whole, and with their stripes is creation healed."[141]

Conclusions

This exploration of κληρονόμος in Rom. 8:17 confirms Adolf Schlatter's proposal that "The promise 'you will inherit the world' (4:13) thus receives its premise and interpretation [in Rom. 8:17]. Humanity is God's possession, and it will become the kingdom handed to Christ. Because he gives the community a share in his dominion, the community inherits with Christ that which comes from God."[142] In other words, Rom. 4:13 and 8:17 are not isolated ideas but different ways of expressing the concept of God's eschatological renewal of the whole physical cosmos, the entire world. "Heirs of God" should not be interpreted as the people of God who are God's "inheritance," but as the people who inherit God's promise to Abraham. As Wright concludes in a discussion of Romans 8:

> The cosmos itself will be redeemed, set free from slavery, liberated to share the freedom of the glory of God's children. God's children in turn have their inheritance, the new covenant equivalent of the promised land, in this entire new world. They will therefore, as Romans 5 stresses, share the *reign* of Jesus over

---

138 Hays, *Echoes of Scripture in the Letters of Paul*, 63.
139 See, for example, verse 26.
140 Hays, *Echoes of Scripture in the Letters of Paul*, 63.   141 Ibid.
142 A. Schlatter, *Romans. The Righteousness of God*, trans. S. S. Schatzmann (Peabody, MA: Hendrickson Publishers, 1995), 182.

the whole new world. This, I suggest, cannot be other than subversive when set as the climax of a letter to the small struggling
church in Rome, whose emperor claimed to rule the world,
whose poets had sung of the new age of peace, freedom and
prosperity that had come to birth through Augustus' defeat of
all enemies.[143]

The discussion of Romans 8 above has thus confirmed the reading of
Romans 4 in the previous chapter: κληρονόμος for Paul involves the heirs
of God in receiving a this-worldly renewal of the earth which includes
a claim to universal sovereignty with Christ. However, Romans 8 also
extends our knowledge of what Paul means when he refers to κληρονόμος.
Paul's understanding of the relationship between this renewed creation
and the people of God has been explained. The wise and nurturing rule of
creation by the people of God is considered by Paul to be a state of "glory"
and all of this is what is included within the concept of κληρονόμος. As
was suggested in the discussion of Romans 4, of course, to make such bold
and expansive claims within the first-century Roman imperial context
was inviting trouble. Paul seems to anticipate this in 8:17, reminding the
Christians in the capital that to be heirs of Abraham's promise is to attract
persecution and hence suffering similar to that of the messiah whom they
follow. Reinforcing the findings of Romans 4, therefore, in Romans 8 not
only the *who* and the *what* of inheritance but also the *how* (or means by
which this occurs) deeply undermines the story being told by first-century
imperial Rome. In these ways, once more, the language of κληρονόμος
in Romans 8 is one means by which Paul presents an eschatology which
is intended to shape and nurture the ethical worldview and imagination
of the Christians at Rome.

[143] N. T. Wright, "Paul and Caesar," 188.

5

"RICHES FOR THE WORLD": INHERITANCE IN ROMANS 11:1

Introduction

In the discussion of the concept of inheritance in Romans 4 and 8 above, several themes have emerged. First, the term refers to a geographical reality which includes the renewal of the earth. While inheritance is often read in individualized and spiritualized terms, an exploration of the concept in Romans 4 and 8 suggests that instead it should be understood as a restoration of the entire cosmos. Closely related to this dimension of the concept is the claim to universal sovereignty which is suggested for those who are considered "heirs of God." On the one hand, this aspect of Paul's eschatology is likely to have been viewed as a bold counter-claim to the worldview being presented by the Roman Empire of Paul's day. On the other hand, as was hinted at in Romans 4 and made more explicit in Rom. 8:17, the language of inheritance seems to have simultaneously been a subversion of all other *paths* to lordship. Those who are "heirs of Christ," Paul insists, will rule not in the manner of imperial power but in line with the example of the crucified messiah whom they follow.

In all English translations of Romans and in the most recent editions of the Greek New Testament, Rom. 8:17 is the last explicit reference to heirs or inheritance. But this is not the case in all manuscripts of the Greek New Testament. While the NA[27] edition of Rom. 11:1a reads "Therefore I ask, God has not rejected his people, has he?" (Λέγω οὖν, μὴ ἀπώσατο ὁ θεὸς τὸν λαὸν αὐτοῦ;) there are witnesses to the verse (most notably p[46]) which include the word κληρονομίαν in place of τὸν λαόν. This textual variant in Rom. 11:1 presents at least two issues of relevance to any study of inheritance in Romans. First, is there any evidence to suggest that κληρονομίαν should be adopted as the preferred reading of the verse? Before attempting any sort of argument regarding the use of the word in Romans 11 it is imperative that a strong case be argued for its inclusion. This will be attempted in detail below. Second, if such a reading can be established, what does it mean for the geographical dimensions of inheritance as argued above? If κληρονομίαν is adopted as a reliable variant for verse 1, to what extent does this necessitate a re-examination of the earthly and physical reading of inheritance advanced so far in this study? These questions emerge because regardless of whether τὴν κληρονομίαν *or* τὸν λαόν is adopted as the preferred reading of Rom. 11:1a, there is little doubt that the question in verse 1 conveys parallel themes and synonymous language to verse 2. After expressing the question in 11:1 – "Therefore I ask, has God rejected his [either "inheritance" or] "people" – Paul responds clearly and emphatically in verse 2: "God has not rejected his people" (τὸν λαόν). In other words, even if the variant reading of verse 1 is adopted (τὴν κληρονομίαν), there seems little doubt that here the concept is intended to be synonymous with "people" in verse 2. Whereas in Rom. 8:17 there is strong evidence to suggest that "heirs of God" means something other than "the people of God as God's inheritance," in Rom. 11:1 there are a number of contextual clues that the two ideas are meant to be read together. For example, in addition to the obvious parallelism between verses 1 and 2, there is also the verse immediately preceding 11:1, where, quoting Isa. 65:2, Paul writes, "But of Israel he says, 'All day long I have held out my hands to a disobedient and contrary people (λαόν)" (Rom. 10:21). It seems very likely that the subsequent question in 11:1 – "has God rejected his inheritance?" – relates closely to the λαόν referred to in 10:21 and that therefore, whether κληρονομίαν or λαόν is to be adopted as the better reading of 11:1, the intent of the phrase is reasonably clear – it refers to the people of God.[1]

Clearly there is some synonymity between κληρονομίαν and λαόν in Rom. 11:1–2. The key question for the purposes of this study then becomes: *what* is the meaning of λαόν in this context? Certainly λαός here refers at least in part to the people of Israel. The immediate context requires that the word be read in this way: Paul says in 11:1 that he is an "Israelite" and in 11:2 that Elijah pleads with God against "Israel." But although this is so, the significant issue for a study of inheritance is the semantic range of λαός in these verses. Is it the case that λαός refers exclusively to the *people* of Israel – as opposed to the land and sovereignty in any sense – or is it true that for Paul λαός includes not only *people* but land and earth as part of this concept? The issue is worth exploring

---

[1] As Wright points out, the NIV translation is technically correct in expressing the aorist sense – Did God reject his people? But the better sense seems to be that of the NRSV and most translations – Has God rejected his people?; N. T. Wright, "Romans," 675.

because if κληρονομίαν and λαός are here synonymous and if λαός refers narrowly to *people* and nothing more, then the judgment could be made that inheritance is here spiritualized by Paul. To make such an assessment has clear consequences for how inheritance is read in Romans because without a concrete reference to land then the socio-political voice of inheritance becomes either muffled or muted.

Before considering the semantic range of λαός, however, there is a need to evaluate the evidence for adopting κληρονομίαν as the preferred reading of Rom. 11:1a. Mark Given, in his article "Restoring the Inheritance in Romans 11:1," acknowledges that as with many textual variants it will never be possible to have absolute certainty with regard to Paul's original wording in Rom. 11:1a. But Given draws on external evidence, intertextual arguments and intratextual factors to present a strong case for κληρονομίαν being the preferable reading in this verse.[2]

As well as the κληρονομίαν variant in Rom. 11:1, some manuscripts also have, at the conclusion of the sentence, ὃν προέγνω, "whom he foreknew." While the κληρονομίαν variant is usually either ignored or rendered undecideable, the variant conclusion, ὃν προέγνω, is unanimously discarded.[3] The external evidence is as follows:

1. τὴν κληρονομίαν αὐτὸν ἣν προέγνω p[46] (*c.* 200 CE)
2. τὸν λαὸν αὐτοῦ א B C D PΨ 33 (many other minuscules), it[ar,d,dem,e,z], vg, syr[p,h,]cop[sa,bo], arm, Origen[lat], Eusebius, Chrysostom, Augustine, Theodoret
3. τὸν λαὸν αὐτοῦ ὃν προέγνω א[2], A, D̂
4. τὴν κληρονομίαν αὐτοῦ F G it[b,f,g,x], Goth, Ambrosiaster, Ambrose, Pelagius[4]

The earliest attested reading is τὴν κληρονομίαν αὐτὸν ἣν προέγνω. This comes from p[46], the earliest witness to the Alexandrian text type. One of the arguments presented by Given is that the same logic be applied to the κληρονομίαν variant as is applied to the ὃν προέγνω variant. Interpreters rightly acknowledge that ὃν προέγνω appears to be an attempt by a later scribe to harmonize verse 1 with verse 2, where Paul writes: οὐκ ἀπώσατο ὁ θεὸς τὸν λαὸν αὐτοῦ ὃν προέγνω. As Cranfield puts it, "The variant reading which adds these words in v. 1 after αὐτοῦ

---

[2] M. Given, "Restoring the Inheritance in Romans 11:1," *JBL* 118.1 (1999): 89–96. For similar arguments see Wagner, *Heralds*, 221–22; Keesmaat, "Psalms in Romans," 153–54.

[3] Those who ignore both variants include, for example: Käsemann, *Commentary on Romans*, 298–99; Byrne, *Romans*, 330–33.

[4] From Given, "Restoring the Inheritance," 91.

is clearly an assimilation to this verse [v. 2]."[5] But Given argues that this same harmonizing tendency may well be the reason for the absence of κληρονομίαν in some manuscripts. This is because while it is easy to explain the use of τὸν λαόν in verse 1 as a harmonization with τὸν λαόν in verse 2, it is more difficult to explain why a later scribe would have added or exchanged κληρονομίαν for τὸν λαόν. After all, as Given observes, there is little question that κληρονομίαν is the more obscure of the two references, especially since this form of the word is not part of Paul's normal vocabulary; it appears in this form only once in Paul's undisputed letters (Gal. 3:18), and in all of Pauline literature it refers only one other time to *God's* inheritance (Eph. 1:18).[6] There is little doubt that κληρονομίαν is therefore the more difficult reading.[7] On the other hand, as noted above, given the occurrence of τὸν λαόν in the preceding verse (10:21) and in the subsequent verse (11:2), it is possible to understand why κληρονομίαν may have been altered to τὸν λαόν – the word could be considered to fit more easily within this immediate context.

Adding further support to this possibility is Paul's allusion to Ps. 93 (94):14 in verse 1.[8]

> For the Lord will not reject his people,
> nor will he forsake his inheritance. (Ps. 93[94]:14)
>
> ὅτι οὐκ ἀπώσεται κύριος τὸν λαὸν αὐτοῦ καὶ
> τὴν κληρονομίαν αὐτοῦ οὐκ ἐγκαταλείψει.

It will be important, in the argument that follows, to consider the significance which the content and context of Psalm 93 have for an understanding of inheritance in Romans 11. At this stage, however, it is enough to identify the allusion and to tease out how this echo may have influenced scribal emendations of Rom. 11:1. Ulrich Wilckens observes that there is a parallelism between verses 1 and 2 which seems to correspond to the chiastic structure of Ps. 93:14a and 14b.[9] Wilckens therefore asks: "Ist das eine sehr geschickte und wirksame Teständerung nach Ψ 93, 14, oder

---

[5] Cranfield, *A Critical and Exegetical Commentary on the Epistle to the Romans*, 545.

[6] Wagner, *Heralds*, 222; Given, "Restoring the Inheritance," 92. Wagner points out that "Given is thus mistaken in asserting that nowhere in the NT (besides Rom 11:1) does κληρονομίαν refer to the people of God"; Wagner, *Heralds*, 222.

[7] Given, "Restoring the Inheritance," 92; Wagner, *Heralds*, 222.

[8] Paul may also have been alluding to 1 Sam. 12.22 in Rom. 11:1. This will be considered in more detail below. For the lexical similarities and differences between the three texts see Wagner, *Heralds*, 223. Wagner considers that an allusion to Psalm 93 is "virtually certain."

[9] Wilckens, *Rom 6–11*, 236. See similarly Cranfield, *A Critical and Exegetical Commentary on the Epistle to the Romans*, 543.

ist τὸν λαὸν αυτοῦ sekundäre Angleichung?"[10] While Wilckens does not conclude either way, it seems that the second of these possibilities is more likely and that Paul himself chose τὴν κληρονομίαν because he was consciously echoing the language and structure of Psalm 93.[11]

The problem with Paul's use of the Psalm is that he uses a different verb than the one connected with κληρονομίαν in Psalm 93 and this may have presented a misunderstanding for later scribes. Given argues that if Paul had used the verb ἐγκαλείπω instead of ἀπωθέω and so written "μὴ ὁ θεὸς ἐγκατέλιπε τὸν λαὸν αὐτοῦ," the text might never have been emended. If the scribe was not familiar with the LXX allusion he might have assumed that Paul was saying the same thing in two different ways, or if the scribe *was* aware of Paul's allusion to scripture then again he would have left the text unaltered.[12] But Paul does use a different verb than the one used with κληρονομίαν in Psalm 93, and perhaps it is this that creates problems for later scribes. Given posits that one of two things might have occurred when a scribe read Paul's original manuscript. A scribe could have found Paul's reference to the people of God as God's inheritance too cryptic and could have been tempted to change the wording to harmonize with the more familiar language of verse 2. Or, if the scribe *was* familiar with the LXX wording, he might have concluded that an earlier scribe had erroneously inserted κληρονομίαν on the basis of the Psalm and, knowing that ἀπωθέω belongs with λαόν *not* κληρονομίαν in the LXX allusion, would have been tempted to emend the text.[13] As Wagner points out, the weight of probability in these cases is always in favor of a later scribe's harmonizing a quotation to the LXX rather than inserting a variant.[14] In light of this external evidence, Mark Given weighs the relative probability of the various scenarios and seems right to conclude that κληρονομίαν should be the preferred reading:

> Are we to imagine that a scribe who has just copied 10:21 in which Israel is referred to as λαός, upon encountering τὸν λαόν again in 11:1 suddenly decided to get creative and introduced the more obscure τὴν κληρονομίαν? Or is it not far more likely that one of two things happened. In one possible scenario, a scribe who did not recognize the LXX allusion in 11:1, and

---

[10] Wilckens, *Rom 6–11*, 236 n. 1053.   [11] Given, "Restoring the Inheritance," 92.
[12] Ibid., 93.   [13] Ibid.
[14] Wagner, *Heralds*, 84 n. 126. On this principle of textual criticism in more general terms, see J. K. Elliott, "Thoroughgoing Eclecticism in New Testament Textual Criticism," in *The Text of the New Testament in Contemporary Research: Essays on the Status Quaestionis*, ed. B. D. Ehrman and M. W. Holmes (Grand Rapids: Eerdmans, 1995), 326.

who had just copied λαόν in 10:21, balked at κληρονομίαν and wondered what Paul meant by such a strange expression – God's inheritance? Then, upon reading λαόν used with the same verb in 11:2 decided to go back and "clarify" 11:1. In another scenario, a scribe who did recognize the LXX allusion in 11:1, and who had just copied λαόν in 10:21, balked at κληρονομίαν and wondered why Paul used ἀπωθέω with it? Then, upon reading λαόν used with ἀπωθέω in 11:2, decided to go back and "correct" 11:1.

As Given concludes, "Either way, 'the inheritance' was lost."[15]

The text-critical case for the originality of the variant κληρονομίαν in 11:1a is therefore substantial and this variant will be adopted and assumed in the rest of this chapter. Given presents a strong case for accepting the p[46] reading on the basis both of external evidence and of transcriptional probabilities. But Given himself points out that while arguments based on the text-critical evidence are compelling, there are ways in which his proposal can be expanded. One way in which this might be pursued, he suggests, is to "listen for possible intratextual resonances between κληρονομίαν in 11:1 and κληρονόμοι in 4:13–14 and 8:16–17."[16] In other words, in addition to the external evidence and the transcriptional probabilities, a third way of approaching the variant is in terms of its intrinsic probabilities: *what* Paul is most likely to have written. It is necessary to explore the ways in which the context and themes of inheritance in Rom. 4:13–25 and Rom. 8:17–39 might be present in Paul's use of κληρονομίαν in Rom. 11:1. What if Paul's use of inheritance is not only echoing OT and LXX uses of the word but is also resonating within the text of Romans? There is a degree to which such questions impinge on interpretive approaches to Romans 9–11 in general.

Romans 11:1: interpretive possibilities

Traditional approaches to Rom. 11:1 and the verses which follow have often defined Paul's argument in rather narrow terms; one reason for this is that (in earlier scholarship at least) interpreters have often seen little connection, thematically or stylistically, between Romans 1–8 and

---

[15] Given, "Restoring the Inheritance," 93. Similarly Keesmaat, "Psalms in Romans," 153–54. Given notes that Paul could have changed ἀπωθέω to ἐγκατέλιπε but that the tendency towards assimilation with λαός in 10:21 is more likely.

[16] Given, "Restoring the Inheritance," 96.

Romans 9–11.[17] It has been common for interpreters to argue that these chapters are mostly unrelated to Paul's "main" argument in Romans 1–8 and that they are best read as a treatise which deals with themes such as the problem of predestination and free will.[18] This overall approach to the letter has in turn shaped how Rom. 11:1 is understood. If Paul is thought to have "finished his main argument"[19] by the end of Romans 8, then it is little wonder that discussion of Romans 11 has focused on such issues as the tension between "divine sovereignty and human responsibility" and has given less thought to the ways in which these verses might cohere with the preceding eight chapters.[20]

Not all interpreters, of course, propose such a discontinuity between Romans 9–11 and the rest of the letter.[21] But even when interpreters argue for a close relationship between Romans 9–11 and Romans 1–8, it is still the case that the content of Romans 11 is often read in predominantly individualistic terms. This is particularly true of those who approach the letter within a Lutheran framework, with the accompanying belief that Romans should be read as dealing with an individual's struggle with a guilty conscience.[22] For example, according to a traditional Lutheran perspective, Romans 9–11 is best interpreted as a specific example of the wider theme of justification by faith. Paul explores the question of the people of Israel in these chapters because he understands them as one example of humanity's position before God.[23] Most tellingly, even Ernst Käsemann, who gives sustained attention to the cosmic dimensions of Romans, finds little of the "cosmic" in Romans 9–11. For example, Käsemann concludes that in these chapters "the justification of the ungodly is here again the secret theme of the problem raised"[24] and

---

[17] Perhaps the most direct articulation of this comes from C. H. Dodd who suggests that Romans 9–11 "can be read quite satisfactorily without reference to the rest of the epistle." See further Dodd, *The Epistle of Paul to the Romans*, 148–51.

[18] Noted, for example, by Käsemann, *Commentary on Romans*, 253.

[19] Sanday and Headlam, *Romans*, 225.

[20] For examples of this tendency see Dodd, *The Epistle of Paul to the Romans*, 148; Bultmann, *Theology of the New Testament*. Barrett refers to a "predestinarian account of the fall of Israel in 9:1–29, 9:30–10:21." C. K. Barrett, "Romans 9:30–10:21: Fall and Responsibility of Israel," in *Die Israelfrage nach Röm 9–11*, ed. D de Lorenzi (Rome: Abtei von St. Paul vor den Mauern, 1977), 99–100. For further discussion of this problem see E. Elizabeth Johnson, *The Function of Apocalyptic and Wisdom Traditions in Romans 9–11*, SBLDS (Atlanta, GA: Scholars Press, 1989), 111–12.

[21] Abasciano observes that "The vast majority of scholars today have rightly rejected the notion that Romans 9–11 is merely an appendix to Romans 1–8"; Abasciano, *Paul's Use of the Old Testament in Romans 9:1–9*, 34.

[22] Perhaps the clearest critique of this approach remains K. Stendahl, *Paul among Jews and Gentiles* (Philadelphia: Fortress Press, 1976), 78–96.

[23] E. E. Johnson, *The Function of Apocalyptic*, 114.

[24] Käsemann, *Commentary on Romans*, 260.

that this section is a further example of "God's faithfulness and man's unfaithfulness in conflict."[25] According to Käsemann, "In and with Israel [Paul] strikes at the hidden Jew in all of us."[26] This means that despite Käsemann's intention to argue for the broad world-embracing scope of Romans, he misses the potential which Romans 11 has to advance his purposes. Yet in this chapter Paul refers to the "riches for the world" and to the "reconciliation of the world" and to "life from the dead." Also, Paul begins the chapter by asking whether God has "rejected his people/inheritance." Käsemann fails to explore the considerable significance which these phrases and concepts have within the letter as a whole.[27]

A third approach is to suggest that there is an integral relationship between Romans 9–11 and the rest of the letter. More than this, such an approach argues that Romans 9–11 is not just using the Jewish people as an example of the point Paul has made in the first eight chapters but in fact represents the *climax* of Paul's argument. One way of understanding this climax has been argued by N. T. Wright: in Romans 1–11 Paul is dealing with the issue of God's faithfulness and the claim Paul makes is that, through Jesus Christ, God has been faithful to the promises God made to Abraham. Wright explains that, understood in these terms, Romans 9–11 is an expected climax to Paul's argument, where Paul provides a historical survey of how these promises have worked out, from Abraham to the prophets, to Jesus Christ and the mission of the church.[28] Regarding Romans 11, Wright argues that Paul shows that

> "the events of Israel's rejection of the gospel of Jesus Christ *are* the paradoxical outworking of God's covenant faithfulness. Only by such a process – Israel's unbelief, the turning to the Gentiles, and the continual offer of salvation to Jews also – can God be true to the promises to Abraham, promises which declared *both* that he would give him a worldwide family *and* that his own seed would share in the blessing.[29]

As Douglas Harink has demonstrated, there are problems with Wright's argument, particularly the tendency towards supersessionism, which Wright's reading seems to reinforce.[30] Despite this, however, there is

---

[25] Ibid., 256.   [26] Ibid.

[27] Others who read Romans 9–11 as an illustration of the early justification-by-faith argument, or as a special problem arising from this doctrine, include Cranfield, *A Critical and Exegetical Commentary on the Epistle to the Romans*, 446; Barrett, *The Epistle to the Romans*, 175; R. A. Harrisville, *Romans*, ACNT (Minneapolis: Augsburg, 1980), 142.

[28] N. T. Wright, *The Climax of the Covenant*, 234.   [29] Ibid., 236.

[30] Harink, *Paul among the Postliberals*, 151–207.

now a general scholarly consensus regarding the integral connection between Romans 9–11 and the rest of the letter, even if there is a variety of ways in which this unity can be expressed.[31] But can more be said? In particular, what happens if inheritance is recognized as the preferred reading of Rom. 11:1? Is there any sense in which such a reading, and the direction it sets for the chapter as a whole, would offer additional insights as to the connections between Romans 9–11 and the chapters which precede and follow it, and especially to Romans 11 as a whole? The present chapter therefore has three main purposes. First, to build on Given's evidence by investigating the connections between Romans 4, 8 and 11; this is to inquire into the intrinsic probability of inheritance in 11:1. Second, to consider the ways in which this contributes to interpretations of Romans 11. Third, to observe the ways in which this adds to the exploration of inheritance as a concept in Romans.

Inheritance and pathos in Romans 11:1

Paul's reference to inheritance in Rom. 11:1 intersects, overlaps and resonates with his previous uses of the concept in Romans in at least three ways. First, the word serves to intensify the pathos towards the plight of the people of Israel. Romans 11 takes its place within a wider section (Romans 9–11) which is focused primarily on ethnic Israel's place in God's plan. Just as the two previous chapters have explored the "problem" of Israel, so "inheritance" in Rom. 11:1 refers specifically to the people of "Israel." For example, immediately prior to this, in order to describe the present condition of Israel ("But of Israel he says," Rom. 10:21), Paul quotes Isa. 65:2: "All day long I have held out my hands to a disobedient and contrary people." Further, after asking "Has God rejected his inheritance?" (11:1a), Paul then responds, "By no means! I myself am an Israelite, a descendant of Abraham, a member of the tribe of Benjamin" (Rom. 11:1b).[32]

It is clear, therefore, that inheritance here refers specifically to Israel in a way that the previous occurrences in Romans 4 and 8 do not. But most importantly, it is because of these *earlier* references to the word that the pathos is particularly strong in Rom. 11:1. In relation to Paul's earlier uses of κληρονόμος (Rom. 4:13–25; 8:17–39), it was observed that the

---

[31] For the connections between Romans 9–11 and 1–8 see Dunn, *Romans 9–16*, 519–20; Abasciano, *Paul's Use of the Old Testament in Romans 9:1–9*, 34–36.

[32] μὴ γένοιτο· καὶ γὰρ ἐγὼ Ἰσραηλίτης εἰμί, ἐκ σπέρματος Ἀβραάμ, φυλῆς Βενιαμίν.

concept includes ideas of God's future restoration of the present physical world.

Just as in the Old Testament and LXX κληρονόμος expresses the conviction that Yahweh is guaranteeing Israel's permanent protection and material security, so for Paul there is a decidedly geographical aspect to κληρονόμος. As well as this, there are motifs of universal sovereignty expressed by the concept of inheritance. In Rom. 8:17–39, for example, κληρονόμος has significant connections with the idea that the children of God will one day participate in God's eschatological renewal of the entire cosmos. In both Romans 4 and Romans 8 there is an implicit expectation that those who are counted as κληρονόμοι μὲν θεοῦ will one day reign with Christ over the earth. As the discussion of Romans 8 observed, this is a different kind of reign than the people of God had previously been led to expect – a rule exemplified in the crucified messiah – but it remains a strong expression of the sovereignty of God.

All of this, I suggest, feeds into the point which Paul intends to make when he uses the word κληρονομίαν in Rom. 11:1. By contemplating the possibility that God has "rejected his inheritance" Paul is asking a question which evokes all that has been said about the inheritance in Romans 4 and 8. It is therefore a shorthand way of asking whether the promise of the people of God inheriting a redeemed earth has been abandoned. Having just concluded that the children of God will one day participate in God's renewal of the earth (Rom. 8:17–39), he now highlights the issue of whether "the people to whom these assurances pre-eminently belong" will also participate in this restoration.[33] As Dunn observes, most of Paul's audience would have little difficulty in appreciating that Paul here "deliberately picks up the language so often used at times of Israel's deepest shame, particularly prior to and during the exile (e.g. 2 Kgs. 21:14; Jer. 7:29). Has what the prophets spoke of generations ago happened again or, rather, happened now at last with eschatological finality? Has God rejected his covenant people once and for all?"[34] While Dunn's observation is not made with reference to the language of inheritance, the point is an important one and is made even more poignant in light of the use of this word. In this verse, through the use of "inheritance" Paul evokes the "declared purposes"[35] of the inheritance as described in Romans 4 and 8, and he therefore contemplates

---

[33] Quotation from N. Elliott, *The Rhetoric of Romans*, 263.

[34] Dunn, *Romans 9–16*, 644.

[35] Hays, *Echoes of Scripture in the Letters of Paul*, 64. This is not to imply that Hays accepts the "inheritance" reading of Rom. 11:1.

the possibility that the original recipients of the promise have now been disinherited. Paul's assumption seems to be that if the original recipients of the inheritance are no longer going to benefit from it, then the original extent and scope of the promise has been truncated. As Paul reminded his audience in Romans 4, the intent of the promised inheritance was always that *all* nations would be blessed through Abraham and his descendants. The apostle wants his audience to call to mind the intent of the original heritage (as alluded to in Romans 4 and 8) in order to draw attention to the disjunction between the present situation and the hoped-for fulfillment. Through the interplay of inheritance in Romans 4, 8 and 11, therefore, Paul calls to mind the question of whether the Jews will one day "embrace the fulfillment of what is properly *their* destiny."[36]

Such pathos-creating language is entirely in keeping with the tone and flow of Paul's argument in Romans 9–11. Neil Elliott, in his analysis of Paul's rhetorical strategy in Romans, proposes that one of Paul's primary purposes in Romans 9–11 is to encourage his Gentile-Christian audience "to share his profound and anxious compassion *for the Jews* who have not yet embraced the fulfillment of what is properly *their* destiny."[37] Elliott observes that Paul's deliberate rhetorical ploy is particularly evident at the beginning of Romans 9. In 9:1–2, for example, there is an abrupt shift in tone and language from the exultant climax of Rom. 8:31–39 to the "great sorrow and unceasing anguish" which he expresses in the verses which follow.[38] It is important to understand that in taking the argument in this direction Paul's purpose is *not* to offer a kind of moral history of Judaism.[39] What is at stake here is not *Israel's* actions but *God's* action. Paul's theme is "not who is in the family and who is out, but who is in charge and to what purposes."[40]

It is these ideas which similarly resonate in Rom. 11:1 when Paul asks, "Has God rejected his inheritance?" Just as in 9:1–6 Paul highlights the distance between God's intention for Israel and what his audience would have known to be the present situation of the people of God – "to them belong the adoption, the glory, the covenants, the giving of the law, the worship, and the promises; to them belong the patriarchs, and

---

[36] N. Elliott, *The Rhetoric of Romans*, 263.   [37] Ibid.; emphasis original.

[38] Ibid., 261. Also Abasciano, *Paul's Use of the Old Testament in Romans 9:1–9*, 35.

[39] Harink makes this point strongly and persuasively; Harink, *Paul among the Postliberals*, 151–207.

[40] E. Johnson, *The Function of Apocalyptic*, 361. See also N. Elliott, "Figure and Ground in the Interpretation of Rom 9–11," in *The Theological Interpretation of Scripture: Classic and Contemporary Readings*, ed. S. Fowl (Oxford: Blackwell, 1997), 371–89.

from them, according to the flesh, comes the Messiah" (9:4–5)[41] – so in 11:1 Paul is observing the gap between the intent of the inheritance and the lack of consummation of that heritage. While interpreters sometimes acknowledge this if "people" is taken to be the word used in 11:1,[42] it is clear that if "inheritance" is adopted as the preferred reading then the idea is expressed in an even more poignant and sharply focused manner. Such observations regarding the function of inheritance in Rom. 11:1 have merit but are not by themselves conclusive, so we also need to explore the degree to which Paul's response in the rest of Romans 11 is a good fit with the language and themes expressed by inheritance.

Inheritance and God's enduring faithfulness in Romans 11:1

This is certainly the case with regard to the second way in which inheritance intersects with the previous uses of the word. As well as intensifying the pathos towards the situation of the people of Israel the concept emphasizes the *permanent nature* of God's promises to Abraham and his descendants.[43] This is evident in the phrase immediately following, 11:1a, where Paul writes, "I ask then, has God rejected his inheritance? *By no means!* (μὴ γένοιτο)." In other words, after hinting at the possibility that God has abandoned the vision of the original promise, Paul immediately rejects this idea. Once more Paul's use of the word relies on the earlier contexts in Romans in which it is used. This is particularly so with regard to the parallelism between λαόν and κληρονομία in Rom. 11:1–2. After asking, "Has God rejected his inheritance" (11:1), Paul then responds "No, God has not rejected his people" (οὐκ ἀπώσατο ὁ θεὸς τὸν λαὸν αὐτοῦ, 11:2).

Richard Hays, in his discussion of this verse, suggests that there are several resonances here with the language of scripture.[44] Although Hays does not explore the possibility that Paul here uses the word "inheritance," Hays does observe that what undergirds this verse is the meanings and themes of "earlier narratives and liturgical utterance."[45] As the discussion

---

[41] ὧν ἡ υἱοθεσία καὶ ἡ δόξα καὶ αἱ διαθῆκαι καὶ ἡ νομοθεσία καὶ ἡ λατρεία καὶ αἱ ἐπαγγελίαι ὧν οἱ πατέρες, καὶ ἐξ ὧν ὁ Χριστὸς τὸ κατὰ σάρκα.

[42] So for example Dunn, *Romans 9–16*, 644.

[43] T. H. Tobin, *Paul's Rhetoric in Its Context. The Argument of Romans* (Peabody, MA: Hendrickson Publishers, 2004), 313.

[44] Hays, *Echoes of Scripture in the Letters of Paul*, 70. So also Wagner who suggests that because of "a textual difficulty" [i.e. reading "people" instead of "inheritance"] the full significance of Paul's allusion has often been obscured; Wagner, *Heralds*, 222.

[45] Hays, *Echoes of Scripture in the Letters of Paul*, 70.

above noted, there is an *assumed* association between "land" and "people" in Romans 4 and 8, even if it is not always acknowledged by Paul's interpreters. In relation to Rom. 4:13–25, for example, it was argued that Paul's use of "descendants" and "father of many nations" in conjunction with "inherit the world" indicates one of the ideas which undergirds this passage, namely that the inheritance includes the concept of the people of God living on the restored earth. This close association between "people" and "inheritance" and "land" is similarly apparent in Rom. 8:17–39, where it was seen that there is an intimate connection in Paul's mind between the restoration of physical creation and the renewal of God's people.

The synonymous nature of these two words, "people" and "inheritance" (in relation both to Romans 4 and 8 and here in Romans 11), is an obvious echo of earlier OT and LXX uses of the "inheritance." As Mark Given points out, "In many [OT/LXX] contexts it is difficult or impossible to decide whether κληρονομία refers to the land, the people, or both, especially when λαός and κληρονομία appear together."[46] What becomes apparent in the OT use of the word is that although it refers primarily to the land of Israel it also functions as a metonym for the people who inhabit the land, those who are considered to be the people of God.[47] The earliest example of this close connection between the two words is in Deuteronomy. For example in Deut. 9:26–29, where Moses is recounting his prayer on behalf of the unfaithful Israelites, there is an obvious fluidity and interchangeability between "people" and "land":

> I prayed to the Lord and said, "Lord God, do not destroy the people who are your very own possession, whom you redeemed in your greatness, whom you brought out of Egypt with a mighty hand. Remember your servants, Abraham, Isaac, and Jacob; pay no attention to the stubbornness of this people, their wickedness and their sin, otherwise the land from which you have brought us might say, 'Because the Lord was not able to bring them into the land that he promised them, and because he hated them, he has brought them out to let them die in the wilderness.' For they are the people of your very own possession, whom you brought out by your great power and by your outstretched arm."

In these verses, therefore, the word "possession" or "inheritance" is used in terms of Israel as God's special treasure or "inheritance." In other

---

[46] Given, "Restoring the Inheritance," 94.   [47] Ibid.

words the people are themselves the inheritance. But intimately linked is the concept of the land, which here refers specifically to the land of Canaan. In this context "people" carries with it the "land" which the people will one day inhabit, all of which is a gift from YHWH.

When Paul draws on one of Israel's foundational narratives in Romans 11, it is not the first time he has done so in this letter. In Romans 10:19, for example, Paul vividly recounts the story of Deut. 32:8–9 – which describes God as distributing the other nations among the heavenly court but reserving Israel as his own special portion – as the basis for his scandalous announcement that God has now chosen Gentiles in order to make Israel jealous.[48] The particular purpose which this foundation narrative serves in Romans 11 is to emphasize God's unchangeable commitment to Israel.

This close link between "land" and "people" is similarly evident in 1 Sam. 10:1 when Saul is anointed by Samuel and also in 1 Kgs. 8:51–53. The two words paired together also occur in the Psalms. For example, in Ps. 27 [28]: 9 the psalmist writes,

> O save your people, and bless
> your heritage (κληρονομίαν);
> be their shepherd, and carry
> them forever.[49]

The prophets similarly use these two words interchangeably, as is evident in Isa. 47:6 – "I was angry with my people | I profaned my heritage (τὴν κληρονομίαν)" – and in Joel 2:17 – "Let them say, 'Spare your people O LORD | and do not make your heritage (τὴν κληρονομίαν) a mockery.'"[50] Significant also is the use of this metaphor in Second Temple texts. Even an initial glance reveals that the metaphor of Israel as God's own inheritance "was a vital component of Israel's self-conception up to and beyond the time of Paul."[51] Often in these texts the conviction is that God has a vested interest in the well-being of his people and that he will therefore intervene to restore, protect and preserve Israel, whom he has called to be his own.[52] For example, this perspective is evident

---

[48] Wagner, *Heralds*, 225.

[49] See also Pss. 32[33]:12; 77[78]:70–71; 93[94]:5; 105:40.

[50] See also Joel 4[3]: 2; Mic. 7:14.

[51] Wagner, *Heralds*, 226. Wagner lists the following as examples: *Pss. Sol.* 14:5; *Jub.* 16:8, 17–18; 22:9–10, 15; 33:20; *LAB* 12:9; 19:8–9; 21:2, 4; 27:7; 28:2; 30:4; 39:7; 49:6; *4 Ezra* 8:15–16, 45. The metaphor is also appropriated in the Dead Sea Scrolls: for example 1QHª 14[6].8; 4Q501 line 2; 4Q511 fr. 2 1.5–6; 11QMelch (11Q13) 2.5.

[52] Wagner, *Heralds*, 226.

in Moses' final prayer for Israel in Pseudo-Philo's *Liber Antiquitatem Biblicarum (LAB)*:

> And now I beg, may your mercy toward your people and your pity toward your portion (*hereditas*), Lord, be firm; may your long-suffering be directed toward your place upon the chosen nation, because you love them beyond all others ... Unless your patience abides, how will your portion (*hereditas*) be secure, unless you be merciful to them? Who will yet be born without sin? Chastise them for a time, but not in anger.
>
> (*LAB* 19:8–9)[53]

Similarly, in *LAB* 12:9 Moses pleads with God after Israel's sin with the golden calf. Here, because God has chosen Israel as his inheritance, he can be petitioned to restore and deliver Israel. To do so will enhance God's own glory:

> Therefore, if you do not have mercy on your vine, all things, Lord, have been done in vain, and you will have no one to glorify you ... And now let your anger be kept from your vine ... let not your labor be in vain, and let not your portion (*hereditas*) be sold cheaply.[54]

Finally, the combination is also known to the Apocrypha. For example in Sirach's Song of Wisdom there is this use of the words: "I took root in an honored people, in the portion of the Lord, his inheritance (κληρονομίας)" (Sir. 24:12).[55] The conviction which undergirds these texts – that God will preserve his special interest in Israel – takes its place within a much larger cluster of convictions in Second Temple Judaism regarding the enduring election of Israel. This means that even where there is the threat of God's rejection of his people,[56] this risk eventually leads to fresh hope that God will finally redeem his people.

Given suggests that Israel can be described both as God's people and as God's "inheritance," in the Old Testament and LXX, because both concepts were considered to be irreversible transactions and relationships: both the people and the land were a gift of God which would never be reversed. Just as God's gift of land to Israel will last forever, so the relationship between God and Israel will be permanent. Even when themes of the judgment of Israel emerge (for example Pss. 77[78]:62[59] and

---

[53] H. Jacobson, *A Commentary on Pseudo-Philo's Liber Antiquitatem Biblicarum, with Latin Text and English Translation*, AGJU (Leiden: Brill, 1996), vol. II, 121–22.

[54] Ibid., 112. See also *LAB* 39:6–7; 30:4; 49:6; *4 Ezra* 8:15–16, 45.

[55] See Given, "Restoring the Inheritance," 94–95.

[56] Cf. Hos. 4:6; Jer. 7:29; Ezek. 5:11; 11:16; *LAB* 12:4; 13:10; 19:2, 6; 21:1.

105[106]:40), these are always regarded as temporary in the face of God's faithfulness to his people. As W. Foerster puts it: "To call both Israel and Canaan God's κληρονομία, and to apply the term in eschatological contexts, was both meaningful and possible because here we have a lasting possession which rests, not on the basis of a reversible transaction, but on the gift of God."[57]

This theme of God's faithfulness is strengthened even further when it is understood that Paul is probably echoing Ps. 94:14 (93:14 LXX) in Rom. 11:1. In Ps. 94:14 (TDNIV) the psalmist writes:

> For the Lord will not reject his people,
> nor will he forsake his inheritance.

This psalm contributes to a tradition within Israel's scriptures which reminds God's people that although they sometimes feel as if they have been rejected by God, this is not the case, or that at least it would not be the *final* story. Frequently, language is used in scripture which suggests that the people have been rejected by God.[58] But in Romans 11 Paul insists that this is not so. Like the psalmist in Psalm 94, Paul "taps into one of the cultural narratives that shaped Israel's understanding of its special relationship to God: the story that out of all the nations, God chose Israel to be his own particular possession."[59]

A second echo present in 11:1 is from 1 Samuel 12. In this context the people of Israel are asking Samuel to intercede for them because they have sinned against God by asking for a king. Samuel responds with the following speech:

> Do not be afraid; you have done all this evil, yet do not turn aside from following the LORD, but serve the LORD with all your heart... For the LORD will not cast away his people, for his great name's sake, because it has pleased the Lord to make you a people for himself. Moreover, as for me, far be it from me that I should sin against the LORD by ceasing to pray for you.

It is likely that Paul's message in Rom. 11:1–2 is intended to resonate with Samuel's speech.[60] Certainly there are parallels between Samuel

---

[57] Foerster, " κληρονόμος," 769.
[58] Judg. 6:13; 2 Kgs. 23:27; Pss. 44:9, 23; 60:1, 10; 74:1; 78:60, 67; 108:11; Jer. 7:29; 31:37; Lam. 2:7; 5:22; Ezek. 5:11; 11:16; Hos. 9:17.
[59] Wagner, *Heralds*, 225. For example Exod. 19:5; 23:22 [LXX]; 33:16; Lev. 20:24, 26; Deut. 7:6, 14; 10:15; 14:2; 26:19; 28:1.
[60] So Hays, *Echoes of Scripture in the Letters of Paul*, 69–70; Given, "Restoring the Inheritance," 96 n. 25; Keesmaat, "Psalms in Romans," 154 n. 46; Wagner, *Heralds*, 229.

and Paul in their petitions to God that he not cast off his people despite their sin and unfaithfulness.

In these ways, therefore, Paul's use of inheritance in 11:1, because of the way it is combined with "people," once more draws on his earlier uses of the word in Romans 4 and 8 and also on OT and LXX uses of the concept. In 11:1–2 the word λαός has a semantic range which includes not only the people of God but also, in line with its OT usage, the people who inhabit *a particular land*. There is thus no weakening of the geographical dimension of the inheritance concept when it is used in tandem with λαός in 11:1–2. The two words κληρονομία and λαός are here used in parallel because together they convey (and this is what is distinct about the Romans 11 text) the *permanent nature* of God's relationship to Israel. Here the word explicitly expresses the concept of God's enduring faithfulness. It is a reminder that the original promise to Abraham and his descendants is one which God, at least ultimately, intends to keep.

This becomes especially apparent when it is noted that the possibility of God's rejection of Israel is a credible alternative for Paul. A few verses later, for example, Paul assumes that apart from the remnant, Israel *is* rejected: "For if their rejection is the reconciliation of the world, what will their acceptance be but life from the dead!" (Rom. 11:15).[61] In similar fashion, Paul has stated earlier in this section that apart from the chosen few, the Israelites are "objects of wrath that are made for destruction" (9:22). The serious possibility that Israel could be rejected by God is therefore what makes Paul's use of inheritance so significant in this verse. By alluding to Psalm 94 Paul is reminding his audience that although "God frequently rejects his people, he will never *finally* reject them, not even the majority in favor of a remnant."[62] Sylvia Keesmaat, who similarly argues for the inclusion of inheritance in 11:1, observes that whereas previously in Romans there have been "whispered affirmations" of God's steadfast love, here they come to explicit expression.[63]

> Whereas in Romans 3, 4 and 8, Paul relied on the unstated correspondences to keep the subtext of God's faithfulness to Israel a strong thread running through his arguments concerning Jewish and Gentile unfaithfulness, here the urgency of Paul's argument requires that the subtext be made explicit through his

---

[61] εἰ γὰρ ἡ ἀποβολὴ αὐτῶν καταλλαγὴ κόσμου, τίς ἡ πρόσλημψις εἰ μὴ ζωὴ ἐκ νεκρῶν;

[62] Given, "Restoring the Inheritance," 96.   [63] Keesmaat, "Psalms in Romans," 153.

echo. The subtext that whispers through these verses, only to become the text again as Romans 11 progresses, is that of God's faithfulness in spite of Israel's unfaithfulness.[64]

As Keesmaat observes, the theme of God's faithfulness simultaneously signals the direction in which Paul intends to take the argument in this chapter. In other words, while the enduring nature of God's promises is an important point here, there is more that needs to be said. If there are such strong echoes of Romans 4 and 8 in this text, and if there is the explicit theme of God's unending faithfulness to Israel, then it would be expected that the argument which follows will in some way explore the outworking of these themes. As Wagner concludes after his survey of the use of inheritance in Second Temple texts, the implications of these texts for a reading of Rom. 11:1–2 are both clear and profound.

> When set against the broad backdrop of contemporary Jewish understandings of Israel's election and heard in concert with the scriptural citations Paul has repeatedly employed in Romans 9–10 – citations whose wider contexts reverberate with the motif of God's unshakeable commitment to Israel[65] – Paul's question "God hasn't rejected his *inheritance*, has he?" all but answers itself before μὴ γένοιτο escapes his lips.[66]

To put it another way, if all that Paul has said with regard to the promised inheritance is true, then what does this mean for the final state of the world and God's people?

Inheritance and the future restoration of Israel and the world

This is the third aspect of inheritance which resonates with the earlier uses of the word in Romans 4 and 8. The role which inheritance plays in illuminating the disparity between the intention of the promise and the current situation of Israel was noted above. In part, this discussion of Paul's pathos-creating language identified the eschatological nature of inheritance. But it is worth examining the future-oriented themes of inheritance separately, particularly in relation to the direction signaled in

---

[64] Ibid., 154.   [65] For a full discussion of these see Wagner, *Heralds*, 43–218.
[66] Ibid., 228.

Romans 4 and the way the idea unfolds in the argument which follows in Romans 11.

One of the observations made with regard to the use of inheritance in Romans 4 was its close connection with the phrases "father of many nations" (4:17, 18), "father of all of us" (4:16) and numerous "descendants" (4:13, 16, 18). It was proposed that these expressions reverberate throughout Rom. 4:13–25 and combine with the "inherit the world" idea to evoke further themes of the heirs of Abraham reigning on the land that God has gifted to them. In Romans 4 Paul is drawing from and adapting the original Abrahamic promise, which set in motion a trajectory whose ultimate fulfillment would take place in the time of Israel's restoration. In Romans 4 Paul suggests that part of this promise is beginning to come true: the Gentiles are now receiving the blessings of Abraham and his seed.[67]

Ernst Käsemann suggests that much of Romans 11 (for example vv. 11a, 12b, 15b and 23f.) takes up the problem posed in 11:1a.[68] I propose to explore the possibility that 11:1 signals the issue of the future restoration of Israel, and that the direction which is hinted at in this verse is explored further in the verses which follow. When Paul uses inheritance in Rom. 11:1, one of his purposes – as well as creating pathos and emphasizing God's enduring faithfulness – is to echo the understanding of the concept in Romans 4. When he asks, "Has God rejected his inheritance?" – followed by a swift denial – part of what he is doing is evoking the trajectory of the inheritance alluded to in Romans 4. If the ultimate purpose of the promised inheritance was that eventually the whole world, including Jew and Gentile, would be restored, and if God's faithfulness to his promise is unending, then what does this mean for the final state of the world? The implication seems to be that this ultimate fulfillment is still to take place.

That this is what Paul has in mind is hinted at when he uses the phrase "a descendant of Abraham" (ἐκ σπέρματος Ἀβραάμ) in 11:1b. It seems likely that this phrase is a deliberate echo of his earlier uses of "descendant" in Romans 9,[69] and therefore a reminder that his argument has already been heading in the direction of the eventual restoration of Israel. By using this phrase in 11:1b he is evoking the entire complex

---

[67]   J. M. Scott, *Paul and the Nations*, 121.

[68]   Käsemann, *Commentary on Romans*, 304. Tobin proposes that Paul structures Romans 11 by use of three rhetorical questions: 11:1, 11, and 25; Tobin, *Paul's Rhetoric in Its Context*, 353.

[69]   Dunn, *Romans 9–16*, 634; Wagner, *Heralds*, 221.

of ideas accompanying the word "seed" (and the closely related word "remnant") in his argument so far.[70]

This is particularly so in Rom. 9:27–29:

> And Isaiah cries out concerning Israel, "Though the number of the children of Israel were like the sand of the sea, only a remnant of them will be saved; for the Lord will execute his sentence on the earth quickly and decisively." And as Isaiah predicted, "If the Lord of hosts had not left survivors (σπέρμα) to us, we would have fared like Sodom and been made like Gomorrah."[71]

J. Ross Wagner explores Paul's citation of Isa. 1:9 in Rom. 9:29. Wagner argues that when Paul uses σπέρμα in Rom. 9:29 and "remnant" (ὑπόλειμμα) in Rom. 9:27, the words function together "not only to evoke the severe judgment of God on wayward Israel, but also to foreshadow God's *ultimate restoration of his people*."[72] Wagner reaches this conclusion based on how the word "seed" functions in LXX Isa. 1:9, the text which Paul follows exactly. Isaiah 1 introduces some of the main problems of the book of Isaiah, including Israel's unfaithfulness to God, the consequent chastisement of Israel by God and also God's invitation to repentance and forgiveness. Within these themes Isa. 1:7–9 expresses a situation of desolation, a city which is "besieged" and "overthrown by foreigners." Significantly, however, in 1:9 Isaiah stops short of comparing Zion's fate with that of Sodom and Gomorrah, terms which are often bywords for total annihilation.[73] Why is Isaiah able to do this? Because, "The Lord of hosts has left us σπέρμα." Wagner argues that in this context, "God's preservation of Israel's 'seed' vouchsafes the ultimate restoration of the nation."[74] The concept of "seed" therefore includes future growth for all rather than future condemnation for some. Such a concept is similarly conveyed in other texts in Isaiah which Wagner lists:

> But you, Israel, Jacob my servant, whom I chose, seed of Abraham, whom I loved ... I chose you and did not abandon you. Don't be afraid, for I am with you.
>
> (41:8–10a)

---

[70] Dunn, *Romans 9–16*, 574. So also Byrne, *Romans*, 307.

[71] καὶ καθὼς προείρηκεν Ἠσαΐας, Εἰ μὴ κύριος Σαβαὼθ ἐγκατέλιπεν ἡμῖν σπέρμα, ὡς Σόδομα ἂν ἐγενήθημεν καὶ ὡς Γόμορρα ἂν ὡμοιώθημεν.

[72] Wagner, *Heralds*, 116; emphasis added. Dunn similarly notes that Rom. 9:29 ends this section of the argument on a more hopeful note; Dunn, *Romans 9–16*, 576.

[73] Wagner, *Heralds*, 111 n. 214. See Amos 4:11; Zeph. 2:9; Isa. 13:19; Jer. 27:40; 30:12.

[74] Wagner, *Heralds*, 112.

> Don't be afraid, for I am with you. I will bring your seed from
> the east, and I will gather you from the west.
>
> (43:5)

> Thus says the Lord God who made you and who formed you
> from the womb: "You will still be rescued – do not fear, my
> servant Jacob, and my beloved Israel, whom I chose. For when
> they thirst, I will give water to those who travel in a waterless
> land; I will place my spirit on your seed and my blessings on
> your children . . . "
>
> (44:2–3)

> By the Lord they will be vindicated, and in God they will be
> glorified – all the seed of the sons of Israel.
>
> (45:25)

> And I will lead seed from Jacob and seed from Judah out [of
> exile], and they will inherit my holy mountain. My elect and my
> servants will inherit [it] and they will dwell there.
>
> (65:9)

> Just as the new heaven and new earth which I am making remain
> before me, says the Lord, so will your seed and your name
> endure.
>
> (66:22)

In each of these texts, therefore, one of the themes expressed is that God
has elected Israel and that on this basis their "seed" will be redeemed
and restored. Often the idea set against this understanding is that other
nations will be annihilated through the destruction of their "seed."[75] The
concept that the preservation of "seed" safeguards a nation's ongoing
protection and future growth continues to be expressed in the Second
Temple Period.

> For even in the beginning, when arrogant giants were perishing,
> the hope of the world took refuge on a raft, and guided by your
> hand left to the world the seed of a new generation.
>
> (Wis. 14:6 NRSV)

> But in all of them [i.e. previous epochs] he raised up for himself
> those called by name in order to leave survivors for the land and
> to fill the face of the world with their seed.
>
> (CD-A 2.11–12)

---

[75] See for example Isa. 14:22; 14:30; 15:9; 48:14; 33:2.

> "Were you not angry enough with us to destroy us without
> leaving a root or seed or name? O Lord of Israel, you are faithful;
> for we are left as a root to this day."
>
> (1 Esdras 8:88–89 NRSV [8:85–86 LXX])

In this last text, and in the prayer of *4QWords of the Luminaries* (4Q504)
one of the themes is that Israel's seed has not been abandoned by God
because of his covenant faithfulness.

> In spite of all this [Israel's sin and exile] you did not despise
> the seed of Jacob and you did not abhor Israel so as to destroy
> them and break your covenant with them. For you alone are the
> living God and there is none beside you. You remembered your
> covenant by bringing us out [of captivity] in the sight of the
> nations and not abandoning us among the nations. You showed
> favor to your people Israel in all the lands to which you had
> scattered them so that they would return to their senses and turn
> back to you and heed your voice, just as you had commanded
> by the hand of Moses, your servant.[76]

In light of these Isaianic texts and the continuation of these themes in
later Jewish texts, Wagner deduces that "[w]hen Paul appropriates Isaiah's
oracle . . . it is with full knowledge of this widely used metaphor of 'seed'
as the pledge of a *future* for Israel."[77]

This means that Rom. 9:29 signals the conclusion which Paul will reach
in 11:26 regarding the salvation of "all Israel." The use of "seed" in 9:29
(and the earlier reference to "remnant" in v. 27) therefore foreshadows
the dramatic conclusion of Romans 11, which is that God will ultimately
restore all God's people. As Wagner concludes,

> Israel's present tragedy by no means fades from view, but
> through these quotations Paul insists that because God has in
> the present time preserved a remnant and seed, Israel's hope
> of restoration remains very much alive. The "remnant" spo-
> ken of by Isaiah does not refer to barren survivors destined to
> die off one by one . . . but to seed that will germinate, sprout, and
> blossom into a renewed Israel. Because God remains faithful to
> his covenant with Israel, a remnant – and ultimately, "all Israel" –
> *will* be saved.[78]

---

[76] 4Q504 frs. 1–2, 5:6–14.   [77] Wagner, *Heralds*, 115; emphasis original.
[78] Ibid., 116; emphasis original. Similarly Harink, *Paul among the Postliberals*, 174.

Given the direction of Paul's argument up to this point, therefore, it is not surprising that he uses κληρονομία in 11:1 as a way of evoking the future restoration of all Israel. As the chapter progresses this theme becomes more pronounced, so that, for example, Paul can insist in 11:26 that "all Israel will be saved." But before he reaches this dramatic conclusion the argument returns once more to the possibility that Israel may have in fact "stumbled so as to fall." In verses 7–10, for example, Paul concludes that Israel has "failed to obtain what it was seeking." While "the elect" obtained it, "the rest were hardened" (11:7). The language of these verses is similar to that of Romans 9, with Paul (in Romans 11) suggesting that just as in the time of Elijah there was a minority of faithful people, "So too at the present time there is a remnant, chosen by grace" (11:5). Significantly, just as in Romans 9 the word "remnant" signals the first-fruit of God's future restoration of his people, so here the concept should be understood as a sign of the nation's final restoration.[79] Paul does not use the word "remnant" for the purpose of demarcating one group of people (the present remnant) from the other (the rest who are "hardened"). Instead, both "Israel" and "remnant" in this context are eschatological categories for Paul. The "remnant" language of Romans 11, as in Romans 9, is the offering of "first fruits," the sign that there is a much greater harvest to come (Rom. 11:16). Thus the presence of an elect is for Paul an indication of God's continuing faithfulness and election for Israel because ultimately, God's redemptive intent includes "all Israel" (Rom. 11:26).

While this is the conclusion that Paul will reach by the end of the chapter, his argument takes several turns before he arrives there. In 11:11, for example, he asks a question which is almost identical to the question of 11:1: "have they stumbled so as to fall?" While, as Käsemann observes, the question is put even more precisely in verse 11,[80] it is still a question which contains the three overlapping themes identified in 11:1. Not only is it a pathos-creating question but it is also an affirmation of God's faithfulness to Israel: "have they stumbled so as to fall? *By no means!*"[81] Equally significant is the future-oriented nature of verse 11. It is a question which again is concerned with whether Israel has failed to take hold of all that was promised to them. Paul's strong denial of this is then followed by a description, in broad terms, of the restoration which will come to Israel

---

[79] Wagner, *Heralds*, 235.

[80] As Käsemann notes, verse 11 "repeats the question of v. 1a more precisely"; *Commentary on Romans*, 304.

[81] μὴ ἔπταισαν ἵνα πέσωσιν; μὴ γένοιτο.

and the world, in fulfillment of God's promises. Rom. 11:12 and 15 are particularly important for identifying the eschatological, cosmic scope of this restoration. A discussion of these verses will offer further insights into how "inheritance" is best understood in this context, and it will also help to show that adopting "inheritance" as the preferred reading of 11:1 fits very comfortably with the rest of the chapter.

> (12) Now if their [Israel's] stumbling means riches for the world (κόσμου), and if their defeat means riches for Gentiles, how much more will their full inclusion mean![82]

> (15) For if their rejection is the reconciliation of the world (καταλλαγὴ κόσμου), what will their acceptance be but life from the dead! (ζωὴ ἐκ νεκρῶν;)[83]

While I propose that these verses follow the kind of redemptive world-affirming direction signaled in Romans 4, 8 and 11:1, this is not how the verses are always understood: interpreters have often read them in narrow spiritualized terms. For example, Moo suggests that "riches" (πλοῦτος) here refers to "the richness of spiritual blessing," which the Gentiles now experience as a result of Israel's "stumbling."[84] Interpreting verse 15 in similarly spiritualized terms, Moo suggests that the "reconciliation" which Paul refers to is unlikely to be reconciliation between Jews and Gentiles[85] and that it is preferable to understand it in terms of "God's act of bringing sinners into a rightful relationship with himself."[86] According to this approach, therefore, there is little connection between the inheritance themes described above and the κόσμου language used twice in these two verses.

In part, such a conclusion is understandable. After all, the word "inheritance" is absent from many manuscripts, and interpreters often give little thought to the possibility that inheritance themes might undergird this context just as they do in Romans 4 and 8. And yet, as the discussion in previous chapters has shown, there is a clear link in Paul's mind between concepts such as "world" and "inheritance." For Paul, these are all words and phrases which are drawn from the same underlying narrative, a story which includes God's redemption of his people and the whole of creation. This is particularly evident in Rom. 4:13, where Paul says that the descendants of Abraham will one day *"inherit the world."* This suggests

---

[82] εἰ δὲ τὸ παράπτωμα αὐτῶν πλοῦτος κόσμου καὶ τὸ ἥττημα αὐτῶν πλοῦτος ἐθνῶν, πόσῳ μᾶλλον τὸ πλήρωμα αὐτῶν.

[83] εἰ γὰρ ἡ ἀποβολὴ αὐτῶν καταλλαγὴ κόσμου, τίς ἡ πρόσλημψις εἰ μὴ ζωὴ ἐκ νεκρῶν;

[84] Moo, *The Epistle to the Romans*, 688.   [85] Ibid., 693 n. 58.   [86] Ibid., 693.

that there is a strong connection in Paul's mind between "inheritance" and the "world." The "world" in that context (Rom. 4:13) was shown to include a redeemed and restored cosmos, the eschatological world which God has promised to his people. This is not to say, of course, that there can be a simple transference of the meaning of "world" in one text and context to that of another. It is important to note, for example, that in the Rom. 11:12 context the immediately parallel phrase which Paul uses for "riches for the world" in verse 12 is "riches for Gentiles." In other words, it is easy to understand why interpreters have sometimes read "the world" in this context as referring solely to the world outside Judaism, namely the Gentile world.[87]

While an uncritical transference of the meaning of "world" needs to be avoided, it is also important to give more attention to the possibility that Paul's use of κόσμος language is closely linked to the earlier inheritance themes. Significantly, there are thematic links between Rom. 4:13–25 and Romans 11. But even more important are the connections between Rom. 8:17–39 and the chapters which follow. Rather than seeing Rom. 9:1 as marking an entirely different direction of thought, it is best to understand Paul's abrupt shift in tone and style as capitalizing on the exultant doxology of Rom. 8:17–39. Neil Elliott shows in his discussion of the transition between Romans 8 and 9 that the themes of Romans 8 are continued (and adapted) through to Romans 9–11 in order to try to reshape the sympathy of Paul's audience.[88] It is therefore the assumption of the themes of Romans 8 in the chapters which follow that makes Paul's point such a powerful one. And this is similarly the case in Rom. 11:12 and 15, with Paul's use of "riches" and "the world." Just as 11:1 and 11:11 relate to whether Israel will still receive the promised inheritance, so κόσμος in the verses which follow refers to a similar concept to that used in Romans 4 and 8. This is what Grant Osborne recognizes when he suggests that in Rom 11:12 "riches for the world" refers not only to "spiritual" riches, but to "all the wealth of being children and heirs of God (8:14–16)."[89]

Paul's argument in Rom. 8:17–39 includes themes of the benefits and riches which will one day be experienced by those who are "heirs of God." It is likely that he is similarly referring to these riches in 11:12 – the benefits which are promised for those who are "children and heirs of God." Just as in verse 11 the "salvation" which Paul refers to includes

---

[87] So ibid., 689 n. 29.   [88] N. Elliott, *The Rhetoric of Romans*, 261.
[89] G. Osborne, *Romans*, The IVP New Testament Commentary Series (Illinois and Leicester: InterVarsity Press, 2004), 293.

"the broad sweep of both present anticipation and final consummation,"[90] so "riches for the world" should be thought of in the eschatological terms indicated in Romans 8.[91] In a similar way the phrase "reconciliation of the world" (11:15) should not be limited to reconciliation only between individuals or ethnic groups. While it is certainly the case that Paul is referring to the salvation which has now come to the Gentiles because of Israel's rejection, and undoubtedly one of his primary purposes in Romans is to encourage unity between Jews and Gentiles, this again should not be thought of solely in individualized and spiritualized terms. When in 11:15 Paul refers to the reconciliation of the "world" he has in mind the renewal of the cosmos to which he has referred in Romans 4 and 8 and which he has raised again in 11:1.[92] Israel's rejection, as Paul sees it, has had cosmic, universal consequences. As Fitzmyer puts it, in this context, "reconciliation expresses not only an anthropological effect of the Christ-event, but also a cosmic effect."[93]

Perhaps the most significant feature of Paul's argument in these verses, however, is not only the ways in which these phrases – "riches for the world," "reconciliation of the world" – draw from the earlier references to inheritance. These concepts are not, for Paul, the end-point of God's work in the world. Instead, they serve to emphasize that the original promise to Abraham envisaged even more than this. The basic idea conveyed in these parallel verses is that Israel's "stumbling" or "rejection" will bring blessing to the wider world, and in both cases Paul argues from the lesser to the greater.[94] For him, while the "riches for the world" (11:12) and the "reconciliation of the world" (11:15) are benefits to be celebrated, they are not the final state of things. Instead, in each case he indicates that this is only the first installment of God's blessing of the world. If this is what has already been experienced (or at least has been promised), Paul says, "how much more will their [the Jews'] full inclusion mean!" (v. 12). And then in verse 15, taking this line of thought to its ultimate

---

[90] Byrne, *Romans*, 344.

[91] The "riches" which Paul refers to, as well as echoing the "riches" of Romans 8, also intersects and overlaps with "the wealth of God's salvation as in 10:12, the wealth of God's glory as in 9:23, and the wealth of God's kindness as in 2:4, the 'fulness of eschatological blessing' whose depth Paul praises in the concluding hymn"; E. E. Johnson, *The Function of Apocalyptic*, 129.

[92] Note also Paul's use of γῆ in Rom. 9:17; 9:28; 10:18, where, as Williams points out, the word refers to "the whole inhabited earth"; S. K. Williams, "The *Promise* in Galatians," 717.

[93] Fitzmyer, *Romans*, 120. Similarly Tobin, *Paul's Rhetoric in Its Context*, 362.

[94] As Dunn points out, the structure of these two verses is precisely the same. Dunn, *Romans 9–16*, 657. Similarly Schreiner, *Romans*, 596.

conclusion, he says that if the rejection of the Jews has meant the "reconciliation of the world," "what will their acceptance be but life from the dead!" (11:15).

What is often not appreciated is that Paul's phrase here – "life from the dead" (ζωὴ ἐκ νεκρῶν) – has important connections with the argument of Rom. 4:13–25. This is especially so with regard to Rom. 4:17, where Paul writes of God "who gives life to the dead and calls into existence the things that do not exist (θεοῦ τοῦ ζωοποιοῦντος τοὺς νεκροὺς καὶ καλοῦντος τὰ μὴ ὄντα ὡς ὄντα)." This phrase – "life to the dead" – takes its place within the broader narrative of Israel's bringing blessing to the nations. One of the underlying purposes of Paul's argument in Rom. 4:13–25 is to remind the Christians at Rome that one day the entire world will be blessed through the descendants of Abraham. The phrase "life to the dead" contributes to this purpose because by alluding to the Isaianic use of the Abrahamic tradition it is a reminder that the people of God, not the rulers of the Empire, will one day inherit the earth. Just as Abraham had faith that God would do what he promised, so it will be an act of God which brings about the promised inheritance of the earth for the Christians at Rome.

But how does all of this relate to the argument which follows in Romans, particularly Romans 9–11? Neil Elliott observes that the closest context of meaning of Rom. 4:17 for Paul's Gentile-Christian audience is likely to be their own desire to be "brought to life" out of death (cf. 6:21–23). But as Elliott goes on to point out, the phrase "life to the dead" also has meaning within the broader context of the letter. For the Gentiles at Rome it is a reminder that the life which they now have in Christ is not something they can boast about because it is always the gift of God, who is also able to bring Israel to life again (11:15). Elliott therefore believes that "it is not going too far to suggest that Romans 4 lays the groundwork for the discussion in Romans 9–11 by characterizing Abraham's faith as trust in God's ability to 'do what has been promised' (4:21)."[95]

In what ways is this the case? To what extent does Romans 4, and particularly the phrase "life to the dead" lay the groundwork for Romans 9–11? In part, it sets up the theme of God's blessing of the nations through Israel. As Dunn observes, Paul in Romans 11 can continue to insist on the eventual outworking of God's purposes "presumably because for him it was always part of Israel's vocation from God, to bring blessing to

---

[95] N. Elliott, *The Rhetoric of Romans*, 221. As Harink observes, an emphasis on the trustworthiness of *God*'s actions rather than on Israel's moral history is an appropriate reading of Rom 9–11; Harink, *Paul among the Postliberals*, 171.

the world, to mediate the promise of Abraham to 'many nations' (4:13–18), to share the riches of its covenant heritage (9:4–5) with all who believe."[96] Romans 11 is the inevitable outworking of the trajectory set up in Romans 4.

But perhaps the other crucial idea signaled in Romans 4 is that this blessing will come about in an unexpected way – the "life" promised to Abraham and his descendants will come about in the midst of "death." So it is in Romans 11. While this chapter assumes that the concept of the promised inheritance has not been abandoned, it also indicates that this will come about in a way not envisaged by the descendants of Abraham. The phrase "life from the dead" is usually interpreted in one of two ways. Some read it figuratively and suggest that it encompasses the unprecedented spiritual progress of the gospel in the world or the "coming back to life" of Israel or the whole world.[97] While this has some merit, it is preferable to understand it as literally referring to "life from the dead" and therefore as a reference to the final resurrection of the dead and the "life" which will follow this resurrection.[98] As Dunn observes,

> Here more clearly than anywhere else so far in the letter Paul expresses a sense of the nearness of the final consummation of God's purposes for the world. The "more than" the riches of the reconciliation is the resurrection of the body, the complete redemption of the world (8:21–23). Nothing less than this is Paul's goal, the goal of the mission to the Gentiles: to (help) trigger off that final crescendo, when Gentile "riches" will result in Jewish "fullness", will result in "life from the dead."[99]

In the midst of Israel's unfaithfulness and apparent "death" God is able to bring "life" and the renewal of all creation, both Jew and Gentile. All nations will be blessed through Israel, and yet it will happen not through Israel's shining example but through Israel's suffering and stumbling.[100] Israel *has* (as envisaged in Rom. 4:13–25) blessed the nations even

---

[96] Dunn, *Romans 9–16*, 668.

[97] See, for example, D. P. Fuller, *Unity of the Bible: Unfolding God's Plan for Humanity* (Grand Rapids: Zondervan, 1992), 437–48; M. Nanos, *The Mystery of Romans* (Minneapolis: Fortress Press) 264–74.

[98] This is how most scholars understand the phrase. See for example Käsemann, *Commentary on Romans*, 307; Wilckens, *Rom 6–11*, 245; E. E. Johnson, *The Function of Apocalyptic*, 128; Byrne, *Romans*, 339.

[99] Dunn, *Romans 9–16*, 670.

[100] See further D. C. Allison, "Romans 11:11–15: A Suggestion," *Perspectives in Religious Studies* 12 (1985).

though, tragically, they have so far failed to realize the blessing themselves. This certainly makes sense of Paul's phrase later in the chapter when he refers to God's not "sparing" Israel (11:21) just as earlier he refers to God's not sparing "his own Son" (8:32). Both phrases refer to vicarious suffering. In the case of Israel in Rom. 11:21, it is a continuation of the thought that Israel has experienced rejection and stumbling for the sake of the world, in order that the world might ultimately be blessed.[101] Wagner sums it up well:

> [F]or Paul, Israel still plays the crucial role in the redemption of the cosmos. It is their refusal to respond to the gospel that has opened the way for the mission to the Gentiles. Moreover, the inclusion of "the rest" of Israel will be the event that ushers in the restoration of the entire created order . . . *the consummation of the long-awaited renewal of the entire cosmos.*[102]

Read in this way, therefore, inheritance in Rom. 11:1 signals the direction which Paul's argument will take in the chapter which follows. This is hinted at, as has been observed, in 11:12 and 11:15. In the verses which follow (vv. 16–25), Paul continues to use metaphors which express hope that the "rest" of Israel will be restored. For example, he writes of part of the "dough" which is "holy" and makes "the whole batch" holy (11:16). Similarly he refers to the "roots" and "branches" of a tree, emphasizing the importance of the "rich root of the olive tree" that supports the branches (11:17–25). Both images are employed to remind his audience that the present "remnant" of believers is not to be understood as a sign that God has rejected the rest of ethnic Israel but that God has begun the process of the restoration of his people.

But perhaps the climax of the inheritance language in 11:1 is when Paul concludes in 11:25–26 that once the "full number of Gentiles has come in" (11:25) then "all Israel will be saved" (καὶ οὕτως πᾶς Ἰσραὴλ σωθήσεται, 11:26). What Paul is referring to when he uses the phrase πᾶς Ἰσραήλ here has been the subject of considerable debate.[103] For example, does it refer

---

[101] Hays, *Echoes of Scripture in the Letters of Paul*, 61.

[102] Wagner, *Heralds*, 271, 273; emphasis added.

[103] The literature on this question is vast. A full discussion and evaluation of this debate is outside the limits of this chapter. Wright notes that the main positions can be grouped according to the responses given to three questions: *who* is "all Israel"?; *when* will it be accomplished?; *how* will it happen?; N. T. Wright, "Romans," 689. For recent treatments of this see Fitzmyer, *Romans*, 619–20; S. Kim, "The 'Mystery' of Rom 11:25–26 Once More," *NTS* 43 (1997), 412–29; Nanos, *The Mystery of Romans*, 239–88; C. Stanley, "'The Redeemer Will Come *from Zion*': Romans 11:26–27 Revisited," in *Paul and the Scriptures of Israel*, ed. C. A. Evans and J. A. Sanders, JSNTSup 83 (Sheffield: JSOT, 1993), 192–98.

to the "remnant" of Jews throughout history who have believed?[104] Or alternatively, does it refer to *all* Jews throughout history, including those who were hardened by God (Rom. 11:7–10)?[105] While some interpreters have proposed that the term includes both Jews *and* Gentiles who have believed in the messiah,[106] Dunn suggests that "there is now a strong consensus that πᾶς Ἰσραήλ must mean Israel as a whole, as a people whose strong corporate identity and wholeness would not be lost even if in the event there were some (or indeed many) individual exceptions."[107] While it is important not to try to push the term further than was intended – to mean every single Jew without exception[108] – it does seem that Paul is referring here to ethnic Jews. While Paul is "not necessarily asserting that each and every individual Israelite will find salvation" the reference is communal and far-reaching.[109] Paul's dramatic conclusion therefore has obvious importance for an understanding of the way in which inheritance functions in 11:1: when he refers to Israel's "salvation" here, he has in mind the eschatological climax of God's working in history, the time which will include the redemption of the body, all people, and creation itself.[110] At the beginning of the chapter (11:1) Paul insists that God has not rejected the inheritance promised to his people, a guarantee of a redeemed and restored land and people. The far-reaching nature of this inheritance language is then touched on again in 11:12–15 and is brought to a full and dramatic conclusion in 11:26.

Romans 11:1 in the context of first-century imperial Rome

All of this has significance for one of the key questions of this study, namely the extent to which the language of inheritance contributes to a counter-imperial narrative in Romans. In relation to Romans 4 and 8, three interconnected themes have emerged: to be promised the inheritance is to anticipate a time when the present earth will be renewed and when the people of God, through sacrifice and self-giving (rather than through

---

[104] So, for example H. N. Ridderbos, *Paul: An Outline of His Theology*, trans. J. R. de Witt (Grand Rapids: Eerdmans, 1975), 358–59.

[105] So, for example, Wilckens, *Rom 6–11*, 256; Fitzmyer, *Romans*, 623.

[106] See, for example, N. T. Wright, *The Climax of the Covenant*, 246–51. For a critical repudiation of this approach see particularly Harink, *Paul among the Postliberals*, 151–207.

[107] Dunn, *Romans 9–16*, 681. As Wagner points out, this does not exclude the possibility that Gentiles are implicitly included in the phrase "all Israel," but that Paul's focus is on "the rest" of Israel; Wagner, *Heralds*, 278 n. 193.

[108] Schreiner, *Romans*, 615.

[109] Byrne, *Romans*, 354. Similarly, Wagner, *Heralds*, 278.

[110] Dunn, *Romans 9–16*, 682.

domination) will possess this world. Similar themes are evoked when Paul uses the word "inheritance" in Rom. 11:1. Particularly apparent is the concept of God's restoration of his people, Israel, to a particular land. Israel has stumbled towards this goal but even this has brought in the Gentiles and will ultimately result in the anticipated blessing of the nations, the consummation of all that was promised. What has been observed in relation to inheritance in Romans 4 and 8 is similarly true of Romans 11. The concept in this context contributes to an overall counter-imperial narrative in Romans, Paul's story which claims that it is God, not the Roman Empire, who determines who has a share of the world to come and which people are to participate in this gift. To state that God is the one who is in control of the world and that God is the one who will bring about the full redemption of all people and earth is to state that Rome, the emperor of Rome and the elite who benefit from imperial policies will one day no longer be in control. The present state of things is therefore not final. Instead – and here the grand, cosmic scale of inheritance is climactic – God will one day restore the world, which will mean that all God's people, Jew and Gentile, will experience the blessing which is inheritance. This will be a time when all will have access to land and the benefits which this brings. The language of inheritance therefore contributes to a picture of the world when "all will be saved" not through the blessings of Caesar but through the gracious gift of God.

But how might such an inheritance transpire? As argued in Chapters 3 and 4 above, one function of the language of inheritance is to implicitly observe the disparity between the vision of inheritance and the current socio-political situation of the Roman Christians. At the heart of this dissonance is the issue of how the promised world will come about in the midst of the poor conditions in which most of the Roman Christians lived. To put it briefly, it is to ask what it means to be promised the world when one is presently living (predominantly) in squalor.

Here the context of Romans 9–11 in general, and Romans 11 in particular, is instructive. I suggest that perhaps more than at any other stage of his argument to date, the logic of Romans 9–11 reveals the way in which Paul wants his audience to hold in tension the disparity between the present state of things (living in first-century imperial Rome) and the future world to come (to which the concept of inheritance contributes). The use of inheritance in Romans 11 contributes to a way of thinking about the *how* of inheritance, or of what it means for the people of God to live in the shadows of Empire.

Here the work of Scott Bader-Saye is particularly instructive. In his book *Church and Israel after Christendom: The Politics of Election*,

Bader-Saye argues persuasively that the doctrine of Israel's election by God, when identified as central to the biblical narrative, provides the theological foundation for what it means to be the people of God in the world.[111] Bader-Saye particularly challenges the tendency towards a supersessionist reading of Israel in the New Testament in general and in Paul in particular.[112] As has been suggested in the discussion of Rom. 11:25 above, it seems unlikely that Paul envisages the end of God's plan for Israel as a distinct group of people. In other words, the doctrine of election – understood in the broad sense of God choosing the Jewish people in order that *they* might be the means of redemption for the world – is taken seriously by Bader-Saye. One aspect of Bader-Saye's argument which is especially relevant for our purposes is his observation that Israel's historical experience of being a people without land or of being strangers in a foreign land means that burned into Jewish consciousness is what it is to be the people of God in the world when one is not in control of one's land. "Israel's politics of election thus differs fundamentally from the politics of the nations. The remarkable ability of the Jews to remain a people while scattered and landless is but a witness to God's ability to form a people for whom place is a gift to be received rather than a status to be defended."[113] In other words the Jews "endure as a 'sign' of God in the world."[114] The doctrine of election, as Bader-Saye shows, is crucial to such an understanding of the place of Israel in the world. It is this which enables Israel to hold in tension the decidedly physical and material nature of their covenant with God, alongside the hope for a redeemed world, a world where there will be peace and plenty. Bader-Saye argues that even when Israel no longer knows what it is to live in their own land, or to rule their own territory, their hope remains physical and material rather than being spiritualized. As Bader-Saye puts it, "The peoplehood of Israel is established neither as an abstract entity in the heavens nor as an eschatological hope at the end of time. This is neither a *spiritual* covenant floating above earthly engagements nor a *formal* covenant lacking substantive content. Rather, God's covenant with Israel is almost embarrassingly material and political."[115]

---

[111] S. Bader-Saye, *Church and Israel after Christendom: The Politics of Election* (Colorado: Westview Press, 1999), *passim*.

[112] Bader-Saye, *Church and Israel after Christendom*, *passim*. Harink, *Paul among the Postliberals*, 151–207.

[113] Bader-Saye, *Church and Israel after Christendom*, 36.

[114] Ibid., 25; Harink, *Paul among the Postliberals*, 203–207.

[115] Bader-Saye, *Church and Israel after Christendom*, 40; emphasis original.

It is not Bader-Saye's purpose to consider Romans 9–11 in any depth but it is possible to use his argument as a way of understanding one of the purposes of inheritance in Rom. 11:1. As suggested above, one of the goals of Paul's use of inheritance in this verse is to create pathos. I suggest that there are two levels on which his argument regarding God's faithfulness to Israel will have been heard. First, as has been shown, Paul concludes that despite appearances in the present, God will be faithful to the original promise to Israel and will bring redemption and reconciliation to the whole world through them. In the face of strong evidence to the contrary, Paul insists that God has elected a people and that he has chosen to bring redemption to the world through this group. Although it is not made explicit in this context, there is woven throughout Paul's argument an implicit awareness of the riskiness of God's having chosen a particular gathered community through which to bring redemption to the world: "God chooses to be present in the world not as a cosmic force or a transcendent principle but through a people. And thus God's witness in the world relies on this people. So it has always been with Israel."[116] Or to put it the terms of first-century imperial Rome, unlike the political powers of the day, God chooses to bring peace not through violence or military might but through the existence of a people, even a people who in the present time seem to have "stumbled so as to fall" (Rom. 11:11). To put the issue in these terms is simply to make more specific one of the commonly acknowledged central themes of Romans, which is whether God can be considered faithful to God's promises in spite of evidence to the contrary.

Paul's primary concern in this context is therefore the question of Israel's place in God's plan. But I suggest that on another level it cannot help but have been heard as a reminder of what it means to be the people of God in the world. This is not to imply that Israel is merely being adopted by Paul as a paradigm or as an example to illustrate his point but it is to observe that in the course of wrestling with God's faithfulness to Israel, there is an implicit reflection on the role of God's people in the world. As has already been established, the language of inheritance is likely to have resulted in a degree of cognitive dissonance for the Christians in Rome because the disparity was vast between Paul's future vision and their current circumstances. The ideas established in Rom. 11:1 and continued throughout the chapter once more need to be read within this context. Paul's message is that the stance of God's people is to be one of waiting for God's action; God will be able to bring life out of death

---

[116] Ibid., 109.

(Rom. 11:15; cf. Rom. 4:17), which is to say that God will fulfill God's promises. There is no need to resort to the violence of Empire in order to achieve God's plans of redemption for the world. To the Christians at Rome, therefore, both Jew and Gentile, Paul is retelling the narrative of Israel's election in order to help these small and fragile communities in the heart of the Empire to be able to hold together the promise of inheritance with the difficulties of living within the present power of the Empire. Just as in Romans 4 the concept of inheritance evokes themes of Abraham's peaceful blessing of all nations, and similarly in Romans 8 there is the insistence that the people of God are to embody a different path to lordship, so here in Romans 11, in the midst of wrestling with the place of Israel, Paul's point is that to be the people of God in the world is to trust in the purposes and faithfulness of God and not be tempted to take matters into one's own hands.

Conclusions

In this chapter I have argued that the previously marginalized reading of Rom. 11:1 – κληρονομίαν – should be preferred in place of τὸν λαόν, and that κληρονομίαν is in fact superior in light of both text-critical evidence and intratextual considerations. The text-critical evidence gathered by Mark Given (and subsequently adopted by J. Ross Wagner and Sylvia Keesmaat) is in itself compelling. But Given concludes that more needs to be said about the possible effects of the proposed textual restoration. In particular, he identifies a need to listen for possible intratextual resonances between κληρονομία in 11:1 and κληρονόμοι in 4:13–14 and 8:16–17. This is what has been attempted above. Building on the insights gained from the previous discussion of inheritance in Rom. 4:13–25 and Rom. 8:17–39, it has been possible to explore the role which κληρονομία fulfills in Rom. 11:1.

In paying attention to the ways in which Rom. 11:1 resonates with Rom. 4:13–25 and Rom. 8:17–39, further evidence has been gathered for why κληρονομία should be adopted as the preferred reading of this verse. On one level, as Wagner observes, "[r]estoring the reading κληρονομίαν brings into clearer focus both the identity of Paul's scriptural precursors and the significance of this allusion for Paul's larger argument in Romans 9–11 concerning God's faithfulness to Israel."[117] Certainly a strong argument for adopting κληρονομίαν is the way that it underlines the faithfulness-of-God theme (so important both to Romans 9–11 and

---

[117] Wagner, *Heralds*, 223.

to the letter as a whole) in a way that reading τὸν λαόν does not. Further-more, the κληρονομίαν reading suggests greater continuity with Paul's argument both in the immediate context and the entire epistle. This is because, as observed in previous chapters, κληρονομία has played an important role (albeit a sometimes brief one) in two particularly signif-icant sections of Paul's argument (Romans 4 and 8). That Paul would choose to use κληρονομία as he moves towards the conclusion of various strands of his argument does seem likely given that it enables him to tap into the full weight of a foundational narrative such as inheritance. The importance of inheritance to the cultural story of Israel and also to Paul's argument in Romans means that Paul will have known the potential it has to advance his purposes in Romans 11. By combining κληρονομία with τὸν λαόν, as he does in Rom. 11:1–2, Paul is able to draw from a long tradition in Israel's scriptures of the way in which God will provide land and security for his people.

It is important to remember that the task of the present study is to explore how inheritance should be understood in Romans and what it contributes to Paul's eschatological worldview in this letter. While it has been necessary to evaluate the likelihood that Paul uses κληρονομία in this verse, it is obviously the case that in the course of doing so further insights have been made into the meaning of inheritance in Romans. One of the important gains made is the recognition of the ways in which previous uses of the word contribute to and interact with the use of κληρονομία in Rom. 11:1. For example, there are a number of connections between Rom. 4:13–25 and Rom. 11:1. Parts of Paul's argument in Romans 4 can be understood as laying the eschatological groundwork for his later argument. The themes of the future restoration of people and the earth, which surface in both Romans 4 and Romans 8, continue to play an important part in Paul's thinking in Romans 11. Equally significant is the way in which the eschatological vision of Romans 4 and 8, when set alongside Israel's plight described in Romans 9–11, serves to highlight the distance between the original intent of the promise and the current experience of it. In the face of the considerable tension which this raises for Paul, the concept of inheritance both highlights the emotion Paul feels and also enables him to emphasize once more the enduring promises of God. Through the use of inheritance and the direction it sets for Paul's argument in Romans 11, he is able to argue more stridently than ever that God will be faithful to his promises, which include the guarantee of a restored and renewed land and people. Both Jew and Gentile, Paul signals, will reign on this earth.

Finally, thought has been given once more to how inheritance in Rom. 11:1 might have been heard by the Roman Christians who lived in the first-century Greco-Roman imperial context. Again it has become apparent that inheritance here helps to evoke an alternative story to that being perpetuated by the powerful. The themes of God's final restoration of the world and of all people which are evoked by the inheritance concept and which are woven throughout Romans 11 contribute to an unmistakable claim – that the people of God are the ones who will inherit the land. Such a message is undeniably political and yet, as was noted in relation to Romans 4 and 8, so with Romans 11 the path to this future inheritance is not about force, exclusion and domination, but about patiently being the people of God in the presence of Empire. To trust in the faithfulness of God is to believe and to live as if the story of God and God's people in the world is true regardless of what the present state of things might indicate.

6

"LORDS" OVER ALL THE WORLD:
THE LANGUAGE OF INHERITANCE
IN GALATIANS

Inheritance, Romans and Galatians

The discussion of inheritance in Romans found that for Paul the concept refers to a geographical reality which includes the renewal of creation and that it also expresses the universal sovereignty which will be given to those who are "heirs" of the promise. It is apparent from the discussion of these texts that inheritance should not be understood in spiritualized and individualized terms but is best read as one way in which Paul refers to the future transformation of the earth and God's people. But what of Galatians? To what extent is there such a this-worldly emphasis when Paul uses the word "inheritance" in this letter?

There are certainly some parallels between one of the passages considered above (Rom. 4:13–18) and one of the texts in Galatians (3:15–29) which explicitly uses the language of inheritance. There are, for example, striking similarities between Gal. 3:16, 19, 21, 26–29 and Rom. 4:13 and there is also conceptual affinity between Rom. 4:14 and Gal. 3:18 and Rom. 4:16 and Gal. 3:15–18.[1] In both contexts Paul draws on Genesis 15, 17 and 18 in order to argue that a worldwide family was always envisaged. Paul also suggests in both Romans 4 and Galatians 3 that this family would be characterized by faith, not by the law or circumcision. Common to both texts is also the conviction that this family is marked out by those who believe in Jesus Christ. As N. T. Wright concludes, "[t]here can be little doubt that the passages are both quarried from the same seam of thought in Paul's mind."[2] This is not to say that inheritance in Galatians should be understood on the basis of Paul's usage of the concept in Romans or that the two texts should be forced into some sort of unnatural harmony – after all Romans was written some time after Galatians. Despite this, however, it will be helpful to give some thought

---

[1] N. T. Wright, *The Climax of the Covenant*, 166.
[2] Ibid., 167. See also U. Wilckens for the parallels betweeen Romans 8 and Galatians 4; Wilckens, *Rom 6–11*, 138.

to how inheritance should be understood in Galatians, not only because it plays a significant role there but because this will help to crystallize and clarify the themes which have emerged in Romans, the primary focus of this study. Given the obvious thematic kinship between these two epistles, it is worth testing the findings from Romans against Galatians. If it can be shown that Paul uses the concept in a similar way in Galatians, this would reinforce (though it would not of course prove) the conclusions proposed for Romans. The purpose of this chapter is therefore to explore the extent to which the meaning of inheritance in Galatians is consonant with the theme in Romans.

There are six occurrences of the κληρονόμος word group in the Galatians letter. The noun κληρονομία (inheritance) occurs in Gal. 3:18 and κληρονόμος (heir) in Gal. 3:29; 4:1 and 7. The verb κληρονομέω (to inherit) is used in Gal. 4:30 and 5:21.[3] Although the first occurrence of the word does not come until 3:18 – "For if the inheritance comes from the law, it no longer comes from the promise" – the concept underlies much of Paul's argument prior to this verse. This is particularly noticeable when the thematic connection between "inheritance" and "promise" is acknowledged. In fact, Sylvia Keesmaat seems right to conclude that in Galatians the two concepts are so closely linked "that one could easily describe the promise as the promise of inheritance."[4] The reference to inheritance in 3:18 is therefore intimately related to the earlier references to the concept of "promise," particularly in verses 16–17. Also, after 3:18 the concept of inheritance plays a major role in the subsequent argument, leading Brendan Byrne to suggest that the concept is overarching in 3:1– 5:12.[5] The whole point of Paul's argument in this passage is to insist that the Galatian Christians are now able to be a part of the promises made to Abraham by virtue of their being "in Christ." The various strands of his thinking are summarized and given clarity in the climax to the chapter when he says: "If you belong to Christ, then you are Abraham's offspring, *heirs according to the promise*" (3:29).[6]

If it is the case that inheritance plays an important part in Paul's argument in Galatians, what can be said about the *content* of the inheritance

---

[3] See Foerster, "κληρονόμος."
[4] Keesmaat, *Paul and His Story*, 184. Also S. K. Williams, "The *Promise* in Galatians," 711.
[5] B. J. Byrne, *"Sons of God" – "Seed of Abraham": A study of the Idea of Sonship of God of All Christians in Paul against the Jewish Background*. Analecta Biblica 83 (Rome: Biblical Institute, 1979), 189–90.
[6] Dunn suggests that the word "heir" in 3:29 picks up the theme of 3:18 and uses it as a springboard into the next section; J. D. G. Dunn, *The Epistle to the Galatians*, BNTC (Peabody, MA: Hendrickson Publishers, 1993), 208.

in this context? To what extent is it similar to what has been observed in the exploration of the concept in Romans? At first glance there seem to be some differences. For example, while Paul can refer to inheriting "the world" in Rom. 4:13, the concept is never referred to in such this-worldly terms in Galatians. This has led many interpreters to conclude that although the story of Abraham is central to the letter, as is the closely associated language of "promise" and "inheritance," these references to OT concepts are devoid of the original focus on land. For example, F. F. Bruce insists that the reference to the OT concept of land "plays no part in the argument of Galatians."[7]

A "spiritual" inheritance?

Such a conclusion is not surprising. One of Paul's primary concerns in Galatians is to address the question of *who* becomes the recipient of the promise and *who* receives the inheritance. Since one of the chief purposes of the letter is to respond to the pressing issue of *who* the heirs of Abraham are, then the question of *what* the inheritance includes is given little thought by Paul's interpreters. Moreover, in Gal. 3:14 Paul explicitly writes of receiving "the promise of the *Spirit* through faith." In view of the close connection between "promise" and "inheritance" in Galatians, it is not surprising that the inheritance tends to be understood in spiritualized terms. After all, for Paul to refer to the promised inheritance as "the Spirit" would seem to support the belief that the inheritance in Galatians should not be understood in the this-worldly terms of Romans.

But need this be the case? Does Paul's reference to the promised inheritance as the "Spirit" inevitably lead to an understanding of it in spiritualized terms? This is one of the questions which Sam Williams considers in his important article "*Promise* in Galatians: A Reading of Paul's Reading of Scripture."[8] Williams begins by discussing Gal. 3:14, particularly the meaning of the phrase τὴν ἐπαγγελίαν τοῦ πνεύμα-τος. This text holds considerable significance for Williams' purposes (to explore Paul's use of "promise" language) and also for any discussion of inheritance in Galatians because, as Williams notes, "here Paul virtually defines the term *promise* for his readers"[9] and, as noted above, the over-lapping nature of "promise" and "inheritance" in Galatians means that the text therefore has importance for an understanding of inheritance. So

---

[7] F. F. Bruce, *The Epistle to the Galatians*, NIGTC (Grand Rapids: Eerdmans, 1982), 172. Similarly J. Ziesler, *The Epistle to the Galatians*, Epworth Commentaries (London: Epworth Press, 1992), 43.

[8] S. K. Williams, "The *Promise* in Galatians."   [9] Ibid., 712.

what does Paul mean by the phrase τὴν ἐπαγγελίαν τοῦ πνεύματος? Williams argues that the reading "the Spirit's promise," in terms of *what the Spirit promised*, does not fit either Paul's theology in general or the argument of Galatians in particular. Neither can Paul mean the promise to the Galatians that the Spirit would be given in the future, for it is clear from Gal. 3:2–5 that the Galatians had already received the Spirit.[10] A third possibility which Williams considers is that the Spirit is the *present* guarantee of *future* salvation: "that is, the Spirit is God's guarantee of the final salvation which lies still in the future."[11] In this case the concept is eschatological, so that Paul is using it to refer to God's guarantee of the salvation which is in store *in the future* for believers.[12] However, as Williams points out, while there is the expectation of future salvation in Rom. 8:32 and 2 Cor. 5:5, this is not the case in Galatians, where the temporal scheme is then/now rather than now/not yet. Perhaps the clearest example of this is in Gal. 3:22, where Paul explicitly says that what was promised has already been given to believers.[13] In light of this, Williams concludes that the most accurate rendering of the phrase τὴν ἐπαγγελίαν τοῦ πνεύματος is the one preferred by most commentators, where the genitive is read as epexegetic: "Paul is talking about the promised Spirit, the Spirit which had been promised in the past and had now been poured out upon believers."[14] In other words, the Spirit is the *present* fulfillment of the *past* promise of salvation.

The inevitable question which this raises, of course, is where in the Old Testament the Spirit was promised. Various proposals have been put forward, including that Paul is thinking of the promise of the Spirit made to Israel by the prophets.[15] While this suggestion has some merit, however, it needs to be remembered that in Galatians 3 and 4 Paul draws primarily from Genesis and Deuteronomy and that the Abraham story is always at the center of Paul's argument: in 3:16 Paul says explicitly that the promise was made *to Abraham*. The problem with this, of course, is that nowhere in the Genesis text is God said to have promised the Spirit to Abraham. Williams discusses two texts in Galatians which offer insights into what Paul may therefore have meant by the phrase "the promise of the Spirit." First there is Gal. 3:6, where Paul quotes from a divine promise to Abraham: "Just as Abraham 'believed God, and it was reckoned to him as righteousness,' (7) so, you see, those who believe are the descendants of Abraham." The text which Paul quotes from here is

---

[10] Ibid., 711.   [11] Ibid.   [12] Byrne, "*Sons of God*," 156–57.

[13] S. K. Williams, "The *Promise* in Galatians," 712.   [14] Ibid.

[15] J. A. Fitzmyer, "The Letter to the Galatians," in *Jerome Biblical Commentary* (Englewood Cliffs, NJ: Prentice-Hall, 1968), vol. II, 242; J. L. Martyn, *Galatians*, AB 33A (New York: Doubleday, 1998), 323 n. 121.

Gen. 15:5–6 (LXX), which reads: "He brought him outside and said to him, 'Look up at the heavens and count the stars, if you are able to count them.' And he said, 'So shall your *sperma* be.' And Abram believed God, and it was reckoned to him as righteousness." In some sense, therefore, the promise of numerous descendants is for Paul the promise of the Spirit. But how is this so? What allows Paul to read the promise in this way? Paul's belief is that it is the Spirit who begets true sons of Abraham. God keeps the promise *through* the work of the Spirit – that is, the promise is the *means by which* children of Abraham are created. "In other words, Paul reads beyond the explicit words of scripture to the implicit meaning that for him they contain."[16] This is perhaps clearest in Gal. 4:28–29 (cf. also Gal. 4:4–5), where the act of creating children of Abraham is the work of the Spirit. Here there is a very close connection between the promise and the Spirit – just as Isaac was a child of the promise, so too those who are "born according to the Spirit" are "children of the promise."

A second important text for understanding the ways in which the promise *is* the Spirit, is Gal. 3:16: "Now the promises were made to Abraham and to his offspring." Here Paul is clearly quoting from a particular text (after all he is at pains to point out what the text does and does not say regarding "offspring"). The two texts which qualify here are Gen. 13:15 and Gen. 17:18, and in both cases the promise referred to is the promise of "land" (γῆ), unmistakably the land of Canaan, which will be given to the people of Israel. In what sense, then, does Paul understand the believers at Galatia to have received the promise of land? Williams suggests that what Paul has in mind here is not the possession of real estate but the exercise of authority. As has been observed in the discussion of inheritance in Romans 4 and 8 above, this way of reading the word fits comfortably within the wider context of Romans. But what of Galatians? To explore fully the implications of what this means and to consider more specifically what the concept of *the exercise of authority* might mean in Galatians it will be helpful to focus on Gal. 4:1–7, where the word "heir" occurs twice in the space of seven verses.

Inheritance and authority: Galatians 4:1–7 and believers as "lords over all the world"

One of the features of this section of Galatians is the rhetorical structure which Paul uses. Of particular interest to a study of inheritance is the

---

[16] S. K. Williams, "The *Promise* in Galatians," 716.

repeated allusions to, and examples of, the fact that time is characterized by two periods: the period of enslavement and the period of freedom. The main contrasts in the passage illustrate the point. The all-embracing contrast is between two lordships, one good and one evil. Those who believe are no longer slaves (4:1, 3, 7, 8, 9) but are children (4:7) and heirs (4:1, 7); those who believe are no longer under the στοιχεῖα (4:3, 9) but have the Spirit of God (4:6); believers no longer exist in a state of not knowing God (4:8) but are known by God and know God (4:9); they are no longer subjected to those who "are not gods" (4:8) but have entered into a relationship with God who is their Father (4:6, 9).[17] The concept of inheritance is at the heart of these contrasts, with κληρονόμος being paired with "slave" in both 4:1 and 4:7. The effect of this is to create an inclusio for the intervening material.[18]

> 4:1 – "My point is this: heirs (ὁ κληρονόμος), as long as they are minors, are no better than slaves (δούλου), though they are the owners of all the property."[19]
>
> 4:7 – "So you are no longer a slave (δοῦλος) but a child, and if a child then also an heir (κληρονόμος), through God."[20]

Why does Paul use "inheritance" and "slave" together to begin and conclude this section? A common way of understanding Paul's use of these concepts is to suggest that they are legal terms drawn from a particular first-century legal system, although there has been considerable debate about exactly which system this is – Hellenistic, Roman, Semitic or a type of Greco-Roman-Seleucid combination.[21] There are, however, difficulties which arise from all of these proposals.[22] These problems, combined with the "slave"/"inheritance" inclusio, lead James M. Scott to suggest that a better approach is to explore an OT exodus background to the language, concepts and argument in these verses.[23]

There are several terms used in Gal. 4:1–2 which indicate that Paul is probably drawing from the exodus tradition. For example νήπιος

---

[17] C. E. Arnold, "Returning to the Domain of the Powers: *Stoicheia* as Evil Spirits in Galatians 4:3, 9," *Nov T* 38 (1996): 69.

[18] J. M. Scott, *Adoption*, 121.

[19] Λέγω δέ, ἐφ᾽ ὅσον χρόνον ὁ κληρονόμος νήπιός ἐστιν, οὐδὲν διαφέρει δούλου κύριος πάντων ὤν.

[20] ὥστε οὐκέτι εἶ δοῦλος ἀλλὰ υἱός· εἰ δὲ υἱός, καὶ κληρονόμος διὰ θεοῦ.

[21] The options and advocates of each are noted by R. N. Longenecker, *Galatians*, WBC 41 (Dallas: Word Books, 1990), 161.

[22] James M. Scott gives extensive discussion of these problems in *Adoption*, 126–45.

[23] Ibid.

(Gal. 4:1), which is commonly understood to be a technical term referring to legal guardianship (a "minor"), is better read as an allusion to Hos. 11:1, where the term recalls Israel as "young" at the time of the exodus when God brought Israel out of Egypt as his "son."[24] In support of this is the fact that just as ὁ κληρονόμος in Gal. 4:1 is used in the singular to refer to collective Israel, so νήπιος in Hos. 11:1 is used in the singular to refer to collective Israel. One of the reasons why Paul may use νήπιος in Gal. 4:1, therefore, is in order to evoke the traditional divine-sonship imagery which is associated with the exodus (cf. Exod. 4:22; Deut. 1:31, 14:1; Isa. 63:16; Wis. 18:13; *m. Abot* 3:14 [citing Deut. 14:1]).[25] One of the objections to this proposal could be that Paul would then be referring to a historical reference while using the present tense (cf. ἐστιν and διαφέρει in v. 1). Scott points out, however, that it could be that Gal. 4:1 picks up the argument from 3:17 (the repetition of Λέγω δέ would certainly suggest this) and Paul therefore is taking up the historical present of ἀκυροῖ in 3:17.[26] It is common for Paul, when describing OT events, to slide into the present tense because of his belief that the scriptures always speak in the present.

There is also good evidence to suggest that the terms ἐπίτροπος and οἰκονόμος (4:2) stem from an exodus narrative rather than from the context of Greco-Roman guardianship as has traditionally been suggested. One of the problems which is often identified by interpreters is that the connection between the two terms seems awkward.[27] This is because while ἐπίτροπος sometimes denotes "guardian,"[28] οἰκονόμος does not at all fit the milieu of Greco-Roman guardianship.[29] On this basis, James Scott examines other contexts where the two terms *are* used together and proposes that they are often used together to refer to *state officials*.[30] There is considerable evidence too to suggest that in the time of the New Testament ἐπιτρόπος and οἰκονόμος are often used separately as common official titles, with οἰκονόμος especially used to refer to financial

---

[24] For the allusion to Hosea see ibid., 129. Those who argue that νήπιος is not a technical term for "minor" include, for example, Byrne, "*Sons of God*," 175; A. Oepke, *Der Brief des Paulus an die Galater*, THKNT 9 (Berlin: Evangelische Verlagsanstalt, 1973), 127.

[25] J. M. Scott, *Adoption*, 130.   [26] Ibid., 146.

[27] See for example R. N. Longenecker, *Galatians*, 162–63; H. D. Betz, *Galatians: A Commentary on Paul's Letter to the Churches in Galatia* (Philadelphia: Fortress Press, 1979), 203.

[28] However, ἐπιτρόπους does not always denote "guardian." See, for example, Erwin Seidl, *Rechtsgechichte Ägyptens als römischer Provinz: die Behauptung des ägyptischen Rechts neben dem römischen* (Sankt Augustin: Hans Richarz, 1973), 223–24.

[29] So H. D. Betz, *Galatians* 203–204; Longenecker, *Galatians*, 163.

[30] J. M. Scott, *Adoption*, 135–140.

administrators in the Greek city-states and in Ptolemaic Egypt. In light of this evidence it therefore seems likely that in Gal. 4:1–2 the terms refer to official titles. But which government officials is Paul referring to in these verses? A third term in this verse, προθεσμία, offers some clues.

The common understanding of προθεσμία is that it denotes the date set by the father for the termination of the guardianship.[31] There is no evidence, however, that this is how the term was used in the context of the first century.[32] Instead, προθεσμία is used to refer to a "set date" or a "predetermined time limit."[33] Given the lack of evidence for the guardianship view of Gal. 4:1–2, it is likely that the articular noun ἡ προθεσμία refers anaphorically to a date or time limit mentioned previously.[34] In other words, as noted above, the Λέγω δέ of 4:1 continues the train of thought from 3:17 (τοῦτο δὲ λέγω) where the 400/430 years alludes to Exod. 12:40. According to Gen. 15:13 the 430 years is a time limit which Yahweh had predetermined to Abraham that Israel would remain in slavery in Egypt. After this there is the promise of the exodus (15:14–16) and of the land (vv. 18–21). As Scott concludes, "It seems possible, therefore, that ἡ προθεσμία in Gal. 4:2 refers back to 3:17, looking this time at the 400/430 years as a divinely appointed date in Israel's *Heilsgeschichte*, rather than as just a fixed period in Israel's chronology."[35]

If therefore προθεσμία refers to the time of Israel's enslavement in Egypt, then this helps to make sense of the phrase οὐδὲν διαφέρει δούλου in Gal. 4:1. When these verses are understood in terms of Greco-Roman legal guardianship, it is not surprising that the phrase οὐδὲν διαφέρει δούλου is often considered an exaggeration – that the heir is not really enslaved to the "guardians and trustees."[36] But given the exodus clues in these verses, it is more likely that Paul is here taking up the traditional theme of Israel's being no different from a slave in Egypt. In Gal. 4:1 Paul is evoking Israel's story of enslavement in Egypt and Israel's subsequent liberation from this slavery; this provides further indications of what ἐπίτροπος and οἰκονόμος probably refer to in 4:2. If the framework is

---

[31] See, for example, B. Witherington, *Grace in Galatia: A Commentary on St Paul's Letter to the Galatians* (Grand Rapids: Eerdmans, 1998), 284. Similarly Dunn, *The Epistle to the Galatians*, 211.

[32] J. M. Scott, *Adoption*, 140.

[33] J. B. Lightfoot, *St Paul's Epistle to the Galatians* (London: MacMillan, 1896), 166; J. M. Scott, *Adoption*, 140.

[34] J. M. Scott, *Adoption*, 141.   [35] Ibid., 142.

[36] So, for example, Longenecker, *Galatians*, 162. For him the statement is "a hyperbole for the sake of the illustration."

Israel in Egypt, these two terms may refer to the traditional taskmasters in Egypt.[37]

Such an understanding of these terms in verses 1–2 invests the term κύριος πάντων (4:1) with particular significance. While there is relatively little evidence to support the view that κύριος πάντων refers to the heir as (potential) owner of all the property, there is considerable evidence which suggests that the expression is a *Hoheitstitel* ("lord of/over all"). Scott gathers material which demonstrates that in the Septuagint, in Josephus and in other Greek literature the term is used in both the religious and the political spheres and that in both contexts the aspect of universal sovereignty is particularly clear.[38] As Scott points out, it is not difficult to understand why Paul would use this *Hoheitstitel* in the context of the Abrahamic promise. The discussion of Rom. 4:13 above noted that within Judaism the Abrahamic promise of land was often interpreted in terms of the eschatological hope that Israel would one day rule the world. "The fact that Israel was a slave in Egypt under the taskmasters presented merely a temporary and foreseen contrast to this eschatological expectation. According to Dan. 7:18, 22, 27, the eschatological people of God ('the saints of the Most High') were to receive an everlasting kingdom with universal sovereignty (cf. 1 Cor. 6:2)."[39]

If therefore Gal. 4:1–7 draws on the language and concepts of the exodus tradition, what does this mean for how inheritance should be understood in this context? Sylvia Keesmaat points out that while Scott's analysis is helpful, it leaves a number of issues unresolved. This is particularly the case with regard to Paul's use of inheritance language and the way this relates to such suggestive phrases as κύριος πάντων:

> Even though Scott links the language of κύριος πάντων with κληρονόμος, he does not explore how the repetition of κληρονό-μος between v. 1 and v. 7 functions in these verses. Does the heir referred to in v. 7 also have the status of κύριος πάντων? And if so, what does this mean? Also, how does the language of inheritance as it is found throughout Galatians (3:18, 29; 4:29; 5:21) relate to the heirs of 4:7? Moreover, if in contemporary Jewish texts the heirs of Abraham are portrayed as inheriting the whole world, how does the language of inheritance relate

---

[37] For further evidence see J. Reumann, "The Use of Oikonomia and Related Terms in Greek Sources to about AD 100, as a Background for Patristic Application" (Ph.D. thesis, University of Pennsylvania), 266–67.

[38] See J. M. Scott, *Adoption*, 131–34.   [39] Ibid., 147.

to Paul's reference to the "new creation" in 6:15? Does the language of κύριος πάντων not need to be related to this verse as well?[40]

Keesmaat's observations hold obvious importance for the present study and will provide the focus for the argument which follows.

In order to address these issues, Keesmaat notes that when Paul uses the phrase "lord (κύριος) of all" in 4:1 it is an expression which carries implications of universal sovereignty.[41] In this verse the one who is referred to as "lord of all" is said to be the "heir" (κληρονόμος). This term, "heir," is then repeated in 4:7, where Paul says, "So you are no longer a slave but a child, and if a child then *also an heir*, through God." In light of verse 1, where Paul says that the heir is "lord of all," Paul intends his audience to perceive themselves also as having the status of "lord of all." "That is to say, the Galatian believers are now the heirs, the ones who as lord of all are to inherit the whole of creation."[42] Before Christ, humanity was "under the law" (3:23) and "enslaved" to τὰ στοιχεῖα τοῦ κόσμου (4:3). Now, however, the people have been liberated from the control of the law and they are therefore the "lords" of the whole world.[43] In future, creation will be set free from bondage (Rom. 8:21), and now "God's people are already possessing it. No longer slaves, they are already exercising their authority as heirs (Gal. 4:1–7)."[44]

In what sense is this true? How can Paul imply that the Galatian believers are now "lords" of the whole world? Furthermore, how does all of this connect back to his statement in 3:14 regarding "the promise of *the Spirit*"? Just as in Rom. 4:13–25 it was observed that there is a connection in Paul's thinking between Abraham's "numerous descendants" and the inheriting of the world, so too in Galatians 4 there seems to be a link for Paul between the Spirit's work in the Galatian communities and the universal sovereignty of Christ and his followers. As Sam Williams suggests,

> the reality of believers assuming possession of the world is in Paul's mind but the other side of God's keeping his promise of descendants as numerous as the stars of heaven. The promise of numerous descendants and the promise of the world converge;

---

[40] Keesmaat, *Paul and His Story*, 160.

[41] Ibid., 182; S. K. Williams, "The *Promise* in Galatians," 718.

[42] Keesmaat, *Paul and His Story*, 182.

[43] S. K. Williams, "The *Promise* in Galatians," 718. Wright hints at a similar reading of Galatians 3:10–14. N. T. Wright, *The Climax of the Covenant*, 141.

[44] S. K. Williams, "The *Promise* in Galatians," 718.

indeed, they are essentially identical. And as Abraham's descendants possess the world, the Spirit through them is bringing the world under the lordship of Christ. Thus does God keep the promise to the single seed: Christ is being given the world.[45]

"One in Christ Jesus": Galatians 3:28 and the extension of equality

To a certain degree this helps to explain why Paul says that the Galatians are now "lords" of the world. But this can be taken further. There is an often missed association between the phrase τὰ στοιχεῖα τοῦ κόσμου (4:3) and inheritance in this context. To appreciate this relationship it is helpful first to unpack the radical vision of community life which Paul describes in the immediately preceding sentence in Gal. 3:28: "There is no longer Jew or Greek, there is no longer slave or free, there is no longer male and female." Even a cursory glance at the verse suggests that Paul here cuts to the heart of some of the most important socio-cultural distinctions in the first century. Placing these three couplets within the socio-political-religious context of the first century helps first to lay the groundwork for understanding τὰ στοιχεῖα τοῦ κόσμου, because if (as will be argued) this phrase is referring to the powers, both supernatural and earthly, then perhaps the kinds of relationships depicted in 3:28 are meant to be read as one way in which these powers can be subverted and undermined. Such logic has obvious significance to a reading of inheritance in these verses because the vision of Gal. 3:28 is said to be available to all those who "belong to Christ" and who are therefore "Abraham's offspring, heirs according to the promise."

Gal. 3:28, sometimes referred to as the "Magna Carta of Humanity,"[46] stands in bold contrast to a first-century Greek statement which expresses gratitude: "that I was born a human being and not a beast, next a man and not a woman, thirdly, a Greek and not a barbarian."[47] This statement reflects a common Greco-Roman assumption that one's destiny, role and status were determined at birth.[48] Preserving the status quo and maintaining a sense of order were very important in such a context because this differentiation and ranking (particularly of men and women) was a powerful symbol for the foundation and stability of the world order.

---

[45] Ibid., 719–20.

[46] R. Jewett, *Man as Male and Female* (Grand Rapids: Eerdmans, 1975), 142.

[47] Attributed to Thales and Socrates in Diogenes Laertius' *Vitae philosophorum* 1.33.

[48] Witherington, *Grace in Galatia*, 271.

The entrenched belief was that these ethnic, social, economic and gender distinctions were the way the world should be structured.[49] It is this belief that Paul challenges in Gal. 3:28.

The couplet which particularly concerns Paul in 3:28 and in the entire letter is the first one: "There is neither Jew nor Greek" (οὐκ ἔνι Ἰουδαῖος οὐδὲ Ἕλλην).[50] This is simply a compressed statement of what Paul has argued in 2:11–21. In Paul's day, for both Jews and Gentiles, the religious distinction between the person of the law (the Jew) and the person of the Not-law (the Gentile) was one of the basic elements which provided structure to the world.[51] The people of the "Not-law" in this case are characterized as "Greeks" rather than Gentiles; Ἕλλην in the New Testament always means a Greek of Gentile origin, which probably reflects the ubiquity of Hellenistic culture in the Mediterranean world.[52] This distinction, as F. F. Bruce observes, "was for Judaism the most radical within the human race."[53] To cross the gulf between Jew and Gentile was possible, but significantly the gulf (at least from the Jewish perception) remained. It is this deeply ingrained ethnic distinction which Paul challenges in Gal. 2:11–21 and again here in 3:28. Whereas in Galatians 2 the language of "justification" enabled him to make his point, here the language of inheritance (which is the consequence of "justification") is the vehicle for his argument.

Paul's subversion of ethnic exclusivism is then extended to include the two other "most profound and obvious differences in the ancient world."[54] Although it is difficult to be precise about the extent of slavery in the Roman Empire, most studies estimate that slaves comprised about one-third of the entire population of the Roman Empire, being anywhere from three to five times more numerous than Roman citizens.[55] While it is also difficult to ascertain exact figures for the provinces, the percentage was probably comparable.[56] Consequently, the institution of slavery was

---

[49] Martyn, *Galatians*, 376.

[50] Verses 26–28 are probably a confessional statement of the early church which Paul is here quoting. Verse 29 seems to be Paul's own words. See, for example, W. A. Meeks, "The Image of the Androgyne: Some Uses of a Symbol in Earliest Christianity," *HR* 13 (1973/4): 180–89.

[51] Martyn, *Galatians*, 376.

[52] Dunn, *The Epistle to the Galatians*, 205. Paul's use of "Greek" as a synonym for Gentile is not unnatural since most of the Gentiles he knew were probably Greeks, in the sense that Greek was their first language; F. F. Bruce, "One in Christ Jesus, Thoughts on Galatians 3:26–29," *JCBRF* 122 (1991): 8.

[53] Bruce, "One in Christ Jesus," 188.   [54] Dunn, *The Epistle to the Galatians*, 206.

[55] A. A. Rupprecht, "Slave, Slavery," in *DPL* (Leicester: InterVarsity Press, 1993), 881.

[56] O. Patterson, *Slavery and Social Death: A Comparative Study* (Cambridge, MA: Harvard University Press, 1982), 105–31.

accepted as being part of the Greco-Roman economy and it was so ingrained in the lives of the middle and upper classes and in society that these people could hardly have survived without it.[57]

Regarding the range of conditions which slaves experienced at this time, sometimes the occupations of slaves covered a similar range to the occupations of the free.[58] Dale Martin argues that there existed "managerial slaves," who sometimes had the opportunity to advance up the social ladder while still remaining slaves.[59] Exploring why the early Christians seem to have regarded the phrase "slave of Christ" as a positive designation, Martin concludes that it was the potential for upward mobility for managerial slaves which served as an inspiration of hope for the lower classes of Paul's congregations. Martin's conclusions have been strongly questioned, however, and, as Bradley points out, even though some slaves were of higher rank, this did not protect them from the type of abuse and maltreatment to which other slaves were subjected.[60] Although slavery was not always an entirely negative experience, there was still a great distinction between the two groups, particularly in the minds of the traditional aristocracy. This distinction was often believed to be one of character as well as status, with some citizens believing that slaves could be distinguished by their appearance. Perhaps most tellingly, the genuinely free person would find enslavement intolerable, and "one in which serious resistance would be simply suicidal."[61] Slaves were often violently removed from their families;[62] they had no legal rights at all and they had to do whatever their owners instructed without question,[63] thus rendering them effectively marginalized and powerless.[64] "They were socially dead persons, without birthright, isolated from the social heritage of their

---

[57] J. M. G. Barclay, "Paul, Philemon and the Dilemma of Christian Slave-Ownership," *NTS* 37 (1991); Rupprecht, "Slave, Slavery," 881.

[58] Barclay, "Paul, Philemon," 166.

[59] D. B Martin, *Slavery as Salvation: The Metaphor of Slavery in Pauline Christianity* (New Haven: Yale University Press, 1990).

[60] K. R. Bradley, *Slavery and Society at Rome* (Cambridge University Press, 1994). For further critique see, for example, J. Byron, *Slavery Metaphors in Early Judaism and Pauline Christianity*, WUNT (Tübingen: Mohr Siebeck, 2003), 7–15; Horsley, "Paul and Slavery": 175–76.

[61] Horsley, "Slave Resistance in Classical Antiquity," in *Slavery in Text and Interpretation*, *Semeia* 83/4, ed. A. D. Callation, R. A. Horsley and A. Smith (Atlanta: Scholars Press, 1998), 134.

[62] Ibid., 135. C. S. Keener, *Paul, Women and Wives: Marriage and Women's Ministry in the Letters of Paul* (Peabody, MA: Hendrickson Publishers, 1992), 199.

[63] Barclay, "Paul, Philemon," 166; Bruce, "One in Christ Jesus," 9.

[64] M. Harris, *Slave of Christ: A New Testament Metaphor for Total Devotion to Christ* (Leicester: Apollos, 1999), 37.

ancestors"[65] and there was the assumption that slaves should expect to be disciplined by flogging or other forms of torture.[66] The Jewish attitude to slavery was certainly less exploitative than that in the Roman world, but this did not significantly alter the way in which slaves in the first century were perceived and treated:[67] "The most oppressive thing about slavery, of course, was that a slave was considered merely 'a thing' (*res*), 'a mortal object' (*res mortale*), simply 'chattel' (*mancipum*), not a person, and had no personal rights except as permitted him by his master."[68]

It is this distinction, so important to the ancient world, which Paul directly challenges in Gal. 3:28b: οὐκ ἔνι δοῦλος οὐδὲ ἐλεύθερος. Some interpreters have suggested that neither this distinction nor the one which follows has any relevance for Paul's immediate argument and that they are only quoted to complete the confession formula of which they are a part.[69] Such an assertion is not entirely unwarranted. The slave/free pairing is elsewhere presupposed and used as a metaphor in Galatians (4:21–5:1) but it is never explicitly dealt with by itself. This does not mean, however, that it has little relevance to Paul's argument. Since slaves were commonplace in the Christian community, as they were in wider society, issues concerning their role and the desirability of manumission were bound to arise, as 1 Corinthians 7 indicates.[70] Although we have no other indication that such issues had emerged in Galatia, it is probable that they were constantly just below the surface of this community and that Paul deals with the question of slavery here because it is an inevitable elaboration of his argument regarding ethnic distinction.

By affirming the need for equality between ethnic groups in Galatia, Paul is simultaneously encouraging equal participation for all groups in the community. His radically egalitarian vision for community life

---

[65] Horsley, "Slave Resistance in Classical Antiquity," 137.

[66] Barclay, "Paul, Philemon," 167. A. Jones Jr., "Paul's Message of Freedom: What Does It Mean to the Black Church?," in *The Bible and Liberation: Political and Social Hermeneutics*, ed. N. K. Gottwald and R. A. Horsley (Maryknoll, NY: Orbis Books, 1993), 516.

[67] On Jewish slavery see particularly Byron, *Slavery Metaphors*, 22–74.

[68] R. N. Longenecker, *New Testament Social Ethics for Today* (Grand Rapids: Eerdmans, 1984), 49. See also S. Briggs, "Paul on Bondage and Freedom in Imperial Roman Society," in *Paul and Politics: Ekklesia, Israel, Imperium, Interpretation*, ed. R. A. Horsley (Harrisburg, PA: Trinity Press, 2000), 110.

[69] See R. N. Longenecker, *Galatians*, 157.

[70] In a study such as this, it is not possible to compare Paul's argument in Gal. 3:28 with his advice to slaves in 1 Cor. 7:21–24. However, it is worth noting here that there seem to be different reasons why Paul uses the example of slavery in each case. See G. W. Dawes, "'But If You Can Gain Your Freedom' (1 Corinthians 7:17–24)," *CBQ* 52 (1990): 681–97. See further Horsley, "Paul and Slavery."

(2:11–21) set in place beliefs about the way in which human relationships should be structured and ordered which were always going to have
wider implications. It would not be credible for Paul on the one hand
to critique communities structured according to ethnic hierarchy, while
on the other hand having nothing to say about similarly oppressive community relationships. If the institution of slavery is maintained within
the Christian community, then this serves to elevate free people above
slaves. While there was considerable variation in slave–master relationships in the first century, there is little question that such a relationship
was based on an unequal power structure and that it stripped a person of
her/his personal dignity. Paul therefore sees this distinction as intolerable
because slavery destroys the heart of communal relations and damages
what it means to be human.[71] If the prevailing character of this relationship is unaffected in the Christian communities, it means that slaves are
considered less than full members of the people of God.

The third divide identified in this verse, οὐκ ἔνι ἄρσεν καὶ θῆλυ, was
equally ubiquitous in the ancient world. It is true that, influenced by
Etruscan and Hellenistic ideas, women in Roman society experienced
a degree of social mobility and achieved some independence under the
private law.[72] However, there is little doubt that women were at a permanent disadvantage in society as a whole and in the public sector in
particular.[73] While the Greek philosophical schools often affirmed in
principle the equality of women and men, in practice such a status was
hardly ever attained.[74] These very schools remained a community from
which women were excluded. So unfavorable was the position of women
in society that there have even been doubts whether they were Roman
citizens.[75] Several sources illustrate well the attitude towards women's
involvement in the political realm:

> No offices, no priesthoods, no triumphs, no spoils of war. Ele-
> gance, adornment, finery – these are a woman's insignia, these
> are what our forefathers called the woman's world.
>
> (The Tribune L. Valerius, 195 BCE)

[71] R. N. Longenecker, *New Testament Social Ethics for Today*, 48.

[72] C. C. Kroeger, "Women in Greco-Roman World and Judaism," in *Dictionary of New
Testament Background*, ed. C. A. Evans and Stanley E. Porter (Leicester: InterVarsity Press,
2000), 1276–80.

[73] R. A. Bauman, *Women and Politics in Ancient Rome* (London: Routledge, 1992),
1–2; Kroeger, "Women in Greco-Roman World and Judaism," 1276–80.

[74] Meeks, "The Image of the Androgyne," 170.

[75] Noted by Bauman, *Women and Politics in Ancient Rome*, 2. He points out that these
doubts are "unfounded."

Women are barred from all civil and public functions. They may
not be judges or jurors, or hold magistracies, or appear in court
or intercede for others, or be agents.

(The jurist, Ulpian, *c.* 200 CE)

Why should we pay taxes when we have no part in the
sovereignty, the offices, the campaigns, the policy-making for
which you contend against each other with such pernicious
results?

(The matron Hortensia, 42 BCE)

Some women in the Greco-Roman world did rise to prominence and
positions of authority, and Richard Bauman shows that there are examples of women involved in public protests and other forms of political
engagement. These seem to have been the exception, however, and they
appear to have done little to alter the dominant male chauvinism of the
times.[76] Charles Carlston therefore summarizes well the attitude of many
men to women in ancient society when he says that in the literature of
antiquity,

> on balance ... the picture drawn is a grim one. Women, if
> we were to trust the ancient wisdom, are basically ineduca-
> ble and empty-headed; vengeful, dangerous and responsible
> for men's sins; mendacious, treacherous and unreliable .... In
> short, women are one and all "a set of vultures" the "most
> beastly" of all the beasts on land or sea, and marriage is at best
> a necessary evil.[77]

Attitudes in the Jewish world were not dissimilar. The status of a
woman was directly related to her place in the family. While the unmarried
girl was under the authority of her father, a married woman's role "was
essentially that of a homemaker and a mother, with her praise coming
through the wisdom, influence, and exploits of her husbands and sons."[78]
As in the Greco-Roman world, there were examples of Jewish women
who rose to positions of prominence within the nation but once again

---

[76] Ibid., 1–2; Kroeger, "Women in Greco-Roman World and Judaism."

[77] C. Carlston, "Proverbs, Maxims and the Historical Jesus," *JBL* 99 (1980): 95–96.
Similarly Meeks, "The Image of the Androgyne," 179.

[78] R. N. Longenecker, *New Testament Social Ethics for Today*, 73. This is evidenced by
statements in the Mishnah which depreciate the role of women. For example *m. Abot* 1:5;
m. Sotah 3:4.

there was no real attempt within Judaism to advocate or practice the social equality of the sexes.[79]

As he has already done, Paul again says that this ubiquitous discrimination in the ancient world has no place in the Christian community. Once again we should understand "no longer male and female" as an important extension of his main point. In order to note the ways in which this is so, and to further an understanding of Paul's point in this verse, there is a need to examine the background to this phrase.

In Gal. 3:28c Paul breaks the symmetry of the three pairs by inserting καί rather than οὐδέ between ἄρσεν and θῆλυ. It seems likely that the reason for this is a conscious allusion to Gen. 1:27 in the LXX. This inclusion is heightened by the fact that elsewhere (e.g. 1 Cor. 12:13 and Col. 3:10–11) he does not mention the male–female couplet at all.[80] The terms Paul uses, ἄρσην and θῆλυ, are not typically used in Greek to speak of man and woman, but they are specifically used to emphasize the gender distinction, male and female.[81]

There have been various suggestions for why Paul uses this phrase and what he means by it. One interpretation is that the concept of androgyny lies behind Paul's words. There is the possibility that he is drawing on the idea of an androgynous Christ figure, which enables him to call for the abolition of sexual differences in Christ's corporate "body."[82] A related suggestion is that Paul has in mind the "myth of the androgyne," an interpretation of the creation story in which Adam was made after a divine masculo-feminine image.[83] While each proposal represents a good attempt to make sense of this final phrase, they are both difficult to embrace with certainty. Most importantly, the adrogyne interpretations tend to distract interpreters from Paul's intention because they do not demonstrate how this issue then connects with the overall argument of Galatians.

A second way of understanding Paul's phrase has been put forward by Ben Witherington. It is clear from Galatians that circumcision was a major issue for Paul. Yet his opponents at Galatia seem to have been going beyond this. In Gal. 4:10, for example, Paul says that his opponents

---

[79] J. R. Wegner, *Chattel or Person: The Status of Women in the Mishnah* (New York: Oxford University Press, 1988), 146–59. J. Lieu, "Circumcision, Women and Salvation," *NTS* 40 (1994): 361.

[80] It is possible, therefore, that Paul has added this pairing to the existing liturgy he took over. Witherington, *Grace in Galatia*, 279.

[81] A. Oepke, " ἄρσην," in *TDNT* I (Grand Rapids: Eerdmans, 1964–76), 362. The phrase is not unique to Paul.

[82] For evidence of this see H. D. Betz, *Galatians*, 197–98.

[83] Meeks, "The Image of the Androgyne," 185.

had succeeded in getting the Galatians to observe special days, months, seasons and years. This is significant, since if the Galatians were observing circumcision as well as extra dates on the Jewish religious calendar, then a woman's place in the community would be seen as inferior to that of a man.[84] Living by the law would foster inequality within the community since women could not be circumcised and they would not be able or expected to fulfill various demands of the law because they were periodically unclean owing to menstruation.[85] How then were women to be recognized as full members of God's community? Perhaps the answer being offered in the churches at Galatia was similiar to the one given in rabbinic Judaism: in order to assume a place in the community of God, women must marry and bear children. In this way, through their connection to a circumcised husband or son, they would be included.[86] Paul's response in rejecting gender discrimination is therefore that neither marriage nor procreation is necessary for full participation in the community of God.

The strength of this proposal is the way it ties in the phrase "no male and female" to Paul's overall argument. Circumcision seems to have been the main issue the Galatians and therefore Paul were concerned about. However the belief that women were considered second-class citizens because of their inability to be circumcised has been strongly questioned.[87] Paul, after all, gives no clues that this is what he has in mind, and it is doubtful whether anyone thought in these terms.

E. Schüssler Fiorenza proposes a third interpretation which explores the association that Paul's allusion to Gen. 1:27 would have had for his listeners. In the Genesis text, the phrase "male and female" introduces the theme of procreation and fertility. Jewish exegesis understood "male and female" primarily in terms of marriage and family.[88] To be married would be complying with the scriptural mandates that humankind should be fruitful and multiply, a command which immediately follows the statement that God made human beings male and female (Gen. 1:27–28). Paul's reply is that in Christ the coupling of male and female is not mandatory. He is therefore asserting that patriarchal marriage and

---

[84] Lieu, "Circumcision, Women and Salvation," 369; B. Witherington, "Rite and Rights for Women: Galatians 3:28," *NTS* 27.5 (1980): 595.

[85] Witherington, *Grace in Galatia*, 279.

[86] Witherington, "Rite and Rights for Women," 595.

[87] Lieu concludes that "the question remains unanswered"; Lieu, "Circumcision, Women and Salvation," 369; Martyn, *Galatians*, 380–81.

[88] E. Schüssler Fiorenza, *In Memory of Her: A Feminist Theological Reconstruction of Christian Origins* (New York: Crossroads, 1983), 211.

sexual relationships between male and female are no longer constitutive of God's new community; that kinship ties do not form the basis of the Christian community.[89] Such an understanding of Gal. 3:28c explains well Paul's allusion to Gen. 1:27 and it also agrees with his statements in 1 Cor. 7:1ff. that marriage is not necessary for a Christian.

Again, why does Paul make such a statement? What is it about the patriarchal marriage relationship that he sees as inappropriate for Christian community? Once more the egalitarian direction of his thought seems to be at the heart of the issue. The ethnic distinctions being proposed at Galatia would have given Jews exclusive privileges over Gentiles. Slavery, being based on domination and exploitation, leads to a similar hierarchical structure in the community, which in turn creates disunity and division. In the same way, the belief that women in the community must marry in order to be full participants leads to relationships in which men are given more rights than women, and unmarried women are given the lowest status in these groups. Gal. 3:28 is therefore advocating not only the undoing of religious-cultural divisions and of the oppression which slavery brings but also of control based on sexual divisions.[90] In the same way that Jews have no exclusive status over Gentiles, and free people have no exclusive advantage over slaves, so men have no exclusive rights over women.

On the basis of this new community vision, some interpreters suggest Paul is seeking to eradicate all ethnic, gender and class differences. For example, Daniel Boyarin reasons that Paul is "motivated by a Hellenistic desire for the One, which among other things produced an ideal of a universal human essence, beyond difference and hierarchy."[91] Boyarin understands Gal. 3:28 to be a classic example of Paul erasing all ethnic and gender distinctions so that all can become one in Christ's spiritual body.[92]

However, while Christ provides an entirely new identity for these groups, this does not mean that Paul believes all distinctions are completely erased "in Christ." Rather than searching for some abstract "essence" or disembodied "ideal," Paul is seeking "to enable an

---

[89] Witherington, "Rite and Rights for Women," 599.

[90] Schüssler Fiorenza, *In Memory of Her*, 213; S. Briggs, "Slavery and Gender," in *On the Cutting Edge*, ed. J. Schaberg *et al.* (New York: Continuum, 2003), 175.

[91] D. Boyarin, *A Radical Jew: Paul and the Politics of Identity* (Berkeley: University of California Press, 1994), 7.

[92] Ibid., 85. Similarly, P. Esler, "Group Boundaries and Intergroup Conflict in Galatians: A New Reading of Galatians 5:13–6:10," in *Ethnicity and the Bible*, ed. M. G. Brett (Leiden: Brill, 1996), 233.

alternative form of community which could bridge ethnic and cultural divisions by creating new patterns of common life."[93] Instead of encouraging a community of "sameness,"[94] where union with Christ abolishes all differences, the distinctions remain (one could not cease to be a Jew or a male), but their importance is weakened and relativized to the point where they are no longer used as a means of exclusion from full participation in the people of God. This means that no one's culture is condemned, nor is a particular tradition allowed to gain hegemony or be used as a means of maintaining social power at the expense of others: "Jews and Gentiles are simultaneously *affirmed* as Jews and Gentiles and *humbled* in their cultural pretensions."[95]

Of course there is a sense in which this tolerance and inclusion of cultural difference turns out to be a subtle intolerance of those for whom maintaining cultural traditions is the very core of their identity. Paul could be accused of proposing a new type of "centrism" – an "ecclesio-centrism" which prioritizes one social group at the expense of another.[96] For example, his insistence that Jews and Gentiles should eat together undermines the cultural integrity of Jews in the communities at Galatia. But Paul seems comfortable with risking this reverse cultural imperialism because the new social group he is proposing is so radically different from all other social groups. The social cohesion he envisages does not derive from anything of their own doing but is only possible because of the life and death of Christ. Most importantly, his statement is made in an overwhelmingly self-sacrificial context. Perhaps he believes his vision of *cruciform* community will allow for a retention of some ethnic specificity alongside a deeply felt and enacted human solidarity.[97]

Galatians 4:3 and the meaning of τὰ στοιχεῖα τοῦ κόσμου

Appreciating the egalitarian direction of Paul's thinking in verse 28 is an important first step towards a better understanding of inheritance in Galatians. After all, Paul suggests in 3:26–29 that all of this is available for those who are "in Christ" and are therefore "heirs" of the promise. But in what ways does this relate to the phrase τὰ στοιχεῖα τοῦ κόσ-μου in 4:3? In order to understand the connection between these two

---

[93] J. M. G. Barclay, "'Neither Jew nor Greek': Multiculturalism and the New Perspective on Paul," in *Ethnicity and the Bible*, ed. M. G. Brett (Leiden: Brill, 1996), 210.
[94] Boyarin, *A Radical Jew*, 9, 156.   [95] Barclay, "'Neither Jew nor Greek,'" 211.
[96] B. W. Longenecker, *The Triumph of Abraham's God: The Transformation of Identity in Galatians* (Edinburgh: T. & T. Clark, 1998), 77.
[97] Barclay, "'Neither Jew nor Greek,'" 212.

concepts – the "heirs" who participate in a new way of life and τὰ στοι-χεῖα τοῦ κόσμου – it is necessary first to evaluate the various proposals for how τὰ στοιχεῖα τοῦ κόσμου should be understood.

There have been three main ways in which the phrase has been understood. Based on Paul's earlier references to being "under the law" (3:23) and "under a pedagogue" (3:24), and the fact that the term στοιχεῖα originally had the sense of something rudimentary, simple and elementary, some interpreters suggest he is referring to a basic set of philosophical or religious principles or beliefs, the fundamental or elementary principles or teachings of the world.[98] For Jews these elementary principles would be the Mosaic law (4:3), and for Gentiles it may have been their worship of nature and their cultic rituals.[99] In 4:8 Paul says that the Gentile Christians were formerly enslaved to other gods, so his overall point would be that to submit to the elemental principles (in this case the Mosaic law), for both Jews and Gentiles, would be to return to that previous life of enslavement (4:9).[100]

A second understanding of τὰ στοιχεῖα is that it refers to the basic physical elements of which the natural world is made, or that it is a way of referring to the four elements of the world: earth, water, air and fire.[101] This interpretation has been acknowledged as the most common meaning of the term τὰ στοιχεῖα and the only meaning attested for the wider expression τὰ στοιχεῖα τοῦ κόσμου.[102]

This interpretation makes little sense of the context, however, leading some interpreters to argue that Paul begins with this background and then develops it. Martyn, for example, offers a reading of this phrase which attempts to link it closely with Gal. 3:28 and 6:14–15. Martyn argues that in 6:14–15 Paul begins with the ancient tradition of the "cosmos" as being made up of pairs of opposites (such as "odd and even") and extends this to include religious pairs of opposites (such as "circumcised and uncircumcised"). With this background in mind, and because 4:3 and 3:28 are in the same context, Martyn suggests that it is "a reasonable hypothesis that, when he speaks in 4:3 and 9 of the elements of that cosmos, Paul himself has in mind not earth, air, fire and water, but rather

---

[98] Proponents of this approach include R. N. Longenecker, *Galatians*, 164–66; Witherington, *Grace in Galatia*, 284–87; F. J. Matera, *Galatians*, Sacra Pagina 9 (Collegeville, MN: The Liturgical Press, 1992), 149–50.

[99] R. N. Longenecker, *Galatians*, 166.   [100] Witherington, *Grace in Galatia*, 286.

[101] στοιχεῖον, BAGD, 768–69.

[102] Martyn, *Galatians*, 395. E. Schweizer, "Slaves of the Elements and Worshippers of Angels: Gal 4:3, 9 and Col 2:8, 18, 20," *JBL* 107 (1988): 468. However, Schweizer acknowledges that often these "elements" are spoken of in terms of power and they are personified.

the elemental pairs of opposites listed in 3:28, emphatically the first pair, Jew and Gentile, and thus the Law and the Not-Law."[103]

The strength of this reading of τὰ στοιχεῖα τοῦ κόσμου lies in its allowing a natural link between 3:26–29 and 4:1–11 and the rest of the letter. Rather than there being little immediate connection between τὰ στοιχεῖα τοῦ κόσμου and its context, and Paul's overall argument in Galatians, it finds its place at the centre of his concerns. Since his main focus is the Jew/Gentile issue, it makes good sense to understand τὰ στοιχεῖα τοῦ κόσμου as directly referring with this issue.

The main problem with both of these interpretations, however, is that they fail to account for the references to the *personal nature* of the spiritual forces in this linguistic context. This is signaled early in the section (4:2), where Paul uses the personal terms ἐπίτροπος and οἰκονόμος in his initial illustration of the στοιχεῖα.[104] In the preceding verse he says that the στοιχεῖα are masters (κύριος) by virtue of the way they enslave. His point is that Jews and Gentiles, before redemption, are in some sense slaves to these masters.[105] The personal nature of the στοιχεῖα is picked up again in 4:8–9. In verse 8, for example, Paul compares the στοιχεῖα with *beings* that the pagans considered to be *gods*. Paul assumes the existence of these "beings" and characterizes the Galatians' enslavement to them as a time when they "did not know God."[106] As Edgar Krentz observes, this suggests that the apostle considers it to be a more serious matter than simply reverting back to the elementary principles of the world; instead "it is tantamount to allowing the former lords to reassert their control."[107] These ideas are continued in verse 9, where Paul asks, "how can you turn back again to the weak and beggarly στοιχεῖα?" The expression "weak and beggarly" is particularly suggestive since it is drawn from the world of demonology.[108] All of this makes it unlikely that τὰ στοιχεῖα τοῦ κόσμου should be understood as impersonal phenomena, such as basic religious teachings or as "pairs of opposites."

In light of this, a third proposal is that the phrase refers to supernatural influences over the world. This interpretation is often rejected on the grounds that such concepts are not attested until well after Paul's

---

[103] Martyn, *Galatians*, 404.

[104] Arnold, "Returning to the Domain of the Powers," 60–61; D. Reid, "Elements/Elemental Spirits," in *DPL* (Leicester: InterVarsity Press, 1993), 230.

[105] Arnold, "Returning to the Domain of the Powers," 61.

[106] Adams, *Constructing the World*, 230. Cf. 1 Cor. 8:5 and 10:19–20.

[107] E. F. Krentz, *Galatians, Philippians, Philemon, 1 Thessalonians*, ACNT (Minneapolis: Augsburg Press, 1985), 59–60.

[108] H. D. Betz, *Galatians*, 216 n. 32.

time.[109] While there is some validity to this criticism, Clinton Arnold has demonstrated well that a number of first-century traditions do in fact use the term στοιχεῖα in terms of broad supernatural powers.[110] The evidence Arnold presents should at least prevent interpreters from an a priori dismissal only on the basis of dating problems.[111]

Understanding τὰ στοιχεῖα τοῦ κόσμου in a personal, supernatural sense has good support from the Jewish tradition, one strand of which depicts the angels ruling as deities over the nations or over the elements. This is particularly so with regard to the nations other than Israel. While other nations are protected by heavenly beings such as angels, the nation of Israel is said to have a direct relationship with God.[112] In contrast to other nations, who are ruled by tribal angels and are associated with evil spirits and polluted demons,[113] the people of Israel are privileged to have God as their protector. Deut. 32:8–9 is a good example of this: "When the Most High apportioned the nations, when he divided humankind, he fixed the boundaries of the peoples according to the number of the gods [LXX "angels of God"]; the LORD's own portion was his people, Jacob his allotted share." In other words, while the Gentile nations are overseen by angels, the Jewish people enjoy God's special oversight and care. Something similar is evident in Deut. 4:6–8. There Moses says that by observing the law diligently, the peoples will say "'Surely this great nation is a wise and discerning people!' For what other great nation has a god so near to it as the Lord our God is whenever we call to him? And what other great nation has statutes and ordinances as just as this entire law that I am setting before you today?" This is also attested in other Jewish literature. In Sirach we read that God "appointed a ruler for every nation, but Israel is the Lord's own portion" (17:17).[114] Similarly, *Jubilees* 15:3 reads: "Over Israel he did not cause any angel or spirit to rule because he alone is their ruler and he will protect them."[115]

The concept of "guardian angels" or "angels of the nations," who are often characterized as "evil" and "demonic," is therefore well established

---

[109] So Witherington, *Grace in Galatia*, 284–87. R. N. Longenecker, *Galatians*, 164–66.

[110] For the three main examples of this see Arnold, "Returning to the Domain of the Powers," 57–59.

[111] Ibid., 59.

[112] B. W. Longenecker, *The Triumph of Abraham's God*, 51. See Deut. 32:8–9; Dan. 10:13–14, 20–21; Sir. 17:17; *1 Enoch* 20:5; *Jub.* 15:31.

[113] *Jub.* 10:1–6.   [114] See also *Jub.* 1:27–29.

[115] *Jub.* 15:31, 32. Further to these examples, the stars are often perceived as being ruled by angels (*1 Enoch* 60:11–22; 80:1, 6–7) or as themselves being spiritual beings (Wis. 13:2). F. Rochberg-Halton, "Astrology in the Ancient near East," in *ABD* I (New York: Doubleday, 1992), 504–507.

in Jewish thought.[116] It is this tradition which seems best to explain Paul's references to the "elements of the world" and which adds to the force of his argument.[117] His opponents were probably drawing on the Jewish tradition that the people of the law are distinctive in their lifestyle and intimacy with God in contrast to the other nations under the rule of evil angels and powers. Paul reworks this belief, suggesting that Israel's life under the law is a variation on the theme of pagan nations under the oversight of other deities. In short, Paul says the law is analogous to the evil powers.

It is important to note, however, that he does not intend explicitly to identify στοιχεῖα or its parallel "guardians and trustees" (4:2) with the law itself. Both expressions, ὑπὸ ἐπιτρόπους ἐστὶν καὶ οἰκονόμους and ὑπὸ τὰ στοιχεῖα τοῦ κόσμου are in the plural, as opposed to νόμος, which is in the singular. Paul does not say that the child is under a *single* guardian (i.e. the law) but that the child is under *many*. While he can say that the Jews were "under law" and that they have now been redeemed from this, he does not explicitly equate law observance with being under the στοιχεῖα. Instead, it is perhaps best to understand Paul to be signaling a conceptual relationship, or a close association, between "law" and στοιχεῖα.[118] In 4:8–9 his tone becomes even more negative, referring to the στοιχεῖα as "weak and beggarly." As F. F. Bruce observes, the στοιχεῖα are here depicted as "demonic forces which hold in thrall the minds of men and women who follow their dictates."[119] Paul's overall point is therefore that in the Galatians' pre-Christian past these evil forces posed as gods and goddesses and drew to themselves cultic worship (4:8). To the Jews, they used the law as a means of holding humanity in bondage (4:3).[120] For the Gentiles to take up strict law observance, therefore, would be to turn back to the powers to whom they were once enslaved.[121]

---

[116] Arnold, "Returning to the Domain of the Powers," 62. Understanding Paul's use of στοιχεῖα as a response to this tradition makes better sense contextually than the suggestion that he is referring to the ancient tradition of stars and constellations as controlling human destinies. Representatives of this argument are Beker, *Paul the Apostle*, 269–70; I. G. Hong, *The Law in Galatians*, JSNTSup 81 (Sheffield: JSOT Press, 1993), 105.

[117] J. D. G. Dunn, "The Theology of Galatians: The Issue of Covenantal Nomism," in *Thessalonians, Philippians, Galatians, Philemon*, ed. J. M. Bassler (Minneapolis: Fortress Press, 1991), 136–37; Adams, *Constructing the World*, 230.

[118] Arnold, "Returning to the Domain of the Powers," 68.

[119] Bruce, *The Epistle to the Galatians*, 204.

[120] Arnold, "Returning to the Domain of the Powers," 72.

[121] Ibid., 71. Through a comparison of κόσμου in Gal. 6:14–15 and 4:3, 9, Adams shows that in both contexts κόσμου is no neutral entity but is the sphere of opposition and hostility to God; Adams, *Constructing the World*, 229–30.

"Lords over all the world": Paul's egalitarian vision and the subversion of the powers

What does this phrase therefore convey when read alongside the radical vision of community equality which Paul describes in 3:26–29? And most importantly for the present study, what light does this bring to the question of how Paul can insist that the "heirs" are now "lords" of the world?

At no stage does Paul make explicit the connection between these two parts of his argument (3:26–29 and 4:1–7), but there is an *implied* relationship between the two which often goes unnoticed. Paul insists that to live under the law is to return to enslavement by the demonic forces, since these powers exploit the law to their own purposes (4:3, 9). In Paul's mind there seems to be a relationship between human and supernatural powers. The demonic powers lie behind and manipulate for their purposes relationships and structures which perpetuate injustice and inequality. They work within cultural and political forms in order to deny human dignity and to perpetuate forms of hierarchical oppression.

Accordingly, to refuse to live under the law and to be guided by its distinctions is therefore a subversion of the powers' dominion; it is to refuse to be captured by the lordship of the powers, both supernatural and earthly.[122] And it is at this point that there is an intersection between the language of "powers" (4:1–7) and Paul's egalitarian vision (3:26–29) and what it therefore means for the "heirs" to be "lords of all the world" (my trans.). The relativizing of ethnic distinctions is understood by Paul to be a challenge to the powers and therefore part of what it means to exercise the authority of Christ over the world. Similarly, the assertion that free people have no exclusive advantage over slaves, and that men have no exclusive advantage over women, is an implicit affront to the powers. As Williams observes, "Abraham is given the world as his descendants become the 'lords of all,' free from the enslaving power of the στοιχεῖα. And Christ is given the world insofar as the peoples of the earth acknowledge him as Lord."[123] At the crossroads of these two units of thought (Gal. 3:26–29 and 4:1–11), Paul is inviting his audience to realize that by embodying a way of life which is radically egalitarian (3:26–29), they are simultaneously witnessing to the erosion of the powers' jurisdiction and showing how the intervention of God is taking hold of the world. The people of God, who model the cruciform community, are

---

[122] Horsley hints at such a connection in "Paul and Slavery," 188.
[123] S. K. Williams, "The *Promise* in Galatians," 719.

a signal and demonstration to the powers that their previous dominion has finished.[124]

Although, as noted above, the language of στοιχεῖα seems to include both supernatural and earthly powers, it is likely that, given the particular geographical location of the Galatian churches, Paul's message about the powers and the law was heard as a challenge to the imperial cult. There has been considerable scholarly discussion of to whom Paul is referring when he writes "to the churches of Galatia" (1:2) and how this connects with Luke's narrative in Acts. One theory is that he is writing to churches he had founded in *North Galatia* during the second missionary journey (Acts 16:6) and which he revisited in Acts 18:23. Most North Galatianists argue that the letter was written during Paul's third missionary journey, at some point between 53 and 58 CE.[125] The other main theory is that he is writing to churches in *South Galatia*, founded during his first missionary journey in the Lucan account (Acts 13–14). An earlier dating of the letter (before the Jerusalem Council in 49 CE) is usually linked with this proposal. Although there is good evidence for both arguments, Graham Stanton has pointed out that there is an "emerging consensus" that Paul is writing to the churches in the south of Galatia: Pisidian Antioch, Iconium, Lystra and Derbe.[126] Stanton notes in particular the work of ancient historians which has led to fresh considerations of an old discussion.

Significantly, if Paul is writing to the churches in and around Pisidian Antioch, then there is clear evidence that the imperial cult would have figured prominently in the lives of those who gathered in the churches. This would then suggest a more specific target for the subversion-of-the-powers concept in Gal. 3:26–4:9. Bruce Winter proposes that the shadow of the imperial cult looms over the argument in Galatians even though there is no explicit mention of it. He argues that the Gentile Christians in Galatia were being encouraged to become circumcised and to keep the law so as to "look Jewish" and thereby avoid their obligation to the imperial cult. The Jewish Christians believed that "undergoing circumcision and keeping the law was one way of convincing the authorities that Christianity was part of a *religio licita,* for in Galatia these were cultural hallmarks of the one group that was recognised as being exempted from worship of the emperors."[127] By observing the law and thus "looking

---

[124] H. Berkhof, *Christ and the Powers* (Scottdale, PA: Herald Press, 1962), 41–42.

[125] For one proponent of the North Galatian theory see J. L. Martyn, *Galatians,* 15–17.

[126] Stanton, *Jesus and Gospel*, 36.

[127] B. Winter, "The Imperial Cult and the Early Christians in Pisidian Antioch (Acts 13 & Gal 6)," in *Actes du ler congrès international sur Antioche de Pisidie*, ed. T. Drew-Bear (Lyon: Université Lumière-Lyon, 2002), 69.

Jewish," the Christians at Galatia would protect themselves from persecution by taking advantage of the respect which Jews enjoyed in society
at large.[128] If this suggestion is correct, it means that Paul's relativizing
of social and cultural distinctions is not only a challenge to the powers
in general but to the authority and structures of the imperial cult in particular. As Stanton concludes with regard to Winter's proposal, however,
the scenario is "highly likely" but it is still "difficult to take a further step
and suppose that the pressures on the Jewish Christian agitators were
quite specific and involved the imperial cult."[129] Even if it cannot be
conclusively demonstrated that Paul has in mind the Roman authorities,
however, there is little doubt that here the early Christian communities
were being encouraged to become a symbol of "metaphysical rebellion,"
and to engage in an act "of cosmic audacity" which subverts and attacks
the conventional picture of what is real and what is properly human.[130]

But how does all of this happen? If the Galatian believers are to embody
a new way of life and thereby simultaneously exercise their inherited
authority as "lords" over all the world and undermine the "powers" of
the world, including the rulers of the imperial cult, how will such an
audacious claim come about? For Paul, it is the Spirit who does this, and
this is why Paul refers to the "promise of the Spirit" (3:14):

> It is the Spirit's creative, transforming power that makes sons
> and heirs out of those who had been slaves (4:1–7, 21–31), and
> it is those who walk by the Spirit, are led by the Spirit, who are
> 'of Christ' (5:16–24)... For Paul... the promise of numerous
> descendants (alluded to at Gal. 3:6) and the promise of the world
> (cf. 3:16) are both, as well, God's promise of the Spirit.[131]

Another important relationship for Paul in Gal. 3:26–29, besides that of
the Spirit and the people of God, is the intimate association between Christ
and the Christian community, expressed through the phrase ἐν Χριστῷ.
In Gal. 3:26 and 28 the phrase has three main uses, each of which is
broadly reflected in Paul's other letters. It is used once to designate a
corporate group of Christians (1:22); it occurs three times instrumentally
(2:17; 3:14; 5:10, i.e. "by/through Christ"); and four times it is used
locally (2:4; 3:26, 28; 5:6). The instrumental use of this phrase, or when
it is used as a locution for "Christian," is not too difficult to understand.
But how can Paul speak of the believer being "in Christ" in a local and

---

[128] Stanton, *Jesus and Gospel*, 45.   [129] Ibid., 44.
[130] Meeks, "The Image of the Androgyne," 207.
[131] S. K. Williams, "The *Promise* in Galatians," 719.

personal sense? Neither the suggestion that believers actually live in the ethereal Spirit and pneumatic Christ, as Deissmann suggested,[132] nor the argument that this is an instance of "Pauline mysticism," as Schweitzer proposed,[133] adequately explains Paul's use of this phrase. No doubt Paul would have been unable to give a definitive psychological analysis of his relationship with Christ, but he did know that he had experienced an intimacy with Christ and that his audience had experienced this as well. Thus, being "in Christ" seems to be Paul's way of referring, amongst other things, to "communion with Christ in the most intimate relationship imaginable, without destroying or minimizing – rather, only enhancing – the distinctive personalities of either the Christian or Christ."[134]

That this is the case is reinforced by Paul's words in Gal. 3:27. Here he seems to be describing the "moment in which, and action by means of which, their lives and destinies and very identities became bound up with Christ."[135] It was by being baptised "into Christ" (εἰς Χριστὸν) that the Galatians had been so intimately linked with Christ. Of primary importance, however, is the image of being "clothed with Christ" which Paul uses in this verse. Sam Williams notes how apt such a metaphor would have been in Paul's culture. During this period, only a person's face, hands and feet would have remained uncovered. A person's public appearance, therefore, was determined largely by the clothes he or she wore. In many places, it would be one's clothes which told others of one's occupation and social class or of the country one came from. To say that the believers at Galatia were "clothed with Christ," therefore, was significant. It meant that "differences that earlier might have separated them have now disappeared because everyone looks like Christ... believers are so closely identified with Christ that Christ provides them with the only identity, personal and social, that any longer counts."[136] When Paul uses the language of "putting on Christ," therefore, it seems to be another way of figuratively describing the mysterious personal union with Christ portrayed in Gal. 2:20. Since the metaphor can also refer to the idea of "playing the part," some suggest that Paul may have had in mind something similar to the transformation of personality which a good actor would be able to achieve through immersion in a character, by "living a part."[137] Whatever the case, the force of the metaphor is clear: when

---

[132] For example, G. A. Deissmann, *Paul: A Study in Social and Religious History* (London: Hodder and Stoughton, 1926), 140.

[133] A. Schweitzer, *Mysticism*, 10, 19.   [134] R. N. Longenecker, *Galatians*, 154.

[135] Dunn, *The Epistle to the Galatians*, 203.

[136] S. K. Williams, *Galatians*, ANTC (Nashville: Abingdon Press, 1997), 106.

[137] Dunn, *The Epistle to the Galatians*, 205.

believers are involved in this intimate union with Christ, in other words, when they are "in Christ" or "clothed with Christ," they begin to take on his character; their identity is transformed by the identity of Christ. He is therefore "the center of gravity" in this section; he is "the transformative locus" of the Galatians' faith.[138]

Paul reminds his audience of this close relationship between Christ and the community partly because he believes that the motivation and resources necessary for the revolutionary community described in 3:28 are only possible for people who are shaped by Christ.[139] For Paul, the Galatians find the *internal impetus* and the *resources* for this new community life "in Christ." The "oneness" (πάντες γὰρ ὑμεῖς εἷς ἐστε ἐν Χριστῷ Ἰησοῦ) between Jew and Gentile and the relativizing of the significance of gender and class distinctions is enabled only through the love of Christ. It seems to be the case too that for Paul being an "heir" and therefore "lord" of all can never be separated from participation with the suffering Son. The inheritance of the world does not come about through the power displayed by the Roman Empire but through the sacrifice and commitment exemplified by Christ. It is the self-giving demonstrated by Christ on the cross that is for Paul what it means to be an "heir" of the world.[140] As Keesmaat concludes, it is "identification with the suffering Son which means that one is an heir and lord of all (Gal. 4:7; cf. 4:1)."[141]

There are therefore some similarities between the language of inheritance in Romans and the use of the concept in Galatians. In both contexts the word encompasses the future universal sovereignty of the people of God and in both cases this is intimately related to the suffering which being an "heir" involves. In the discussion of Rom. 8:17 it was observed that although Paul's argument envisages the "heirs of God" having sovereignty over the world, he is not calling for his communities to mimic the conquering with which they will have been most familiar, namely that of the Roman Empire. Instead, at the heart of Paul's argument in Rom. 8:17, inheritance is not only a direct confrontation to other *claims* to rule but also a reversal of all other *paths* to lordship and rule. Something similar is evident in Paul's use of inheritance in Galatians. But there are also some differences between the concept of inheritance

---

[138] L. A. Jervis, *Galatians*, NIBC (Peabody, MA: Hendrickson Publishers, 1999), 107.

[139] The concept of union with Christ does not capture all that Paul means by this phrase, but the cruciform motif is nevertheless an important one in the immediate context and in the whole letter.

[140] B. W. Longenecker, *The Triumph of Abraham's God*, 74. Also Schüssler Fiorenza, *In Memory of Her*, 218.

[141] Keesmaat, *Paul and His Story*, 204.

in Romans and in Galatians. One of these is in 5:21, where, after listing the "works of the flesh," Paul warns that "those who do such things will not inherit (κληρονομήσουσιν) the kingdom of God."

Inheritance and the kingdom of God

It is often noted that the expression Paul uses here – inherit the kingdom of God – is unusual and is perhaps "not quite Pauline at a number of points."[142] Not only is the phrase βασιλείαν θεοῦ rare in Paul's letters[143] but the substantival participle οἱ πράσσοντες ("those who do") is an unexpected way for Paul to express "doing" in this letter.[144] Most importantly for the present study, however, is the discrepancy between the use of inheritance here and the other uses in Galatians (3:18, 29; 4:1, 7, 30). On the one hand, the concept as used in 5:21 seems closer to the Synoptic sayings which refer to "entering into the kingdom of Heaven/God."[145] Also, it is not usual in Galatians and Romans for Paul to use the promised inheritance in the context of a warning. As has been observed with regard to Romans, for example, the concept of inheritance functions eschatologically and in terms of the transformation of all things.

In light of these differences within Galatians and between Romans and Galatians, how should this expression be understood? At first glance, it could be understood to have spatial connotations and to some degree be conveying a political concept. But not surprisingly interpreters have more often suggested that the phrase is referring to a spiritual, rather than a geographical-spatial reality.[146] For example, Richard Longenecker observes that while the OT background to the concept of inheritance "had principally to do with territorial, material possessions (cf. Gen. 13:14–17; 15:7, 18–21; 17:3–8)," the concept became spiritualized in later Jewish traditions. Longenecker therefore concludes that "[t]he territorial and material features of the Abrahamic inheritance are not mentioned here by Paul, for in Christian thought 'inheritance' had become thoroughly spiritualized (cf. 5:21; also Acts 2:32; 1 Cor. 6:9–10; Eph. 5:5; Col. 3:24) and Paul's opponents would undoubtedly have thought

---

[142] R. N. Longenecker, *Galatians*, 258.
[143] Cf. Rom. 14:17; 1 Cor. 4:20; 6:9–10; 15:50. See also 1 Cor. 15:24; 1 Thess. 2:12.
[144] R. N. Longenecker, *Galatians*, 258.
[145] Cf. Mark 10:15, par; Matt. 7:21; 18:8–9; 19:17; etc.
[146] See, for example, Longenecker, who does not make this conclusion explicitly in his comments on 5:21 but implies this from his comment on 3:18; R. N. Longenecker, *Galatians*, 134.

along such lines as well."[147] Similarly, Oscar Blackwelder suggests that when Paul lists the fruit of the Spirit in 5:21–23 he is describing the "essentials of the kingdom" and therefore the content of the inheritance concept.[148]

Not all interpreters, of course, have understood the phrase "inherit the kingdom of God" in such spiritualized terms. James Hester, for example, suggests that there remains a geographical reality to the kingdom of God when Paul uses the phrase in Gal. 5:21. Hester accepts that the land of Canaan no longer plays an important role in Paul's thinking[149] but argues that this does not therefore mean that the phrase "kingdom of God" has been thoroughly spiritualized. The term still refers to a *place*, a location where people live under the rule of God.[150] Paul therefore refers to the kingdom as the "inheritance" because it has all the characteristics of the "inheritance": "The Kingdom also fulfils the Old Testament characteristic as the Land-inheritance, because it is the place where the people of God will be gathered into a great nation and will enjoy the full blessings of the reign of God. This, then, is how the Land was conceived as, or developed into, the Kingdom, and why the Kingdom came to be called the inheritance."[151]

While Hester's proposal makes sense of "inherit the kingdom of God" in 5:21, he makes no attempt to demonstrate the ways in which such a reading would fit within its immediate context. In particular, how does this geographical sense relate to the vices which Paul lists in 5:19–21, a list which defines those who will not receive the inheritance of the kingdom of God? These "works of the flesh" are predominantly relational in nature, so could it be that here (while not undermining the geographical nature of inheritance) the word "inheritance" primarily concerns relationships within the community. Similar questions arise with regard to inheritance in 5:21 and the wider context of the letter. For example, if "inheritance" in 5:21 refers to a this-worldly renewal of the world, then one possibility is that the phrase "new creation" in Gal. 6:15 could be understood in similarly this-worldly terms. While Hester suggests that this is true for "new creation" in Romans 8, he does not attend to the possibility that this might also be evident in Galatians 6. What then needs to be considered is how best to understand "new creation" in Gal. 6:15.

---

[147] Ibid.
[148] O. Blackwelder, "The Epistle to the Galatians," in *Corinthians, Galatians, Ephesians*, ed. G. A. Buttrick, The Interpreter's Bible 10 (Nashville: Abingdon, 1953), 565.
[149] Hester, *Paul's Concept of Inheritance*, 79–80.   [150] Ibid., 83.   [151] Ibid., 80.

Inheritance and new creation

Sylvia Keesmaat addresses some of these possibilities, beginning with an observation of the ways in which Paul's use of "new creation" has links to his earlier uses of "inheritance." The association is apparent in 6:14–15, where Paul juxtaposes the cross of Christ with the new creation: "May I never boast about anything except the cross of our Lord Jesus Christ, through whom the world has been crucified to me, and I to the world. For neither circumcision nor uncircumcision is anything; but a new creation is everything!" As Keesmaat points out, "Given the close connection between participation in the Son and receiving the inheritance throughout the letter, this linking of participation in the crucified Christ and the new creation reinforces the suggestion that the inheritance is precisely this new creation."[152] As further support for this proposal, Keesmaat observes the parallels between the exodus story, (which as mentioned above, is strongly evoked by Paul in Galatians 3–4) and Paul's telling of this story in Galatians. Just as the exodus story culminates with the receiving of the inheritance, and possession of the land, so

> Paul's telling of the Galatian story as such a narrative, from slavery to sonship (3:26–4:7), to the desire to return to slavery (4:8–5:1) and the resultant threat of disinheritance (5:21) should rightly end, if they are not enslaved again, with the inheritance itself: the new creation (6:15). The story of a new exodus is complete in Galatians.[153]

To what extent is this plausible? Paul's use of "new creation" without explanation or elaboration suggests that it was a concept with which his audience was familiar. But how should the phrase be understood? Does it refer to the individual believer[154] or to a new cosmic order?[155] Several factors point to the wider, cosmic reading being preferable.

J. L. Martyn provides strong evidence for a corporate or cosmic reading. He begins by noting the similarities between Jewish apocalyptic literature and Paul's worldview. Common to both is a dualism of the ages; the present age of evil will one day be transformed and renewed, resulting in a new age. Martyn argues convincingly that in this verse Paul

---

[152] Keesmaat, *Paul and His Story*, 185.   [153] Ibid.

[154] W. D. Davies, *Paul and Rabbinic Judaism: Some Rabbinic Elements in Pauline Theology* (London: SPCK, 1962), 119.

[155] Dunn, *The Epistle to the Galatians*, 343; Adams, *Constructing the World*, 225–28.

is drawing from "apocalyptic antinomies," which were a feature of Jewish apocalyptic literature. By "antinomy" Martyn means "the numerous expressions by which the ancients referred (in many languages) to a pair of opposites so fundamental to the cosmos, being one of its elements, as to make the cosmos what it is."[156] Martyn shows that in the ancient world there was a widespread belief that the fundamental building blocks of the cosmos were pairs of opposites. The thought of cosmic polarity was nearly ubiquitous in Paul's day, so that it is almost certain that the Galatians were familiar with it. It is this, argues Martyn, which Paul presupposes in Gal. 6:15.[157]

The significance of this background becomes apparent when we observe what Paul does with these accepted antinomies. He denies the existence of the antinomy of circumcision/uncircumcision, therefore making a statement no less radical than that the cosmos has suffered its death, that the building blocks of the cosmos are deficient. In this pivotal verse he explains to the Galatians that they should know the old world has died because its fundamental structures, which consist of certain identifiable pairs of opposites, have gone.[158]

This corporate reading of καινὴ κτίσις is confirmed by the immediate context. In Gal. 6:15–16 Paul makes his point by contrasting the "world" with the "new creation." The "world" (κόσμῳ) is characterized by circumcision/uncircumcision and is considered to be "nothing." In comparison, Paul boasts in the "new creation" (καινὴ κτίσις) which is inaugurated through Christ and is "everything." Therefore the primary antithesis is not Christ–law or cross–circumcision. Rather, these are subsets of the overall contrast between κόσμῳ and κτίσις.[159] It would therefore seem to make less sense of his argument to limit καινὴ κτίσις to a solely individual sense, since Paul's contrast would then be between the entire world and an individual creation.[160]

Such a distinction between individual and corporate realities, of course, may reflect a modern mindset. It is possible that first-century thinkers would not have understood the post-enlightenment division between public and private thought and lifestyle. Bruce Longenecker may therefore

[156] J. L. Martyn, *Theological Issues in the Letters of Paul* (Nashville: Abingdon Press, 1997), 115.

[157] Ibid.   [158] Ibid., 118.

[159] See B. R. Gaventa, "The Singularity of the Gospel," in *Philippians, Galatians, Philemon*, ed. J. M. Bassler (Minneapolis: Fortress Press, 1991), 156.

[160] Dunn, *The Epistle to the Galatians*, 343; J. T. Carroll and J. B. Green, *The Death of Jesus in Early Christianity* (Peabody, MA: Hendrickson Publishers, 1995), 127.

be correct when he suggests that the individual and corporate dimensions to this term are "intricately interrelated," with the individual dimension always affecting, and being affected by, the corporate dimension.[161] Although there is certainly a cosmic dimension to Paul's use of the phrase "new creation" it is not necessarily intended in the same physical sense as in Rom. 8:17–39. Instead, in Galatians "new creation" signifies a reordering of social relationships in which the old social division between "circumcised" and "uncircumcised" is done away with and a new social entity is created.[162] This is demonstrated when Paul speaks in anthropological terms ("the world has been crucified *to* me," ἐμοί, 6:14) rather than in physical terms. He thus seems to take the Jewish hope for the restoration of the world and invest it with new meaning in relation to the community at Galatia. He asserts that the exclusive religious and social boundaries which his opponents are wanting to maintain have been broken down as a result of God's (partial) renewal of creation. In this way, at the heart of Paul's statement concerning the new creation is the life of the Christian community at Galatia, in particular the issue of circumcision. His concept of "new creation" does not exist in a vacuum; it is a new pattern of existence which is lived out in community.

Conclusions

The discussion of inheritance in Galatians has been necessarily brief. There has been no effort to engage in the detailed analysis applied to the texts in Romans nor has this chapter endeavored to provide a major comparison between inheritance in Romans and inheritance in Galatians. The purpose here has been more limited: to consider the degree to which there are similarities in the uses of the word "inheritance" in these epistles and to consider the points at which there are differences. Is the interpretation of inheritance in Galatians consonant with the themes identified in Romans? By considering inheritance as it is used in different environments it is possible to reinforce the findings of the work on Romans.

As has been observed, there are many points at which inheritance in Galatians conveys similar ideas to those identified in Romans. For example, there are clear overtones of universal sovereignty which are closely associated with inheritance in Galatians. For Paul, to be an "heir" is to

---

[161] B. W. Longenecker, *The Triumph of Abraham's God*, 37 n. 6.
[162] J. M. G. Barclay, *Obeying the Truth. A Study of Paul's Ethics in Galatians* (Edinburgh: T. & T. Clark, 1988), 102.

be a "lord" of all. Read alongside the egalitarian message of Gal. 3:28 and understood against the backdrop of τὰ στοιχεῖα τοῦ κόσμου in 4:3, it seems likely that Paul believes that it is as the Galatian communities adopt a new way of relating to each other and to wider society that that they will subvert the "powers" and therefore exercise their authority as "lords" of the world. It is worth noting, however, that in Galatians this notion of universal sovereignty is more clearly situated in the realm of relationships: the implication of these texts, which is not as clear in Romans, is that how one relates to others is evidence of who is one's "Lord." This nuance is similarly apparent in the language of 5:21 and 6:15. There the connection between inheritance and "new creation," like the texts examined in Romans, assumes a future renewal of creation. But one of the distinctives of these texts is that the nature of this renewal principally involves relationships within the community of God. And yet once more it is worth pointing out that while there are these different shades of meaning of inheritance in Galatians, there are also points of striking similarity. One of these is the link which Paul understands there to be between "inheritance" and the suffering of those who are "heirs" of the promise. In both Romans and Galatians there is little possibility of missing Paul's conviction that in order to reign with Christ, one must also be "baptized with Christ" and "clothed with Christ" and therefore "crucified with Christ." The language of inheritance in Galatians, therefore, similar to that in Romans, includes simultaneously a claim to universal sovereignty and also a "lordship" which means participating in the self-giving suffering of Christ. In sum, although there is a need to engage in further detailed exegesis in order to do justice to the theme of inheritance in Galatians, even this initial exploration suggests that Paul's usage in this letter is coherent with his meaning in Romans.

7

INHERITANCE IN 1 CORINTHIANS
AND COLOSSIANS

Having considered the uses of inheritance in Romans and having then compared these with the use of the word in Galatians, I propose in this chapter to ask how the term should be understood in 1 Corinthians, the only other undisputed Pauline letter where the word occurs, and also in Colossians, a letter whose authorship is contested. Once more the focus of this chapter is determined by the findings from the study on Romans, where themes of earthly renewal, universal sovereignty, and self-sacrifice were shown to be closely associated with the language of inheritance. When the word is used in 1 Corinthians and Colossians, to what degree are these themes similarly evident and to what extent do they challenge the reading of inheritance proposed above? To ask these questions is to seek both support and critique for the proposed understanding of inheritance and to allow the different subject matter of these letters to bring further clarity to how inheritance is conceptualized.

The primary question which needs to be addressed with regard to inheritance in 1 Corinthians is whether Paul is thinking in spiritual, non-material terms when he uses the word or whether he is intending it in this-worldly, corporeal terms. Once more there will also be an attempt to explore what it would have meant to use the language of inheritance within first-century imperial society: to what degree was such language subversive of the social and political context? There are two texts which need to be explored – 1 Cor. 6:9–10 and 1 Cor. 15:50–54 – both of which use the verb "inherit" (κληρονομέω) twice in the space of only a few verses. Of these four occurrences, the two uses in 1 Cor. 15:50 reveal the most about the content of inheritance. Despite the compressed nature of the references to inheritance here, there are a number of clues in the wider passage (1 Corinthians 15) which enable fruitful comparisons with Romans. The uses of κληρονομέω in 6:9–10, while similarly brief, offer very little by way of insight into the content of inheritance. It is worth observing these references first, however, because of the way they anticipate the themes developed more fully in 1 Corinthians 15.[1]

1 Corinthians 6:9–10

In 1 Cor. 6:9–10 the phrase "will not inherit the kingdom of God" (θεοῦ βασιλείαν οὐ κληρονομήσουσιν) brackets the catalogue of sins listed in these verses: "Do you not know that wrongdoers will not inherit the kingdom of God? Do not be deceived! Fornicators, idolaters, adulterers, male prostitutes, sodomites, (10) thieves, the greedy, drunkards, revilers, robbers – none of these will inherit the kingdom of God." Richard Horsley suggests that these verses and the ones which surround them (particularly 1 Cor. 6:1–11) convey an apocalyptic orientation and framework. This perspective, argues Horsley, helps to convey the clear "political implications" which are at the heart of these verses. The experience of having been dominated by the Seleucid and Roman imperial regimes leads to certain subversive themes in Jewish apocalyptic literature: "The very purpose of Jewish apocalyptic literature was to bolster the resolve of Jewish communities to persist in their traditional way of life and maintain their independence of the dominant imperial society."[2] Horsley thus points to the social and political subversion which is conveyed when Paul uses the phrase "inherit the kingdom of God" in 1 Cor. 6:9–10.

Although it is debatable whether these verses in 1 Corinthians are best categorized as "apocalyptic,"[3] it is certain that in this text in general (6:1–11), and through the use of inheritance in particular (6:9–10), there is an eschatological perspective which invites the Corinthians to a transformed life. Paul puts it in negative terms when he says that there is no place for "fornicators, idolaters, adulterers, male prostitutes, sodomites, thieves, the greedy, drunkards, revilers, robbers" in God's kingdom. Paul's forceful words therefore insist on a changed way of life because of how God's rule will be characterized in the future. This is why Anthony Thiselton translates the phrase as "*cannot* inherit" (in the logical sense of "cannot," not in its causal sense) rather than "*will* not inherit." This rendering of the phrase is not intended to deny its future element (κληρονομήσουσιν) but it does help to capture Paul's point that there is a change which must take place in those who wish to inherit the kingdom of God. In 6:9–10, therefore, Paul is

---

[1] N. T. Wright, *The Resurrection and the Son of God*, 288.

[2] R. A. Horsley, *1 Corinthians*, ANTC (Nashville: Abingdon Press, 1998), 88.

[3] With regard to 1 Cor. 15 Gorden Fee suggests that the language is less "apocalyptic" than it is "eschatological." It may be that a similar observation applies here; G. Fee, *The First Epistle to the Corinthians*, NICNT (Grand Rapids: Eerdmans, 1987), 752 n. 30.

comparing habituated actions, which by definition can find no place in God's reign for the welfare of all, with those qualities in accordance with which Christian believers need to be transformed if they belong authentically to God's new creation in Christ... For people who do evil to inherit God's lordship is self-contradiction. Hence it entails a tacit invitation to change.[4]

1 Corinthians 15:50

By itself, 1 Cor. 6:9–10 does not offer much help in terms of the *content* of the inheritance in 6:9–10. It is clear that for Paul the advent of the kingdom of God has consequences for the present behavior of believers but there is little evidence regarding the *nature* of this future kingdom: what will be the shape of God's reign, apart from the fact that it will mean the absence of evil? For this it is necessary to explore the use of inheritance in chapter 15. When Paul writes in 15:50 that "flesh and blood cannot inherit the kingdom of God, nor does the perishable inherit the imperishable,"[5] the two main concepts he uses here – inheriting the "*kingdom of God*" and the *nature* of that kingdom ("imperishable") – have already been referred to earlier in the chapter (15:23–25 and 15:42–45). These two previous texts reveal important insights into the meaning which Paul intends when he uses inheritance language in verse 50. These insights are that (1) there is a socio-political subversiveness evoked by the language of inheritance in 1 Corinthians 15 and (2) there is a clear this-worldly, physical nature attached to inheritance in 1 Corinthians 15. In other words, at least two of the themes identified in relation to inheritance in Romans are also present in 1 Corinthians.

The kingdom of God, the powers and the inheritance (1 Cor. 15:23–25)

In 15:23–25 Paul writes,

> But each in his own order: Christ the first fruits, then at his coming those who belong to Christ. (24) Then comes the end, when he hands over the kingdom to God the Father, after he has destroyed every ruler and every authority and power. (25) For he must reign until he has put all his enemies under his feet.

---

[4] A. C. Thiselton, *The New International Greek Commentary on the First Epistle to the Corinthians*, NIGTC (Grand Rapids: Eerdmans, 2000), 439. Similarly D. E. Garland, *1 Corinthians*, BECNT (Grand Rapids: Baker, 2003), 211.

[5] σὰρξ καὶ αἷμα βασιλείαν θεοῦ κληρονομῆσαι οὐ δύναται, οὐδὲ ἡ φθορὰ τὴν ἀφθαρσίαν κληρονομεῖ.

The use of "kingdom" here anticipates the use of "kingdom of God" in verse 50 and it is particularly useful for understanding the inheritance language in verse 50 because it signals the socio-political nature of the "inheritance" of the "kingdom" (15:50). This does not mean that all interpreters agree that there is a politically subversive element to the idea that "God the Father" will reign over "every ruler and every authority and power (πᾶσαν ἀρχὴν καὶ πᾶσαν ἐξουσίαν καὶ δύναμιν)." For example, often interpreters argue that in general the terms can refer to either "good or evil spirits"[6] and that here Paul is referring to "spiritual powers" or "malevolent, demonic powers."[7] When interpreters use this language to explain the terms "rulers, authorities and powers" there is often little thought given to whether these "powers" are in any sense earthly or terrestrial. Such an approach is understandable because the terms do refer, at least in part, to supraterrestrial or cosmological powers. But the question which is particularly significant for a reading of inheritance in 1 Corinthians 15 is the degree to which there is a link in Paul's thinking between these supraterrestrial powers and the earthly (for example imperial) powers of the first century. Konrad Weiss argues that, when the first of these terms (ἀρχή) – and this is especially the case when it is linked with ἐξουσία – is referring to "primacy of *rank*" (rather than primacy of *time* or *place*) then "only context can clarify whether the reference is to earthly or supraterrestrial spheres or figures of power."[8]

If this is so, to whom is Paul referring here? One contextual clue is the preceding verse, where Paul refers to the "coming" (παρουσία) of Christ. The political connotations of this word are increasingly appreciated.[9] Hellenistic literature uses παρουσία to refer both to the epiphany of God or a god and to the official visit of an emperor or another high-ranking official to a provincial city.[10] Thus when Paul uses the word παρουσία in 15:23, it is highly likely to be a deliberate attempt to subvert the claims made by Caesar. Paul "associates salvation not with the coming of Caesar, but with the coming and return of Christ."[11] The Corinthians, as inhabitants of a Roman colony, would have been fully

---

[6] Hans Conzelmann, *1 Corinthians*, Hermeneia (Philadelphia: Fortress Press, 1975), 272.

[7] For example Fee, *First Corinthians*, 754 n. 41.

[8] K. Weiss, "ἀρχή," *EDNT* I (Grand Rapids: Eerdmans, 1990), 162.

[9] See for example, Garland, *1 Corinthians*, 708; N. T. Wright, *The Resurrection and the Son of God*, 337.

[10] Thiselton, *First Corinthians*, 1230; Weiss, "ἀρχή."

[11] B. Witherington, *Conflict and Community in Corinth: A Socio-Rhetorical Commentary on 1 and 2 Corinthians* (Grand Rapids: Eerdmans, 1995), 297.

aware of the festivities and ideology associated with imperial visits. Paul undermines this ideology by using the term in reference to Christ, not Caesar.[12]

This evocation of the first-century political environment in 15:23 signifies how the subsequent verse should be read, particularly the phrase "every ruler and authority and power" (15:24) – there is clearly an earthly aspect to it. This was certainly the normal, daily usage of ἀρχή, where it described the political, economic and religious structures and functionaries with which people had to deal.[13] This does not mean that the supraterrestrial sense can be minimized or ignored. Rather (and this is what was argued with relation to the use of similar terms in Romans 8 and Galatians 4) the terms are best understood as a combination of earthly and cosmological rulers. After all, although the majority of the uses of this term in the New Testament refer to human powers, ἀρχή is also occasionally used to designate spiritual powers, good or evil (and the same general pattern is evident in the New Testament for the word ἐξουσία, which Paul here uses in combination with ἀρχή).[14] It is therefore best to understand Paul's use of ἀρχή as relating to *all* oppressive systems and structures which hinder God's purposes in the world, whether these are supernatural powers or earthly political and social powers or, alternatively, supernatural powers *working through* human rulers and structures.[15] With regard to the first-century context within which Paul writes, therefore, it is likely that the terms signify Christ's future reign over "every structural power" which brings oppression to humanity;[16] "they are the imperial political institutions with superhuman power, not simply 'demons' in a heavenly or spiritual realm."[17] Acknowledging the fluid nature of these terms as they are used in the first-century context is particularly appropriate in relation to 1 Cor. 15:24–35, because here, alongside the terms ἀρχή and ἐξουσία, Paul uses the word δύναμις. Whereas in Jewish sources of the period the word is most often used of military or political power, the New Testament ignores this and instead focuses on the spiritual dimension of

---

[12] Garland, *1 Corinthians*, 708.

[13] So W. Wink, *Naming the Powers: The Language of Power in the New Testament* (Philadelphia: Fortress Press, 1984), 14, 15–16. Horsley suggests that the terms refer to "the rulers of the Roman imperial system"; R. A. Horsley, "1 Corinthians: A Case Study of Paul's Assembly as an Alternative Society," in *Christianity at Corinth: The Quest for the Pauline Church*, ed. E. Adams and D. G. Horrell (Louisville: Westminster John Knox Press, 2004), 231.

[14] Wink, *Naming the Powers*, 15.

[15] Thiselton, *First Corinthians*, 1232.   [16] Ibid.

[17] Horsley, *1 Corinthians*, 205. Although against Horsley I would argue that there still remains a supranatural referent to the terms.

power.[18] Thus in 1 Cor. 15:24 when Paul uses the terms ἀρχή, ἐξουσία and δύναμις, there is considerable overlap between the supraterrestrial and the earthly dimension of power and authority.

It is very likely, therefore, that Paul's Corinthian audience would have grasped the political overtones of verses 23–25. The use of "Father" in verse 24 gives further support to this reading. Frequently in imperial ideology the emperor is described as "father of the fatherland (*pater patriae*)." For example, an inscription dedicated to the emperor, dating from 47–50 CE in Corinth, refers to the emperor as both *pontifex maximus* and *p(ater) p(atriae)*.[19] As Ben Witherington observes, "Paul is trying to supplant the imperial eschatology, which was clearly extant in Corinth and which looked to the emperor as the father and benefactor providing the current blessings, with an eschatology that involves Christ and a truly divine Father."[20] While the link between this subversive claim and the language of inheritance is not made explicit by Paul, there is a connection which needs to be acknowledged. For Paul, the coming "kingdom" of God will involve Christ's reign over every earthly power, including but not limited to the first-century Roman imperial powers (1 Cor. 15:23–24). And as 15:50 makes clear, in this context it is precisely the "kingdom of God" which believers will inherit. In other words, there are significant socio-political implications in the language of inheritance in 1 Corinthians.

Inheriting an imperishable body: 1 Corinthians 15:42–44 and 53–54

In addition to this link between inheritance and the socio-political powers of the day, there is a reference to the this-worldly nature of the inheritance, a reference which (as was argued in relation to Romans) has similar socio-political significance. This concept is unpacked from 1 Cor. 15:42 through to 15:54. Although our concern is primarily the language of inheritance (which does not occur until 15:50), the verses which precede it (especially 15:42–44) and those which follow it (15:53–54) similarly express the material or physical nature of the future kingdom of God. Whereas in 15:50 Paul's focus is the inheritance in its broadest political

---

[18] Horsley, "1 Corinthians: A Case Study," 230; Wink, *Naming the Powers*, 17.

[19] J. H. Kent (ed.), *The Inscriptions 1926–1950*, vol. VIII/3 (Princeton: ASCSA, 1966), no. 77. See further E. M. Lassen, "The Use of the Father Image in Imperial Propaganda and 1 Corinthians 4:14–21," *TynBul* 42 (1991), 127–36.

[20] Witherington, *Conflict and Community in Corinth*, 305.

terms ("kingdom of God"), in verses 42–44 and 53–54 the concept is expressed in terms of an individual's physical body.

There is disagreement amongst interpreters as to why in this specific context and throughout the letter Paul repeatedly considers the notion of the body. One suggestion is that Paul's primary concern in this letter is to confront the Corinthians' "over-realized" eschatological view which resulted in a "spiritualized eschatology."[21] This argument proposes that the Corinthians' eschatology led to an understanding of "spirituality" in decidedly non-material terms. The "pneumatics" in the Corinthian congregation believed they had transcended the material world (4:8; 15:12) and that they had risen with Christ, through baptism, into a new primordial perfection (1:21–2:16; 3:18–23). Consequently, the Corinthians seem to have considered the present moral conduct of the body to be inconsequential to Christian experience (5:1–13; 6:12–20).[22] Not all interpreters agree, however. Others insist that the issue at Corinth was not *too much* eschatology, but too little.[23] According to this line of thinking, the Corinthians' puffed-up spirituality was a mixture of Christianity with paganism and one of the results of this was a belief that there could be no such thing as a resurrection of the body.[24]

Whatever the reason for Paul's focus on the notion of the body, the crucial point for the purposes of the present chapter is understanding *what* Paul says about the nature of the resurrected body. In verses 42–44 he puts it this way: "So it is with the resurrection of the dead. What is sown is perishable, what is raised is imperishable. (43) It is sown in dishonor, it is raised in glory. It is sown in weakness, it is raised in power. (44) It is sown a physical body, it is raised a spiritual body. If there is a physical body, there is also a spiritual body."

The term Paul uses in verse 44, "a spiritual body" (σῶμα πνευματικόν), has led some to insist that Paul is here suggesting that the resurrection body will be something other than physical. For example, Louw and Nida place 15:44 in a brief category under the heading "pertaining to not being physical."[25] But there are several problems with this interpretation. First, such a reading of πνευματικόν is at odds with Paul's use of the word earlier in the letter. In 1 Cor. 2:14–15, for example, the word πνευματικός

---

[21] The phrase was coined by Fee, *First Corinthians*, 12.

[22] J. H. Neyrey, "Body Language in 1 Corinthians: The Use of Anthropological Models for Understanding Paul and His Opponents," *Semeia* 35 (1986), 129–70.

[23] N. T. Wright, *The Resurrection and the Son of God*, 279. R. B. Hays, "The Conversion of the Imagination: Scripture and Eschatology in 1 Corinthians," *NTS* 45 (1999), 391–412.

[24] N. T. Wright, *The Resurrection and the Son of God*, 352.

[25] Louw–Nida, 141–43 (sections 12–18, 12–21) and 509 (sections 40.41; cf. 79.86).

clearly is not intended to describe a person who is non-physical but rather is expressing the idea that some people (the πνευματικά) are indwelt by the Spirit, and are thus able to discern the things of the Spirit. On the other hand there are those who are ψυχικός and therefore "do not receive the gifts of God's Spirit." In this context there is no thought that Paul is making a distinction between physical and non-physical when he uses the terms.[26] Similarly in 1 Corinthians 12, when Paul refers to "spiritual gifts" there is no possibility that he means "spiritual" in the sense of "non-physical." Furthermore, understanding πνευματικόν as meaning non-physical goes completely against the grain of what Paul is arguing in 1 Corinthians 15. Rather than simply confirming the Corinthians' misinformed spirituality by suggesting that the resurrection body will be non-physical, Paul's words are more likely to have jolted the Corinthians because the idea of σῶμα πνευματικόν – a spiritual body – would have seemed an oxymoron.[27]

This is not to say that Paul is describing the resurrection body as *only* physical. To understand his argument in these terms would similarly be to miss his point. On the one hand, Paul implies that there will be a genuine continuity between the present body and the future resurrection body. For example, in each of the four clauses in verses 42–44, although there is no stated subject, it is likely that Paul intends σῶμα as the subject for both verbs in each set, thus conveying a continuity between the present body and the future body.[28] The concept is the same when Paul uses the clothing imagery in verses 53–54. Four times in the space of two verses Paul says that the "mortal body" must "put on immortality" (15:53–54). As Richard Horsley notes, by using this metaphor Paul is "intentionally addressing and blocking the idea that the soul becomes disembodied when it takes on immortality."[29] While Paul makes no attempt to explain the detail of this transformation in verses 42–44 and 53–55, he understands it as something like the seed miraculously changing into a plant – just as a beautiful plant transcends the seed of grain from which it grows, so the resurrection body will transcend the earthly body.[30] Just as is implied in verses 42–45, so in verses 53–55 the resurrected body will be

---

[26] N. T. Wright, *The Resurrection and the Son of God*, 349–50.

[27] Thiselton points out that the NRSV and REB do not help matters by translating the contrast as between "physical" and "spiritual," rather than, as seems more appropriate, "natural" and "spiritual." Thiselton, *First Corinthians*, 1275.

[28] Fee, *First Corinthians*, 784.   [29] Horsley, *1 Corinthians*, 214.

[30] P. Lampe, "Paul's Concept of a Spiritual Body," in *Resurrection. Theological and Scientific Assessments*, ed. T. Peters, R. J. Russell and W. Welker, (Grand Rapids: Eerdmans, 2002), 107.

an enhancement of the present physical body, both in continuity with it and yet qualitatively transcending it in some way.[31]

On the other hand, Paul implies that the resurrection body will transcend the present physical body. The future body which Paul describes here will involve an enhancement of the physical body, a moving beyond the present body in ways that both "assimilate and transcend" our earthly bodies.[32] The present physical body – which Paul will suggest is in the order of "the first man, Adam" who was "from the earth, a man of dust" (15:45–49) – was animated by and empowered by the physical life principle or force. The resurrection body – which Paul will refer to as in the order of "the last Adam" who is "from heaven" (15:45–49) – will in contrast be animated by the Spirit. As Fee puts it, "The transformed body, therefore, is not composed of 'spirit'; it is a *body* adapted to the eschatological existence that is under the ultimate domination of the Spirit. Thus for Paul, to be truly pneumatikos is to bear the likeness of Christ (v. 49) in a transformed body, fitted for the new age."[33]

Inheriting the kingdom of God: 1 Corinthians 15:50

What does this mean for an understanding of inheritance in this context? Although the word is not mentioned directly in verses 42–44 and 53–55, there is a logical and thematic flow between these verses and the use of inheritance in verses 50. These bracketing texts provide the basis from which Paul will go on to refer to inheriting "the kingdom of God" in verse 50, where he writes, "What I am saying, brothers and sisters, is this: flesh and blood cannot inherit the kingdom of God, nor does the perishable inherit the imperishable." How best to read these parallel phrases has been the subject of considerable discussion; is it an example of *synthetic* parallelism, in which case each clause refers to a different category of believers,[34] or is it an example of *synonymous* parallelism, which would mean that the second clause simply restates the first? Jeremias argues that this is synthetic parallelism and that the first clause – "flesh and blood" – relates to the living and that the second clause – "the

---

[31] 1 Cor. 15:39–49 continues this idea; Lampe, "Paul's Concept of a Spiritual Body," 108.
[32] Thiselton, *First Corinthians*, 1279.   [33] Fee, *First Corinthians*, 786.
[34] So for example C. K. Barrett, *A Commentary on the First Epistle to the Corinthians* (London: A. & C. Black, 1971), 379–80; J. Jeremias, "Flesh and Blood Cannot Inherit the Kingdom of God," *NTS* 2 (1956): 151–59.

perishable" – concerns the dead. Jeremias posits that this antithesis is then repeated throughout verses 51–54 in a form of chiasm.[35]

This view, however, has been challenged and it seems more likely that here the second clause makes the same point as the first.[36] In this case both "flesh and blood" and "perishable" refer to the present physical bodies of believers whereas "the imperishable" refers to the resurrection body. Paul says that "flesh and blood" cannot inherit the kingdom of God, presumably because the present physical body, which is subject to weakness, decay and death, is not fit for future life in the kingdom of God. There must therefore be a transformation of the present body into a body which is more suited to the new existence, which is the "kingdom of God." In this context, "spiritual," as established above, means that the Spirit of God is the only force that creates the new body.[37] Importantly, as argued, this does not mean that the transformed body will be of an entirely different order than the present body.

There are at least two conclusions which can therefore be drawn with regard to the use of inheritance in this context. First, Paul's emphasis in 1 Corinthians 15 is on the bodily nature of salvation for the Corinthians. The language used is predominantly in terms of an individual's resurrected body but there are also clues that this extends to creation more broadly. For example, the fact that one must experience transformation in order to be a part of the kingdom of God is a clear indication that he expects the inheritance to include the restoration of creation. This suggests that Paul expects God not to destroy but to restore, renew and transform the created order. Far from God's abandoning creation or physical bodies, there are indications that for Paul the inheritance involves the redemption of creation.

Second, this eschatological picture which Paul paints is closely allied to the ethical life of believers in a way not so evident in Romans. This is particularly clear at the conclusion of the chapter (15:58), which can be considered the *peroratio*. Here Paul sums up the ethical implications and significance of the eschatological worldview he has presented so far: "Therefore, my beloved, be steadfast, immovable, always excelling in the work of the Lord, because you know that in the Lord your labor is not in vain." Paul is thus ending on the same note as he began with in verses 1–2 and so is tying the entire chapter together. Paul presumably concludes in this way because he believes that if God is going to

---

[35] Jeremias, "Flesh and Blood," 151–59.

[36] So, for example, most of the older commentaries. Also Fee, *First Corinthians*, 798.

[37] Lampe, "Paul's Concept of a Spiritual Body," 109.

transform the present world and renew physical bodies, then what believers do in the present time with their bodies, and with the world, is of considerable importance.[38] In other words the resurrection (both Christ's and the believers'), as Paul understands it, is the basis for a new moral order. He is not saying that the resurrection of Christ leads to a new Eden but that there is now one place where God's reign will begin to be manifest on earth.[39] As observed in the discussion of verses 23–25 above, there are obvious connections in Paul's thinking between this new way of life and the present rulers and authorities. As Wright points out, "The whole paragraph is about the Messiah through whose 'kingdom' the one true God will overthrow all other authorities and rulers ... every first-century Jew knew that kingdom-of-God theology carried inescapable political meaning."[40] Paul is evoking a new way of viewing history which would in turn influence one's perspective on the social structures of the world, including political institutions and the entrenched views of social status in the first century.[41]

Conclusions (1 Corinthians)

One of the main purposes of this chapter is to assess the degree to which the themes identified in relation to inheritance in Romans are similarly present in 1 Corinthians. This is not to attempt to read 1 Corinthians through Romans but it is to provide a focus for what would otherwise be a vast landscape to explore on its own. The method here has been initial exegetical aerial reconnaissance rather than on-the-ground examination.

In terms of the *content* of the inheritance in 1 Corinthians there are similarities with Romans but the particular aspects of the word which are revealed in 1 Corinthians are inevitably determined by the audience to whom he writes. One of the obvious differences in this letter is the connection Paul makes between an individual's resurrection body and the future inheritance. This is not to say that the broader this-worldly nature of inheritance is entirely absent from 1 Corinthians. As observed, there is a conceptual extension implied by Paul from a resurrected, physical/spiritual body to the resurrection or restoration of creation more

---

[38] N. T. Wright, *Paul for Everyone: 1 Corinthians* (London: SPCK, 2003), 228. As Keener puts it, "Eschatology has moral implications"; C. S Keener, *1–2 Corinthians*, NCBC (Cambridge University Press, 2005), 135.

[39] Witherington, *Conflict and Community in Corinth*, 311.

[40] N. T. Wright, *The Resurrection and the Son of God*.

[41] Witherington, *Conflict and Community in Corinth*, 311.

broadly. Also one of the emphases in 1 Corinthians is on the need for Christians to live changed lives in the present, with the implication that this is because the future inheritance of the kingdom of God will be a physical, embodied reality. This is reinforced by Paul's indication that the future kingdom of God will challenge and confront the earthly rulers and powers of the day: there is a socio-political nature to the inherited kingdom of God. If the believers at Corinth live in light of Paul's eschatological worldview then any human realized eschatologies become pointless, as 1 Corinthians 7 also makes apparent.

As for *who* will receive the inheritance, the evidence is again different in this letter from what was discovered in Romans. In 1 Corinthians the language of inheritance is not bound so tightly to the language of "heirs": for example, Abraham's descendants' being the heirs is paramount to Paul's purpose in Romans and Galatians but is entirely absent from 1 Corinthians. Instead (and this is almost inseparable from the issue noted above) the emphasis in this letter is on the fact that those who wish to receive the inheritance must evidence a changed way of life in the present. So the people who inherit the kingdom of God are those who live in line with the story of God in the present.

The question of *how* the inheritance comes about, which surfaced at a number of points in Romans, is not attached to the concept in any obvious way in 1 Corinthians. As noted above, the primary response to the *how* question is approached in terms of a transformed life in the present – this is how one prepares for the kingdom of God, by doing the "work of the Lord," for example (1 Cor. 15:58). It is possible to argue that themes such as the "crucified messiah," so important to the early stages of Paul's argument in this letter (1 Corinthians 1–2), convey something similar to the idea of "suffering conquerors" which was identified in Rom. 8:17 for example, but the link here is not explicit and it is outside the bounds of this chapter to attempt to establish the connection.

All of this suggests that although there are different emphases in 1 Corinthians, the themes of this-worldly renewal and the closely allied political dimension of this claim are in no way undermined or challenged in this letter. The use of inheritance in 1 Corinthians helps to delineate more clearly some of the broader brushstrokes applied in Romans but it does not limit the scope of these more far-reaching concepts. For, in the language of 1 Corinthians, the political and social implications of the belief that God's eschatological reign has already begun are dramatic: believers are to live in the Empire without conforming to its dominant structures and systems. Such a conclusion serves to reinforce rather than erode the conclusions reached with regard to Romans.

Inheritance in Colossians

Now that I have considered each of the uses of inheritance in the undisputed Pauline letters it will be helpful to finish by reflecting on the use of the word in Colossians. Although this letter is not judged to be among the seven undisputed Pauline epistles, many scholars suggest that the case against Colossians is not as strong as that against Ephesians and the Pastorals.[42] As John Barclay points out, "the evidence for pseudonymity is not decisive, and strong arguments can still be mounted for Pauline authorship."[43] The question of the authorship of Colossians differs from that of most of the other disputed letters in that the evidence against Pauline authorship is cumulative (including, for example, nuances of style, theology and historical plausibility) and there is thus no overwhelming proof for one's position on authorship.[44] In this chapter, therefore, I will proceed on the basis that Colossians is not assuredly Pauline but that, as Barclay concludes, "Whether by Paul, by a secretary, by an associate or by a pupil, Colossians is clearly a 'Pauline letter.'"[45] For the purposes of this chapter, I will follow the traditional practice of referring to the author as "Paul." Exploring the use of inheritance in this epistle will therefore round out a "Pauline" perspective on the word.

Colossians 1:12

The term κληρονομία occurs only once in Colossians (3:24) but a cognate of the term – κλῆρος – is also used in 1:12. What does Paul mean when he writes, in 1:12, of "giving thanks to the Father, who has enabled you to share in the inheritance of the saints in the light (εὐχαριστοῦντες τῷ πατρὶ τῷ ἱκανώσαντι ὑμᾶς εἰς τὴν μερίδα τοῦ κλήρου τῶν ἁγίων ἐν τῷ φωτί·)"?[46] Often interpreters begin by noting the obvious OT echoes in the verse but conclude by insisting that the term has been spiritualized by Paul. More specifically, although the reference to Canaan is often noted, there is little serious attention given to the degree to which Paul

---

[42] J. M. G. Barclay, *Colossians and Philemon*, New Testament Guides (Sheffield Academic Press, 1997), 22; A. T. Lincoln, "The Letter to the Colossians," in NIB 11 (Nashville: Abingdon Press, 2000), 551–60.

[43] Barclay, *Colossians and Philemon*, 23.

[44] Lincoln, "The Letter to the Colossians," 588.

[45] Barclay, *Colossians and Philemon*, 35.

[46] By using the authorial designation "Paul" in what follows I am acknowledging that although there is good evidence for Paul's being the author of Colossians, this is disputed terrain. I therefore use it in the sense described by Barclay above – that Colossians is clearly, in the broad sense of the word· a "Pauline" letter.

has retained such this-worldly content. Perhaps the clearest example of this spiritualizing of Canaan is from H. C. G. Moule, who explains this phrase as referring to "the light of spiritual knowledge, purity and joy; *the mystical Canaan of the redeemed.*"[47] This last phrase – "the mystical Canaan of the redeemed" – encapsulates well the interpretive leap which is often made by commentators. While rightly observing that Paul's use of inheritance does not have the same narrow territorial features as the OT use of the word, interpreters then proceed on the assumption that this also means Paul's inheritance is non-physical or other-worldly. But need this be the case? If it is true that Paul no longer understands the concept of inheritance to refer only to the land of Canaan, is it also true that the concept in Colossians should be read solely in spiritualized terms? The examination of Romans and Galatians above showed that this kind of hermeneutical jump is unwarranted and does not adequately account for the Jewish worldview out of which Paul works. But what of Colossians?

Once again the language and concepts which surround inheritance in 1:12, as well as the term itself, are unmistakably Jewish in character. As James Dunn points out, "For anyone familiar with the Jewish scriptures, it would immediately evoke the characteristic talk of the promised land and of Israel as God's inheritance."[48] The observation is an important reminder of the promised-land narrative which informs Paul's thinking here. In particular, the combination of κλῆρος with μερίς has a fixed place within the OT context of the partition of the land, as do their Hebrew equivalents in the Qumran literature.[49] Both κλῆρος and μερίς and the Hebrew equivalents are often used to describe the part or share received in the apportionment of the land.[50] The following texts are examples of this:

> Deut. 10:9: Therefore Levi has no allotment or inheritance (κλῆρος) with his kindred; the LORD is his inheritance (κλῆρος), as the LORD your God promised him.

---

[47] H. C. G. Moule, *Studies in Colossians and Philemon* (Grand Rapids: Kregel Publications, 1977), 74; emphasis added. Similarly P. T. O'Brien, *Colossians, Philemon*, WBC 44 (Waco, TX: Word Books, 1982), 26.

[48] J. D. G. Dunn, *The Epistles to the Colossians and to Philemon. A Commentary on the Greek Text*, NIGTC (Grand Rapids: Eerdmans, 1996), 75–76.

[49] So M. Barth and H. Blanke, *Colossians. A New Translation with Introduction and Commentary*, trans. A. B. Beck, AB 34B (New York: Doubleday, 1994), 187.

[50] E. Lohse, *Colossians and Philemon*, trans. W. R. Poehlmann and R. J. Karris, Hermeneia (Philadelphia: Fortress Press, 1971), 35.

Deut. 32:9: The LORD's own portion (μερίς) was his people, Jacob his allotted share (κληρονομίας).

Josh. 19:9: The inheritance (κληρονομία) of the tribe of Simeon formed part of the territory (κλήρου) of Judah; because the portion (μερίς) of the tribe of Judah was too large for them, the tribe of Simeon obtained an inheritance (ἐκληρονόμησαν) within their inheritance (κλήρου).

Not only is Paul drawing from texts which evoke the promised land of Canaan but he is also echoing the wider story of Israel's exodus from Egypt. This is particularly clear in Col. 1:13–14, where he writes: "He has rescued us from the power of darkness and transferred us into the kingdom of his beloved Son, (14) in whom we have redemption, the forgiveness of sins." The phrases "he has rescued us" (ὃς ἐρρύσατο ἡμᾶς) and "in whom we have redemption" (ἐν ᾧ ἔχομεν τὴν ἀπολύτρωσιν) are clear references to God's rescue operation, delivering God's people from the power of Egypt into a new land.[51]

Understanding this promised-land/exodus background to the inheritance language is an important first step towards challenging an exclusively spiritualized reading of the word.[52] In the examination of the word in Romans and Galatians (above) for example, the OT exodus and promised-land narrative were shown to be an integral part of how Paul uses the term. All of what was described in these earlier chapters similarly helps to elucidate the backdrop to inheritance in Col. 1:12 and it is not necessary to recount the detail again. But although identifying the OT echoes *is* an important first stage in questioning a primarily spiritualized reading of inheritance, it is still evident (as with interpretations of Romans) that even the most spiritualized and individualized readings of inheritance begin by acknowledging this background. Often these spiritualized readings of 1:12 conclude that there are other more significant factors which determine how inheritance should be explained here. The phrase which is given the most interpretive weight is "in the light" (ἐν τῷ φωτί). Perhaps it is because the phrase is often understood in spiritualized terms that inheritance is also frequently interpreted as here referring to an inward or spiritual domain rather than as describing the kinds of this-worldly characteristics noted in the discussion of the term in Romans

---

[51] D. M. Hay, *Colossians*, ANTC (Nashville: Abingdon Press, 2000), 48; M. MacDonald, *Colossians and Ephesians*, Sacra Pagina 17 (Collegeville, MN: The Liturgical Press, 2000), 51.

[52] For a sustained study of this connection see especially Keesmaat, *Paul and His Story*.

and Galatians. This is particularly evident in Ralph Martin's approach to the verse: "The last phrase ['in the light'] qualifies all that precedes it, for Paul wishes to make clear that while Israel was allotted Canaan as God's promised land to His elect people, *the inheritance of the new Israel is no territorial possession but a spiritual dimension*, the realm of light."[53] Should, therefore, the phrase "in the light" be understood in exclusively spiritualized terms and should this determine how inheritance is understood in this context?

There are three main ways in which this prepositional phrase – ἐν τῷ φωτί – can be construed.[54] First, it can be understood as "who has qualified you . . . *by* his light," in which case Paul would most likely be meaning "the light" of the gospel. Second, it can be read as "God's people who are *in* the kingdom of light," further explaining the nature of God's people. Most commentators, however, conclude that ἐν τῷ φωτί modifies "the inheritance of the saints" so that it reads "the inheritance . . . that *consists of* the kingdom of light."[55] But what does it mean for Paul to say that the "inheritance of the saints" consists of the kingdom of "light"? Is it necessary to conclude, along with many interpreters, that this is another way by which Paul refers to the "inward transformation" of believers[56] or of a "spiritual dimension"[57] of the original promised land – the "mystical Canaan of the redeemed"?[58]

There are two particularly striking parallels to this phrase in the Dead Sea Scrolls:[59] 1QS 11:7–8 – "God has given them (wisdom, knowledge, righteousness, power and glory) to his chosen ones as an everlasting possession and has caused them to inherit the lot of the saints"; 1QH 11:10–12 – "For the sake of your glory you have purified man of sin that he may be holy for you . . . that he may be one [with] the children of your truth and partake of the lot of your saints." Common to these Qumran texts and Paul in 1:12–13 is the contrast between two domains: there is an antithesis between the kingdom of "light" and the "power of darkness." But this contrast need not be understood in exclusively

---

[53] R. P Martin, *Colossians: The Church's Lord and the Christian's Liberty. An Expository Commentary with a Present-Day Application* (Grand Rapids: Zondervan, 1972), 38; emphasis added.

[54] See M. Harris, *Colossians and Philemon*, EGGNT (Grand Rapids: Eerdmans, 1991), 35.

[55] So, for example, ibid., 35; O'Brien, *Colossians, Philemon*, 26; Lohse, *Colossians and Philemon*, 36n.28.

[56] So P. Pokorny, *Colossians: A Commentary*, trans. S. S. Schatzmann (Peabody, MA: Hendrickson Publishers, 1991), 35.

[57] So O'Brien, *Colossians, Philemon*, 26.

[58] H. C. G. Moule, *Studies in Colossians and Philemon*, 74.

[59] Noted by Dunn, *Colossians*, 76.

spiritualized terms. Underlying the phrase "kingdom of his beloved Son" in Col. 1:13 is the promise of the coming kingdom of the Son of God which was made to David in 2 Sam. 7:16: "Your house and your kingdom shall be made sure forever before me; your throne shall be established forever."[60] Paul also picks up this theme in 1 Cor. 15:24–28, where the kingdom of the Son is characterized as a preliminary period before the end. Both 1 Corinthians 15 and Col. 1:12–14 are rooted in the Davidic tradition, therefore, indicating that in both texts what is intended is not the idea of a kingdom of light in another, transcendent, world, but the sphere or domain in which Christ reigns.[61]

This suggests that the word "light" (φῶς) here does not refer to a transcendent domain of salvation where God is present but denotes the sphere or realm into which God has transferred the saints and which therefore shapes and influences their life in the present.[62] Instead of understanding "in the light" to be referring to a non-material world, therefore, so that inheritance is similarly defined in these exclusively metaphysical terms, it should be read as indicating a new kind of inheritance – not *spiritual* inheritance as opposed to *physical* but a transformation of the world which reshapes how believers now live.[63] Margaret MacDonald rightly observes the ways in which these verses contribute to one of the overall messages of Colossians, namely that of belonging: "The reference to 'sharing in the inheritance of the saints in the light' is language of belonging, boldly announcing that *believers ultimately belong to a transformed world.*"[64] By comprehending the physical and this-worldly nature of inheritance in the Old Testament and by noting that Paul does not fundamentally alter this meaning of the term, we see that the function of inheritance in 1:12 becomes increasingly important. Paul wants the believers at Colossae to remember that the world is in the process of being physically transformed and that they must now live in accordance with this new world, this new kingdom of "light."

Colossians 3:24

The other occurrence of inheritance in Colossians is in 3:22–24 where Paul writes,

---

[60] Note also Ps. 2:7; 4QFlor 1:11; Luke 1:33.
[61] E. Schweizer, *The Letter to the Colossians. A Commentary*, trans. A. Chester (Minneapolis, MN: Augsbury Publishing House, 1982), 52.
[62] Lohse, *Colossians and Philemon*, 36 n. 30.
[63] N. T. Wright, *Colossians and Philemon*, TNTC (Grand Rapids: Eerdmans, 1986), 61.
[64] MacDonald, *Colossians and Ephesians*, 56; emphasis added.

(22) Slaves, obey your earthly masters in everything, not only while being watched and in order to please them, but wholeheartedly, fearing the Lord. (23) Whatever your task, put yourselves into it, as done for the Lord and not for your masters, (24) since you know that from the Lord you will receive the inheritance as your reward; you serve the Lord Christ (εἰδότες ὅτι ἀπὸ κυρίου ἀπολήμψεσθε τὴν ἀνταπόδοσιν τῆς κληρονομίας. τῷ κυρίῳ Χριστῷ δουλεύετε).

Just as "inheritance" in 1:12 is often read in terms of a transcendent afterlife, so interpretations of this verse commonly understand it to be referring to the non-material realm. David Hay's reading of the word is indicative; for Hay, the key phrase "the inheritance as your reward" is referring to "an after-death heavenly compensation making up for the fact that Roman law did not permit slaves to inherit anything."[65] Although Paul's words would have given an element of hope to slaves in first-century Rome, this hope is consigned to the eternal, transcendent realm and it is expected only in the future.

To what extent is such a reading warranted? First, it is important to realize that Paul is here evoking the laws and regulations surrounding the tradition of slave release which are described in three OT texts. There are slavery laws found in Deut. 15:12–18 which seem to be based on Exod. 21:2–6. Both of these texts address the situation of debt slavery in Israel. Debt slavery was the only way in which someone within the Israelite community could become permanently enslaved.[66] Although there are slight differences between these two texts,[67] the emphasis of both is that debt slavery was a temporary status and that the creditor was to free the debtor after a period of six years. This ensured that an Israelite would not remain disconnected from society but be able to retain family and ethnic ties.[68]

A third text which similarly guarantees that debt slavery is not permanent for an Israelite is Lev. 25:39–43. The main difference between this text and the previous two is that instead of a six-year limit to debt slavery, the Leviticus text puts in place a release after the period of jubilee.[69] The reason for the debt slavery described in Leviticus 25 is that because

---

[65] Hay, *Colossians*, 146.   [66] Byron, *Slavery Metaphors*, 41.
[67] See here G. C. Chirichigno, *Debt-Slavery in Israel and the Ancient Near East*, JSNTSup 141 (Sheffield Academic Press, 1992), 286.
[68] Byron, *Slavery Metaphors*, 42.
[69] The other difference is that whereas in Exod. 21:3–4 the slave's release does not include the release of his wife and children, in Leviticus 25 the slave's family is released with him.

of financial difficulty the head of household has to sell his property (25:25). If the person has no kin to redeem the property, he is forced to enslave himself and his family to a fellow Israelite (25:39). The debtor "shall remain with" the purchaser until the year of the jubilee: "Then they and their children with them shall be free from your authority; they shall go back to their own family and return to their ancestral property" (Lev. 25:40–41). In contrast to this scenario in which a slave returns to the family's inheritance, the Leviticus text then goes on to describe the expectations regarding foreign slaves or "domestic slaves."[70] Rather than receiving an inheritance, these slaves themselves become someone else's inheritance: "You may keep them as a possession for your children after you, for them to inherit as property" (25:46).

Paul's words in Col. 3:24 would therefore have been somewhat shocking for his audience. Addressing slaves, he reminds them that "from the Lord you will receive the inheritance as your reward" (3:24). Clearly Paul is evoking here the OT tradition of slave release rather than that of slaves being passed on as inheritance. But what is being envisaged by Paul and how might this have been heard by his audience? As in Romans and Galatians, so in this context, one of the neglected areas of interpretation is the extent to which Paul is drawing on, and is shaped by, the Abrahamic promise tradition. Dunn is one who notes the ways in which the phrase "the inheritance as your reward" "picks up the theme of the inheritance promised to Abraham, that is, primarily the land of Canaan as consistently in Jewish usage."[71] Dunn goes on to suggest that although the concept is sometimes subject to eschatological reference in the Old Testament (e.g. Ps. 37:9; Isa. 54:17), here it is clear that what is being offered to slaves is "a share in the inheritance promised to Abraham – that is, in the blessing promised to the nations through Abraham."[72]

This of course addresses only part of the question. For Paul to suggest that slaves will receive the Abrahamic inheritance is one thing, but how would such words have been received by his audience – what does it mean to say that slaves will have a part in the blessing promised to the nations through Abraham? After all, Paul is evoking this jubilee tradition within a context where, under Roman law, slaves could own little and

---

[70] This is the category used by, for example, I. Mendelsohn, *Slavery in the Ancient Near East: A Comparative Study of Slavery in Babylonia, Assyria, Syria and Palestine from the Middle of the Third Millenium to the End of the First Millenium* (New York: Oxford University Press, 1949). D. E. Callender, "Servants of God(s) and Servants of Kings in Israel and the Ancient Near East," in *Slavery in Text and Interpretation, Semeia* 83/4, ed. A. D. Callahan, R. A. Horsley and A. Smith (Atlanta: Scholars Press, 1993), 73–76.
[71] Dunn, *Colossians*, 256–57. [72] Ibid., 257.

inherit nothing and where conditions for slaves were harsh.[73] Exactly what Paul envisages to be the outworking of his inheritance language in Col. 3:24 is open to considerable debate.

One way of dealing with this verse is for interpreters to suggest that Paul is here being ironic or that the concept is a paradox, presumably based on the assumption that Paul cannot really have expected there to be any outworking of this inheritance while on earth.[74] In conjunction with this, the suggestion is then made that this is a vision which is meant entirely for the future. Certainly there is an eschatological tone to Paul's words.[75] This is true not only in earlier sections of the letter (for example 2:6, 20; 3:1–17) but also in verse 24 and the subsequent verse, where Paul suggests that the "wrongdoer *will be paid back* for whatever wrong has been done."[76]

The problem with such an approach is not in recognizing the eschatological nature of Paul's words, but in failing to identify the connection between a future vision and what this means for how one lives in the present. In Chapter 3 above (and this approach has been implicit throughout this study) it was pointed out that Paul's vision of the way things were meant to be must also be read as a critique of the ways things currently were. Even if Paul here does intend his words to be read as an eschatological reference, he is still proclaiming a dramatic reversal of cultural and political expectations.[77] To suggest that real slaves should, according to the ways of God's kingdom, be given the reward of an actual inheritance is to proclaim "a countereconomics of sabbath and jubilee rooted in the forgiving love of Jesus."[78] By telling slaves that they have an inheritance, Paul is recalling the traditions of jubilee; he is reminding his audience that Israel's story – and now, through Jesus, their own story – is a slave-freeing story.[79] As Robert Wall concludes, "To 'mind the things above'

---

[73] Lincoln, "The Letter to the Colossians," 658.

[74] N. T. Wright, *Colossians and Philemon*, 150.

[75] There is considerable debate as to the nature of eschatology in Colossians. Often it is suggested that the eschatology is entirely realized and that there is no future aspect to it; for example, E. Lohse, *Theological Ethics of the New Testament* (Philadelphia: Fortress Press, 1991), 148. However, as Todd Still shows, there is still a strong "not yet" aspect to Colossians; T. D. Still, "Eschatology in Colossians: How Realized Is It?" *NTS* 50 (2004): 137.

[76] Still, "Eschatology in Colossians: How Realized Is It?."

[77] MacDonald, *Colossians and Ephesians*, 158; Still, "Eschatology in Colossians: How Realized Is It?," 134.

[78] S. C. Keesmaat and B. J Walsh, *Colossians Remixed: Subverting the Empire* (Downers Grove, IL: InterVarsity Press, 2004), 208.

[79] Ibid.

is to hope for an inheritance that reverses socioeconomic conditions *on earth,* where many people are oppressed and denied humanity."[80]

Conclusions (Colossians)

What can therefore be said about the use of inheritance in Colossians when it is set alongside the use of the concept in Romans? As in 1 Corinthians, so here, what Paul understands to be the content of the inheritance is not made as clear as it is in Romans. There is no language here, for example, of inheriting "the world." This does not mean, however, that the conclusions made in relation to Romans are in any way undermined. Instead, as in 1 Corinthians, the meaning of the word in Colossians is distinct from, but not fundamentally different to, that in Romans. There does seem to be more of a realized nature to the inheritance, especially in Col. 1:12, but as has been argued, this does not also mean that the word has been spiritualized. Inheritance there includes the realm into which God has transferred the Christians at Colossae and which therefore should shape their life in the present. As was observed, inheritance in 1:12 does not mean *spiritual* inheritance as opposed to *physical* but signifies the transformation of the world. The word in this verse echoes OT themes of exodus and land and refers to how believers are to live in the new domain which is the inheritance. This is particularly evident in 3:24, where Paul makes a connection between inheritance and the situation of slaves in the first century. The way in which Paul uses the word here is eschatological, so that he exposes a disparity between what slaves currently experience and what they ought to experience. More directly than in Romans, Paul here shows that the *who* of inheritance is undeniably socio-political. Far from the wealthy and powerful being the ones entitled to the inheritance, it is actually one of the most marginalized groups in the Empire who will one day receive this reward. With more socio-political bite than in Romans, Galatians and 1 Corinthians, therefore, Paul here specifically applies the inheritance to those who walk in the shadows of the Empire. Once more, therefore, the language of inheritance opens up a world of possibilities. It encourages the Christians at Colossae to critique and question the supposedly permanent and immutable character of the present order of the world.

Regarding the *how* of inheritance, again no association is made here between inheritance and suffering (as there is in Romans). Having said

[80] R. Wall, *Colossians & Philemon,* IVPNT (Downers Grove, IL: InterVarsity Press, 1993), 163.

this, I find it difficult to believe that Paul equates the slaves' claim to inheritance with the Empire's path to power, because in the text immediately preceding 3:24 he describes a community which is to be marked out by "compassion, kindness, humility, meekness and patience" (3:12), a group of people who "bear with one another" and "forgive each other" (3:13). Paul summons the people who will receive the inheritance to a life of love, harmony and peace (3:14–15). It is therefore inconceivable that such a community would appropriate the inheritance in ways which mirror the hegemonic approach of Rome.

8

CONCLUSIONS

When Colin McCahon produced his painting *I Paul, to you at Ngatimote* it was the first step towards an important development in his artistic career. One of the features which became distinctive of McCahon's body of work was his ability to relocate the Christian story in a recognizably Aotearoa New Zealand context. The particular significance of McCahon's *Paul* was that it was the first painting in which he placed a cast of biblical characters in a New Zealand landscape. Subsequently McCahon explored what it might mean to locate the crucifixion of Jesus amongst the hills of New Zealand. But it was the apostle Paul whom McCahon first positioned in the artist's own country, in solidarity with McCahon's own people. We do not know why he chose first to work with Paul, but whatever the reasons, whether conscious or unconscious, the development seems fitting, because it is Paul who, after Jesus, is acknowledged to be the person most responsible for directing and shaping the way the Christian church has reflected on and articulated its faith.[1] Paul has been called the "second founder of Christianity" and his writings have influenced Christianity more than any other single individual.[2] It therefore seems appropriate that at the earliest stage of his painting of biblical characters McCahon chose first to embed Paul's narrative within the context of New Zealand.

Not all interpreters of Paul would agree with McCahon's choice of landscape. One observation in the study above is that many students of Paul prefer to envisage him as elevated above the earth rather than with his feet placed firmly upon it. As well as discussion of the context of Paul's message and the extent to which this both influenced, and was influenced by, his letters, there has been considerable discussion of the content of the scroll which Paul brought to his communities. Some of his readers have argued that the content of his message is primarily spiritual

---

[1] J. D. G. Dunn, *The Theology of Paul the Apostle* (Grand Rapids: Eerdmans, 1998), 2.
[2] W. Wrede, *Paul* (London: Green, 1907), 180.

and that his concerns are of a transcendent, rather than a physical and material nature.

As noted in Chapter 1, such conclusions remain puzzling given the important work carried out by James Hester in 1968, in which he argues that Paul's inheritance concept maintains the focus on "land" which is so central to the Old Testament's use of the word. Hester shows that for Paul the inheritance retains a strongly geographical reality but that this is now extended to the whole world rather than limited to Canaan. Hester's emphasis on the earthly and physical nature of inheritance planted the seed for a reading of the concept which is attentive to its socio-political content; his work has therefore provided an important starting point for the present study. However, the argument above has added exegetical depth and socio-political scope to Hester's findings by narrowing the focus of the task primarily to Romans (and then comparing this with Galatians, 1 Corinthians and Colossians) and by placing the concept more firmly within its first-century context.

Three questions emerged as a way of exploring the social and political shape of the inheritance language within the context of first-century imperial Rome: *what* is the nature of the inheritance; *who* is to receive this inheritance; and *how* will this transpire? The inheritance concept which is woven throughout Romans 4, 8 and 11 evokes the expectation that a certain group of people (the people of God) will one day receive an earth which will be renewed and which stands in continuity with the present world. In Rom. 4:13–25 the phrase "inherit the world" is not an isolated theme but contributes to a whole complex of ideas (including "descendants" and "father of many nations") which encompasses the people of God, who will one day receive actual physical territory and bring blessing to the nations.

But what of the language of inheritance in Romans 8? Although interpreters have suggested the possibility that the two texts are connected in some way – that Romans 4 perhaps signals ideas which will be developed more fully in Romans 8 – few have given any sustained attention to the degree to which this is the case. More common amongst readers of Romans is the conclusion that there is little lexical or logical continuity in the use of inheritance in Rom. 4:13 and Rom. 8:17. The consequence of this assumption is that Rom. 4:13 is seen as ultimately disconnected from Paul's "main argument" and that Rom. 8:17 is read in predominantly individualized and spiritualized terms. Chapter 4 challenged this common reading of Romans 8. Just as in Romans 4 the language of inheritance is thoroughly integrated into Paul's overall argument, so in Rom. 8:17 the apparently brief and elusive word dovetails with the terms "glory"

(8:17, 18, 21), "creation" (vv. 19, 21, 22) and "children of God" (v. 21). Together these concepts demonstrate that the Rom. 4:13 and 8:17 texts are not isolated ideas but different ways of expressing God's eschatological renewal of the entire world – in 8:17 "heirs of God" is best understood as referring to the people who inherit God's promise to Abraham. In this context even more light is shed on the nature of the relationship between the children of God and the renewal of creation. The wise and nurturing rule of creation by the people of God is considered by Paul to be a state of "glory" and all of this is included within the meaning of κληρονομία. Furthermore, to be "joint heirs with Christ" (συγκληρονόμοι δὲ Χριστοῦ, v. 17) is to be given "everything" (τὰ πάντα, v. 32); and to be considered the "firstborn (πρωτότοκον) within a large family" (v. 29c) and "at the right hand of God." Together with the language of inheritance these phrases convey the idea of the universal sovereignty which believers will share with the Son.

The themes of the future restoration of people and the earth which emerge in both Romans 4 and Romans 8 continue to play a significant role in Paul's argument in Romans 11. The present study therefore has contributed to the debate surrounding the textual variant in 11:1. In particular Chapter 5 demonstrated the ways in which the inheritance themes of Romans 4 and 8 serve to increase the pathos of Paul's argument in Romans 11. For example, when set alongside Israel's plight as described in Romans 9–11, the inheritance language from Romans 4 and 8 helps Paul to highlight the distance between the original intent of the promise and the current experience of it. In the face of the considerable anxiety which this raises for Paul, the concept of inheritance intensifies the emotion he feels but also allows him to emphasize again the enduring promises of God. Included in these promises, according to the allusions and claims of Romans 11, is the most climactic description to date in Paul's argument of what the inheritance includes: the guarantee that "all will be saved" (11:26), which means the guarantee of a restored and renewed land and of a time when Jew and Gentile will reign on this earth.

If the inheritance language were read in isolation, it could be considered politically innocuous. However, when the themes associated with inheritance are situated within the context of first-century imperial Rome it is difficult to overlook their socio-political bite. The belief perpetuated by the Roman emperors and accepted by many of the people of the empire was that there would be peace, stability and abundance through the actions and guidance of the emperor. The expectation created was that the people of Rome would be "lords of creation" and that this would involve a life of order, tranquility and stability. The means by which this "blessing" would occur was stated unambiguously: the gods would enable the emperor to achieve military victory and thus to subdue and dominate other peoples. Or, to put it in the categories adopted throughout this study, the *who* (the emperor and the people of Rome) would ultimately achieve the *what* (prosperity, abundance and peace in the world) through aggression and violence.

Paul's language of inheritance therefore contributes to an overall counter-imperial narrative in Romans. But one of the other findings of this study has been the observation that the inheritance is not only a direct confrontation to other *claims* to rule, but also simultaneously a reversal of all other *paths* to lordship and rule. In other words the *how* of inheritance is also undeniably counter-imperial. This is expressed to varying degrees in each of the three passages examined.

First, in relation to Romans 4 it was noted that Paul's appropriation of the Abraham narrative suggests that there is here an echoing of an "immigrant ideology" from the Old Testament. This tradition was that the original intent of the Arahamic promise would not come about through conquering annihilation but in the course of the people of God bringing "blessing to the nations." There are signals in Romans 4 that Paul remains in step with this idea of living at peace with other people and that he therefore rejects the kind of ideology which sought theological legitimation for the violent overthrow of people and their land.

Such a counter-imperial perspective becomes even stronger in Rom. 8:17–39. Paul makes it clear that to be an heir is to "suffer with Christ" (v. 17) and that suffering is integral to the life of those "in Christ." Just as the messiah, who suffered and died (vv. 32, 34) at the hands of Empire, is now "at the right hand of God" (v. 34) and is our "lord" (v. 39), so too those who "suffer with him" (v. 17) are also "glorified with him" (v. 17) and therefore "conquerors" through Christ (v. 37). In a bold reversal of the imperial worldview, therefore, Paul in Rom. 8:17–39 proclaims that the way to lordship and rule is not through military victory and aggression but through suffering love. The "sheep to be slaughtered" (v. 36) are the ones who will one day inherit the earth.

The third and final way in which Paul's inheritance language deeply undermines the story being told by first-century imperial Rome is through the situation of the people of Israel, which is the central concern of Romans 9–11. One of the conclusions which can be drawn with regard to these chapters in general and Romans 11 in particular is that unlike the political powers of the day, God chooses to bring peace not through violence or military might but through the existence of a people, even a people who at the present time seem to have "stumbled so as to fall." For

Paul the path to inheritance is not about force, exclusion and domination but about patiently being the people of God in the presence of the Empire.

In light of the socio-political significance of the language of inheritance, what might the concept have sounded like to the Christians in the heart of the Empire? More particularly, to a group of people who were in marginal social circumstances and excluded from the domain of power, to Christians who had ongoing troubles with persecution, poverty and conflict, what would it have meant to be told that they would inherit the earth? Clearly there was a vast disparity between Paul's vision for the world and the current experience of being under Roman rule. One of the possibilities repeatedly proposed in this study has been the cognitive dissonance experienced by Paul's audience. What has been suggested, however, is that although Paul's eschatological vision creates a dissonance for his audience, it also simultaneously signals an alternative vision which is to be worked towards and which implicitly critiques the present state of things. In the discussion of Rom. 4:13–25 (Chapter 3) it was suggested that in verses 19–21 Paul is echoing Isa. 54:1–3 and that he is doing so because that text and context has something to offer the historical and socio-political situation of the people to whom he writes. This reading of Rom. 4:19–21, which has not previously been proposed, suggests that both the author of Isaiah and Paul in Romans 4 make available to the people of God a memory which can be actualized and fulfilled in the present in order to subvert the empire of the day. The significance of this reading reaches beyond its immediate context because it offers a way of thinking about the eschatological language and imagery which is threaded throughout Romans 8 and 11. In Romans 8 Paul describes the present state of creation as "groaning" for a new world and waiting for "liberation" in the future. Paul evokes a time when the children of God and also the entire creation will be renewed and restored. The nature of Paul's alternative vision, therefore, is that it critiques life in the Empire (things are not as good as they are made out to be) and it invites a critique of the status quo with regard to ownership and distribution of the land. Similarly in Romans 11 the themes of God's final restoration of the world and of all people contribute to an unmistakable eschatological vision – that the people of God (not the people of the Empire) are the ones who will inherit the land. In other words, one of the functions of the language of inheritance in Romans is to contribute to an eschatological vision which reveals the contradictions between what is and what ought to be. The language of inheritance encourages and enables Paul's audience to distance themselves from reality so that they can begin to think about alternative ways of living. It therefore opens up a world of possibilities for the Christians at Rome. Certainly there is a sense in which the language is utopian but it is precisely this which helps to expose the supposedly impermanent and immutable character of the present order of the world.

However, to observe that the language of inheritance is eschatological is not to relegate the concept to the political wastelands of first-century Rome. Ironically W. D. Davies (who, as noted in Chapter 1, has been one of the most influential proponents of an a-political reading of "land" in Paul) hints at this when he suggests that one of the reasons for the absence of the concept of "land" in Paul's writings is because it might have been politically unwise for the apostle to include any reference to "land" in his letter to the Roman church: "There is the possibility that he was anxious not to cause any misunderstanding that might disturb Rome."[3] The study of inheritance above has demonstrated that Davies is wrong to suggest that the concept of "land" in Paul's writings is entirely spiritualized. And yet Davies is right to suggest that if Paul's concept of "land" *had* been understood in material and physical (rather than spiritual and transcendent) terms, it would have been too politically dangerous within the context of first-century imperial Rome. After all it seems virtually certain that Nero was the emperor during Paul's time of imprisonment in Rome and it is likely that Nero was the final judge over Paul's case.[4] Against Davies, therefore, the present study has argued that Paul's language of inheritance continues in a geographical, physical direction *and that* using this kind of language in the first-century context was undeniably subversive of the message perpetuated by the powers of the day.

All of this, of course, raises the question of how Rom. 13:1–7 should be read in light of the inheritance concept explored above. If the language of inheritance does contribute to an overall counter-imperial narrative in Romans, what does this mean for interpretations of Rom. 13:1–7, a text which has commonly been understood to be encouraging the Christians at Rome to maintain the social and political status quo and encouraging the believers to comply to all demands of the state? It is here that Paul advises that "every person be subject to the governing authorities" (13:1) and that "whoever resists authorities resists what God has appointed" (13:2). Paul refers to the governing authority in Rome as "God's servant for your good" (13:4) and he says that the Christians at Rome should therefore offer the present rulers "respect" and "honor" (13:7).

Such glowing references to the imperial powers at first glance seem to stand in stark contrast to the kinds of themes which have been identified

---

[3] Davies, *The Gospel and the Land*, 178.   [4] Cassidy, *Paul in Chains*, 142.

in this study. The language of inheritance evokes a number of counter-imperial ideas and expectations and contributes to an overall counter-imperial narrative in Romans. How should Rom. 13:1–7 be understood in light of this (often implied rather than directly stated) imperially subversive narrative? If, as traditionally understood, Rom. 13:1–7 is encouraging compliance to all demands of the state, this seems to clash conceptually with the language of inheritance and with the other ideas in Romans which are subversive of the social and political status quo. This suggests that either Paul has contradicted himself in Romans 13, or alternatively, that something else is going on here – that there is another way of reading Rom. 13:1–7 which identifies how the text is conceptually akin to the language of inheritance proposed above rather than conceptually jarring. Such a possibility will be explored briefly below. It is not the purpose of what follows to catalogue and assess all of the main ways in which the text has been interpreted. Not only has this been done well in many other places but, given that the proposed argument for inheritance is coherent and strong, all that remains to be done is to ask how this reading might fit with Romans 13. The focus of what follows is therefore limited in scope: its purpose is to suggest that Rom. 13:1–7 does not stand in bold contrast to the language of inheritance, but, rather, that the inheritance reading proposed above might provide further impetus for understanding these apparently ruler-respecting words as subtly undermining the governing authorities. Or, to put it more simply, it is to fossick for clues which suggest that, like the language of inheritance, Rom. 13:1–7 is subtly subverting the social and political status quo.

One way of bringing Romans 13 conceptually closer to the inheritance texts is by proposing that Paul's opening sentence lays the subversive groundwork for what follows. Having begun with words which appear to encourage absolute submission to the state he then says: "there is no authority except from God, and those authorities that exist have been instituted by God" (13:1). The idea that a ruler has no power except through God's appointment is conventional OT and Jewish teaching, a tradition which, by subordinating human rulership to the authority of God, serves ultimately to qualify and diminish the perceived power of human government.[5] There is a degree to which these opening words

---

[5] Moo, *The Epistle to the Romans*, 798. Moo's conclusion is that "balance is needed. On the one hand . . . Government is more than a nuisance to be put up with; it is an institution established by God to accomplish some of his purposes on earth (cf. vv. 3–4)." On the other hand . . . "we should also refuse to give to government any absolute rights and should evaluate all its demands in the light of the gospel." In what follows I will argue that Paul is suggesting nothing as "balanced" as Moo's reading.

therefore encourage a qualified obedience to the authority of Rome. On the one hand, the verse seems to suggest that the communities of Christians at Rome should submit to earthly government because it has a divinely ordained status, but on the other, there is also the idea that government does not have absolute rights over the believer because the rulers are themselves subordinate to God. The implication is that there may be instances when the Christian communities are required to "obey" God and thus to "disobey" the government.

Although this phrase therefore encourages a qualified obedience, it is also true that ultimately Paul's words are politically innocuous. While there is a sense in which Paul's words limit human authority, Kaylor does not seem too far wrong when he suggest that the first few verses of Romans 13 "could have been written by the emperor himself!"[6] This is because it is common within agrarian societies and aristocratic empires for the rulers to place a high value on traditional forms of legitimation for their power, such as theological or religious validation. The authorities are able to do this by co-opting the temples, priests and sacred sects of their society. "Most temples, therefore, support the ruler's claim to a mandate from heaven and are handsomely rewarded for their efforts. So Paul's opening remarks recognize the reality of how politics works in his world."[7]

Besides the ultimate political harmlessness of this reading it is also the case that if Paul is only situating the rulers of Rome within a divinely ordained role then he does very little to address the realities of Roman rule for the majority of the Empire. After all, within ten years of Paul's writing of Romans, the emperor Nero, whom Paul is here commending, would let loose a violent persecution against the church.[8] After Rome was destroyed by fire in 64 CE Nero blamed the Christians. The consequences were that a vast number of believers were tossed to the dogs, nailed to crosses, or used as human torches to illuminate Nero's gardens.[9] Furthermore the tradition is that Paul himself was beheaded as part of this persecution.[10] As T. L. Carter therefore rightly points out, "Paul's ignorance of the fate that he and his readers would suffer at the hands of Nero lends an element of tragic irony to his claim that the authorities are not to be feared, because they exist for the benefit of his readers and all those

---

[6] D. R. Kaylor, *Paul's Covenant Community: Jew and Gentile in Romans* (Atlanta: John Knox Press, 1989), 204.

[7] W. R. Herzog, "Dissembling, a Weapon of the Weak: The Case of Christ and Caesar in Mark 12:13–17 and Romans 13:1–7," *Perspectives in Religious Studies* 21. 4 (1994): 355.

[8] T. L. Carter, "The Irony of Romans 13," 210.   [9] Tacitus, *Annals* 15.44.2–8.

[10] Eusebius, *Historia Ecclesiastica* II.25.5–8.

who do good deeds."[11] In addition, as established in Chapter 2, most of Paul's audience are likely to have been poor, to have had no legal status and to have had an uncertain official status. Given this context, it is difficult to avoid the conclusion that Paul's words regarding the Roman authorities would have sounded either naïve or tactless to those who daily experienced oppression and injustice at the hands of the Roman Empire.

It is on this basis that Carter, William Herzog II and Neil Elliott propose that Paul's words in Rom. 13:1–7 may have been intended to be read on two levels. To the authorities of Rome the straightforward meaning of the text (that Christians should obey the emperor) would have been apparent. Yet to those on the margins of society the text would have been read as implausible and thus potentially ironic. It is therefore possible to understand Paul's text as sifting the audience into two groups – those who categorise it as unacceptable and therefore look for an alternative meaning and those who expect the socially marginalized to adopt such a subordinate stance and therefore take the text at face value. Significantly, irony is the most difficult to detect when it is one's own beliefs that are being subverted.[12]

> A surface reading of Rom. 13 is perfectly plausible to those who perceive political power as an instrument of divine rule . . . Yet the original audience of the letter would not have heard the text in this way. If the letter's original readers shared with the author an experience of oppression at the hands of the authorities, that shared experience would have paved the way for the readers' understanding of Paul's use of irony, by rendering the surface meaning of Paul's commendation of the authorities blatantly implausible to them.[13]

Irony can thus simultaneously blind one's opponents and acquire a closer bond between the ironist and those in the audience who perceive the irony.[14]

In what specific way, therefore, can irony (or what has also been referred to as "dissembling" or "hidden transcripts") be detected in this text? One important phrase in this regard comes in verse 4, where Paul says that the governing authority "is *God's servant* (διάκονος) for your good" and that "It is the servant of God to execute wrath on the wrong-doer." Crucial to acknowledging the potential irony here is an awareness of the way in which the phrase creates a disparity between what Paul is

---

[11] T. L. Carter, "The Irony of Romans 13," 210.
[12] Ibid., 215.   [13] Ibid.   [14] Ibid.

suggesting and how things actually are. Paul's words would have been more likely to have been taken at face value if those citizens who lived upright lives were rewarded for doing so and had no reason to be afraid of those in authority. There is much to suggest, however, that the Roman Empire fell well short of rewarding the good and punishing the bad in society. Instead the nature of Roman "justice" was that "peace" and "stability" were imposed upon the local communities through domination, violence and intimidation.[15] Paul is therefore describing an empire which does not exist:[16] "By portraying the authorities as those who worked for the benefit of upright citizens and who wielded the sword in order to punish evildoers, Paul highlights the ways in which the authorities in Rome were actually falling short of the ideal of good government that he portrayed."[17] What may have further reinforced this gap between the expectation of government and the reality of rulership is Rom. 13:13, where Paul says, "Let us live honorably as in the day, not in reveling and drunkenness, not in debauchery and licentiousness, not in quarreling and jealousy." It seems very likely that Paul's audience would not have missed the echo here of Nero's decadent behavior and that this would have provided further evidence for the irony of Paul's remarks that the governing authority is "God's servant." In other words Paul's reference to the rulers as "God's servants" in verse 4a comes like "a surgical strike. In the midst of reiterating the 'public transcript,' Paul introduces a coded message from the 'hidden transcript.'"[18]

Further on in the text Paul then refers again to the authorities as "God's servants," λειτουργοί, a word very similar to διάκονος. This time the term is used specifically in relation to those who collect taxes. The λειτουργοί were those who functioned as "an authorized representative of an administrative body"[19] and the people who "carried out public works in the service of the state."[20] The reputation of this group was that they were dishonest and rapacious. The λειτουργοί were those who are "busy with this very thing" (Rom. 13:6), which was to provide the revenue needed by the emperor to run his Empire. In a startling move Paul refers to the tax collectors as "God's servants," the very people whose role was to extract everything except the barest essentials from the local populations. Adding to the effect of Paul's words is the fact that λειτουργοί (unlike

---

[15] Ibid. 220–21.   [16] Herzog, "Dissembling, a Weapon of the Weak," 357.

[17] T. L. Carter, "The Irony of Romans 13," 222.

[18] Herzog, "Dissembling, a Weapon of the Weak," 356; see p. 357 for the chiasm which serves to highlight the phrase "God's servants."

[19] Käsemann, *Commentary on Romans*, 353.

[20] Barrett, *The Epistle to the Romans*, 247.

διάκονος above) can be translated as "God's priests." Though it is not usually translated as such (because it appears so inappropriate); it is true that, especially for readers familiar with the LXX, this term would normally carry the meaning of "God's priests."[21] Carter's observation is important: "The designation of rapacious tax collectors as 'God's priests' is a case of hyperbole: the use of religious language to denote the activity of the tax collectors stretches the meaning of the language to breaking point and highlights the way in which the tax collectors fail to live up to the designation applied to them."[22] It is therefore likely that, for Paul's audience, the idea that these tax collectors are "priests of God" could not be further from the truth. Once more, then, it appears that Paul is deliberately using a term which highlights the lack of correspondence between that term and the way things actually are in order to signal the presence of irony.

Given this inappropriateness of Paul's word choice, why does he then go on to insist that the Christians at Rome should not only pay taxes and revenue to these "priests" but that they should also give them "respect" and "honor" (Rom. 13:7)? The most likely answer is that Paul understands that to do anything else would be foolhardy and ultimately fatal: "Rome holds all the cards. Just as rebellion was futile because Rome held all the military cards, so in the case of taxes and tribute, Rome holds all the bureaucratic cards. Just as the military devotes itself to physical control, the financial bureaucrats devote themselves to economic control. It is useless to fight them."[23] But how should the exhortation to offer "respect" and "honor" be understood? Bearing in mind the ironic nature of his argument, we may deduce here that Paul intends the Christians at Rome to show the necessary public deference that is asked of the oppressed towards their masters. Sociologist James C. Scott has argued that although minority groups in society rarely display public acts of defiance, this does not mean that resistance is entirely absent. Instead, these groups are more likely to express their resistance in more covert, hidden ways, using methods which will not get them killed for their actions; they practice the art of appearing to conform while strongly believing something entirely different.[24] Something similar appears to be being recommended by Paul in this text:

> Paul advises the Romans to practice the arts of resistance but in ways that will not threaten the community lodged near the heart

---

[21] T. L. Carter, "The Irony of Romans 13," 225.   [22] Ibid.
[23] Herzog, "Dissembling, a Weapon of the Weak," 358.
[24] J. C. Scott, *Domination and the Arts of Resistance*; J. C. Scott, *Weapons of the Weak*.

of the Roman system of domination. He has managed to sound obedient and loyal, but he has granted nothing to the actual empire, and his apparent advice about loyalty is coded language for how to survive in an authoritarian environment."[25]

Furthermore this way of approaching the Empire fits well with what Paul advised in the text immediately preceding this one: to "live peaceably with all" and "not be overcome with evil, but overcome evil with good" (Rom. 12:18, 21). To resort to violent revolution in order to bring about change would therefore be to ignore or to contradict the principle of non-violent resistance which is so clearly articulated in Romans 12.[26]

Clearly this is only to scratch the surface of an alternative approach to how Rom. 13:1–7 is commonly read. There is much more that needs to be said but it has been enough here lightly to sketch the ways in which the language of inheritance as proposed above need not be understood as a conceptual clash with a conventional reading of Romans 13. But it is not only these indications of irony in Romans 13 which draw the text conceptually closer to the language of inheritance in Romans. The potential link between the texts is further reinforced by the socio-political and theological perspective common to both. One of the themes which emerged from the exploration of the inheritance texts was the way in which the concept holds two ideas in balance. On the one hand the present state of things is not likely to change dramatically in the near future; for the moment the powerful and the wealthy are those who have inherited the earth. Paul is writing to the powerless in the Empire and he is realistic about what it means to survive in such a situation.[27] On the other hand, it has also been demonstrated that at no stage does this realistic appraisal of the way things are revert to an otherworldly perspective. Instead, the language of inheritance creates the expectation that the current state of the world is not permanent; it is not the way things will always be. There will come a time when situations will be inverted and the believers at Rome, the ones supposedly powerless to change anything, will be the people who will inherit the world.

---

[25] Herzog, "Dissembling, a Weapon of the Weak," 359.

[26] "Given the exuberant currents of political rhetoric in the Neronian age, Paul's phrases encouraging submission are remarkably ambivalent. I suspect that in a Roman official's ear, Paul's language would have seemed to offer a peculiarly grudging compliance, rather than the grateful contentment of the properly civilized"; N. Elliott, "Strategies of Resistance," 120–21. "Any reasonable Jew could have imagined what the probable imperial response would have been to even modest popular agitation . . . "; ibid., 121.

[27] Meggitt, *Paul, Poverty and Survival*, 155–78. Similarly Dunn, *Romans 9–16*, 679–80.

I propose that (although the connection is seldom made) it is this perspective which is carried through to Rom. 13:1–7. Just as the language of inheritance invites an eschatological realism, so too the perspective of Romans 13 encourages something similar. This is to suggest that on the one hand Paul is mindful of the caution which is always needed when dealing with the powerful and dangerous powers of the day. Paul's first strategy is survival and in order to survive he and his audience must (at least publicly) be heard to be expressing the accepted doctrine of Empire. Such realistic caution was necessary for all people of the Empire.[28] On the other hand, embedded in Romans 13, is the acknowledgement of the absurdity of the imperial claims and an ironic critique of the way things are. As is clear from Romans 12, Paul expects that there will be resistance to the Empire, but that such gentle revolution will not take the same path as that of Empire:

> Paul expresses no fantasy that the powers that be are about to vanish in a miraculous puff of smoke, but neither are they permanent (13:11–12). The Christians' arena of responsibility is much closer, in any event, for the Christian must be diligent for the common good (12:3–21) and fulfill the obligation of mutual love (13:8–10).[29]

To reiterate, therefore, the purpose of this section has not been to argue in detail that Rom. 13:1–7 should be read as ironically subverting the socio-political status quo. Instead I have attempted to demonstrate that it is possible to build a conceptual bridge between the language of inheritance and Rom. 13:1–7. Even if this were not to be accepted, however, the argument regarding inheritance would not crumble. Instead, in light of the subversive nature of inheritance in Romans, and bearing in mind the similarly counter-imperial nature of other terms and concepts in the letter, thought would need to be given to which voice (if it is the case that Romans 13 is to be read in the conventional way) is assigned priority. At the very least the argument for inheritance above should stimulate discussion of whether the traditional reading of Romans 13 should continue to be allowed to be the loudest interpretive voice in the room.

The primary purpose of this study has been to explore the language of inheritance in Romans. A secondary task has then been to consider the use of the concept in the two other undisputed Pauline letters where it occurs (Galatians and 1 Corinthians) and also in the disputed (although

---

[28] N. Elliott, "Strategies of Resistance," 121.   [29] Ibid.

less so than other letters) letter to the Colossians. To what extent does a discussion of the inheritance in these epistles reinforce the findings from Romans, to what degree does it challenge the conclusions and in what sense are the arguments refined when these letters are considered? The overriding impression is that there is nothing in Galatians, 1 Corinthians or Colossians which significantly challenges the this-worldly, political nature of the language of inheritance in Romans. This is not to say that the concept is identical in each of these letters; it has become apparent that the particular needs of Paul's audience dictate the shape of the inheritance. For example in Galatians the inheritance remains "of this world" and political but it is focused more specifically on relationships within the community rather than on the eschatological world. One of the associations specific to Galatians is the suggestion that a community with transformed relationships challenges and confronts the powers of the day. This is particularly apparent in Gal. 5:21 and 6:15. There is in these texts a connection between inheritance and a future renewal of creation. But one of the distinctives of these passages is that the nature of this renewal refers primarily to relationships within the community of God. Significantly, interwoven with these points of difference there remain many striking similarities. One of these is the link which Paul understands there to be between inheritance and the path of suffering. As in Romans, so in Galatians the language of inheritance includes both a claim to universal sovereignty and a "lordship" which means participating in the self-giving suffering of Christ.

In 1 Corinthians the language of inheritance was also seen to be undermining of first-century imperial Rome but this was expressed particularly through the concept of the renewal of the individual's body. In itself this was seen to have importance for an embodied eschatological world; there is a conceptual extension assumed by Paul from a resurrected body to the resurrection of creation more generally. One emphasis in 1 Corinthians is on the necessity for believers to live transformed lives in the present because the future inheritance of the "kingdom of God" will be a physical, embodied world. It is also the case that Paul believes that the future "kingdom of God" will resist, challenge and confront the earthly powers of the day – the phrase is therefore rich in socio-political overtones. One of the notable differences between the inheritance in Romans and in 1 Corinthians is the question of *who* will receive it. Whereas in Romans and Galatians the question of Abraham's descendants is of paramount importance to Paul's audience, in 1 Corinthians the issue is entirely absent. In 1 Corinthians the emphasis is instead on the need for the recipients of the inheritance to live changed lives in anticipation of the eschatological world. A final difference is the question of *how* the inheritance comes about – the issue which emerges at a number of places in Romans is not associated with the language of inheritance in any obvious way in 1 Corinthians.

As in Galatians and 1 Corinthians, so in Colossians the terrain of inheritance is distinct from, but not fundamentally different to, the territory in Romans. Although the word is used in a more realized sense in Colossians, there is no justification for suggesting that the word has been spiritualized or individualized. Instead, inheritance in Colossians is about the realm into which God has brought the believers at Colossae and which is therefore expected to shape their lives in the present. One obvious implication which Paul signals is for the life of slaves: of all the uses of inheritance noted in this study, Paul's suggestion that slaves will one day receive the reward of the inheritance is perhaps the most striking of all. In a particularly arresting reference Paul applies the inheritance to those who walk at the outskirts of the Empire. Such an association, while not immediately realizable, once more serves to critique and question the supposedly permanent nature of the present order of the world.

What has been established here is that Paul, at key points in his letter to the believers at Rome, uses the language of inheritance in a way which has profound socio-political significance. He reminds the Christians at Rome that, contrary to accepted opinion, it will not be Nero but God who brings peace and wholeness to the world. Paul encourages the Christians at the heart of the Empire not to mirror the hegemonic claims of Rome but to live in communities which embody love and self-sacrifice. To do so is to appreciate and to be nurtured by the politics of inheritance.

BIBLIOGRAPHY

Abasciano, B. *Paul's Use of the Old Testament in Romans 9:1–9. An Intertextual and Theological Exegesis.* Library of New Testament Studies, 301. London: T. & T. Clark, 2005.

Adams, E. *Constructing the World: A Study in Paul's Cosmological Language.* Edinburgh: T. & T. Clark, 2000.

Alföldy, G. "Subject and Ruler, Subjects and Methods: An Attempt at a Conclusion." In *Subject and Ruler: The Cult of the Ruling Power in Classical Antiquity, Papers Presented at a Conference Held in the University of Alberta on April 13–15, 1994, to Celebrate the 65th Anniversary of Duncan Fishwick,* ed. A. Small. Journal of Roman Archeology Supp. Series, 17. Alberta: Journal of Roman Archeology, 1996: 254–61.

The Social History of Rome. 2nd edn. Baltimore: The Johns Hopkins University Press, 1998.

Alford, H. *The Acts of the Apostles, the Epistle to the Romans and Corinthians.* The Greek Testament. 4th edn. 4 vols. Vol. II. Chicago: Moody, 1958.

Allison, D. C. "The Background of Romans 11:11–15 in Apocalyptic and Rabbinic Literature." *Studia Biblica et Theologica* 10 (1980): 229–34.

"Romans 11:11–15: A Suggestion." *Perspectives in Religious Studies* 12 (1985): 23–30.

The End of the Ages Has Come. Philadelphia: Fortress Press, 1987.

"Jesus and the Victory of Apocalyptic." In *Jesus and the Restoration of Israel: A Critical Assessment of N. T. Wright's Jesus and the Victory of God,* ed. C. Newman. Carlisle: Paternoster Press, 1999: 126–41.

Arnold, C. E. "Returning to the Domain of the Powers: *Stoicheia* as Evil Spirits in Galatians 4:3, 9." *NovT* 38 (1996): 57–76.

Aune, D. E. "Eschatology (Early Jewish)." In *ABD* II. New York: Doubleday, 1992: 594–609.

Bader-Saye, S. *Church and Israel after Christendom: The Politics of Election.* Colorado: Westview Press, 1999.

Bailey, Kenneth E. "St Paul's Understanding of the Territorial Promise of God to Abraham. Romans 4:13 in Its Historical and Theological Context." *Theological Review,* 15.1 (1994): 59–69.

Baltzer, K. *Deutero-Isaiah: A Commentary on Isaiah 40–55,* trans. M. Kohl. Hermeneia. Minneapolis: Fortress Press, 2001.

Barclay, J. M. G. "Paul and the Law: Observations on Some Recent Debates." *Themelios* 12 (1986): 5–15.

Obeying the Truth. A Study of Paul's Ethics in Galatians. Edinburgh: T. & T. Clark, 1988.

"Paul, Philemon and the Dilemma of Christian Slave-Ownership." *NTS* 37 (1991): 161–86.

Jews in the Mediterranean Diaspora. From Alexander to Trajan (323 BCE – 117 CE). Edinburgh: T. & T. Clark, 1996.

" 'Neither Jew nor Greek': Multiculturalism and the New Perspective on Paul." In *Ethnicity and the Bible*, ed. M. G. Brett. Leiden: Brill, 1996: 197–214.

Colossians and Philemon. New Testament Guides. Sheffield Academic Press, 1997.

Barre, M. "Paul as 'Eschatological Person': A New Look at 2 Cor 11:29." *CBQ* 37 (1975): 510–12.

Barrett, C. K. *The Epistle to the Romans*. BNTC. London: A. and C. Black, 1957.

A Commentary on the First Epistle to the Corinthians. London: A. & C. Black, 1971.

"Romans 9:30–10:21: Fall and Responsibility of Israel." In *Die Israelfrage nach Röm 9–11*, ed. D. de Lorenzi. Rome: Abtei von St. Paul vor den Mauern, 1977: 99–121.

Freedom and Obligation: A Study of the Epistle to the Galatians. London: SPCK, 1985.

Barth, M. and H. Blanke. *Colossians. A New Translation with Introduction and Commentary*, trans. A. B. Beck. AB 34B. New York: Doubleday, 1994.

Bartlett, D. L. *Romans*. Westminster Bible Companion. Louisville: Westminster John Knox Press, 1995.

Bartsch, H. W. "Die Historische Situation des Römerbriefes." *Studia Evangelica* 4 (1968): 282–91.

Bauman, R. A. *Women and Politics in Ancient Rome*. London: Routledge, 1992.

Becker, J. "Paul and His Churches." In *Christian Beginnings: Word and Community from Jesus to Post-Apostolic Times*, ed. J. Becker. Louisville: John Knox Press, 1993: 132–212.

Beker, J. C. *Paul the Apostle: The Triumph of God in Life and Thought*. Philadelphia: Fortress Press, 1980.

"Vision of Hope for a Suffering World: Romans 8:17–30." *The Princeton Seminary Bulletin* 3 (1994): 26–32.

Benko, S. "The Edict of Claudius of AD 49 and the Instigator Chrestus." *Theologische Zeitschrift* 25 (1969): 406–18.

Berger, P. L. *The Social Reality of Religion*. London: Faber and Faber, 1969.

Berkhof, H. *Christ and the Powers*. Scottdale, PA: Herald Press, 1962.

Betz, H. D. *Galatians: A Commentary on Paul's Letter to the Churches in Galatia*. Philadelphia: Fortress Press, 1979.

Betz, O. *Jesus und das Danielbuch*, vol. I: *Die Menschensohnworte Jesu und die Ziekunftserwartung des Paulus (Daniel 7, 13–14)*. Frankfurt: Peter Lang, 1985.

Beuken, W. A. M. "Isaiah LIV: The Multiple Identity of the Person Addressed." *Oudtestamentische studiën* 19 (1974): 29–70.

Bickerman, E. J. *Chronology of the Ancient World*. 2nd edn. New York: Cornell University Press, 1980.

Blackwelder, O. "The Epistle to the Galatians." In *Corinthians, Galatians, Ephesians*, ed. G. A. Buttrick. The Interpreter's Bible 10. Nashville: Abingdon Press, 1953: 429–593.

Blenkinsopp, J. *Isaiah 40–55: A New Translation with Introduction and Commentary*, AB 19A. New York, London, Toronto, Sydney and Auckland: Doubleday, 2000.

Blumenfeld, Bruno. *The Political Paul: Justice, Democracy and Kingship in a Hellenistic Framework*. JSNTSup 210. London: Sheffield Academic Press, 2001.

Boorer, S. "Review of *The Land Is Mine*." *Pacifica* 10 (1997): 93–95.

Borg, M. J. *Conflict, Holiness and Politics in the Teachings of Jesus*. New York: The Edwin Mellen Press, 1984.

Boyarin, D. *A Radical Jew: Paul and the Politics of Identity*. Berkeley: University of California Press, 1994.

Bradley, K. R. *Slaves and Masters in the Roman Empire: A Study of Social Control*. New York: Oxford University Press, 1982.

Slavery and Society at Rome. Cambridge University Press, 1994.

Briggs, S. "Paul on Bondage and Freedom in Imperial Roman Society." In *Paul and Politics: Ekklesia, Israel, Imperium, Interpretation*, ed. R. A. Horsley. Harrisburg, PA: Trinity Press, 2000: 110–23.

"Slavery and Gender." In *On the Cutting Edge: The Study of Women in Biblical Worlds. Essays in Honor of Elisabeth Schüssler Fiorenza*, ed J. Schaberg, A. Bach and E. Fuchs. New York: Continuum, 2003: 171–92.

Bruce, F. F. "Christianity under Claudius." *BJRL* 44 (1961): 309–26.

The Epistle of Paul to the Romans. TNTC. Grand Rapids: Eerdmans, 1980.

The Epistle to the Galatians. NIGTC. Grand Rapids: Eerdmans, 1982.

The Epistles to the Colossians, to Philemon, and to the Ephesians NICNT. Grand Rapids: Eerdmans, 1984.

"One in Christ Jesus, Thoughts on Galatians 3:26–29." *JCBRF* 122 (1991): 7–10.

Brueggemann, W. *The Land: Place as Gift, Promise, and Challenge in Biblical Faith*. Overtures to Biblical Theology. Philadelphia: Fortress Press, 1977.

Hopeful Imagination: Prophetic Voices in Exile. Philadelphia: Fortress Press, 1986.

"Land: Fertility and Justice." In *Theology of the Land*, ed. B. F. Evans. Collegeville, MN: The Liturgical Press, 1987: 41–68.

"Reflections on Biblical Understandings of Property." In *A Social Reading of the Old Testament: Prophetic Approaches to Israel's Communal Life*, ed. P. D. Miller. Minneapolis: Fortress Press, 1994: 276–84.

Theology of the Old Testament. Testimony, Dispute, Advocacy. Minneapolis: Fortress Press, 1997.

Isaiah 40–66. Westminster Bible Companion. Louisville: Westminster John Knox Press, 1998.

"Hope." In *Reverberations of Faith. A Theological Handbook of Old Testament Themes*. Louisville and London: Westminster John Knox Press, 2002: 101–102.

"Land." In *Reverberations of Faith. A Theological Handbook of Old Testament Themes*. Louisville and London: Westminster John Knox Press, 2002: 120–23.

Brunt, P. and J. M. Moore, eds. *Res Gestae Divi Augusti*. Oxford University Press, 1967.

Bultmann, R. "History and Eschatology in the New Testament." *NTS* 1 (1954): 5–16.

Theology of the New Testament. London: SCM Press, 1956.

Jesus Christ and Mythology. New York: Scribner's, 1958.

Burton, E. D. W. *A Critical and Exegetical Commentary on the Epistle to the Galatians*. ICC. Edinburgh: T. & T. Clark, 1921.

Byrne, B. J. *"Sons of God" – "Seed of Abraham": A Study of the Idea of Sonship of God of All Christians in Paul against the Jewish Background*. Analecta Biblica 83. Rome: Biblical Institute, 1979.

Romans. Sacra Pagina 6. Collegeville, MN: The Liturgical Press, 1996.

"Creation Groaning: An Earth Bible Reading of Romans 8:18–22." In *Readings from the Perspective of Earth*, ed. N. C. Habel. Sheffield Academic Press, 2000: 193–203.

"Interpreting Romans Theologically in a Post-'New Perspective' Perspective." *Harvard Theological Review* 94.3 (2001): 227–41.

Byron, J. *Slavery Metaphors in Early Judaism and Pauline Christianity*. WUNT. Tübingen: Mohr Siebeck, 2003.

Caird, George B. *Principalities and Powers*. Oxford: Clarendon Press, 1958.

The Language and Imagery of the Bible. London: Duckworth, 1980.

Callender, D. E. "Servants of God(s) and Servants of Kings in Israel and the Ancient Near East." In *Slavery in Text and Interpretation*, Semeia 83/4, ed. A. D. Callahan, R. A. Horsley and A. Smith. Atlanta: Scholars Press, 1998: 67–82.

Calvin, J. *Romans*. Grand Rapids: Eerdmans, 1973.

Campbell, D. "The Story of Jesus in Romans and Galatians." In *Narrative Dynamics in Paul. A Critical Assessment*, ed. B. W. Longenecker. London: Westminster John Knox Press, 2002: 97–124.

Carlston, C. "Proverbs, Maxims and the Historical Jesus." *JBL* 99 (1980): 87–105.

Carroll, J. T. and J. B. Green. *The Death of Jesus in Early Christianity*. Peabody, MA: Hendrickson Publishers, 1995.

Carter, T. L. "The Irony of Romans 13." *NovT* 46.3 (2004): 209–28.

Carter, W. *Matthew and the Margins. A Socio-Political and Religious Reading*. JSNTSup 204. Sheffield Academic Press, 2000.

"Vulnerable Power: The Roman Empire Challenged by the Early Christians." In *Handbook of Early Christianity: Social Science Approaches*, ed. J. Anthony, J. Duhaime Blasi, and P. A. Turcotte. Walnut Creek, CA: AltaMira Press, 2002: 453–88.

Cassidy, R. J. *Paul in Chains. Roman Imprisonment and the Letters of St. Paul*. New York: The Crossroad Publishing Company, 2001.

Castelli, E. *Imitating Paul: A Discourse of Power*. Louisville: Westminster John Knox, 1991.

Chirichigno, G. C. *Debt-Slavery in Israel and the Ancient Near East*. JSNTSup 141. Sheffield Academic Press, 1992.

Christofferson, O. *The Earnest Expectation of the Creature: The Flood Tradition as Matrix of Romans 8:18–27*. Coniectenea Biblica 23. Stockholm: Almqvist and Wiksell, 1990.

Clark, Mark Edward. "Images and Concepts of Hope in the Early Imperial Cult." In *Society of Biblical Literature: Seminar Papers*, ed. K. H. Richards. California: Scholars Press, 1982: 39–43.

Collins, A. Y. *Crisis and Catharsis. The Power of the Apocalypse*. Philadelphia: Westminster Press, 1984.

Collins, J. J. "Sibylline Oracles." In *Dictionary of New Testament Background*, ed. C. A. Evans and Stanley E. Porter. Leicester: InterVarsity Press, 2000: 1107–12.

Collins, R. *First Corinthians*. Sacra Pagina. Collegeville, MN: The Liturgical Press, 1999.

Combes, I. A. H. *The Metaphor of Slavery in the Writings of the Early Church: From the New Testament to the Beginning of the Fifth Century*. JSNTSup 156. Sheffield Academic Press, 1998.

Conzelmann, Hans. *1 Corinthians*. Hermeneia. Philadelphia: Fortress Press, 1975.

Coote, R. B. *Amos among the Prophets*. Philadelphia: Fortress Press, 1981.

Coppes, L. J. "Nahal, NahᵃLâ." In *Theological Wordbook of the Old Testament*, ed. R. L. Harris. Chicago: Moody Press, 1980: vol. II, 569–70.

Cottrell, J. *Romans*. The College Press NIV Commentary. Missouri: College Press, 1996.

Cranfield, C. E. B. *A Critical and Exegetical Commentary on the Epistle to the Romans*. ICC 1. Edinburgh: T. & T. Clark, 1975.

Dahl, N. A. "The Atonement: An Adequate Reward for the Akedah? (Rom 8:32)." In *Neotestamentica et Semitica: Studies in Honour of Matthew Black*, ed. E. E. Ellis and M. Wilcox. Edinburgh: T. & T. Clark, 1969: 15–29.

Danker, F. W. *Benefactor*. St. Louis, MS: Clayton, 1982.

Davies, W. D. *Paul and Rabbinic Judaism: Some Rabbinic Elements in Pauline Theology*. London: SPCK, 1962.

The Gospel and the Land. London: University of California Press, 1974.

"Paul and the People of Israel." In *Jewish and Pauline Studies*, ed. W. D. Davies. Philadelphia: Fortress Press, 1984: 123–52.

Dawes, G. W. " 'But If You Can Gain Your Freedom' (1 Corinthians 7:17–24)." *CBQ* 52 (1990): 681–97.

de Boer, M. C. "Paul and Apocalyptic Eschatology." In *The Encyclopedia of Apocalypticism*, ed. J. J. Collins. New York: Continuum, 1998: I, 345–83.

Deissmann, G. A. *Light from the Ancient East*, trans. L. R. M Strachan. London: Hodder and Stoughton, 1910.

Paul: A Study in Social and Religious History. London: Hodder and Stoughton, 1926.

Delling, G. "στοιχεῖον." In *TDNT* VII. Grand Rapids: Eerdmans, 1964–76: 670–87.

Denton, D. R. "Inheritance in Paul and Ephesians." *EQ* 53.3 (1982): 157–62.

Dihle, A. *Greek and Latin Literature of the Roman Empire: From Augustus to Justinian*, trans. M. Malzahn. London: Routledge, 1994.

Dodd, C. H. *The Epistle of Paul to the Romans*. Moffat New Testament Commentary. London: Hodder and Stoughton, 1932.

Donaldson, T. *Paul and the Gentiles: Remapping the Apostle's Convictional World*. Minneapolis: Fortress Press, 1997.
Duff, J. W. and A. M. Duff. "Introduction to Einsiedeln Eclogues." In *Minor Latin Poets*, ed. J. W. Duff and A. M. Duff. London: William Heinemann Ltd, 1954: 319–22.
Duling, D. C. "Empire: Theories, Methods, Models." In *The Gospel of Matthew in Its Roman Imperial Context*, ed. J. Riches and D. C. Sim. London: T. & T. Clark, 2005: 49–74.
Duncan-Jones, R. *The Economy of the Roman Empire: Quantitative Studies*. Rev. edn. Cambridge University Press, 1982.
Structure and Scale in the Roman Economy. Cambridge University Press, 1990.
Dunn, J. D. G. "The New Perspective on Paul." *BJRL* 65 (1983): 95–122.
Romans 1–8. WBC 38A. Dallas: Word Books, 1988.
Romans 9–16. WBC 38B. Dallas: Word Books, 1988.
"The New Perspective on Paul." In *Jesus, Paul and the Law*, ed. J. D. G. Dunn. London: SCM Press, 1990: 183–214.
"The Theology of Galatians: The Issue of Covenantal Nomism." In *Thessalonians, Philippians, Galatians, Philemon*, ed. J. M. Bassier. Minneapolis: Fortress Press, 1991: 125–46.
The Epistle to the Galatians. BNTC. Peabody, MA: Hendrickson Publishers, 1993.
The Theology of Paul's Letter to the Galatians. Cambridge University Press, 1993.
The Epistles to the Colossians and to Philemon. A Commentary on the Greek Text. NIGTC. Grand Rapids: Eerdmans, 1996.
The Theology of Paul the Apostle. Grand Rapids: Eerdmans, 1998.
Eichholz, G. *Die Theologie Des Paulus Im Umriss*. Neukirchen-Vluyn: Neukirchener, 1972.
Eichler, J. "Inheritance, Lot, Portion." In *NIDNTT* II. Grand Rapids: Zondervan, 1975–85: 295–304.
Elliott, J. K. "Thoroughgoing Eclecticism in New Testament Textual Criticism." In *The Text of the New Testament in Contemporary Research: Essays on the Status Quaestionis*, ed. B. D. Ehrman and M. W. Holmes. Grand Rapids: Eerdmans, 1995: 321–33.
Elliott, N. *The Rhetoric of Romans. Argumentative Constraint and Strategy and Paul's Dialogue with Judaism*. JSNTSup 45. Sheffield: JSOT Press, 1990.
Liberating Paul: The Justice of God and the Politics of the Apostle. Maryknoll, NY: Orbis, 1994.
"Figure and Ground in the Interpretation of Rom 9–11." In *The Theological Interpretation of Scripture: Classic and Contemporary Readings*, ed. S. Fowl. Oxford: Blackwell, 1997: 371–89.
"Romans 13 in the Context of Imperial Propaganda." In *Paul and Empire*, ed. R. A. Horsley. Harrisburg, PA: Trinity Press, 1997: 184–204.
"The 'Patience of the Jews': Strategies of Resistance and Accommodation to Imperial Cultures." In *Pauline Conversations in Context. Essays in Honor of Calvin J. Roetzel*, ed. J. C. Anderson, P. Sellew and C. Setzer. London: Sheffield Academic Press, 2002: 32–41.
"Strategies of Resistance in the Pauline Communities." In *Hidden Transcripts and the Arts of Resistance. Applying the Work of James C. Scott to Jesus*

and Paul, ed. R. A. Horsley. Atlanta: Society of Biblical Literature, 2004: 97–122.

Ellis, E. E. *Pauline Theology: Ministry and Society*. Grand Rapids: Eerdmans, 1989.

Esler, P. "Group Boundaries and Intergroup Conflict in Galatians: A New Reading of Galatians 5:13–6:10." In *Ethnicity and the Bible*, ed. M. G. Brett. Leiden: Brill, 1996: 215–40.

Conflict and Identity in Romans. The Social Setting of Paul's Letter. Minneapolis: Fortress Press, 2003.

"Rome in Apocalyptic and Rabbinic Literature." In *The Gospel of Matthew in Its Roman Imperial Context*, ed. J. Riches and D. C. Sim. London: T. & T. Clark, 2005: 9–33.

Evans, C. A. and J. A. Sanders, eds. *Paul and the Scriptures of Israel*. JSNTSup 83. Sheffield Academic Press, 1993.

Fee, G. *The First Epistle to the Corinthians*. NICNT. Grand Rapids: Eerdmans, 1987.

God's Empowering Presence. The Holy Spirit in the Letters of Paul. Peabody, MA: Hendrickson Publishers, 1994.

Fergusson, D. "Eschatology." In *The Cambridge Companion to Christian Doctrine*, ed. C. E. Gunton. Cambridge University Press, 1997: 226–44.

Finlay, M. I. *Ancient Slavery and Modern Ideology*. New York: Viking, 1980.

Fitzmyer, J. A. "The Letter to the Galatians." In *Jerome Biblical Commentary*, Englewood Cliffs, NJ: Prentice-Hall, 1968: vol. II, 242.

Romans. AB 33. London: Doubleday, 1993.

Fletcher-Louis, H. T. *All of the Glory of Adam: Liturgical Anthropology in the Dead Sea Scrolls*. STDJ 42. Leiden: Brill, 2002.

Foerster, W. "κληρονόμος." In *TDNT* III. Grand Rapids: Eerdmans, 1964–76: 767–85.

Forshey, R. O. "The Hebrew Root Nhl and Its Semitic Cognates." Harvard University Press, 1972.

Friedrich, J. H. "κληρονομία." In *EDNT* II. Grand Rapids: Eerdmans, 1993: 298–99.

Friesen, S. J. *Imperial Cults and the Apocalypse of John. Reading Revelation in the Ruins*. Oxford University Press, 2001.

"Poverty in Pauline Studies: Beyond the So-Called New Consensus." *JSNT* 26.3 (2004): 323–61.

Fuller, D. P. *Unity of the Bible: Unfolding God's Plan for Humanity*. Grand Rapids: Zondervan, 1992.

Funk, R. W. *A Greek Grammar of the NT and Other Early Christian Literature*. Rev. edn. Cambridge University Press, 1961.

Gager, J. G. "Functional Diversity in Paul's Use of End-Time Language." *JBL* 89 (1970): 325–37.

Kingdom and Community: The Social World of Early Christianity. Englewood Cliffs: Prentice-Hall, 1975.

Galinsky, Karl. *Augustan Culture: An Interpretive Introduction*. Princeton University Press, 1996.

Garland, D. E. "The Composition and Unity of Philippians: Some Neglected Literary Factors." *NovT* 27 (1985): 141–73.

1 Corinthians. BECNT. Grand Rapids: Baker, 2003.

Garnsey, P. *Food and Society in Classical Antiquity.* Cambridge University Press, 1999.

Gaston, L. *Paul and the Torah.* Vancouver: University of British Columbia Press, 1987.

Gathercole, S. *Where Is Boasting? Early Jewish Soteriology and Paul's Response in Romans 1–5.* Grand Rapids: Eerdmans, 2002.

Gaventa, B. R. "The Singularity of the Gospel." In *Philippians, Galatians*, ed. J. M. Bassler. Minneapolis: Fortress Press, 1991: 147–59.

Geertz, C. "Ethos, World View, and the Analysis of Sacred Symbols." In *The Interpretation of Cultures: Selected Essays by Clifford Geertz*, ed. C. Geertz. London: Hutchinson, 1975: 126–41.

Georgi, Dieter. *Theocracy in Paul's Praxis and Theology*, trans. David. E. Green. Minneapolis: Fortress Press, 1991.

"Who Is the True Prophet." In *Paul and Empire: Religion and Power in Roman Imperial Society*, ed. R. A. Horsley. Harrisburg, PA: Trinity Press International, 1997: 36–45.

Gibbs, J. G. *Creation and Redemption: A Study in Pauline Theology.* NovTSup 26. Leiden: Brill, 1971.

Given, M. "Restoring the Inheritance in Romans 11:1." *JBL* 118 (1999): 89–96.

Gottwald, N. K. *The Tribes of Yahweh: A Sociology of the Religion of Liberated Israel 1250–1050 BCE.* London: SCM Press, 1979.

The Hebrew Bible. A Socio-Literary Introduction. Philadelphia: Fortress Press, 1985.

Gow, A. S. F and D. L. Page. *The Greek Anthology: The Garland of Philip and Some Contemporary Epigrams*, vol. I: *Introduction, Text and Translation.* Cambridge University Press, 1968.

Gowan, Donald. *Eschatology in the Old Testament.* Philadelphia: Fortress Press, 1986.

Gren, E. "Augustus and the Ideology of War and Peace." In *The Age of Augustus*, ed. R. Winkes. Louvain: Brown University Press, 1985: 51–72.

Grenholm, C. and D. Patte, eds. *Gender, Tradition and Romans.* Romans through History and Culture Series. London: T. & T. Clark, 2005.

Grimshaw, M. "Believing in Colin: 'A Question of Faith' from 'Celestial Lavatory Graffiti' to 'Derridean Religious Addict.'" *Pacifica* 18 (2005): 175–222.

Grudem, W. *1 Peter.* TNTC. Leicester: InterVarsity Press, 1988.

Habel, N. C. *The Land Is Mine: Six Biblical Ideologies.* Overtures to Biblical Theology. Minneapolis: Fortress Press, 1995.

Hahn, F. "Zum Verständnis von Römer 11:26a '. . . Und so wird ganze Israel gerettet werden.'" In *Paul and Paulinism: Essays in Honour of C. K. Barrett*, ed. M. Hooker and S. G. Wilson. London: SPCK, 1982: 221–36.

Halpern-Amaru, B. "Land Theology in Josephus' *Jewish Antiquities.*" *JQR* 71 (1981): 202–29.

"Exile and Return in Jubilees." In *Exile: Old Testament, Jewish, and Christian Conceptions*, ed. James. M. Scott. Leiden: Brill, 1997: 127–44.

Hammer, P. L. "A Comparison of *Klēronomia* in Paul and Ephesians." *JBL* 79.3 (1960): 267–72.

Hanson, P. D. "Apocalypse, Genre." In *IDBSup* 29. Nashville: Abingdon Press, 1976: 27–34.

Hardwick, L. "Concepts of Peace." In *Experiencing Rome. Culture, Identity and Power in the Roman Empire*, ed. J. Huskinson. London: Routledge, 2000: 335–68.

Harink, D. *Paul among the Postliberals. Pauline Theology Beyond Christendom and Modernity*. Grand Rapids: Brazos Press, 2003.

Harrill, J. A. "Review of Dale B. Martin, *Slavery as Salvation: The Metaphor of Slavery in Pauline Christianity*." *Journal of Religion* 72 (1992): 426–27.

The Manumission of Slaves in Early Christianity. Tübingen: Mohr-Siebeck, 1995.

Harris, M. "Appendix: Prepositions and Theology in the Greek New Testament." In *NIDNTT* III. Grand Rapids: Zondervan, 1975–85: 1192–98.

Colossians and Philemon. EGGNT. Grand Rapids: Eerdmans, 1991.

Slave of Christ: A New Testament Metaphor for Total Devotion to Christ. Leicester: Apollos, 1999.

Harrison, E. "Romans." In *EBC* X, ed. Frank Gaebelein. Grand Rapids: Zondervan, 1976: 3–171.

Harrison, J. R. *Paul's Language of Grace in Its Graeco-Roman Context*. Wissenschaftliche Untersuchungen zum Neuen Testament. Tübingen: Mohr-Siebeck, 2003.

Harrisville, R. A. *Romans*. ACNT. Minneapolis: Augsburg, 1980.

Hauerwas, S. *A Community of Character: Toward a Constructive Christian Social Ethic*. Notre Dame, IN: University of Notre Dame Press, 1981.

Hay, D. M. *Colossians*. ANTC. Nashville: Abingdon Press, 2000.

Hays, R. B. *The Faith of Jesus Christ: An Investigation of the Narrative Substructure of Galatians 3:1–4:11*. Ph.D. thesis Emory University 1981; Atlanta: Scholars Press, 1983.

"'Have We Found Abraham to Be Our Forefather According to the Flesh?' A Reconsideration of Rom 4:1." *NovT* 27 (1985): 76–98.

Echoes of Scripture in the Letters of Paul. New Haven; London: Yale University Press, 1989.

"The Conversion of the Imagination: Scripture and Eschatology in 1 Corinthians." *NTS* 45 (1999): 391–412.

The Letter to the Galatians. NIB 11. Nashville: Abingdon Press, 2000.

"Review of J. L. Martyn, Galatians." *JBL* 119.2 (2000): 373–79.

"Is Paul's Gospel Narratable?" *JSNT* 27 (2004): 217–39.

Hegermann, H. " δόξα." In *EDNT* II. Grand Rapids: Eerdmans, 1993: 344–49.

Herzog, W. R. "Dissembling, a Weapon of the Weak: The Case of Christ and Caesar in Mark 12:13–17 and Romans 13:1–7." *Perspectives in Religious Studies* 21.4 (1994): 339–60.

Hester, J. D. "The 'Heir' and Heilsgeschichte: A Study of Gal 4:1ff." In *Oikonomia, Festschrift für Oscar Cullmann*, ed. F. Christ. Hamburg-Bergstedt: Reich, 1967: 118–25.

Paul's Concept of Inheritance. Edinburgh: Oliver & Boyd, 1968.

Hoegen-Rohls, C. "Ktisis and Kaine Ktisis in Paul's Letters." In *Paul, Luke and the Greco-Roman World*, ed. O. Christofferson, C. Clausen, J. Frey and B. W. Longenecker. JSNTSup 217. Sheffield Academic Press, 2002: 102–22.

Hoftijzer, J. *Die Verheissung an die drei Erzvater*. Leiden: Brill, 1956.

Holmberg, B. *Sociology and the New Testament: An Appraisal.* Philadelphia: Fortress Press, 1990.

"The Methods of Historical Reconstruction in the Scholarly 'Recovery' of Corinthian Christianity." In *Christianity at Corinth: The Quest for the Pauline Church*, ed. E. Adams and D. G. Horrell. Louisville: Westminster John Knox Press, 2004: 255–71.

Hong, I. G. *The Law in Galatians.* JSNTSup 81. Sheffield: JSOT Press, 1993.

Hooker, M. *From Adam to Christ: Essays on Paul.* Cambridge University Press, 1990.

Horne, C. M. "The Meaning of the Phrase 'and Thus All Israel Will Be Saved' (Romans 11:26)." *JETS* 21 (1978): 329–34.

Horrell, D. G. *Solidarity and Difference: A Contemporary Reading of Paul's Ethics.* London: T. & T. Clark, 2005.

Horsley, R. A. "The Gospel of Imperial Salvation." In *Paul and Empire: Religion and Power in Roman Imperial Society*, ed. R. A. Horsley. Harrisburg, PA: Trinity Press International, 1997: 10–24.

1 Corinthians. ANTC. Nashville: Abingdon Press, 1998.

"Paul and Slavery." In *Slavery in Text and Interpretation, Semeia* 83/4, ed. A. D. Callahan, R. A. Horsley and A. Smith. Atlanta: Scholars Press, 1998: 153–200.

"Slave Resistance in Classical Antiquity." In *Slavery in Text and Interpretation, Semeia* 83/4, ed. A. D. Callahan, R. A. Horsley and A. Smith. Atlanta: Scholars Press, 1998: 133–52.

"Rhetoric and Empire and 1 Corinthians." In *Paul and Politics: Ekklesia, Israel, Imperium, Interpretation*, ed. R. A. Horsley. Harrisburg, PA: Trinity Press, 2000: 72–102.

Jesus and Empire: The Kingdom of God and the New World Disorder. Minneapolis: Fortress Press, 2003.

"1 Corinthians: A Case Study of Paul's Assembly as an Alternative Society." In *Christianity at Corinth: The Quest for the Pauline Church*, ed. E. Adams and D. G. Horrell. Louisville: Westminster John Knox Press, 2004.

Horsley, R. A., ed. *Paul and Politics: Ekklesia, Israel, Imperium, Interpretation.* Harrisburg, PA: Trinity Press, 2000.

ed. *Paul and the Roman Imperial Order.* Harrisburg, PA: Trinity Press International, 2004.

Howard, G. *Crisis in Galatia.* Cambridge University Press, 1979.

Howgego, C. *Ancient History from Coins.* London: Routledge, 1995.

Jacobson, H. *A Commentary on Pseudo-Philo's Liber Antiquitatem Biblicarum, with Latin Text and English Translation.* Arbeiten zur Geschichte des antiken Judentums und des Urchristentum 2. Leiden: Brill, 1996.

James, P. "The Language of Dissent." In *Experiencing Rome. Culture, Identity and Power in the Roman Empire*, ed. J. Huskinson. London: Routledge, 2000: 277–303.

Jeffers, J. S. *Conflict at Rome. Social Order and Hierarchy in Early Christianity.* Minneapolis: Fortress Press, 1991.

Jeremias, J. "Flesh and Blood Cannot Inherit the Kingdom of God." *NTS* 2 (1956): 151–59.

Jervis, L. A. *Galatians.* NIBC. Peabody, MA: Hendrickson Publisher, 1999.

Jewett, R. *Man as Male and Female.* Grand Rapids: Eerdmans, 1975.

Paul, the Apostle to America: Cultural Trends and Pauline Scholarship.
Louisville: Westminster John Knox Press, 1994.

"Impeaching God's Elect: Romans 8.33–37 in Its Rhetorical Situation." In
Paul, Luke and the Greco-Roman World, ed. O. Christofferson, C. Clausen,
J. Frey and B. W. Longenecker. JSNTSup 217. Sheffield Academic Press,
2002: 37–58.

"The Corruption and Redemption of Creation. Reading Rom 8:18–23 within
the Imperial Context." In *Paul and the Roman Imperial Order,* ed. R. A.
Horsley. Harrisburg, PA: Trinity Press International, 2004: 25–46.

Johnson, E. Elizabeth. *The Function of Apocalyptic and Wisdom Traditions in
Romans 9–11.* SBLDS. Atlanta: Scholars Press, 1989.

Johnson, L. T. *Reading Romans: A Literary and Theological Commentary.* New
York: The Crossroad Publishing Company, 1997.

Jones Jr., A. "Paul's Message of Freedom: What Does It Mean to the Black
Church?" In *The Bible and Liberation: Political and Social Hermeneutics,*
ed. N. K. Gottwald and R. A. Horsley. Maryknoll, NY: Orbis Books, 1993:
504–40.

Kaiser, W. C. and M. Silva. *An Introduction to Biblical Hermeneutics: The Search
for Meaning.* Grand Rapids: Zondervan, 1994.

Käsemann, E. *New Testament Questions of Today.* London: SCM Press, 1965.

"Justification and Salvation History in the Epistle to the Romans." In *Perspectives on Paul.* London: SCM Press, 1971: 68–70.

Commentary on Romans. Grand Rapids: Eerdmans, 1980.

Kaylor, D. R. *Paul's Covenant Community: Jew and Gentile in Romans.* Atlanta:
John Knox Press, 1989.

Kee, A. "The Imperial Cult: The Unmasking of an Ideology." *Scottish Journal
of Religious Studies* 6 (1985): 112–28.

Keener, C. S. *Paul, Women and Wives: Marriage and Women's Ministry in the
Letters of Paul.* Peabody, MA: Hendrickson Publisher, 1992.

1–2 Corinthians. NCBC. Cambridge University Press, 2005.

Keesmaat, S. C. *Paul and His Story: (Re)Interpreting the Exodus Tradition.*
Sheffield Academic Press, 1999.

"Crucified Lord or Conquering Saviour: Whose Story of Salvation?" *Horizons
in Biblical Theology* 26.2 (2004): 70–90.

"The Psalms in Romans and Galatians." In *The Psalms in the New Testament,* ed. S. Moyise and M. Menkes. Edinburgh: T. & T. Clark, 2004:
139–62.

Keesmaat, S. C. and B. J Walsh. *Colossians Remixed: Subverting the Empire.*
Downers Grove, IL: InterVarsity Press, 2004.

Kent, J. H., ed. *The Inscriptions 1926–1950.* Vol. VIII/3. Princeton: American
School of Classical Studies at Athens, 1966.

Kim, S. "The 'Mystery' of Rom 11:25–26 Once More." *NTS* 43 (1997): 412–
29.

Klein, W. W., C. L. Blomberg and R. L. Hubbard. *Introduction to Biblical
Interpretation.* Dallas: Word Books, 1993.

Kreitzer, L. J. "Eschatology." In *DPL.* Leicester: InterVarsity Press, 1993: 253–
69.

Striking New Images: Roman Imperial Coinage and the New Testament World.
JSNTSup 134. Sheffield Academic Press, 1996.

Krentz, E. F. *Galatians, Philippians, Philemon, 1 Thessalonians*. ACNT. Minneapolis: Augsburg Press, 1985.

Kroeger, C. C. "Women in Greco-Roman World and Judaism." In *Dictionary of New Testament Background*, ed. C. A. Evans and Stanley E. Porter. Leicester: InterVarsity Press, 2000: 1276–80.

Kuss, O. *Der Römerbrief*. Vol. I. Regensburg: Pustet, 1957.

Der Römerbrief. Vol. III. Regensburg: Pustet, 1978.

Lampe, P. "Paul's Concept of a Spiritual Body." In *Resurrection. Theological and Scientific Assessments*, ed. T. Peters, R. J. Russell and W. Welker. Grand Rapids: Eerdmans, 2002: 103–14.

From Paul to Valentinus. Christians at Rome in the First Two Centuries, trans. Michael Steninhauser. Minneapolis: Fortress Press, 2003.

Lang, B. "The Social Organization of Peasant Poverty in Biblical Israel." *JSOT* 24 (1982): 47–63.

Lassen, E. M. "The Use of the Father Image in Imperial Propaganda and 1 Corinthians 4:14–21." *TynBul* 42 (1991): 127–36.

Leenhardt, J. *The Epistle to the Romans*. London: Lutterworth, 1961.

Lempke, W. "Review of *The Land Is Mine*." *JBL* 116 (1997): 332–34.

Lenski, R. C. H. *The Interpretation of St. Paul's Epistle to the Romans*. Columbus, OH: Wartburg Press, 1945.

Levine, A., ed. *A Feminist Companion to Paul*. Cleveland, OH: The Pilgrim Press, 2004.

Lichtenberger, H. " 'Im Lande Israel zu wohnen, wiegt alle Gebote der Tora auf' – Die Heiligkeit des Landes und die Heiligung des Lebens." In *Die Heiden. Juden, Christen und das Problem des Fremden*, ed. R. Feldmeier and U. Heckel. Tübingen: Mohr-Siebeck, 1993: 92–107.

Lieu, J. "Circumcision, Women and Salvation." *NTS* 40 (1994): 358–70.

Lightfoot, J. B. *St Paul's Epistle to the Galatians*. London: MacMillan, 1896.

Lincoln, A. T. *Ephesians*. WBC 42. Dallas: Word, 1990.

"The Letter to the Colossians." In NIB 11. Nashville: Abingdon Press, 2000: 551–60.

Lohse, E. "Christologie und Ethik im Kolosserbrief." In *Apophoreta. Festschrift für Ernst Haenchen*, ed. W. Eltester and F. H. Kettler. Berlin: Töpelmann, 1964: 1957–68.

Colossians and Philemon, trans. W. R. Poehlmann and R. J. Karris. Hermeneia. Philadelphia: Fortress Press, 1971.

Theological Ethics of the New Testament. Philadelphia: Fortress Press, 1991.

Longenecker, B. W. *Eschatology and the Covenant. A Comparison of 4 Ezra and Romans 1–11*. JSNTSup 57. Sheffield: JSOT Press, 1991.

The Triumph of Abraham's God: The Transformation of Identity in Galatians. Edinburgh: T. & T. Clark, 1998.

"Narrative Interest in the Study of Paul. Retrospective and Prospective." In *Narrative Dynamics in Paul: A Critical Assessment*, ed. B. W. Longenecker. Louisville: Westminster John Knox Press, 2002: 3–16.

Longenecker, B. W, ed. *Narrative Dynamics in Paul: A Critical Assessment*. Louisville: Westminster John Knox Press, 2002.

Longenecker, R. N. *New Testament Social Ethics for Today*. Grand Rapids: Eerdmans, 1984.

Galatians. WBC 41. Dallas: Word Books, 1990.

Lübking, H. M. *Paulus und Israel im Römerbrief: Eine Untersuchung zu Römer 9–11*. Frankfurt: Lang, 1986.

Luz, U. *Das Geschichtsverständnis des Paulus*. BevTh 49. Munich: Kaiser, 1968.

Lyall, F. "Roman Law in the Writings of Paul – the Slave and Freedman." *NTS* 17 (1970): 73–80.

"Legal Metaphors in the Epistles." *TynBul* 32 (1981): 81–95.

Slaves, Citizens, Sons. Legal Metaphors in the Epistles. Grand Rapids: Acadamie Books, Zondervan Publishing House, 1984.

Lyons, W. J. "Possessing the Land: The Qumran Sect and the Eschatological Victory." *DSD* 3 (1996): 130–51.

MacDonald, M. *Colossians and Ephesians*. Sacra Pagina 17. Collegeville, MN: The Liturgical Press, 2000.

MacGregor, G. H. C. "Principalities and Powers: The Cosmic Background of Paul's Thought." *NTS* 1 (1954): 17–28.

MacMullen, R. *Enemies of the Roman Order*. Harvard University Press, 1966.

Malherbe, A. J. *Social Aspects of Early Christianity*. Baton Rouge: Louisiana State University Press, 1977.

Malina, B. and J. H. Neyrey. *Portraits of Paul: An Archeology of Ancient Personality*. Louisville: Westminster/ John Knox Press, 1996.

Marshall, I. H. "Response to A. T. Lincoln: The Stories of Predecessors and Inheritors in Galatians and Romans." In *Narrative Dynamics in Paul: A Critical Assessment*, ed. B. W. Longenecker. London: Westminster John Knox Press, 2002: 204–14.

Martin, D. B. *Slavery as Salvation: The Metaphor of Slavery in Pauline Christianity*. New Haven: Yale University Press, 1990.

"Review Essay: Justin J. Meggitt, *Paul, Poverty and Survival.*" *JSNT* 84 (2001): 51–64.

Martin, R. P. *Colossians: The Church's Lord and the Christian's Liberty. An Expository Commentary with a Present-Day Application*. Grand Rapids: Zondervan, 1972.

Martyn, J. L. "Apocalyptic Antinomies in Paul's Letter to the Galatians." *NTS* 31 (1985): 410–25.

Theological Issues in the Letters of Paul. Nashville: Abingdon Press, 1997.

Galatians. AB 33A. New York: Doubleday, 1998.

Matera, F. J. *Galatians*. Sacra Pagina 9. Collegeville, MN: The Liturgical Press, 1992.

Matlock, B. *Unveiling the Apocalyptic Paul: Paul's Interpreters and the Rhetoric of Criticism*. Sheffield Academic Press, 1996.

Meeks, W. A. "The Image of the Androgyne: Some Uses of a Symbol in Earliest Christianity." *HR* 13 (1973/74): 165–208.

The First Urban Christians. New Haven: Yale University Press, 1983.

"Social Functions of Apocalyptic Language in Pauline Christianity." In *Apocalypticism in the Mediterranean World and the Near East: Proceedings of the International Colloquium on Apocalypticism*, ed. D. Hellholm. Tübingen: Mohr-Siebeck, 1983: 687–705.

Meggitt, J. J. *Paul, Poverty and Survival*. Studies of the New Testament and Its World. Edinburgh: T. & T. Clark, 1998.

"Response to Martin and Theissen." *JSNT* 84 (2001): 85–94.

Mendels, D. *The Land of Israel as Political Concept in Hasmonean Literature: Recourse to History in Second Century BC. Claims to the Holy Land.* TSAJ 15. Tübingen: Mohr-Siebeck, 1987.

Mendelsohn, I. *Slavery in the Ancient Near East: A Comparative Study of Slavery in Babylonia, Assyria, Syria and Palestine from the Middle of the Third Millenium to the End of the First Millenium.* New York: Oxford University Press, 1949.

Merrill, E. "Review of *The Land Is Mine.*" *Bibliotheca Sacra* 154 (1997): 234–35.

Metzger, B. M. *The Text of the New Testament: Its Transmission, Corruption, and Restoration.* 3rd edn. New York: Oxford University Press, 1992.

Michel, O. *Der Brief an die Römer.* Göttingen: Vandenhoeck & Ruprecht, 1978.

Miles, R. "Communicating Culture, Identity and Power." In *Experiencing Rome. Culture, Identity and Power in the Roman Empire*, ed. J Huskinson. London: Routledge, 2000: 29–62.

Milgrom, J. *Leviticus 23–27.* AB3B. New York: Doubleday, 2001.

Mitchell, Stephen. *Anatolia: Land, Men, and Gods in Asia Minor.* 2 vols. Vol. I. New York: Oxford University Press, 1993.

Momigliano, A. *The Emperor Claudius and His Achievement.* Revised ed. Oxford University Press, 1961.

Moo, D. J. *The Epistle to the Romans.* NICNT. Grand Rapids: Eerdmans, 1996.

Moore-Crispin, D. R. "Galatians 4:1–9: The Use and Abuse of Parallels." *EQ* 61 (1989): 203–23.

Morris, L. *The Epistle to the Romans.* Grand Rapids: Eerdmans; Leicester: Inter-Varsity Press, 1988.

Moule, C. F. D. *The Origin of Christology.* Cambridge University Press, 1977.

Moule, H. C. G. *Studies in Colossians and Philemon.* Grand Rapids: Kregel Publications, 1977.

Murray, J. *The Epistle to the Romans: The English Text with Introduction, Exposition and Notes.* NICNT. Grand Rapids: Eerdmans, 1968.

Mussner, F. *Der Galaterbrief.* HTKNT. Freiburg, Basel and Vienna: Herder, 1974.

Nanos, M. *The Mystery of Romans.* Minneapolis: Fortress Press, 1996.

Neill, S. and N. T. Wright. *The Interpretation of the New Testament: 1881–1986.* Oxford University Press, 1988.

Neyrey, J. H. "Body Language in 1 Corinthians: The Use of Anthropological Models for Understanding Paul and His Opponents." *Semeia* 35 (1986): 129–70.

Nicolet, Claude. *Space, Geography, and Politics in the Early Roman Empire*, trans. Helene Leclerc. Jerome Lectures 19 Series. University of Michigan Press, 1991.

Nisbet, R. G. M. "Horace's *Epodes* and History." In *Poetry and Politics in the Age of Augustus*, ed. T. West and D. Woodman. Cambridge University Press, 1984: 1–17.

Nock, A. D. "Deification and Julian." *JRS* 47 (1972): 115–23.

Nygren, A. *Commentary on Romans.* London: SCM Press, 1952.

Oakes, P. *Philippians. From People to Letter.* SNTS 110. Cambridge University Press, 2001.

"A State of Tension: Rome in the New Testament." In *The Gospel of Matthew in Its Roman Imperial Context*, ed. J. Riches and D. C. Sim. London: T. & T. Clark, 2005: 75–90.

O'Brien, P. T. *Colossians, Philemon*. WBC 44. Waco, TX: Word Books, 1982.

"Was Paul Converted?" In *Justification and Variegated Nomism. The Paradoxes of Paul*, ed. D. Carson, P. T. O'Brien and M. Seifrid. Grand Rapids: Baker Academic, 2004: vol. II, 361–91.

Oepke, A. "ἄρσην." In *TDNT* I. Grand Rapids: Eerdmans, 1964–76: 360–63.

Der Brief des Paulus an die Galater. THKNT 9. Berlin: Evangelische Verlagsanstalt, 1973.

Osborne, G. *The Hermeneutical Spiral: A Comprehensive Introduction to Biblical Interpretation*. Downers Grove: InterVarsity Press, 1991.

Romans. IVPNT Commentary Series. Illinois and Leicester: InterVarsity Press, 2004.

Oswalt, J. N. *The Book of Isaiah: Chapters 40–66*. NICOT. Grand Rapids and Cambridge: Eerdmans, 1998.

Pallis, A. *To the Romans: A Commentary*. Liverpool: Oxford University Press, 1920.

Patterson, O. *Slavery and Social Death: A Comparative Study*. Cambridge, MA: Harvard University Press, 1982.

Pekary, T. *Die Wirtschaft der griechisch-römischen Antike*. Wiesbaden: Franz Steiner, 1976.

Penn, R. G. *Medicine on Ancient Greek and Roman Coins*. London: Seaby, 1994.

Pesch, R. *Römerbrief*. Die Neue Echter-Bibel 6. Wurzburg: Echter-Verl, 1994.

Pietersma, A. and B. G. Wright, *A New English Translation of the Septuagint*. Oxford University Press, 2007.

Pobee, John. S. *Persecution and Martyrdom in the Theology of Paul*. JSNTSup 6. Sheffield: JSOT Press, 1985.

Pokorny, P. *Colossians: A Commentary*, trans. S. S. Schatzmann. Peabody, MA: Hendrickson Publishers, 1991.

Preisigke, F. *Wörterbuch Der Griechischen Papzrusurkunden*, ed. E. Kiessling. Vol. II. Berlin: Selbstverlag, 1924–.

Premnath, D. M. *Eighth Century Prophets. A Social Analysis*. St. Louis, MO: Chalice Press, 2003.

Price, S. R. F. *Rituals and Power: The Roman Imperial Cult in Asia Minor*. Cambridge University Press, 1984.

Räisänen, H. "Did Paul Expect an Earthly Kingdom?" In *Paul, Luke and the Greco-Roman World*, ed. O. Christofferson, C. Clausen, J. Frey and B. W. Longenecker. JSNTSup 217. Sheffield Academic Press, 2002: 2–20.

Ramsaran, R. A. "Resisting Imperial Domination and Influence: Paul's Apocalyptic Rhetoric in 1 Corinthians." In *Paul and the Roman Imperial Order*, ed. R. A. Horsley. Harrisburg, PA: Trinity Press International, 2004: 89–101.

Reichert, A. *Der Römerbrief Als Gratwanderung: Eine Untersuchung Zur Abfassungsproblematik*. Forschungen zur Religion und Literatur des Alten und Neuen Testaments. Göttingen: Vandenhoeck & Ruprecht, 2001.

Reid, D. "Elements/Elemental Spirits." In *DPL*. Leicester: InterVarsity Press, 1993: 229–33.

Reumann, J. "The Use of Oikonomia and Related Terms in Greek Sources to about AD 100, as a Background for Patristic Application." Ph.D. thesis, University of Pennsylvania, 1957.

Ridderbos, H. N. *Paul: An Outline of His Theology*, trans. J. R. de Witt. Grand Rapids: Eerdmans, 1975.

Riecke, R. B. "The Law and This World According to Paul: Some Thoughts Concerning Gal 4:1–11." *JBL* 70 (1951): 259–76.

Rives, J. "Religion in the Roman World." In *Experiencing Rome. Culture, Identity and Power in the Roman Empire*, ed. J. Huskinson. London: Routledge, 2000: 245–76.

Robertson, A. and A. Plummer. *A Critical and Exegetical Commentary on the First Epistle of St Paul to the Corinthians*. 2nd edn. ICC. Edinburgh: T. & T. Clark, 1914.

Robinson, D. W. B. "The Salvation of Israel in Romans 9–11." *Reformed Theological Review* 28 (1967): 81–96.

Robinson, J. A. T. *Wrestling with Romans*. Philadelphia: Westminster, 1979.

Rochberg-Halton, F. "Astrology in the Ancient near East." In *ABD* I. New York: Doubleday, 1992: 504–507.

Rudich, V. *Political Dissidence under Nero. The Price of Dissimulation*. London: Routledge, 1993.

Rupprecht, A. A. "Slave, Slavery." In *DPL*. Leicester: InterVarsity Press, 1993: 881–83.

Sampley, J. P. *Walking between the Times: Paul's Moral Reasoning*. Minneapolis: Fortress Press, 1991.

Sanday, W. and A. C. Headlam. *A Critical and Exegetical Commentary on the Epistle to the Romans*. ICC. 5th edn. Edinburgh: T. & T. Clark, 1902.

Sanders, E. P. *Paul and Rabbinic Judaism*. London: SCM Press, 1977.
  Paul and Palestinian Judaism: A Comparison of Patterns of Religion. Philadelphia: Fortress Press, 1997.

Schlatter, A. *Gottes Gerechtigket. Ein Kommentar zum Römerbrief*. Stuttgart: Calwer, 1935.
  Romans. The Righteousness of God, trans. S. S. Schatzmann. Peabody, MA: Hendrickson Publishers, 1995.

Schlier, H. *Der Brief an Die Galater*. Meyers Kommentar 7. Göttingen: Vandenhoeck & Ruprecht, 1962.
  Der Romerbrief. Vienna: Herder, 1987.

Schmithals, W. *Paul and the Gnostics*. New York: Abingdon Press, 1972.

Schreiner, Thomas R. Romans. BECNT 6. Grand Rapids: Baker Books, 1998.

Schüssler Fiorenza, E. *In Memory of Her: A Feminist Theological Reconstruction of Christian Origins*. New York: Crossroads, 1983.

Schweitzer, A. *The Mysticism of Paul the Apostle*. London: Black, 1931.

Schweizer, E. *The Letter to the Colossians. A Commentary*, trans. A. Chester. Minneapolis, MN: Augsburg Publishing House, 1982.
  "Slaves of the Elements and Worshippers of Angels: Gal 4:3, 9 and Col 2:8, 18, 20." *JBL* 107 (1988): 455–68.

Scobie, C. H. H. "Israel and the Nations: An Essay in Biblical Theology." *TynBul* 43.2 (1992): 283–305.

Scott, J. C. *Weapons of the Weak: Everyday Forms of Peasant Resistance.* Yale University Press, 1987.
Domination and the Arts of Resistance: Hidden Transcripts. Yale University Press, 1990.
Scott, James M. *Adoption as Sons of God. An Exegetical Investigation into the Background of YIOTHEZIA in the Pauline Corpus.* WUNT 48. Tubingen: J. C. B. Mohr (Paul Siebeck), 1992.
"Luke's Geographical Horizon," in *The Book of Acts in its First-Century Setting,* D. W. T. Gill and C. Gempf. ed. Grand Rapids: Eerdmans, 1994: vol. II, 483–544.
Paul and the Nations: The Old Testament and Jewish Background of Paul's Mission to the Nations with Special Reference to the Destination of Galatians. WUNT 84. Tubingen: J. C. B. Mohr (Paul Siebeck), 1995.
On Earth as in Heaven. The Restoration of Sacred Time and Sacred Space in the Book of Jubilees. JSJSup 91. Leiden, Netherlands: Brill, 2005.
Scott, W. "Review of *The Land Is Mine.*" *CBQ* 58 (1996): 708–709.
Scroggs, R. "Paul and the Eschatological Woman." *JAAR* 40 (1972): 283–303.
Seidl, Erwin. *Rechtsgechichte Ägyptens als römischer Provinz: Die Behauptung des ägyptischen Rechts neben dem römischen.* Sankt Augustin: Hans Richarz, 1973.
Seifrid, M. A. "In Christ." In *DPL.* Leicester: InterVarsity Press, 1993: 433–36.
"Unrighteousness by Faith: Apostolic Proclamation in Romans 1:18–3:20." In *Justification and Variegated Nomism. The Paradoxes of Paul,* ed. D. Carson, P. T. O'Brien and M. Seifrid. Grand Rapids: Baker Academic, 2004: vol. II, 105–45.
Seters, J. V. "The Problem of Childlessness in Near Eastern Law and the Patriarchs of Israel." *JBL* 87 (1968): 401–408.
Sherk, R. K, ed. and trans. *The Roman Empire: Augustus to Hadrian.* Translated Documents of Greece and Rome. Cambridge University Press, 1988.
Siegert, F. *Argumentation bei Paulus gezeigt an Röm 9–11.* WUNT 34. Tübingen: J. C. B. Mohr (Paul Siebeck), 1985.
Silva, M. *Explorations in Exegetical Method: Galatians as a Test Case.* Grand Rapids: Baker, 1996.
Snijders, L. A. "Genesis XV. The Covenant with Abram." *Oudestamentische Studien* 12 (1958): 261–80.
Spykerboer, H. "Review of: *The Land Is Mine.*" *Colloquium* 28.2 (1996): 122–23.
Standhartinger, A. "Colossians and the Pauline School." *NTS* 50.4 (2004): 572–93.
Stanley, C. " 'The Redeemer Will Come from Zion': Romans 11:26–27 Revisited." In *Paul and the Scriptures of Israel,* ed. C. A. Evans and J. A. Sanders. JSNTSup 83. Sheffield: JSOT Press, 1993: 118–42.
Stanton, G. " 'I Think, When I Read That Sweet Story of Old': A Response to Douglas Campbell." In *Narrative Dynamics in Paul. A Critical Assessment,* ed. B. W. Longenecker. Louisville: Westminster John Knox Press, 2002: 125–32.
Jesus and Gospel. Cambridge University Press, 2004.
Stegemann, E. W., and W. Stegemann. *The Jesus Movement: A Social History of Its First Century.* Minneapolis: Fortress Press, 1999.
Stendahl, K. *Paul among Jews and Gentiles.* Philadelphia: Fortress Press, 1976.

Still, T. D. "Eschatology in Colossians: How Realized Is It?" *NTS* 50 (2004): 125–38.

Stott, J. R. W. *The Message of Romans*. The Bible Speaks Today. Leicester: InterVarsity Press, 1994.

Stringfellow, W. *Free in Obedience*. New York: Seabury Press, 1964.

Stuhlmacher, P. *Paul's Letter to the Romans: A Commentary*, trans. by S. J. Hafemann. Louisville: Westminster John Knox Press, 1994.

Tannehill, Robert. C. *Dying and Rising with Christ. A Study in Pauline Theology*. Berlin: Alfred Töpelmann, 1967.

Taubenschlag, Raphael. *The Law of Greco-Roman Egypt in the Light of the Papyri 332–640 BCE*. Warsaw: Panvstwowe Wydawnictwo Naukowe, 1955.

Taylor, L. R. *The Divinity of the Roman Emperor*. Middletown, CT: American Philological Association, 1931.

Theissen, G. *The Social Setting of Pauline Christianity*. Philadelphia: Fortress Press, 1982.

"The Social Structure of Pauline Communities: Some Critical Remarks on J. J. Meggitt, *Paul, Poverty and Survival.*" *JSNT* 24 (2001): 65–24.

"Social Conflicts in the Corinthian Community: Further Remarks on J. J. Meggitt, *Paul, Poverty and Survival.*" *JSNT* 25.3 (2003): 371–91.

Thiselton, A. C. *The New International Greek Commentary on the First Epistle to the Corinthians*. NIGTC. Grand Rapids: Eerdmans, 2000.

Thompson, M. *Isaiah 40–66*. Epworth Commentaries. London: Epworth Press, 2001.

Tobin, T. H. *Paul's Rhetoric in Its Context. The Argument of Romans*. Peabody, MA: Hendrickson Publishers, 2004.

Tsumura, D. T. "An OT Background to Rom 8: 22." *NTS* 40 (1994): 620–21.

van Winkle, D. W. "The Relationship of the Nations to Yahweh and to Israel in Isaiah XL–LV." *Vetus Testamentum* 35 (1985): 446–58.

VanderKam, J. C. "The Putative Author of the Book of Jubilees." *Journal of Semitic Studies* 36 (1981): 209–17.

"The Origins and Purposes of the Book of Jubilees." In *Studies in the Book of Jubilees*, ed. M. Albani, J. Frey and A. Lange. TSAJ 65. Tübingen: Mohr–Siebeck, 1997: 3–24.

Calendars in the Dead Sea Scrolls: Measuring Time. London: Routledge, 1998.

"Studies in the Chronology of the Book of Jubilees." In *From Revelation to Canon: Studies in the Hebrew Bible and Second Temple Literature*, ed. J. C. VanderKam. JSJSup 62. Leiden: Brill, 2000: 522–44.

"Studies on the Prologue and *Jubilees*1." In *For a Later Generation: The Transformation of Tradition in Israel, Early Judaism, and Early Christianity*, ed. R. A. Argall. Harrisburg, PA: Trinity Press International, 2000: 266–79.

Vermes, G. "New Light on the Sacrifice of Isaac from 4Q225." *JJS* 47 (1996): 140–46.

Veyne, P. *Bread and Circuses. Historical Sociology and Political Pluralism*, trans. B. Pearce. Penguin History. London: Allen Lane, 1990.

Vögtle, A. *Das Neue Testament und die Zukunft des Kosmos*. Düsseldorf: Patmos, 1970.

Wagner, J. Ross. *Heralds of the Good News: Isaiah and Paul "in Concert" in the Letter to the Romans*. NovTSup 51. Leiden, Boston and Cologne: Brill, 2002.

Wall, R. *Colossians & Philemon*. IVPNT. Downers Grove, IL: InterVarsity Press, 1993.

Wallace-Hadrill, A. "The Golden Age of Sin in Augustan Ideology." *Past & Present* 95 (1982): 19–36.

Wanke, G. "Nahal, NahᵃLâ." In *TLOT* II., ed. E. Jenni and C. Westermann. Peabody, MA: Hendrickson Publishers, 1997: 731–34.

Watson, F. "Is There a Story in These Texts?" In *Narrative Dynamics in Paul. A Critical Assessment*, ed. B. W. Longenecker, 231–39. Louisville: Westminster John Knox Press, 2002.

Wegner, J. R. *Chattel or Person: The Status of Women in the Mishnah*. New York: Oxford University Press, 1988.

Weinfeld, M. *The Promise of the Land. The Inheritance of the Land of Canaan by the Israelites*. Berkeley: University of California Press, 1993.

Weiss, K. "ἀχή." *EDNT* I. Grand Rapids: Eerdmans, 1990: 162.

Wengst, Klaus. *Pax Romana and the Peace of Jesus Christ*, trans. John Bowden. London: SCM Press, 1987.

Westerholm, S. "The 'New Perspective' at Twenty-Five." In *Justification and Variegated Nomism. The Paradoxes of Paul*, ed. D. Carson, P. T. O'Brien and M. Seifrid. Grand Rapids: Baker Academic, 2004: vol. II, 1–38.

Westermann, C. "The Way of Promise in the Old Testament." In *The Old Testament and Christian Faith*, ed. B. W. Anderson. New York: Harper and Row, 1964: 200–24.

Genesis 12–36: A Commentary. Minneapolis: Augsburg Publishing House, 1986.

Westermann, W. L. "Slavery and the Elements of Freedom in Ancient Greece." In *Slavery in Classical Antiquity: Views and Controversy*, ed. M. I. Finlay. Cambridge: Heffer, 1974: 17–32.

Whitelam, K. "Israelite Kingship: The Royal Ideology and Its Opponents." In *The World of Ancient Israel*, ed. R. Clements, Cambridge University Press, 1989: 119–39.

Whittaker, C. R. "The Poor in the City of Rome." In *Land, City, and Trade in the Roman Empire*. Aldershot: Ashgate, 1993: 301–33.

Wilckens, U. *Der Brief an die Römer: Röm 1–5*. EKK. 3 vols. Vol. I. Zurich: Benziger, 1974.

Der Brief an die Römer: Rom 6–11. EKK. 3 vols. Vol. II. Zurich: Benziger, 1980.

Williams, D. J. *Paul's Metaphors. Their Context and Character*. Peabody, MA: Hendrickson Publishers, 1999.

Williams, S. K. "The 'Righteousness of God' in Romans." *JBL* 99 (1980): 241–90.

"The *Promise* in Galatians: A Reading of Paul's Reading of Scripture." *JBL* 107.4 (1988): 709–20.

Galatians. ANTC. Nashville: Abingdon Press, 1997.

Wink, W. *Naming the Powers: The Language of Power in the New Testament*. Philadelphia: Fortress Press, 1984.

Unmasking the Powers: The Invisible Forces That Determine Human Existence. Philadelphia: Fortress Press, 1986.

Engaging the Powers: Discernment and Resistance in a World of Domination. Minneapolis: Fortress Press, 1992.

Winter, B. "The Imperial Cult and the Early Christians in Pisidian Antioch (Acts 13 & Gal 6)." In *Actes du 1er congrès international sur Antioche de pisidie*, ed. T. Drew-Bear. Lyon: Université Lumière-Lyon, 2002: 67–75.

Wire, A. C. *The Corinthian Women Prophets: A Reconstruction through Paul's Rhetoric*. Minneapolis: Fortress, 1990.

Witherington, B. "Rite and Rights for Women – Galatians 3:28." *NTS* 27.5 (1980): 593–604.

  Conflict and Community in Corinth: A Socio-Rhetorical Commentary on 1 and 2 Corinthians. Grand Rapids: Eerdmans, 1995.

  Grace in Galatia: A Commentary on St Paul's Letter to the Galatians. Grand Rapids: Eerdmans, 1998.

  Paul's Letter to the Romans. A Socio-Rhetorical Commentary. Grand Rapids and Cambridge.: Eerdmans, 2004.

Wolff, H. W. "The Kerygma of the Yahwist." *Int* 20 (1966): 131–58.

Woolf, G. "Inventing Empire in Ancient Rome." In *Empires: Perspectives from Archeology and History*, ed. S. E. Alcock, T. N. D Altroy, K. D. Morrison and C. M. Sinopoli. Cambridge University Press, 2001: 311–22.

Wrede, W. *Paul*. London: Green, 1907.

Wright, Christopher. *God's People in God's Land. Family, Land and Property in the Old Testament*. Rev. edn. Carlisle: Paternoster Press, 1997.

  "Nahal, NahᵃLâ." In *NIDOTTE* III, ed. W. A. Van Gemeren. Grand Rapids: Zondervan Publishing House, 1997: 77–81.

Wright, N. T. "The Paul of History and the Apostle of Faith." *TynBul* 29 (1978): 61–88.

  "A New Tübingen School? Ernst Käsemann and His Commentary on Romans." *Themelios* 7 (1982): 6–16.

  Colossians and Philemon. TNTC. Grand Rapids: Eerdmans, 1986.

  The Climax of the Covenant: Christ and the Law in Pauline Theology. Edinburgh: T. & T. Clark, 1991.

  The New Testament and the People of God. Christian Origins and the Question of God 1. London: SPCK, 1992.

  "Gospel and Theology in Galatians." In *Gospel in Paul: Studies on Corinthians, Galatians and Romans for Richard N. Longenecker*, ed. L. A. Jervis and P. Richardson. JSNTSup. 108. Sheffield Academic Press, 1994. 222–39.

  "Putting Paul together Again: Towards a Synthesis of Pauline Theology." In *Pauline Theology*, vol. I: *Thessalonians, Philippians, and Philemon*, ed. J. M. Bassier. Minneapolis: Fortress, 1994: 183–211.

  "Romans and the Theology of Paul." In *Pauline Theology,* vol. III*: Romans*, ed. D. M. Hays and E. Elizabeth Johnson. Minneapolis: Fortress Press, 1995: 30–67.

  Jesus and the Victory of God. Christian Origins and the Question of God 2. Minneapolis: Fortress Press, 1996.

  "New Exodus, New Inheritance: The Narrative Substructure of Romans 3–8." In *Romans and the People of God: Essays in Honour of Gordon D. Fee on the Occasion of His 65th Birthday*, ed. N. T. Wright and S. K. Soderland. Grand Rapids: Eerdmans, 1999: 26–35.

  "Paul's Gospel and Caesar's Empire." In *Paul and Politics: Ekklesia, Israel, Imperium, Interpretation*, ed. R. A. Horsley, Harrisburg, PA: Trinity Press, 2000: 160–83.

"Coming Home to St Paul? Reading Romans a Hundred Years after Charles Gore." *Scottish Journal of Theology* 55.4 (2002): 392–407.

"Paul and Caesar: A New Reading of Romans." In *A Royal Priesthood? The Use of the Bible Ethically and Politically. A Dialogue with Oliver O'Donovan*, ed. C. Bartholomew. Grand Rapids: Zondervan, 2002: 172–92.

"Romans." In NIB 10. Nashville: Abingdon Press, 2002: 395–770.

Paul for Everyone: 1 Corinthians London: SPCK, 2003.

The Resurrection and the Son of God. Christian Origins and the Question of God 3. Minneapolis: Fortress, 2003.

Paul in Fresh Perspective. Minneapolis: Fortress Press, 2005.

Yoder, J. H. *The Politics of Jesus*. 2nd edn. Grand Rapids: Eerdmans, 1995.

Yonge, C. D., trans. *The Works of Philo*. Peabody, MA: Hendrickson Publishers, 1993.

Zahn, T. *Der Brief des Paulus an die Romer*. KNT. Leipzig: Deichert, 1925.

Zanker, P. *The Power of Images in the Age of Augustus*, trans. Alan Shapiro. Jerome Lecture Series 16. University of Michigan Press, 1988.

Ziesler, J. *Pauline Christianity*. Oxford University Press, 1983.

Paul's Letter to the Romans. Harrisburg, PA: Trinity Press, 1989.

The Epistle to the Galatians. Epworth Commentaries. London: Epworth Press, 1992.

Zuntz, G. *The Text of the Epistles: A Disquisition upon the Corpus Paulinum*. The Schweich Lectures of the British Academy, 1946. London: Oxford University Press, 1953.

INDEX

Abrahamic promise
and the "blessing to the nations" 97,
154
and universal sovereignty 69,
180
culmination in Christ 85
expansive nature of 71, 79, 80, 84, 87,
154
in Isaiah 54, 77, 87, 90, 99
in Philo 92
interpretation of 68
physical and social dimensions 71,
79
socio-political significance 79, 85,
98
universal application of 71
Abrahamic tradition 63–64, 99, 106–07,
162
Adams, Edward 82n102, 110–11, 114n52,
124n97, n101, 126n110, 193n106,
195n121.
Aeneid 33, 34, 37n91, 41, 44, 92
Age of Saturn 33, 38, 116
Altar of Peace 29
Antioch Temple 28
apocalyptic language 2, 3, 126, 203–04,
208
Apostolic Council 78
Arnold, Clinton 117n17, 193n104, n105,
194, 195n116, 195n118

Bader-Saye, Scott 166–68
Bailey, Kenneth 69, 85
Barclay, John 8n30, 124n98, 124n100,
n102, 184n57, n58, n63, 185n66,
191n93, n95, n97, 205n162,
219
Barre, Michael 122
Barrett, C. K. 60, 64n20, 114n50, 142n20,
215n34, 238n20

Becker, J. 47
Beker, Christiaan 2, 195n116
Blumenfeld, Bruno 15–16
Boyarin, Daniel 190, 191n94
Bruce, F. F. 124n100, 174, 183,
195
Brueggemann, Walter 5, 8n28, 13n42, n44,
63, 64n19, 67n41, n43, 70, 74n63,
n67, 90n129, 98, 99n151, 115n57
Byrne, B. J 8n28, 59n2, 70n55, 79n97,
80n101, 85, 110n32, 112–13, 117n62,
118n66, 128n118, 138n3, 161n90,
165n109, 173, 175n12, 178n24

Carlston, Charles 187
Carter, T. L. 47, 51n144, 236, 237, 238n17,
239
Carter, Warren 37n75, 54n164
Cassius Dio 31n44, 40, 41, 124
Christ as eschatological firstborn
119
Christians in first-century Rome 44–54,
92–100, 122, 130, 134, 168, 233–43
Cicero 42
Clark, Mark 55, 56
Claudian Edict 123
Colossians
authorship of 219
slavery 224–27
Cranfield, C. E. B. 104, 118, 138, 143n27

Davidic promise 120
Davies, W. D. 5–7, 60, 97n146, 203n154,
234
debt slavery 224
Deissmann, A. 12, 40n90, n91, 41n94,
n95, 45, 46n115, 199
Derbe 197
Dihle, A. 33, 38
Duncan-Jones, R. 49